Praise for *Race, War, and Remembrance in the Appalachian South*

"Deftly combining telling detail with cautious generalization, Inscoe offers us a nuanced interpretation of race, war, and remembrance in the era of Appalachia's 'discovery' and describes how ideas born in this era survive today to shape Appalachia's problematic but persistent identity, both as a region apart and as a part of the South. The book is essential reading for anyone fascinated by this special and complicated part of the world."
—John Alexander Williams, Appalachian State University

"No historian better captures the complex conjunction of Appalachia, race, and the American South before and after the Civil War than does John Inscoe. His greatest contribution in this fine volume of essays lies in his ability, amidst lucid analysis and explication, to illuminate the contradictions and ambiguities inherent in this fascinating region."
—Durwood Dunn, Tennessee Wesleyan College

"For a quarter of a century John Inscoe has dedicated himself to rescuing nineteenth-century Appalachia, and its involvement in the sectional conflict in particular, from the disdain of history. Each essay makes essential reading; together they provide a compelling overview of the political, racial, and familial imperatives governing upcountry survival in the crucible of war."
—Martin Crawford, Keele University

"Over the last two decades, John Inscoe's pathbreaking scholarship did nothing less than redefine what scholars think and write about life in antebellum and Civil War Appalachia. Consistently exciting and enlightening, these essays not only represent penetrating historical research at its best, but stand as milestones in an ongoing revisionist conversation that continues to revolutionize southern history."
—Kenneth W. Noe, author of *Perryville: This Grand Havoc of Battle*

Praise for *Race, War, and Remembrance in the Appalachian South,* continued

"Meticulously researched, unfailingly judicious and balanced, these essays highlight Inscoe's defining strengths as a scholar."
—Robert Tracy McKenzie, University of Washington

"John Inscoe's broad imagination, deep research, and engaging writing over the past two decades have given us new ways to think about Appalachia and the South. He has led the way in shaping how we understand race and the Civil War in these contexts. His deep empathy for the people he studies is balanced by a careful analysis of their thoughts and actions. Inscoe clarifies the complex history of Appalachia and, by extension, enables us to see more clearly the South and the United States."
—David C. Hsiung, author of *Two Worlds in the Tennessee Mountains: Exploring the Origins of Appalachian Stereotypes*

Race, War, and
Remembrance in the
Appalachian South

To Evon —
with warm regards,
John Inscoe
June 2010

Race, War,
and
Remembrance
in the
Appalachian
South

John C. Inscoe

THE UNIVERSITY PRESS OF KENTUCKY

Copyright © 2008 by The University Press of Kentucky
Paperback edition 2009

The University Press of Kentucky
Scholarly publisher for the Commonwealth,
serving Bellarmine University, Berea College, Centre
College of Kentucky, Eastern Kentucky University,
The Filson Historical Society, Georgetown College,
Kentucky Historical Society, Kentucky State University,
Morehead State University, Murray State University,
Northern Kentucky University, Transylvania University,
University of Kentucky, University of Louisville,
and Western Kentucky University.
All rights reserved.

Editorial and Sales Offices: The University Press of Kentucky
663 South Limestone Street, Lexington, Kentucky 40508-4008
www.kentuckypress.com

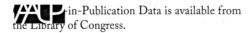

Cataloging-in-Publication Data is available from
the Library of Congress.

ISBN 978-0-8131-9300-7 (pbk: acid-free paper)

This book is printed on acid-free recycled paper meeting
the requirements of the American National Standard
for Permanence in Paper for Printed Library Materials.

Manufactured in the United States of America.

Member of the Association of
American University Presses

To Meg and Clay

Contents

Acknowledgments   xi

Introduction   1

Race

1. Race and Racism in Nineteenth-Century Appalachia: Myths, Realities, and Ambiguities   13

2. Between Bondage and Freedom: Confronting the Variables of Appalachian Slavery and Slaveholding   46

3. Olmsted in Appalachia: A Connecticut Yankee Encounters Slavery in the Southern Highlands, 1854   65

4. Mountain Masters as Confederate Opportunists: The Slave Trade in Western North Carolina, 1861–1865   80

War

5. The Secession Crisis and Regional Self-Image: The Contrasting Cases of Western North Carolina and East Tennessee   103

6. Highland Households Divided: Familial Deceptions, Diversions, and Divisions in Southern Appalachia's Inner Civil War *with Gordon B. McKinney*   124

7. Coping in Confederate Appalachia: Portrait of a Mountain Woman and Her Community at War   144

Contents

8. "Moving through Deserter Country": Fugitive Accounts of Southern Appalachia's Inner Civil War   175

9. "Talking Heroines": Elite Mountain Women as Chroniclers of Stoneman's Raid, April 1865   204

Remembrance

10. The Racial "Innocence" of Appalachia: William Faulkner and the Mountain South   227

11. A Fugitive Slave in Frontier Appalachia: *The Journey of August King* on Film   242

12. "A Northern Wedge Thrust into the Heart of the Confederacy": Explaining Civil War Loyalties in the Age of Appalachian Discovery, 1900–1921   256

13. Unionists in the Attic: The Shelton Laurel Massacre Dramatized   282

14. Appalachian Odysseus: Love, War, and Best-sellerdom in the Blue Ridge   303

15. Guerrilla War and Remembrance: Reconstructing a Father's Murder and a Community's Civil War   322

16. Race and Remembrance in West Virginia: John Henry for a Postmodernist Age   350

17. In Defense of Appalachia on Film: Hollywood, History, and the Highland South   364

Credits   381

Index   385

Acknowledgments

I have incurred many debts over the years in which I have generated this work. Many of us historians moved into and through this brave new world of nineteenth-century Appalachia together, and my efforts have been much enhanced and expanded by collaboration and frequent exchanges, in person and in print, with these fellow travelers. I owe my biggest debt to Gordon McKinney for having provided me with the most rewarding, and lengthiest, of those collaborations. Coauthoring a book on the Civil War in western North Carolina was far more enriching than it would have been to undertake the same project alone, and the sheer fact that it took us so long to do—nearly a decade—allowed us both the chance to spin off separate essays and articles on related topics. Several of them appear here. Whereas we coauthored only one essay (reproduced here with my thanks to Gordon), his fingerprints are on far more of these pieces than authorial attribution indicates, and I am very grateful that we undertook the war together and that we both survived it to move on and fight on other fronts.

I am also indebted to fellow historians Durwood Dunn, Kenneth Noe, Martin Crawford, Ronald Lewis, John Alexander Williams, Richard Drake, David Hsiung, Tracy McKenzie, Paul Salstrom, Altina Waller, John Stealey, Tyler Blethen, Ronald Eller, Curtis Wood, Richard Starnes, Ralph Mann, Marie Tedesco, and Shannon Wilson for their friendship, for their good work, and for the feedback they've provided on my work for many years now. I especially thank Tracy and Ralph for their careful readings of this manuscript and offering useful suggestions and insights, nearly all of which I've incorporated into its final version.

Acknowledgments

One of the great benefits of working on Appalachia has been the opportunity to interact with scholars in other disciplines. The Appalachian Studies Association has provided an invaluable forum for interdisciplinary discussion and exchange of ideas, and I am one of many beneficiaries of contacts and friendships forged through its annual conferences. In addition to the historians just named, I've found some of the most provocative and valuable work on race and gender in Appalachia is coming from sociologists, anthropologists, and literary and film critics, among others. (We historians still have the Civil War pretty much to ourselves.) I am much indebted to the insightful, multifaceted, and often far more sophisticated work on race by Barbara Ellen Smith, Dwight Billings, Kathleen Blee, Larry Griffin, Wilburn Hayden, Cecelia Conway, Phil Obermiller, and Wilma A. Dunaway that has come to inform my own views on the subject. Wilma and I have not always seen eye to eye on matters of mutual interest, but I've enjoyed our friendship over the years and have learned a great deal from her groundbreaking work on slavery and much else about frontier and antebellum Appalachia.

Barbara Ellen Smith and Mary Anglin have much enriched our historical understanding of Appalachian gender as well. Both have chided me—quite rightfully—for my shortcomings in incorporating women into some of my work. I hope I've redeemed myself somewhat in making gender a significant component of many of the essays collected here. Loyal Jones, Jerry Williamson, Jack Wright, Pat Beaver, David Whisnant, Ross Spears, and Jamie Ross all deserve honorary status as historians for the rich and varied ways in which their own work has informed so many people's work, including mine, and I'm grateful for all they've done for and with me over the years. I owe a special thanks as well to George Frizzell, archivist extraordinaire at Western Carolina University, for his proactive efforts to keep me—and I'm sure many other scholars—fully abreast of the rich holdings he oversees in the Hunter Library there.

I have had the great good fortune of working with and learning from a number of graduate students at the University of Georgia, past and present, whose work has in both tangible and intangible ways influenced my own. I am grateful to Mark Huddle, Keith Bohannon, Jonathan Sarris, Craig Brashear, Michael Buseman, Bruce Stewart,

Acknowledgments

Jennifer Lund Smith, Steve Nash, Drew Swanson, Mary Ella Engel, Kyle Osborn, and Alex Massengale, each of whom has made or is making significant contributions to our understanding of nineteenth-century Appalachia. I owe just as much to many more students in our program whom I dare not try to name, who have worked on the Civil War and its aftermath in non-Appalachian settings, though I can't resist thanking Emory Thomas for luring most of them to UGA in the first place, where I—as his trusty sidekick for many years—became the beneficiary of the accomplished history they produced both while here and since. Nor will I try to name the numerous UGA students in other fields—from anthropology and religion to English and landscape design—whose work is set in Appalachia, and on whose committees I've served. All have further reinforced my appreciation for the healthy cross-pollination that has informed so much of our work separately and together. I have gained much from exchanges with fellow UGA colleagues and southern film historians Hugh Ruppersburg and Richard Neupert, that have helped shape some of my thinking on several of the films I discuss in the latter part of this volume.

We in Appalachian studies have been an unusually collaborative group, as far as gathering our work between single book covers. Much of the best and most cutting-edge scholarship on the region has appeared in essay collections, most of which still provide invaluable samplers of different approaches and perspectives to similar topics and issues. These include *Appalachia in the Making*, edited by Dwight B. Billings, Mary Beth Pudup, and Altina Waller (Chapel Hill: University of North Carolina Press, 1995); *Confronting Appalachian Stereotypes: Back Talk from an American Region*, edited by Dwight B. Billings, Gurney Norman, and Katherine E. Ledford (Lexington: University Press of Kentucky, 1999); *Appalachian Frontiers: Settlement, Society & Development in the Preindustrial Era*, edited by Robert Mitchell (Lexington: University Press of Kentucky, 1991); *The Civil War in Appalachia: Collected Essays*, edited by Kenneth W. Noe and Shannon H. Wilson (Knoxville: University of Tennessee Press, 1997); *Diversity and Accommodation: Essays on the Cultural Composition of the Virginia Frontier*, edited by Michael J. Puglisi (Knoxville: University of Tennessee Press, 1997); *High Mountains Rising: Appalachia in Time and Place*, edited by Richard A. Straw

Acknowledgments

and H. Tyler Blethen (Urbana: University of Illinois Press, 2004); *The Handbook of Appalachia: An Introduction to the Region*, edited by Grace Toney Edwards, JoAnn A. Asbury, and Ricky L. Cox (Knoxville: University of Tennessee Press, 2006); *The Civil War's Aftermath in Appalachia*, edited by Andrew L. Slap (forthcoming from the University Press of Kentucky); and *Appalachians and Race* (Lexington: University Press of Kentucky, 2001), which I edited. I feel privileged to have been a part of a few of these projects; several of the pieces here were originally commissioned for such volumes. I am particularly grateful to the various editors who called on me to write them, and for their feedback as they worked their way into print.

I'm especially grateful to Dwight Billings, who served as co-editor of two volumes in which my essays have appeared and as editor of the *Journal of Appalachian Studies*, where another was published, so that three of these pieces bear his imprint in one way or another. I very much appreciate how often Jerry Williamson and Sandy Ballard have asked me to contribute pieces or serve as parts of debates, roundtable discussions, or forums in the *Appalachian Journal*; I've benefited tremendously from those exchanges and from their input as editors.

It's a real pleasure to work with the University Press of Kentucky again, and I'm especially grateful to Joyce Harrison, now an old friend, for her initial and sustained enthusiasm for this project, and her guidance in getting it pulled together. The entire staff, now under Stephen Wrinn's dynamic leadership, has always been a joy to work with, and I'm always delighted to be in their good hands. I especially appreciate the much-improved prose that has resulted from the good, sharp copyediting provided by Penelope Stratton.

I'm grateful to several people who have enabled me to spend much valued time in western North Carolina settings in ways that have contributed to this volume. I've enjoyed parts of two summers on the campus of Mars Hill College in different capacities provided by Kathy Newfont in the history department and Rick Morgan and Bill Gregg of the Southern Appalachian Repertory Theater, who allowed me and Dan Slagle, from whom I've also learned much, to be small parts of an extraordinary theater project, which I write about in chapter 13 of this book.

Acknowledgments

I thank Nancy and Charlie Midgette for their generosity in letting me use their beautiful house in Montreat, North Carolina, as a getaway, where I've enjoyed a great deal of time for uninterrupted writing and thinking. As much as I love Athens, Georgia, it's great to be able to write about the mountains while nestled in them, and somehow whatever I try to say about that world seems to flow more freely at higher elevations and cooler climes.

Finally, I thank my father in Morganton, North Carolina, for his love of our mountains, and for having spent over fifty years now exploring them with my brothers and me and our families and instilling in us all his enthusiasm for the flora and fauna, trails and vistas, people and history of the region.

Introduction

Late in the fall of 1861, James W. Taylor, a Minnesota journalist, published an extraordinary series of articles in the *St. Paul Daily Press* in which he contemplated the Civil War, then well under way, and the demographic and geographic factors that would affect the course of that conflict and the North's chances of victory. More specifically, as the title of a pamphlet comprising these pieces indicates, Taylor's focus was *Alleghania: The Strength of the Union and the Weakness of Slavery in the Mountain Districts of the South.* His contention was that "within the immense district to which the designation of Alleghania is here applied, the slaves are so few and scattered" and that its residents were imbued with a "complete dedication to Free Labor." He proposed that with the federal government's protection and encouragement, southern highlanders—all "ready to strike for Liberty and Union"—could rise up against the Confederacy to which they had been unwillingly bound, and be reinstated into the Union. This "Switzerland of the South . . . a land of corn and cattle, not cotton," could then become a military base of operations from which the Union army in conjunction with native highlanders could launch "a powerful diversion of a hostile character against the insurrectionists."[1]

Taylor was not alone in these assumptions. In March 1862, James R. Gilmore put readers of *The Continental Monthly,* a newly established journal based in New York and Boston, on alert as to the "possibility of a counter-revolution among the inhabitants of the mountain districts, who hold but few slaves, who have preserved a devoted love for the Union, and who are, if not at positive feud, at least on anything but social harmony with their aristocratic neighbors of the lowlands and of the plantation." In those southern highlands, Gilmore declared, there "exists a tremendous groundwork of aid to the north, and weakness for secession. The love of this region for the Union, and its local hatred for planterdom with its arrogance towards free labor, is no chimera"; with aid from the North, it could "light up a flame of counter-revolution . . . that would sweep the slaveocracy from existence."[2]

Of course, such a scenario never became a reality, nor was it ever very likely to. Its significance lies more in the assumptions on which it was based. John Alexander Williams has called *Alleghania* "the first attempt to define Appalachia systematically."[3] If that is indeed the case, it is perhaps fitting that one of the first region-wide generalizations articulated what would rest on two of the most basic and deepseated misconceptions about the region—its aversion to slavery and its solid Unionist stance—both of which would take their place among the even more entrenched stereotypes of Appalachian isolation, backwardness, degeneracy, and violence.

I encountered *Alleghania* early in the research for my dissertation, a study of slavery and the sectional crisis in western North Carolina, and much later I discovered Gilmore's version of the same premise. I was intrigued to see these ideas so boldly put forward for a national audience at this critical—indeed, rare—moment when it seemed as if Southern Appalachia could play an integral part in resolving the national crisis at hand. They are among the first and fullest expressions of assumptions made far more broadly and extending through much of the next century and a half—that Southern Appalachia was basically free of slaves and, as a consequence, had no interest in or commitment to the Confederate cause. Yet, as with so many such regional generalizations, a close examination of these issues at local or intraregional levels quickly reveals their flaws. They were myths, but myths with remarkably strong staying power. Taking issue with those two misconceptions is, in effect, the driving force behind the essays collected here.

The claim that the southern highlands had nothing in common with the rest of the Confederacy and had no vested interest in defending the labor system or racial order that drove most of the rest of the

South out of the Union raised another question that chroniclers of the region have wrestled with ever since: how much can Appalachia be considered an integral part of the South? In work that will be referenced more fully later in this volume, James Klotter and others have argued effectively that the illusion of an all-white, all-Anglo-Saxon populace had much to do with Southern Appalachia's appeal to northern philanthropists, educators, and missionaries in the post-Reconstruction era, after many of them had tired of the biracial complexities that had made rebuilding and reshaping the rest of the South so difficult and unsavory, and that provided an equally refreshing diversion from the problems associated with the ever more foreign and multiethnic makeup of their own cities.

At the turn of the century, Berea College president William G. Frost referred to the region as "one of the grand divisions of our continent, which we are beginning to name Appalachian America," in a conscious effort to generate sympathy—even nostalgia—for a region that still embraced what had once been the premodern traditions and values of the nation as a whole, and with no reference to any geographical linkage to the South.[4] He too stressed the steadfast loyalty of southern highlanders to the Union when that Union split, as did John C. Campbell, who went so far as to label Southern Appalachia "a northern wedge thrust into the heart of the Confederacy." Both had specific rationales and not-so-hidden agendas in distancing the highlands from the rest of the South (some of which will be explored in this volume); noting such commonalities with the North served as one, fairly blatant means of doing so.

Even the terms "southern highlands" and "Southern Appalachia" which came into common usage only in the early twentieth century, served less to link the region with the rest of the South than to distinguish a specific part of the mountain chain that stretches from Georgia and Alabama through New England, and thus carried a very different connotation from the terms "Appalachian South" and "mountain South" that do suggest a subregion within a region.

Scholars continue to disagree on the geographical—or even geocultural—bounds of Southern Appalachia and on the criteria by which those bounds are determined.[5] But the region undeniably consists of what Campbell once called "the backyards" of at least five

3

antebellum states (at its most basic: Virginia, Kentucky, North Carolina, Tennessee, and Georgia).[6] All were slaveholding states, and all but one (Kentucky) joined the Confederacy, though a significant part of highland Virginia remained in the Union and in 1863 became West Virginia, the northernmost of Southern Appalachian states. Those facts alone—whatever the internal sentiment against slavery, secession, or the Civil War—made Southern Appalachia fully a part of the South, and it is upon those facts that much of the more recent scholarship, including my own, has been built.

John Shelton Reed once observed, "Appalachia serves as the South's 'South,'" suggesting that the problems of Appalachia—including its relative poverty and marginalization—make its relationship to the broader South parallel to that of the South's place within the nation as a whole.[7] In a more substantive analysis of those issues, Allen Batteau has referred to the "double otherness" of Appalachia—its distinctiveness from the South as well as from the nation. Seeing both racial issues and the Civil War as major impetuses in the creation of these dual distinctions, he notes that they made it possible "to identify Appalachia as southern and anti-progressive on the one hand, and a critique of the South on the other."[8]

Those of us in the field of Appalachian studies have confronted that dual identity head on in a variety of ways. The theme of an early Appalachian Studies Conference and its published proceedings focused on "Southern Appalachia and the South: A Region within a Region," and both the *Appalachian Journal* and the *Journal of Appalachian Studies* have devoted forums or special issues to the question of Appalachia's southernness.[9] Provocative recent studies of Appalachian identity by Batteau, Jerry Williamson, and Jeff Biggers have assessed the region's significance within both a southern and a national context.[10]

Yet this path of inquiry has thus far been a one-way street. Few of those working on the lowland South have felt the need to lift their eyes unto the hills. Sociologist Larry Griffin has probably done more than anyone in juxtaposing Appalachian and southern identity and the different fields of study entailed by each; he has admitted that he and a colleague approached the field of Appalachian studies fearful of how little they knew of the region and how much there was to learn.

"What we found," he wrote in 2002, "was that the literature on Appalachia and its people is both extraordinarily rich and of great, if somewhat surprising, utility to scholars in Southern Studies."[11] It's hard to think of an Appalachian historian ever saying—or having to say—the same thing about southern history. Anyone who writes about nineteenth-century—or, for that matter, twentieth-century—Appalachia has to be grounded in the broader historical trends and developments taking place elsewhere in the South.

And yet scholars of the rest of the South can—and usually do—assess the larger region without acknowledging Appalachia. My friend and colleague Jim Cobb recently produced an impressively comprehensive and well-received history of southern identity—without any mention of mountain folks.[12] Current textbooks, essay collections, and documentary readers on southern history pay little more than lip service to the mountain South, and it is never mentioned in relation to the antebellum or Civil War years.[13]

Certainly no two topics have been more central to southern history (or, one might argue, to southern identity) than race relations and the Confederacy. Both entail complex issues that defy generalization for any part of the larger region. Perhaps as a result, both fields have spawned multiple localized or regional studies that have allowed scholars to examine in more microcosmic scope the dynamics of race (slavery, emancipation, Jim Crow, and civil rights) and of the war (issues of loyalty and willpower, political and nonpolitical dissent, household hardship and community breakdown, and the traumas of guerrilla warfare). The same has proved true of Appalachian scholarship as well, and yet rarely do these studies overlap or connect with those of the South at large.

One set of scholars has characterized this approach as "an effort to deconstruct the concept of an essential and universalistic Appalachian past," and those of us looking especially at race and war in the region have taken on this challenge with particular gusto.[14] Perhaps because those myths still loom so large, my generation of historians discovered and reconstructed slavery's existence in multiple modes throughout the region that raise new questions about master-slave relationships, the economics of slave labor and slave markets, and the quality of slave life. Others among us have discovered new and somewhat messier realities in terms of both Civil War loyalties and home-front experiences. The regional variants in both cases have continued to contribute to a sense of Appalachian distinctiveness, and yet I think we would acknowledge more fully than was once the case that the differences between the highland and lowland South in regard to these particular topics are more of degree than of kind. As such, there is much of relevance in the Appalachian experience to that of the South as a whole, as Larry Griffin, for one, has discovered.

Consideration of these issues at ground level also allows us to consider the variables that rendered southern highlanders different in behavior, attitude, and experience not only from their lowland counterparts, but from each other as well. The foibles of human nature as reflected in decisions made, attitudes formed, and actions taken have much to do with the exigencies of kinship, household, and community. Individuals, families, and communities provide the core for many of the essays that follow. Both before and even more so during the Civil War, Appalachians left an extraordinary written record of their experiences, which allow us more fully to re-create and appreciate the human dimension of the conflict as they experienced it in all its complexity and variety, which are so often at odds with the generalizations that have, since Taylor and Gilmore, dominated—and distorted—our understanding of the region. By embracing the particular—whether it be place, person, or situation—I, like many of my colleagues, have sought to shed meaningful light on larger historical realities of the Appalachian experience, even as they defy easy categorization or broad assumptions that were applicable to the whole.

By the same token, it is important to remember that many of the behaviors and attitudes in evidence here were by no means exclusive to Appalachia. The further back one pulls his lens on the region, the more contradiction and ambiguity his frame has to take in and to account for. Geography was certainly a crucial factor in determining what was—or merely may have been—exceptional about the mountain South, but it was never the only factor, any more than sugar planters in Louisiana, rice planters on Georgia's Sea Islands, or merchants in Richmond or Baltimore or New Orleans can be defined only by the particular settings or crops that so seemed to distinguish them. Like all of these, southern highlanders were also southerners—sometimes foremost, sometimes more secondarily—and their actions and attitudes were often dictated as much or more by identity with that larger regional entity than by the smaller, more immediate geographical area defined primarily by topography or climate. Nothing brings those dual and overlapping identities into sharper focus in the nineteenth century than do the realities of slavery, race, and Civil War.

To further complicate matters, Appalachian history rarely comes to us unfiltered. Far more than is true for other regional histories, both its filterers and the filtering process are often as revealing and as significant as what is actually being conveyed; as such, those chronicling the region deserve close scrutiny from those of us making use of their writings. Emerging from the juxtaposition of these essays are multiple voices and perspectives of both insiders and outsiders. While many of those outsiders (such as Taylor and Gilmore) created and perpetuated much of the misinformation and stereotypes about the southern highlands without ever having visited the region, others—from Frederick Law Olmsted to fugitive prisoners of war—actually moved through parts of the mountain South and left us with more credible firsthand, if often fleeting, accounts of life and conditions there. Their observations supplement, enhance, reinforce, and sometimes challenge the written expressions of highlanders themselves—most of them privately, through letters, diaries, journals, or memoirs, though some in more self-conscious form as they wrote for publication or posterity.

Those contemporary voices, in various configurations, provide the basis for most of the essays in the first two sections of this book, where I have tried to explore, first, the historical reality of particular aspects of slavery and racial attitudes, and second, the social upheavals of the war years as experienced by a populace far from the center of military action for most of the conflict. But I am equally interested in the depiction of antebellum and Civil War Appalachia in hindsight and how such depictions took shape in insiders' personal or collective memories, in outsiders' observations and assessments, and ultimately in what novelists, filmmakers, and a playwright have made of it all. The distortions and misconceptions inherent in so much of the historical and literary treatments of the region have been widely chronicled; as Allen Batteau once noted, "In the Appalachian studies industry, an entire shop floor is devoted to the labor-intensive task of debunking stereotypes."[15]

Thus, in the third section of the book, called "Remembrance" in a very loose use of the term, I explore the many ways through which misconceptions about race and war have evolved and have been challenged. Many of these works represent serious efforts to move beyond—or rise above—clichés and stereotypes to provide genuine insights and capture certain realities about Appalachia and its people that only the dramatic license of fiction and film can provide. They too focus on the particular, as both genres demand. Although these authors cast their characters as heroes, heroines, and villains, they also depict individuals and communities struggling within a society and a culture often vividly reconstructed and movingly presented to readers or viewers. Most of the works I consider here—novels, short stories, films, and a play—get at least as much historically right as they get wrong, or so I argue. Unlike critics who have faulted these works for factual inaccuracies, more often than not I see glasses half full rather than half empty in terms of the larger "truths" that emerge.

The seventeen essays presented here were produced over the past two decades. A few appeared first as journal articles, but most were commissioned or invited pieces for essay collections or for special thematic issues or forums in journals. I have revised most for this volume, some more than others. I have tried to update citations to reflect the vast and valuable scholarship that has appeared since the original publication of some of these pieces. The editors have indulged me in allowing me to retain slight differences in endnote formats, reflecting the stylistic differences in the various journals and books in which they originally appeared.

As much as possible, I have sought to eliminate any repetitious material. But some stories, quotations, or factual data are so integral to the differing contexts of two or more essays that I have retained them in both places, and beg the reader's indulgence in the occasional passages that may give a slight sense of déjà vu.

Notes

1. James W. Taylor, *Alleghania: A Geographical and Statistical Memoir Exhibiting the Strength of the Union and the Weakness of Slavery in the*

Mountain Districts of the South (St. Paul, Minn.: James Davenport, 1862), v, 15–16, 1–2.

2. [James R. Gilmore,] "Southern Aid to the North," *The Continental Monthly* 1 (March 1862): 142–43. Gilmore cites Taylor's pamphlet in his article.

3. John Alexander Williams, *Appalachia: A History* (Chapel Hill: University of North Carolina Press, 2002), 11.

4. William G. Frost, "Educational Pioneering in the Southern Mountains," in the National Education Association's *Addresses and Proceedings* (1901): 556. See chap. 12 in this volume for more on Frost and Campbell's depictions of the region.

5. For one of several useful overviews of these debates, see John Alexander Williams, "Counting Yesterday's People: Using Aggregate Data to Address the Problem of Appalachia's Boundaries," *Journal of Appalachian Studies* 2 (Spring 1996): 3–28.

6. John C. Campbell, *The Southern Highlander and His Homeland* (New York: Russell Sage, 1921), 18–19.

7. John Shelton Reed, *Southern Folk, Plain and Fancy: Native White Social Types* (Athens: University of Georgia Press, 1986), 42.

8. Allen W. Batteau, *The Invention of Appalachia* (Tucson: University of Arizona Press, 1990), 37.

9. *Journal of the Appalachian Studies Association* 3: "Southern Appalachia and the South: A Region within a Region," ed. John C. Inscoe (1991). Two articles in that issue are still very useful treatments of the subject: John Alexander Williams, "A Regionalism Within Regionalisms: Three Frameworks for Appalachian Studies," 4–17; and Richard B. Drake, "Southern Appalachia and the South: A Region Within a Section," 18–27. See also "Forum on Appalachia and the South," *Appalachian Journal* 29 (Spring 2004): 296–340; and "Whiteness and Racialization in Appalachia," special issue of the *Journal of Appalachian Studies* 10 (Spring/Fall 2004).

10. Batteau, *Invention of Appalachia*; J. W. Williamson, *Hillbillyland: What the Movies Did to the Mountains and What the Mountains Did to the Movies* (Chapel Hill: University of North Carolina Press, 1995); and Jeff Biggers, *The United States of Appalachia: How Southern Mountaineers Brought Independence, Culture, and Enlightenment to America* (Emeryville, Calif.: Shoemaker and Hoard, 2005).

11. Larry J. Griffin and Ashley B. Thompson, "Appalachia and the South: Collective Memory, Identity, and Representation," *Appalachian Journal* 29 (Spring 2002): 296. In addition to this essay (pp. 296–327), see also responses it by Chad Berry, Dwight B. Billings, and John C. Inscoe (pp. 328–40). See Griffin's equally valuable essay, "Whiteness and Southern Identity in the Mountain and Lowland South," *Journal of Appalachian Studies* 10 (Spring/Fall 2004): 7–37.

12. James C. Cobb, *Away Down South: A History of Southern Identity* (New York: Oxford University Press, 2005). (Cobb does give Thomas Wolfe his due, on pp. 135–37, but he never identifies him as a product of Appalachia.) I may as well alienate another friend, W. Fitzhugh Brundage, by noting that his equally valuable study, *The Southern Past: A Clash of Race and Memory* (Cambridge: Harvard University Press, 2005), make no mention of the mountain South either, although he very effectively extended his study of southern lynching into Appalachian regions, in both *Lynching in the New South: Georgia and Virginia, 1880–1930* (Urbana: University of Illinois Press, 1993), and "Racial Violence, Lynchings, and Modernization in the Mountain South," in *Appalachians and Race: The Mountain South from Slavery to Segregation,* ed. John C. Inscoe (Lexington: University Press of Kentucky, 2001), 302–16.

13. William J. Cooper Jr. and Tom E. Terrill, in *The American South: A History* (New York: Alfred A. Knopf, 1991), which includes a three-page discussion of Southern Appalachia in a chapter on "Restoration and Exile, 1919–1929." No mention of the region is made in John B. Boles, *The South through Time: A History of an American Region,* 2nd ed. (Upper Saddle River, N.J., 1999); Paul D. Escott, et al., *Major Problems in the History of the American South,* 2nd ed., 2 vols. (Boston: Houghton Mifflin, 1999); or J. William Harris, *The Making of the American South: A Short History, 1500–1877* (Oxford, England: Blackwell Publishing, 2006). John Boles does include a full essay on Appalachian historiography in *A Companion to the American South* (Oxford, England: Blackwell Publishers, 2002), 369–86.

14. Dwight B. Billings, Mary Beth Pudup, and Altina Waller, eds., *Appalachia in the Making: The Mountain South in the Nineteenth Century* (Chapel Hill: University of North Carolina Press, 1995), 9.

15. Batteau, *The Invention of Appalachia,* 7. Among the major works dealing with regional perception and stereotyping in addition to Batteau's book are Henry Shapiro, *Appalachia on Our Mind: The Southern Mountains and Mountaineers in the American Consciousness, 1870–1920* (Chapel Hill: University of North Carolina Press, 1978); Cratis D. Williams, "The Southern Mountaineer in Fact and Fiction" (Ph.D. diss., New York University, 1961); David Whisnant, *All That is Native and Fine: The Politics of Culture in an American Region* (Chapel Hill: University of North Carolina Press, 1983); Williamson, *Hillbillyland;* and Anthony Harkins, *Hillbilly: A Cultural History of an American Icon* (New York: Oxford University Press, 2004).

Race

1

Race and Racism in Nineteenth-Century Appalachia

Myths, Realities, and Ambiguities

David Whisnant, one of the premier chroniclers of Appalachia, once noted that whenever he read books that generalized about "the South," he amused himself by checking their generalizations against what he knows of the mountain South. Rarely, he said, was the congruence very great. Nowhere, in fact, has the incongruence between the highland and lowland South been more apparent than on matters of race. In one of the most celebrated regional generalizations, U. B. Phillips in 1928 argued that racism—or, more specifically, the quest for white supremacy—was the central theme of southern history. While that claim has been debated ever since, few scholars have objected to the basic premise behind it: that, as Phillips put it quite simply, the Negro was an essential element in "the distinctive Southern pattern of life."[1]

For a significant section of the South—the Southern Appalachians—however, the African American presence has not been central, perhaps not even essential, to its distinctive "pattern of life." That so integral a factor to southern life elsewhere is peripheral to highland society no doubt accounts for the fact that, despite increasingly sophisticated analysis of the complexities of both southern race relations and Appalachian society, the two fields have not yet intersected to any significant degree. Perhaps as a result, no other aspect of the Appalachian character has been as prone to as much myth, stereotype, contradiction, and confusion as have matters of race relations and racial attitudes among mountaineers.

Historians have often skirted the question, but none of them has yet tackled it nearly as directly as have literary interpreters of the region. Two works of early twentieth-century fiction are particularly striking in their portrayals of the contradictory assumptions regarding racism among southern highlanders. Both works, one a short story and one a novel, use the Civil War as the catalyst through which mountain whites confront not only blacks for the first time but their own racist proclivities as well. In so doing, the authors give dramatic form to the deep-seated discrepancies that have long plagued popular and scholarly ideas regarding the relationship between these two groups of southerners.

In his immensely popular 1903 novel, *The Little Shepherd of Kingdom Come,* John Fox chronicled a young orphan boy's move from Kentucky's Cumberland Mountains to the Bluegrass. Until he leaves his home and moves to a nearby valley, where he encounters two slaves, Chad Buford has never seen a black person. Dazed, he stares at them and asks his companion, Tom, "Whut've them fellers got on their faces?" Tom responds, "Hain't you nuver seed a nigger afore?" When Chad shakes his head, Tom says, "Lots o' folks from yo' side o' the mountains nuver have seed a nigger. Sometimes hit skeers 'em." "Hit don't skeer me," Chad replies. A few years later, when the outbreak of the Civil War forces Kentuckians to take a stand for or against the Union, Chad, by then a teenager fully exposed to slavery and plantation society as they existed in central Kentucky, chooses to fight for the Union, despite pressure from his Confederate guardians. Yet his attitude toward slavery or blacks is not central to his decision. His exposure to it has been brief, and the defense of slavery, Fox writes, "never troubled his soul. . . . Unlike the North, the boy had no prejudice, no antagonism, no jealousy, no grievance to help him in his struggle."[2]

Nearly thirty years after the publication of Fox's novel, William Faulkner examined highland racial attitudes from another, far more dramatic angle. In a 1932 short story, "Mountain Victory," he wrote of a Confederate major from Mississippi and his slave, who in heading home from Virginia just after the end of the Civil War, come upon a Tennessee mountain family and ask to spend the night in their cabin. The bulk of the story involves the varied reactions of members of this family to their two strange guests and their racial identity. Only

14

well into the story does it become apparent that the Tennesseans assume that Major Weddel, of French and Creole ancestry, is black as well, which prompts him to taunt his hosts as to the source of their hostility: "So it's my face and not my uniform. And you fought four years to free us, I understand." Ultimately their revulsion toward the black man and the close relationship he enjoys with his master lead to a violent denouement, an ambush by the mountain men that leaves both Mississippians and one of the Tennesseans dead.[3]

This powerful but little-known Faulkner story and Fox's far more widely read saga of Civil War Kentucky offer enlightening comparisons on a number of levels. Both are studies of the culture clashes between plantation aristocrats and poor white mountaineers, and both examine the tensions between Confederate and Unionist values that set southerner against fellow southerner. But perhaps most significant, both Faulkner and Fox depicted highlanders' ignorance—or to use Faulkner's term, innocence—of the biracial character of the rest of the South and described very different responses by highlanders suddenly exposed to the reality of another race.

While more subtle in delineating the reactions of their mountain characters than many, Faulkner and Fox both rely on one of the most basic assumptions regarding preindustrial Appalachian society—the absence of blacks. This chapter explores the implications of that demographic given in terms of both the myths and realities of a far more elusive factor—the racial attitudes of white southern highlanders resulting from that minimal or nonexistent contact with blacks and what, if anything, made their brand of racism unique. Which was a more accurate reflection of mountain racism—John Fox's young humanitarian hero or Faulkner's vicious and violent Tennesseans?

Part of the romanticization of Appalachia that accompanied its "discovery" in the late nineteenth and early twentieth centuries lay in its perceived racial and ethnic homogeneity. "Nowhere will be found purer Anglo-Saxon blood," a journalist wrote of the north Georgia mountains in 1897.[4] Ethnogeographer Ellen Semple extolled the mountain populace of Kentucky on the same grounds. Not only had they kept foreign elements at bay, she observed in 1901, but they had "still more effectively . . . excluded the negroes. This region is as free from them as northern Vermont."[5] After geological expeditions through the Blue Ridge and the Alleghenies in the late 1880s, Harvard professor Nathaniel S. Shaler wrote that there were "probably more white people who have never seen a negro in this part of the United States than in all New England." He was amused at the intense curiosity his own black servants evoked among highland men and women, some of whom traveled more than twenty miles to stare at them.[6]

Appalachian residents themselves contributed to the myth. In 1906 East Tennessee minister Samuel Tyndale Wilson, then president of Maryville College, stated categorically that the mountain region is "the only part of the South that is not directly concerned with the race problem." He even suggested that the commonly used term "mountain whites," which he found pejorative (too much like "poor white trash"), be replaced with simply "mountaineer," with no need for any designation by race. In *The Hills Beyond,* his semifictional interpretation of his region's history, Asheville native Thomas Wolfe claimed that the mountain people had not owned slaves and that in many counties, "Negroes were unknown before the war."[7]

Even Flannery O'Connor based one of her most celebrated stories, "The Artificial Nigger," on the premise that mountaineers had no contacts with blacks. The 1950 story, which O'Connor once said was her favorite, centers on an elderly north Georgia man who brings his ten-year-old grandson on an excursion to Atlanta in order to expose him to the world beyond their isolated backwoods existence. The experience becomes one of continual encounters with blacks, which alternately baffle, intrigue, repel, and traumatize the two highlanders, whose backgrounds have left them totally unprepared for this strange race of people. Once safely back home, the young boy sums up his introduction to the biracial urban South: "I'm glad I've went once, but I'll never go back again."[8]

While O'Connor (like Faulkner and Fox) drew upon the assumption of a pure white mountain South to explore more universal racial themes, more recent scholars have made much of the propagandistic effects of that image. James Klotter has argued convincingly that it was the region's perceived "whiteness" that so appealed to northern interests at the time and inspired them to divert their mission impulses toward deserving highlanders after their disillusionment with similar efforts on behalf of southern blacks during Reconstruction. Nina Silber has suggested that northerners found postwar reconciliation more palatable with the mountain South, due to its racial purity and its loyalty to the Union during the war. These traits provided northerners with identifying links less apparent in poor whites elsewhere in the South, still unreformed rebels caught up in the biracial complexities of the lowland South.[9]

This basic demographic assumption, which Edward Cabbell has called Appalachia's "black invisibility" factor, is simple enough to refute, and a number of studies in recent years have effectively demolished the myth that African Americans were a negligible presence in Appalachia.[10] Slavery existed in every county in Appalachia in 1860, and the region as a whole included a black populace, free and slave, of more than 175,000. Freedmen and freedwomen continued to reside in most areas of the mountain South by century's end, when their numbers totaled more than 274,000.[11] Most of the region's few urban areas, such as Chattanooga, Knoxville, Asheville, Bristol, and Roanoke, saw a dramatic influx of blacks in the decades following the Civil War, and communal experiments, such as North Carolina's "Kingdom of the Happy Land" and Kentucky's Coe Ridge, were established by former slaves moving into the region from antebellum plantation homes elsewhere.[12] From the 1880s on, the coalfields of Kentucky, Virginia, Tennessee, and especially West Virginia attracted thousands of southern blacks and drastically changed the racial demographics of substantial areas of central Appalachia.[13]

There were, however, rural areas of the southern highlands from which former slaves drifted away. At least ten Appalachian counties lost their entire black population between 1880 and 1900, due to a combination of push (scare tactics) and pull (economic opportunity elsewhere) factors.[14] Thus by the end of the century there were large numbers of mountain residents whose contacts with blacks were negligible. It was they who served as the models of racial purity—or to use Faulkner's term, "innocence"—to both contemporary observers and later generations. But the nature of the racial attitudes spawned by this void, whether real or perceived, has proven a difficult aspect of the mythology to come to terms with. Like W. J. Cash's *The Mind of the South,* most treatments of mountain racism have characterized it as a single and simple mentality. But unlike Cash, who took more than 400 pages to describe the regional "mind" as he saw it, most of what has been written about southern highlanders' racial views has been consigned to slight and usually casual references, based on conjecture, exaggeration, and overgeneralization. More often than not, the topic is mentioned only in passing in works with other concerns or priorities. Much is taken for granted, and no one to date has subjected the issue to either serious scrutiny, systematic analysis, or substantial documentation.

What makes the topic so intriguing is the sharp dichotomy that characterizes opinions as to how white mountaineers viewed blacks. On the one hand is the assumption on which Faulkner drew heavily—highlanders' inherent fear of and intense hostility toward the race that they alone among southerners did not know or control. Conversely there is the more extensively supported notion that the mountains were a southern oasis of abolitionism and racial liberality. Despite the pervasiveness of both schools of thought, proponents of one never seem to have acknowledged the other, much less made any direct effort to discredit it.

Cash's *Mind of the South* had much to do with giving widespread credence to the idea of mountain hostility to blacks. His one relevant statement is among the most often quoted: "Though there were few slaves in the mountains," the mountaineer "had acquired a hatred and contempt for the Negro even more virulent than that of the common white of the lowlands; a dislike so rabid that it was worth a black man's life to venture into many mountain sections."[15] This was a belief to which mountain residents and chroniclers of the region had long adhered. Just after the Civil War, John Eaton, as commissioner of Tennessee's Freedman's Bureau, noted that even though there were far fewer blacks in the state's eastern highlands, "the prejudice of the whites against the Negro was even more acute" there than in areas overrun with "colored" refugees, such as Memphis or Vicksburg.[16]

John Campbell, perhaps the region's most influential twentieth-century chronicler, presented a somewhat more judicious view of its racism but confirmed that there were counties "without a single Negro inhabitant and where it was unpleasant if not unsafe for him to go." Muriel Shepherd quoted a North Carolina highlander who, in explaining why there were no blacks, free or slave, in the Rock Creek section of Mitchell County, stated that "colored people have a well-founded belief that if they venture up there they might not come back alive."[17]

The idea of a more intense highland racism was widespread even in other parts of the South. In his memoir of his sharecropping childhood in middle Georgia, for example, black author Raymond Andrews wrote of a particular overseer: "Mister Brown and his family were mountain folks, or 'hillbillies,' but were considered unusual for the breed, as it was often said that folks from up in the hills had no use for lowlanders, particularly colored folks." William Styron made a similar point in *The Confessions of Nat Turner,* perhaps the most insightful portrait of the slaveholding South in modern fiction. In attempting to explain why Joseph Travis split a slave family by selling a mother and child south, he noted that Travis had moved to Southampton County from "the wild slopes of the Blue Ridge mountains." Styron, in Nat's voice, speculates: "Maybe it was his mountain heritage, his lack of experience with Tidewater ways, that caused him to do something that no truly respectable slaveowner would do."[18]

But whereas there is evidence of intense negrophobia among southern highlanders, the diminished presence of slavery there led many to far different conclusions about the reasons behind the institution's relative absence. The belief has long held sway that "Appalachians have not been saddled with the same prejudices about black people that people of the deep South have," as Loyal Jones, one of the region's most perceptive interpreters, has expressed it.[19] This idea of a moral superiority among highlanders in regard to their racial attitudes is deep rooted and is based in large part on the stereotypical "rugged individualism" credited to mountain men. That perception, along with the reality of comparatively fewer slaves in the region, has led many to conclude that the rejection of slavery was a conscious choice.

The concept of Appalachia as a bastion of liberty was well developed by the time the Civil War broke out, largely because the area was seen as a refuge for escaped slaves. The region was considered part of the Underground Railroad out of the South, where according to one contemporary source, "rugged mountaineers forfeited life for the furtherance of the means of justice, and mingled blood . . . with the blood of millions of slaves."[20] More recently, Boston social worker Leon Williams described the region as "settled to a substantial degree by slaves and indentured white servants fleeing from exploitation and angry with established colonial America." "The hills, in their exquisite isolation," he continued, "became havens for the disenchanted black and white . . . who needed to escape burdensome drudgery and slavery."[21]

Historian Barbara Fields has even suggested that the movement of yeomen into the backcountry can be viewed as a southern counterpart to the northern Free-Soil movement. They migrated into the hills, she maintains, "to escape the encirclement of the plantation and create a world after their own image." Highlanders themselves often extolled the "slavelessness" of their region in Calvinistic terms that the abolitionist movement later adopted. "We are more moral and religious and less absorbed . . . than the people of West Tennessee," noted East Tennessean David Deaderick in his journal in 1827, for "where slaves exist in large numbers and where all the work, or nearly all, is performed by slaves, a consequent inaction and idleness are characteristics of the whites."[22]

John Brown long saw the southern highlands as central to his abolitionist schemes. As early as 1847, in a meeting with Frederick Douglass, Brown pointed on a map to the "far-reaching Alleghenies" and declared that "these mountains are the basis of my plan," both as an escape route out of the South and a base of operations from which he could direct uprisings against the plantation South. Douglass quoted Brown as saying, "God has given the strength of the hills to freedom; they were placed here for the emancipation of the negro race; they are full of natural forts . . . [and] good hiding places, where large numbers of brave men could be concealed, baffle and elude pursuit for a long time."[23] When Brown finally attacked Harpers Ferry twelve years later, the highlands were still crucial to his aims. He hoped to move south through Virginia and the Carolinas, liberating the slaves of the plantation piedmont and sending them to a chain of fortresses established in the mountains to their west, from which they would hold their opponents at bay as reinforcements, black and white, gathered to form an army of liberation. "The mountains and swamps of the South," Brown reiterated to a fellow conspirator a year before his 1859 raid on that western Virginia arsenal, "were intended by the Almighty for a refuge for the slave and a defense against the oppressor."[24]

In the early months of the Civil War, a Minnesota journalist suggested that the key to putting down the southern rebellion lay in the federal government's embrace and use of the support it enjoyed within the South, particularly among southern Appalachians. The reason, he maintained, was that "within this Switzerland of the South, Nature is at war with slavery." Bondage, he implied, was incompatible with high altitudes: "Freedom has always loved the air of mountains. Slavery, like malaria, desolates the low alluvials of the globe."[25] Such sentiments became even more prevalent after the war, as northerners acknowledged the Union loyalty of much of the region. In an 1872 sermon Rev. William Goodrich of Cleveland, Ohio, was among those who extolled the virtues of the highland South. "Explain it as we may," he preached, "there belongs to mountain regions a moral elevation of their own. They give birth to strong, free, pure and noble races. They lift the men who dwell among them, in thought and resolve. Slavery, falsehood, base compliance, luxury, belong to the plains. Freedom, truth, hardy sacrifice, simple honor, to the highlands."[26]

So the creation of "Holy Appalachia"—as Allen Batteau termed it in his study of the region's "invention" by outside interests—was under way. It was a creation based on rather convoluted reasoning. The admiration for the Anglo-Saxon purity of mountaineers' identity carried with it the implication that a conscious rejection of slavery on ideological grounds played a major part in their lack of racial or ethnic contamination. Abraham Lincoln became part of this increasingly idealized formula and emerged as a patron saint to a later generation of mountain residents.[27]

Even Harry Caudill, whose haves-versus-have-nots analysis of Kentucky's Cumberland Mountains extended to antebellum tensions between the area's few slaveholders and its vast majority of nonslaveholders, believed that nonslaveholders' Unionist stance during the Civil War stemmed not so much from class resentment as from the fact that in some vague way "these poorer mountaineers, fiercely independent as they were, found something abhorrent in the ownership of one person by another." John Fox's idealistic young hero in *The Little Shepherd of Kingdom Come* was not, Caudill maintained, "the only mountaineer to risk or endure death on the battlefields because of a sincere desire to see the shackles stricken from millions of men and women."[28]

Another major factor that contributed to the image of Appalachia as "holy" ground was the establishment of several abolitionist footholds in the region. The frequently touted claim that the abolition movement began in the mountains rests on early efforts in Wheeling, Virginia; in East Tennessee; and later in Berea, Kentucky. As early as 1797 a Knoxville newspaper advocated the forming of an abolition society, and the next decade saw Benjamin Lundy fulfilling that charge in Wheeling. Lundy later moved to northeastern Tennessee, where he joined a number of "New Light" Presbyterians and Quakers from Pennsylvania and Ohio, who established what were among the nation's first manumission societies and produced the earliest antislavery publications. By 1827, according to one claim, East Tennessee had one-fifth of the abolition societies in the United States and almost a fifth of the national membership.[29] But most organized efforts were phased out or moved elsewhere within a few years; Maryville College in Blount County remained the only substantial base of antislavery activity for the rest of the antebellum period.[30]

Other manifestations of highland antislavery were more sectional. In 1847 Henry Ruffner—a Presbyterian minister and president of Virginia's Washington College, who had small slaveholdings in Rockbridge County—stirred debate over (and, briefly, garnered considerable support for) a proposal that slavery, while firmly entrenched in eastern Virginia, could be gradually abolished west of the Blue Ridge "without detriment to the rights or interests of slaveholders." He proposed that all slaves in the Shenandoah Valley and surrounding mountains be transported to Liberia and that future importation of blacks into the region be banned. But much of Ruffner's agenda and the basis for much of the initial enthusiasm for his proposal grew out of resentment of sectional inequities that benefited the Tidewater slaveholding elite at the expense of westerners. Once constitutional reforms in 1851 alleviated many of those perceived abuses, support for Ruffner's emancipation scheme evaporated.[31]

Although less explicitly abolitionist in purpose, Berea College stood as a model of interracial education from its origins in the 1850s until almost the end of the century, the product of Kentucky-born, Ohio-educated abolitionist John Fee's quest for "a practical recognition of the brotherhood of man." Ellen Semple cited Berea as an example of "the democratic spirit characteristic of all mountain people" and concluded that its location on the western margin of the Cumberland Plateau was "probably the only geographic location south of the Mason and Dixon line where such an institution could exist."[32] As unusual as this experiment was in the postbellum, much less the antebellum, South, one can hardly credit its existence to Appalachian liberality. The school's turn-of-the-century shift to an exclusive mission aimed at mountain whites and preservation of their folk arts bestowed on Berea a reputation as a cultural center of Appalachia. Fee himself never thought of Berea as being located in the mountains. "We are in the 'hill country,'" he wrote in 1867, "between the 'blue grass' & the mountains. From the former region we now draw our colored men, from the latter the young white men & ladies."[33]

Merely on the basis of these rather limited or regionally marginal efforts, however, the concept of Appalachia as a solid bastion of freedom and equality has been difficult to shake, as scholars from Carter Woodson in the 1910s to Don West in the 1970s have implied that Appalachia was thoroughly and deeply abolitionist. Yet all have distorted the evidence to make such a case, and their treatments of the subject are deceptive. Woodson, himself a black Appalachian native, published his landmark 1916 essay, "Freedom and Slavery in Appalachia," in the very first issue of the *Journal of Negro History,* which he founded and edited. He maintained that the Scotch-Irish who settled the southern highlands, a "liberty-loving, and tyrant-hating race," exhibited "more prejudice against the slave holder than against the Negro." He stressed their antislavery sentiment in the region as pervasive and ongoing. Woodson's geographic scope was deceptively broad, however, encompassing far more than the southern highlands. As much of his essay deals with abolitionist activity in piedmont North Carolina and central Kentucky as it does with those short-lived efforts in East Tennessee.[34]

Don West, a native of north Georgia and cofounder of the Highlander Folk School, relied on only scattered evidence—from the East Tennessee abolitionists to incidents of Confederate disaffection in north Georgia—to draw even more generalized conclusions regarding mountain liberalism on racial matters. From these few examples he claimed to demonstrate that the mountain South "consistently opposed slavery" and "refused to go with the Confederacy." The southern mountaineer, West wrote, "may be said to have held the Lincoln attitude generally."[35]

There was more than a touch of presentism in both Woodson's and West's historical claims. Each maintained that the legacy of antebellum racial tolerance was still very much in evidence in the Appalachia in which they were raised. Woodson concluded his essay claiming that "one can observe even day-to-day such a difference in the atmosphere of the two sections, and in passing from the tidewater to the mountains it seems like going from one country into another. . . . In Appalachian America the races still maintain a sort of social contact," working, eating, and worshipping together. West, too, drew on his own childhood memories to make the same case. He recalled that he never saw a black person until he was fifteen years old, when his family had moved from Georgia's mountains to sharecrop in the cotton country of Cobb County. Unfamiliar with the racial mores of the lowland South, the Wests welcomed their black neighbors as guests in their home and at their dinner table, much to the chagrin of local whites. When asked about it, his mother replied that she had always been taught to treat people equally, an attitude West claimed "was indicative of the sentiment of many people in the Appalachian South."[36]

So what is one to make of these extreme contradictions regarding highland attitudes toward blacks? Both contain significant elements of truth and perhaps even accurately convey the sentiments of certain pockets of southern highland society. However, there is another body of evidence that, while by no means either comprehensive or systematic, can be mustered in support of the idea that southern mountaineers were first and foremost southerners and that they viewed slavery and race in terms not unlike those of their yeoman or even slaveholding counterparts elsewhere in the South.

Certainly the most useful contemporary source on the subject is

Frederick Law Olmsted. As a New York journalist, he spent fourteen months traveling through the South in 1853 and 1854, observing and reporting on the region and its peculiar institution. The final month or so of his "journey through the back country," as he called the latter part of his tour, was spent in the highlands of Georgia, Tennessee, North Carolina, and Virginia. Although Olmsted noted some differences in slavery as it existed in the mountains, the comments he evoked from residents in many ways reflected attitudes not unlike those of nonslaveholding yeomen or poor whites elsewhere in the South at the time. Most seemed to be equally contemptuous of slaves, their masters, and the system itself. But given the option of eliminating slavery and the privileged class it supported, highlanders consistently deferred to what they saw as the lesser evil. Few advocated abolishing the institution, and most were blatant in demonstrating that racism dominated their rationales for tolerating its perpetuation. Olmsted said of one Tennessee mountaineer, "He'd always wished there had n't been any niggers here . . . but he would n't think there was any better way of getting along with them than that they had." A highland woman reacted with "disgust and indignation on her face" when Olmsted informed her that blacks in New York were free. "I would n't want to live where niggers are free," she said. "They are bad enough when they are slaves. . . . If they was to think themselves equal to we, I do n't think white folks could abide it—they're such vile saucy things."[37]

Olmsted and others after him recognized the degree to which class resentment was also at the core of whatever opposition mountaineers felt toward slavery and its beneficiaries. In his 1888 paean to the "loyal mountaineers" of Tennessee, Thomas Humes echoed a major theme of Olmsted's by noting that slavery, "even in the modified, domestic garb it wore" among these highlanders, had "a depressing, degrading influence" on them.[38] Slave labor and the plantation system forced yeomen from their seaboard and piedmont homes up into the mountains, where they were somewhat insulated from the system's direct competition but were nevertheless denied the greater economic opportunity the outside world had to offer. Southern highlanders, according to a 1903 analysis, "were penned up in the mountains because slavery shut out white labor. . . . It denied those that looked down from their mountain crags upon the realm of King Cotton a chance to expand, circulate, and mingle with the progressive elements at work elsewhere in the republic."[39] As north Georgia's Lillian Smith phrased it even more eloquently: "A separation began in minds that had already taken place in living: a chasm between rich and poor that washed deeper and deeper as the sweat of more and more slaves poured into it."[40]

At least some mountain masters sensed the potential for lower-class resentment to transform itself into antislavery sentiment. Former Virginia governor David Campbell, a Washington County slave owner, cautioned fellow slave owners in the state's southwestern corner about how tenuous the commitment to the institution was among their nonslaveholding neighbors. Most Virginians west of the Blue Ridge, he observed, "never expect or intend to own" slaves and were thus not susceptible to the fervent proslavery defenses to which they were subjected during the sectional debates of 1850. Whereas he recognized the common bonds of white supremacy that bound whites of all classes, he urged owners to tone down their impassioned rhetoric to their yeoman constituencies, because "they are not at all interested—so far from it [that] many of them feel exactly like the men of Indiana and Illinois or any of the northwestern states."[41]

Yet whatever element of truth there was to these claims of yeoman indifference to slavery's survival—and Olmsted for one offers considerable firsthand verification—a part of the cultural baggage mountain settlers brought from the lowlands was an intense and deeply rooted racism. In that sense they were very much like their "plain folk" counterparts throughout the South. Even nonslaveholding whites living closer to slavery and feeling even more directly victimized by it kept their resentment of the institution in check by more dominant feelings of contempt, hostility, and social superiority toward all blacks, free or slave. Many, in fact, lumped together "crackers" and "rednecks" with "hillbillies" in describing these effects.[42] In short, antislavery sentiment among Appalachians did not mean that they, any more than other southerners, were what Carl Degler has labeled "enemies of slavery on behalf of blacks."[43]

The strong racial prejudices in areas without a black populace were not a phenomenon limited to the mountain South. Other Americans in nonslaveholding parts of the country were hostile to the few blacks, if any, they lived with and felt threatened by future prospects of a black influx. Alexis de Tocqueville had observed this racism without tangible targets during his visit to America in 1831. "In no part of the Union in which negroes are no longer slaves," he wrote, "they have in nowise drawn nearer to the whites. On the contrary, the prejudice of the race appears to be stronger in the states which have abolished slavery, than in those where it still exists; and nowhere is it so intolerant as in those states where servitude has never been known."[44]

Eugene Berwanger, in his study of attitudes toward slavery in the Northwest Territory and other western frontiers, demonstrated that antislavery sentiment there was fueled far more by residents' prejudice against blacks and a desire to keep them out of their region than by any moral qualms about the peculiar institution. It took Rodger Cunningham to point out perhaps the most obvious link between Appalachia and other slaveless areas of the country. Dismissing moral components as causal factors, he stated that "the mountains were largely free of slavery only because their climate, terrain, and soil were mostly unsuited to crops and plantation sizes for which slave labor was profitable." But this, he continued, "was also the reason the North had no slaves."[45]

Just as resentment of slavery rarely sprang from humanitarian impulses toward its black victims, there was also little correlation during the war years between loyalty to the Union and abolitionist sentiment. Nevertheless, the degree to which mountain men were committed to slavery's preservation was long a point of contention. Two nineteenth-century historians of East Tennessee (both natives of the region) have argued that its commitment to slavery was so strong as to endanger its place in the Union. Just before the state voted on June 8, 1861, to secede, Knoxville lawyer Oliver Temple laid out his priorities: "If we had to choose between the government on one side without slavery, and a broken and dissevered government with slavery, I would say unhesitatingly, 'Let slavery perish and the Union survive.'"[46] Thomas Humes contended that most "loyal mountaineers" would have agreed with Temple's choice. "Generally they looked upon slavery as something foreign to their social life," he wrote. "They would have been displeased at its coming near their homes in the imperious majesty it wore in the cotton States. At the same time they were satisfied to let men of the South keep serfs at pleasure, but they counted it no business of theirs to help in the work." Thus, he concluded, they would have had no hesitation in choosing "perpetuity of the Union over that of slavery."[47]

Most mountain Unionists were sensitive to charges that they opposed black bondage, however, and emphatically asserted their full support of the institution. In fact, highland spokesmen such as Zebulon Vance, William Brownlow, and Andrew Johnson argued against secession to their highland constituencies and readerships on the grounds that slavery was safer in, rather than out of, the Union. Alexander H. Jones of Henderson County, one of western North Carolina's most vocal Unionists, asserted that "by throwing off those guarantees—the Constitution and the Union—southern states have done the cause of slavery more injury than anyone else could have done." Others warned of the devaluation of slave property and the difficulties of reclaiming fugitive slaves who went north into what would be foreign territory.[48]

"Parson" Brownlow, whose Knoxville newspaper made him among East Tennessee's most visible opponents of secession, was quick to state that his "contempt for the Abolitionists of the North is only equaled by my hatred of the Disunionists of the South." Nevertheless, he expressed what were likely the sentiments of many mountain residents: "The Union men of the border slave states are loyal to their Government and do not regard the election of Lincoln as any just cause for dissolving the Union. . . . But, if we were once convinced that the Administration in Washington and the people of the North contemplated the subjugation of the South or the abolishing of slavery, there would not be a Union man among us in twenty-four hours." Many mountain Unionists felt betrayed by Lincoln when he issued his Emancipation Proclamation in September 1862, and some even abandoned their loyalist stance as a result. Former congressman Thomas A. R. Nelson, one of East Tennessee's most influential antisecessionist voices in 1861, declared two years later that he would have advocated secession if he "had believed it was the object of the North to subjugate the South and emancipate our slaves." "The Union men of East Tennessee," he declared emphatically, "are not now and never were Abolitionists."[49]

The very fact that mountain slaveholders were among the most ardent Unionists is indication enough that abolition was hardly the basis of their anti-Confederate tendencies. Both Zebulon Vance and Andrew Johnson had modest slaveholdings, and many who owned far more slaves were equally as resistant to secession. Analysis of election returns in western North Carolina on a referendum to hold a secession convention indicates a fairly even split between slaveholders and little or no correlation between a county's slave population and its vote on secession.[50]

Perhaps the most striking example of this pattern—or lack of pattern—was the situation in Kentucky's Tug Valley. In her masterful study of the Hatfield-McCoy feud, Altina Waller noted the paradoxical fact that Harmon McCoy, one of the valley's few slaveholders, was also among the few residents who remained loyal to the Union when the war broke out. But in that area he was not alone. Slaveholders in Pike County were as a rule less likely to support the Confederacy than were most of its nonslaveholding farmers.[51] Studies of north Georgia's mountain counties also indicate that the few residents with substantial slaveholdings were actively Unionist and in several instances served in the Union rather than the Confederate army.[52]

Likewise in those parts of Southern Appalachia where support for secession was strong, highlanders' concerns about slavery's future under a Republican regime was a vital factor in shaping that support. In 1944 historian Henry Shanks argued that the strong secessionist vote in Virginia's southwestern corner (85 percent of its delegates voted to withdraw from the Union in May) was due to substantial ownership of slaves by local farmers and their bitter hostility to "abolitionism, to the Republican party, and to the election of Lincoln."[53] Whereas such sentiments were taken for granted in most other parts of the South, highland support of the Confederacy has generally been attributed to the independence and individualism inherent in mountaineers. Even more vaguely, as a western Carolinian wrapped in the romance of the "lost cause" explained in 1905, the mountain South seceded not as a defense of slavery but, rather, over "the real issue . . . a lofty and patriotic sense of duty which animated the Southern people of all classes."[54]

Until recently such rationales were accepted with little acknowledgment of how central slavery's survival was as a motivating factor for much of Appalachia's support of secession, despite evidence of considerable rhetoric to that effect. The crisis raised even greater fears as to the impact of slavery's abolition on the southern highlands, fears that mountain secessionists were quick and effective in exploiting. Georgia governor Joseph E. Brown, himself a native of the state's mountain region, appealed to his fellow north Georgians' racial fears by urging them to support their state's separation from the Union. Within the Union, slavery was no longer safe, he reasoned, and "so soon as the slaves were at liberty, thousands of them would leave the cotton and rice fields in the lower part of our State, and make their way to the healthier climate in the mountain region. We should have them plundering and stealing, robbing, and killing in all the lovely vallies of the mountains."[55] Western North Carolina politicians were just as vocal in raising the specter of such an influx among their constituents as they described "the terrible calamity of having three hundred thousand idle, vagabond free negroes turned loose upon you with all the privileges of white men." By the same token, in seceding from Virginia, West Virginians were sharply divided as to the future status of slavery in their new state constitution, but they had no problem in agreeing to a Negro exclusion policy that would ban either slave importation or free black migration into the state.[56]

There are other indications that some sections of Appalachia could claim no exemptions from the evils of southern racial prejudice. Slave markets existed in a number of mountain communities, such as Wheeling, Winchester, and Abingdon in Virginia; Bristol, Jonesboro, Knoxville, and Chattanooga in Tennessee; and London and Pikeville in Kentucky. (Witnessing the cruelties of the slave trade in Wheeling, in fact, set Benjamin Lundy on his abolitionist course.)[57] Slave auctions elsewhere in the upper South were apparently dependent on slaves supplied from highland areas, and it was not an uncommon sight, according to British geologist George Featherstonaugh, to see slave coffles moving through southwest Virginia and East Tennessee headed for deep South markets. On an 1844 trip through the southern highlands, he expressed amazement at the sight of slave drivers with more than three hundred men, women, and children in chains, which he encountered both along the New River valley and then again in Knoxville as they moved their human cargo toward Natchez, Mississippi.[58]

At least one observer saw the mere living conditions of mountain slaves to be intolerable and was skeptical of claims for their well-being. Joseph John Gurney, a British Quaker traveling through the Virginia mountains in 1841, encountered black workers at White Sulphur Springs and was distressed at the "miserable manner in which the slaves were clad." After chiding their master, a physician, on their appearance, Gurney reported, "he assured me that the slaves were among the happiest of human beings; but it was nearer the truth, when he afterwards observed that they were remarkably able to endure hardships." He concluded from this encounter that "certain it is, that the negroes here, as elsewhere, are an easy, placid, and long-suffering race."[59]

Former slaves themselves bore witness to the fact that bondage in the southern highlands was no less abusive than elsewhere. Sarah Gudger recalled the visits of a "specalator" to a neighboring plantation near Old Fort, North Carolina. He and "Old Marse" would pick out a slave from the field, and then "dey slaps de han' cuffs on him and tak him away to de cotton country." Mary Barbour, from the same county, testified that her master sold almost all of his slaves, including at least twelve of her brothers and sisters, when they reached age three. Aunt Sophia, a former slave from eastern Kentucky, contended that though her master "wuzn't as mean as most," a nearby owner "wuz so mean to his slaves that I know two gals that kilt themselfs."[60]

After the war the racial violence that plagued so much of the South was evident in the mountains as well. The influx of blacks into such cities as Knoxville, Chattanooga, and Asheville led to open unrest not unlike that in other southern cities. In Asheville, the attempt by a black man to vote in 1868 led to a race riot that left one black dead and several blacks and whites wounded. In his study of this and other such incidents, Eric Olson noted that in terms of reactions expressed in the local newspaper, there was little to differentiate Asheville from Savannah.[61]

Several studies of the north Georgia mountains demonstrate that racial violence was no less apparent there than in other parts of the state during the postwar decades. Edward Ayers has noted that although blacks in Whitfield and other mountain counties posed little political or economic threat to white residents during Reconstruction, the Ku Klux Klan in that area was notorious for the brutal treatment it and other mobs inflicted on the relatively few blacks in their midst. "Honor reigned," Ayers observed, "with as much volatility among the whites of the hills as among their low-country brethren."[62] Yet Ayers argued that the post-emancipation abuse of highland blacks was distinguished from that elsewhere in the South by the fact that it was integral to a long tradition of group violence and extralegal retribution among mountaineers, most of which was inflicted by whites on other whites. In analyses of the "whitecapping" that plagued Georgia's mountain counties during the moonshine wars of the 1880s and 1890s, both Will Holmes and Fitzhugh Brundage confirm the biracial makeup of whitecappers' targets but note that blacks were whipped and murdered for offenses that included insolence or miscegenation as well as any threat they might have posed to moonshiners' security.[63]

In his statistical analysis of racial violence in late nineteenth-century Kentucky, George Wright noted that while mountain residents lynched fewer blacks than did other Kentuckians, they did so at a rate proportionate to the region's African American populace.[64] In a more broadly cast statistical study of racial violence in Appalachia, Robert Stuckert suggests that blacks were more often victimized by white mobs in mountain areas than elsewhere. Though only 6 percent of the black population of seven southern states lived in the highlands, more than 10 percent of the blacks lynched in those states were Appalachian residents.[65] Brundage confirms these findings with his rather startling discovery that no area of Virginia saw more lynchings than did its mountain counties. Of a total of seventy blacks lynched in Virginia between 1880 and 1930, no less than twenty-four lost their lives in southwestern counties, a phenomenon Brundage credits to the "furious pace" of the region's postwar social and economic transformations, particularly the influx of itinerant black and foreign workers into mining and lumber camps. The fact that most lynchings occurred in towns, the centers of this change, rather than in the hills or countryside, confirms the economic roots of this particular expression of mountain racism.[66]

Although some Appalachians exhibited the same violent and abusive treatment toward blacks as other southerners, there are also indications of "kinder and gentler" race relations in the region. I have suggested elsewhere that slaveholders in the Carolina highlands exhibited more benevolent attitudes and lenient treatment toward their black property than was usual in the lowland South. Despite the conclusions of British Quaker Joseph John Gurney that slaves in southwestern Virginia were no better off than those in other parts of the South, other outside observers have provided among the most explicit testimony that there was indeed a qualitative difference in the treatment of highland bondsmen. Charles Lanman, for example, wrote in 1849 that "the slaves residing among the mountains are the happiest and most independent portion of the population." Olmsted noted that in the southern highlands, slavery's "moral evils . . . are less, even proportionately to the number of slaves." He detected that they were "less closely superintended. . . . They exercise more responsibility, and both in soul and intellect they are more elevated."[67] I also detected among mountain masters in North Carolina what seemed to be a preponderance of acts of goodwill, affectionate references to their slaves, unusual efforts—sometimes including financial sacrifice—to ensure their welfare and happiness, and even occasional pangs of conscience about the system.[68]

Other scholars have also noted greater moderation or leniency in highland race relations. In an analysis of political divisiveness in Virginia from 1790 to 1830, Van Beck Hall demonstrated the degree to which western legislators, while fully supportive of slavery itself, often differed from their eastern counterparts on more peripheral issues regarding blacks. On various occasions Appalachian delegates blocked proposals to toughen manumission procedures, to pass retaliatory measures against blacks after Gabriel Prosser's aborted 1800 rebellion, and to ban the distribution of abolitionist publications in the state. At the same time they supported measures to liberalize restrictions on the state's free black population, to end compensation for masters of slave criminals who were executed or banished, and to support Richmond free black efforts to establish their own church.[69]

Even during the intense racist repression of the Reconstruction era, some highlanders showed more restraint in dealing with the new freedman population than southerners elsewhere. In his comprehensive study of the Republican Party in the southern highlands, Gordon

McKinney credited at least part of its success to "the relative lack of hostility between mountain whites and blacks," though he noted that it was an alliance based far more on political pragmatism than humanitarian ideals.[70] Despite John Eaton's observations regarding racism in Reconstruction Tennessee, a recent study has suggested that emancipation was accepted more quickly in East Tennessee than was true elsewhere in the occupied South.[71] Eric Olson concluded his study of racial postwar violence in Asheville with the suggestion that the incidents he described were more the exception than the rule; the disruptions remained more isolated and their effects more easily contained than was the case in similar incidents in Atlanta, for example.[72] J. Morgan Kousser, in documenting racial disfranchisement in the turn-of-the-century South, noted that hill country whites were among the few who opposed denying blacks the political rights they had gained a generation earlier, though such resistance had less to do with any benevolence toward blacks than with the realization that they were often the unacknowledged secondary victims of such measures as literacy tests, poll taxes, and understanding clauses.[73]

So where are we left in terms of characterizing the racism of nineteenth-century Appalachians? The reality seems almost as contradictory and confusing as the myths. If the evidence presented here does not span quite the extremes of the popular assumptions laid out in fictional form by Fox and Faulkner, it fills in much of the intervening space along that vast spectrum of opinion. The nature of the evidence on racism at the grassroots level of any populace is and must remain scattered, speculative, and circumstantial, so that any definitive or comprehensive statement on how mountain whites viewed blacks remains elusive. But the sheer range of experiences—lynchings and race riots occurring in areas where abolitionism had thrived; blacks moving quickly into some parts of the region when given the option, while deserting others just as rapidly; some highlanders willing to leave the Union to protect slavery while others proved relatively receptive to emancipation—demonstrates the dangers of generalizing about highland attitudes and of drawing any hard and fast conclusions about a society that has been subjected to far more than its share of homogenization, stereotyping, and image-making.

Barbara Fields has warned us of the dangers of according race "a transhistorical, almost metaphysical, status," noting that "ideas about color, like ideas about anything else, derive their importance, indeed their very definition, from their context."[74] The variety of white responses to blacks in Southern Appalachia serves as a vivid reminder of the fact that racial attitudes and actions are indeed functions of other social, economic, political, or even sectional forces. The power struggles between a state's mountain region and its state government or lowland elite; the politicization of slavery, emancipation, and later disfranchisement and segregation; the demographic shifts, often dramatic, of populations, black and white, into or out of highland areas; the effects of poverty and other forms of material stagnation or deprivation; the new dynamics of community and class, and accompanying tensions, brought on by colonialism, industrialization, urbanization, and other forces of modernization—all of these were very real aspects of the Appalachian experience that could, and often did, affect racial attitudes. The actual contacts between mountain whites and blacks were of course a crucial—but far from consistent or predictable—factor in shaping race relations in the region. But these other factors were equally significant, if more subtle, determinants of highlanders' perceptions and treatment of blacks. The variations in pace and degree at which these changes were felt throughout the region may be the key to explaining the quiltlike character of highland racism.

Fields reminds us too that racism can be a slippery concept to pin down. "Attitudes," she maintains, "are promiscuous critters and do not mind cohabiting with their opposites."[75] Such was certainly true of racism's highland manifestations. The fluidity and often contradictory expressions of racial opinions among mountaineers reflect the diversity and complexity of experience rarely acknowledged about Appalachia and its historical development. Once that range of experience is recognized, it may be that the most that one can draw from this admittedly sketchy overview is that there was nothing truly unique about Appalachian racial attitudes. The region's residents were first and foremost southerners. Despite demographic deviations in their racial makeup and their political alienation from the South's dominant slaveocracy, white highlanders' views of African Americans in theory and treatment of them in practice were for the most part well within the mainstream of attitudes and behavior elsewhere in the South, a mainstream that was in itself by no means monolithic. Likewise those views manifested in the few areas of Appalachia without a significant black presence were not so different from those of Americans in other nonslaveholding parts of the country. On either side of the Mason-Dixon Line, nineteenth-century white America was racist, varying only in degree and in form of expression. The same was true of Appalachia.

It is one thing simply to chronicle or to categorize the varieties of ways in which white mountaineers viewed or treated blacks, and that is all that has been attempted here. It is quite another to sort out, identify, and explain the more elusive causal factors behind such views. That formidable task still looms large as one of the more exciting challenges confronting Appalachian scholars and can perhaps proceed once the debris of myth and misconception that has for so long obstructed the route to such insights is at long last cleared away.

Notes

1. U. B. Phillips, "The Central Theme of Southern History," *American Historical Review* 34 (1928): 30–43. On the debate among historians since, see John David Smith and John C. Inscoe, eds., *Ulrich Bonnell Phillips: A Southern Historian and His Critics* (Westport, Conn.: Greenwood Press, 1990). The statement by David Whisnant is from a book review in the *Journal of Southern History* 56 (1990): 566.

2. John Fox Jr., *The Little Shepherd of Kingdom Come* (1903; reprint, Lexington: University Press of Kentucky, 1987), 28, 119, 239.

3. William Faulkner, "Mountain Victory," in *Collected Stories* (1950; reprint, New York: Vintage, 1977), 745–80; quote, 751. For a more extensive analysis of this story, see "The Racial 'Innocence' of Appalachia," chap. 10 in this volume.

4. William Brewer, "Moonshining in Georgia," *Cosmopolitan* 23 (June 1897): 132, quoted in Nina Silber, *The Romance of Reunion: Northerners and the South, 1865–1900* (Chapel Hill: University of North Carolina Press, 1993), 144.

5. Ellen Churchill Semple, "The Anglo-Saxons of the Kentucky Mountains: A Study in Anthropogeography," in *Appalachian Images in Folk and Popular Culture*, ed. W. K. McNeil (Ann Arbor, Mich.: UMI Research Press, 1989), 150–51.

6. Nathaniel S. Shaler, "The Peculiarities of the South," *North American Review* 151 (October 1890): 483–84. See also Margaret Ripley Wolfe, "The

Appalachian Reality: Ethnic and Class Diversity," *East Tennessee Historical Society Publications* 52 and 53 (1980–1981): 40–60.

7. Samuel Tyndale Wilson, *The Southern Mountaineers* (New York: Presbyterian Home Missions, 1906), 42, 20–21; Thomas Wolfe, *The Hills Beyond* (1935; reprint, New York: Plume, 1982), 263.

8. Flannery O'Connor, "The Artificial Nigger," in *The Complete Stories* (New York: Farrar, Straus and Giroux, 1971), quote, 129. Curiously, analysts of this story fail to recognize or acknowledge the mountain context of the two characters' background. See, for example, Miles Orvell, *Flannery O'Connor: An Introduction* (Jackson: University of Mississippi Press, 1991), 152–60; Kathleen Feeley, *Flannery O'Connor: Voice of the Peacock* (New York: Fordham University Press, 1982), 120–24; and Jill P. Baumgaertner, *Flannery O'Connor: A Proper Scaring* (Wheaton, Ill.: Harold Shaw, 1988), 56–62.

9. James C. Klotter, "The Black South and White Appalachia," *Journal of American History* 66 (March 1980): 832–49; Silber, *Romance of Reunion,* 143–58. See also Allen W. Batteau, *The Invention of Appalachia* (Tucson: University of Arizona Press, 1990), 59–63, on other uses of Anglo-Saxonism in romanticizing Appalachia. Even more recent studies have focused on turn-of-the-century mission work to Appalachian blacks. See Conrad E. Ostwalt Jr., "Crossing of Cultures: The Mennonite Brethren of Boone, North Carolina," in *Environmental Voices: Cultural, Social, Physical, and Natural,* ed. Garry Barker, *Journal of the Appalachian Studies Association* 4 (1992): 105–12; Conrad E. Ostwalt Jr. and Phoebe Pollitt, "The Salem School and Orphanage [in Elk Park, N.C]: White Missionaries, Black School," in Inscoe, *Appalachians and Race,* 235–44.

10. Useful and varied anthologies on the black experience in the southern highlands, most of which focus on the twentieth century, include William H. Turner and Edward J. Cabbell, eds., *Blacks in Appalachia* (Lexington: University Press of Kentucky, 1985); Edward J. Cabbell, guest ed., "Black Appalachians," special issue of *Now and Then* 3 (Winter 1986); Lenwood Davis, *The Black Heritage of Western North Carolina* (Asheville: Southern Highlands Research Center, University of North Carolina–Asheville, 1986); William H. Turner, guest ed., "Blacks in Appalachia," special issue of *Appalachian Heritage* 19 (Fall 1991); and "Whiteness and Racialization in Appalachia," special issue of *Journal of Appalachian Studies* 10 (Spring/Fall 2004). For an essay collection focused on the nineteenth century, see Inscoe, *Appalachians and Race.*

11. On the distribution of slaves in Appalachia, see Robert P. Stuckert, "Black Populations of the Southern Appalachian Mountains," *Phylon* 48 (June 1987): 141–51; Richard B. Drake, "Slavery and Antislavery in Appalachia," *Appalachian Heritage* 14 (Winter 1986): 25–33; James B. Murphy, "Slavery and Freedom in Appalachia: Kentucky as a Demographic Case

Study," *Register of the Kentucky Historical Society* 80 (1982): 151–69; John C. Inscoe, *Mountain Masters: Slavery and the Sectional Crisis in Western North Carolina* (Knoxville: University of Tennessee Press, 1989), 59–63, 84–86; Wilma A. Dunaway, "Diaspora, Death, and Sexual Exploitation: Slave Families at Risk in the Mountain South," *Appalachian Journal* (Winter 1999): 128–49; and Dunaway, "Put in Master's Pocket: Cotton Expansion and Interstate Slave Trading in the Mountain South," in Inscoe, *Appalachians and Race,* 116–32. For a nineteenth-century perspective, see William E. Barton, "The Cumberland Mountains and the Struggle for Freedom," *New England Magazine* 16 (1897): 65–87.

We are still sadly lacking in scholarly treatments of antebellum free black highlanders. Among the few works dealing with the subject are Stuart Sprague, "From Slavery to Freedom: African-Americans in Eastern Kentucky, 1864–1884," in *Diversity in Appalachia: Images and Realities,* ed. Tyler Blethen, *Journal of the Appalachian Studies Association* 5 (1993): 67–74; and Marie Tedesco, "A Free Black Slave Owner in East Tennessee: The Strange Case of Adam Waterford," in Inscoe, *Appalachians and Race,* 133–53.

12. Sadie Smathers Patton, "The Kingdom of the Happy Land" (Asheville: Stephens Press, 1957); Sam Gray and Theda Perdue, "Appalachia as the Promised Land: A Freedmen's Commune in Henderson County, North Carolina, 1870–1920," paper presented at the meeting of the American Anthropological Association, 1979, Lexington, Ky.; William Lynwood Montell, *The Saga of Coe Ridge: A Study in Oral History* (Knoxville: University of Tennessee Press, 1970). For other treatments of the postwar black population in Appalachia, see William H. Turner, "The Demography of Black Appalachia, Past and Present," in Turner and Cabbell, *Blacks in Appalachia,* 237–61; Michael A. Cooke, "Race Relations in Montgomery County, Virginia, 1870–1990," in Barker, *Environmental Voices,* 94–104; Sprague, "From Slavery to Freedom," 72–73; and Wilson, *Southern Mountaineers,* 41–42.

13. On the migration of blacks in Appalachian coalfields, see Ronald L. Lewis, *Black Coal Miners in America: Race, Class, and Community Conflict, 1780–1980* (Lexington: University Press of Kentucky, 1987), chap. 7; Ronald L. Lewis, "From Peasant to Proletarian: The Migration of Southern Blacks to the Central Appalachian Coalfields," *Journal of Southern History* 55 (1989): 77–102; Emily Jones Hudson, "The Black American Family in Southeastern Kentucky: Red Fox, Kodak, and Town Mountain," in *Reshaping the Image of Appalachia,* ed. Loyal Jones (Berea, Ky.: Berea College Appalachian Center, 1986), 136–45; Joe William Trotter Jr., *Coal, Class, and Color: Blacks in Southern West Virginia, 1915–1932* (Urbana: University of Illinois Press, 1990), pt. 1; Wayne Flynt, *Poor but Proud: Alabama's Poor Whites* (Tuscaloosa: University of Alabama Press, 1989), chap. 5.

None of these works speaks to the issue of local reaction of white Appalachians to this influx of black migrants, although Flynt has a perceptive discussion of race relations between black and Appalachian white workers in northern Alabama's coalfields (pp. 121, 136–38, 257–61).

14. Stuckert, *Black Populations of Southern Appalachian Mountains,* 141 (tab.), 145.

15. W. J. Cash, *The Mind of the South* (New York: Knopf, 1941), 219.

16. John Eaton, *Grant, Lincoln, and the Freedman: Reminiscences of the Civil War* (New York: Longmans, Green, 1907), 119. See also John Cimprich, "Slavery's End in East Tennessee," in Inscoe, *Appalachians and Race,* 190–91.

17. John C. Campbell, *The Southern Mountaineer and His Homeland* (New York: Russell Sage Foundation, 1921), 95; Muriel E. Sheppard, *Cabins in the Laurel* (Chapel Hill: University of North Carolina Press, 1935), 60.

18. Raymond Andrews, *The Last Radio Baby: A Memoir* (Atlanta: Peachtree, 1990), 79; William Styron, *The Confessions of Nat Turner* (New York: Random House, 1967), 326–27.

19. Loyal Jones, "Appalachian Values," in *Voices from the Hills: Selected Readings of Southern Appalachia,* ed. Robert J. Higgs (New York: Ungar, 1975), 507–17.

20. Quoted in William H. Turner, "Between Berea (1904) and Birmingham (1908): The Rock and Hard Place for Blacks in Appalachia," in Turner and Cabbell, *Blacks in Appalachia,* 13. The whole notion of Appalachia as a center of Underground Railroad activity is suspect. Most major treatments of the Underground Railroad make no reference to southern highland locales. See Larry Gara, *The Liberty Line: The Legend of the Underground Railroad* (Lexington: University Press of Kentucky, 1961); William Still, *The Underground Railroad* (Philadelphia: Porter and Coates, 1872); and Eber M. Pettit, *Sketches in the History of the Underground Railroad* (Fredonia, N.Y.: W. McKinstry and Son, 1879). The only such account to refer to even the possibility that Appalachians provided regular routes is Wilbur H. Siebert, *The Underground Railroad from Slavery to Freedom* (New York: Macmillan, 1899), 118–19, but its map (facing p. 113) indicates no routes anywhere in the region.

21. Leon F. Williams, "The Vanishing Appalachian: How to 'Whiten' the Problem," in Turner and Cabbell, *Blacks in Appalachia,* 201.

22. Barbara J. Fields, "Ideology and Race in American History," in *Region, Race, and Reconstruction: Essays in Honor of C. Vann Woodward,* ed. J. Morgan Kousser and James M. McPherson (New York: Oxford University Press, 1982), 157; Samuel C. Williams, ed., "Journal of Events (1825–1873) of David Anderson Deaderick," *East Tennessee Historical Publications* 8 (1936): 121–37.

23. Frederick Douglass, *The Life and Times of Frederick Douglass* (1892; reprint, New York: Macmillan, 1962), 273–74. See also William S. McFeely, *Frederick Douglass* (New York: Norton, 1991), 186–87, 190–92.

24. Richard Hinton interview with John Brown and John Kagi in August 1858, in *John Brown,* ed. Richard Warch and Jonathan F. Fauton (Englewood Cliffs, N.J.: Prentice-Hall, 1973), 54 (second quote). For other treatments of the southern highlands as central to Brown's insurrection plan, see Siebert, *Underground Railroad,* 118, and Jules Abel, *Man on Fire: John Brown and the Cause of Liberty* (New York: Macmillan, 1971), 245–48.

25. James W. Taylor, *Alleghania: A Geographical and Statistical Memoir* (St. Paul, Minn.: James Davenport, 1862), 1–2, 15–16.

26. William Goodrich, *God's Handiwork in the Sea and the Mountains: Sermons Preached after a Summer Vacation* (Cleveland, Ohio: privately published, n.d.), quoted in Jan Davidson's introduction to Frances Louisa Goodrich, *Mountain Homespun* (Knoxville: University of Tennessee Press, 1989), 13.

27. Batteau, *Invention of Appalachia,* 78. On Lincoln's legacy for Appalachia, see Shannon H. Wilson, "Lincoln's Sons and Daughters: Berea College, Lincoln Memorial University, and the Myth of Unionist Appalachia, 1866–1910," in *The Civil War in Appalachia: Collected Essays,* ed. Kenneth W. Noe and Shannon W. Wilson (Knoxville: University of Tennessee Press, 1997), 242–64.

28. Harry M. Caudill, *Night Comes to the Cumberlands: A Biography of a Depressed Area* (Boston: Little, Brown, 1962), 38–39.

29. Asa Earl Martin, "The Anti-Slavery Societies of Tennessee," *Tennessee Historical Magazine* 1 (1915): 261–81; Cratis D. Williams, "The Southern Mountaineer in Fact and Fiction," 2 vols. (Ph.D. diss., New York University, 1961), 1:74–75; North Callahan, *Smoky Mountain Country,* ed. Erskine Caldwell (New York: Duell, Sloan, and Pearce, 1952), 37–49; Thomas W. Humes, *The Loyal Mountaineers of Tennessee* (Knoxville: Ogden Bros., 1888), 31–33; David W. Bowen, *Andrew Johnson and the Negro* (Knoxville: University of Tennessee Press, 1989), 15–16; and Durwood Dunn, *An Abolitionist in the Appalachian South: Ezekiel Birdseye on Slavery, Capitalism, and Separate Statehood in East Tennessee, 1841–1846* (Knoxville: University of Tennessee Press, 1997).

30. Durwood Dunn, *Cades Cove: The Life and Death of a Southern Appalachian Community, 1818–1937* (Knoxville: University of Tennessee Press, 1988), 124–25. On opposition to East Tennessee abolitionists, see Chase C. Mooney, *Slavery in Tennessee* (Bloomington: Indiana University Press, 1957), 70–73; Bowen, *Andrew Johnson and the Negro,* 16; Drake, "Slavery and Antislavery in Appalachia," 31–32. On postwar commitment to biracial education at Maryville, see Lester C. Lamon, "Ignoring the Color Line: Maryville College, 1868–1901," in *The Adaptable South: Essays in*

Honor of George Brown Tindall, ed. Elizabeth Jacoway et al. (Baton Rouge: Louisiana State University Press, 1991), 64–89.

31. Henry Ruffner, *Address to the People of West Virginia: Showing That Slavery Is Injurious to the Public Welfare and That It May Gradually Be Abolished Without Detriment to the Rights and Interests of Slaveholders* (Lexington, Va.: R. C. Noel, 1847), cited and discussed in W. Fitzhugh Brundage, "Shifting Attitudes towards Slavery in Antebellum Rockbridge County," *Rockbridge Historical Society Proceedings* 10 (1980–1989): 333–44. There is no indication that the abolition of slavery was ever a factor in intrastate sectional battles waged by highlanders in antebellum legislatures in North Carolina, Kentucky, or even Tennessee. On Ruffner's role in the American Colonization Society, see Eric Burn, "A Manumission in the Mountains: Slavery and the African Colonization Movement in Southwestern Virginia," *Appalachian Journal* 33 (Winter 2006): 164–86.

32. Richard D. Sears, *"A Practical Recognition of the Brotherhood of Man": John G. Fee and the Camp Nelson Experience* (Berea, Ky.: Berea College Press, 1986), 46; Semple, "Anglo-Saxons of the Kentucky Mountains," 151. See also Richard D. Sears, *The Day of Small Things: Abolitionism in the Midst of Slavery* (Lanham, Md.: University Press of America, 1986). Broader studies of abolitionism in Kentucky include Asa Earl Martin, *The Anti-Slavery Movement in Kentucky Prior to 1850* (Louisville, Ky.: Filson Club Publication no. 25, 1918); Lowell H. Harrison, *The Antislavery Movement in Kentucky* (Lexington: University Press of Kentucky, 1978); Gordon E. Finnie, "The Antislavery Movement in the Upper South before 1840," *Journal of Southern History* 35 (1969): 319–42; Jeffrey Brooke Allen, "Were Southern White Critics of Slavery Racists? Kentucky and the Upper South, 1791–1824," *Journal of Southern History* 44 (1978): 169–90; Stanley Harrold, "Violence and Nonviolence in Kentucky Abolitionism," *Journal of Southern History* 57 (1991): 15–38. None of these works acknowledges any significant abolitionist activity in the state's eastern mountain region. (Another Appalachian institution that embraced biracial education after the war was Tennessee Wesleyan College in Athens, under the auspices of the Northern Methodist Church.)

33. Quoted in Sears, *"Practical Recognition of the Brotherhood of Man,"* 46. On Berea's move away from its commitment to black education, see Klotter, "Black South and White Appalachia," 846–48; Turner, "Between Berea and Birmingham," 13–14; Jacqueline G. Burnside, "Suspicion Versus Faith: Negro Criticisms of Berea College in the Nineteenth Century," in Jones, *Reshaping the Image of Appalachia,* 102–25; and Burnside, "Lessons and Legacies: The Meaning of Berea College's Nineteenth Century Interracial Education in the Twenty-first Century," lecture delivered at Berea College Symposium on the Black Experience in Appalachia and America, September–October 2005.

34. Carter G. Woodson, "Freedom and Slavery in Appalachia," *Journal of Negro History* 1 (April 1916): 132–50. For more on Woodson's essay, see introduction to Inscoe, *Appalachians and Race,* 1–2. Much the same ground is covered in Finnie, "Anti-slavery Movement in the Upper South." See also Barton, "Cumberland Mountains and the Struggle for Freedom."

35. Don West, *Freedom in the Mountains* (Huntington, W.Va.: Appalachian Movement Press, 1973), 3–4, 9.

36. Woodson, "Freedom and Slavery in Appalachia," 147; Don West interview in *Refuse to Stand Silently By: An Oral History of Grass-Roots Social Activism in America, 1921–1964,* ed. Eliot Wigginton (New York: Doubleday, 1992), 68.

37. Frederick Law Olmsted, *A Journey through the Back Country in the Winter of 1853–54* (New York: Mason Brothers, 1860), 239, 237, 263–64. On Olmsted's schedule and route, see Charles E. Beveridge, ed., *The Papers of Frederick Law Olmsted,* vol. 2: *Slavery and the South, 1852–1857* (Baltimore: Johns Hopkins University Press, 1981), 309 (map) and 481–82 (itinerary). For a fuller discussion of his mission and findings, see chap. 3, "Olmsted in Appalachia," in this volume.

38. Humes, *Loyal Mountaineers,* 30.

39. Julian Ralph, "Our Appalachian Americans," *Harper's Monthly Magazine* (June 1903): 37.

40. Lillian Smith, *Killers of the Dream* (1949; rev. ed., New York: Norton, 1961), 171.

41. Kenneth W. Noe, *Southwest Virginia's Railroad: Modernization and the Sectional Crisis* (Urbana: University of Illinois Press, 1994), 17.

42. See, for example, Smith, *Killers of the Dream,* 170; Daniel R. Hundley, *Social Relations in Our Southern States* (1860; reprint, Baton Rouge: Louisiana State University Press, 1979), 258–60; Eugene D. Genovese, "Yeomen Farmers in a Slaveholder's Democracy," *Agricultural History* 49 (1975): 331–42; Steven Hahn, *The Roots of Southern Populism: Yeoman Farmers and the Transformation of the Georgia Upcountry, 1850–1890* (New York: Oxford University Press, 1983), 88–91; J. William Harris, *Plain Folk and Gentry in a Slave Society: White Liberty and Black Slavery in Augusta's Hinterlands* (Middletown, Conn.: Wesleyan University Press), 72–77; F. N. Boney, *Southerners All* (Macon, Ga.: Mercer University Press, 1984), chap. 2. On the commonality of southern and Appalachian values, see Richard B. Drake, "Southern Appalachia and the South: A Region within a Section," in *Southern Appalachia and the South: A Region within a Region,* ed. John C. Inscoe, *Journal of the Appalachian Studies Association* 3 (1991): 18–27.

43. Carl N. Degler, *The Other South: Southern Dissenters in the Nineteenth Century* (Boston: Northeastern University Press, 1982). Quote is title of chap. 2.

44. Alexis de Tocqueville, *Democracy in America,* 4th ed., 2 vols. (New York: Henry G, Langley, 1845), 1:389–90.

45. Eugene H. Berwanger, *The Frontier against Slavery: Western Anti-Negro Prejudice and the Slavery Extension Controversy* (Urbana: University of Illinois Press, 1967); Rodger Cunningham, *Apples on the Flood: The Southern Mountain Experience* (Knoxville: University of Tennessee Press, 1987), 99.

46. Oliver P. Temple, *East Tennessee and the Civil War* (Cincinnati, Ohio: Robert Clarke, 1899), 196–97.

47. Humes, *Loyal Mountaineers,* 31. See also Arthur W. Spaulding, *The Men of the Mountains: The Story of the Southern Mountaineer and His Kin of the Piedmont* (Nashville: Southern Press, 1915), 40–41.

48. Alexander H. Jones, *Knocking at the Door* (Washington, D.C.: McGill and Witherow, 1866), 14; Inscoe, *Mountain Masters,* 236–38.

49. Vernon M. Queener, "William G. Brownlow as an Editor," *East Tennessee Historical Society Publications* 4 (1932): 80; W. G. Brownlow, *Sketches of the Rise, Progress and Decline of Secession* (Philadelphia: George W. Childs, 1862), 109; and Robert Tracy McKenzie, *Lincolnites and Rebels: A Divided Town in the American Civil War [Knoxville]* (New York: Oxford University Press, 2006), esp. 61–70. Nelson quoted in Richard Current, *Lincoln's Loyalists: Union Soldiers from the Confederacy* (Boston: Northeastern University Press, 1992), 50. For a comparison of attitudes in two sections of Appalachia, see "The Secession Crisis and Regional Self-Image," chap. 5 in this volume.

50. Inscoe, *Mountain Masters,* 244–46.

51. Altina L. Waller, *Feud: Hatfields, McCoys, and Social Change in Appalachia, 1860–1900* (Chapel Hill: University of North Carolina Press, 1988), 30.

52. Etheleve Dyer Jones, *Facets of Fannin: A History of Fannin County, Georgia* (Dallas: Curtis Media, 1989), 32; Jonathan Sarris, "Anatomy of an Atrocity: The Madden Branch Massacre and the Guerrilla War in North Georgia, 1861–1865," *Georgia Historical Quarterly* 77 (Winter 1993): 679–710.

53. Henry T. Shanks, "Disloyalty to the Confederacy in Southwestern Virginia, 1861–1865," *North Carolina Historical Review* 21 (1944): 118–19. For more recent confirmation of Shanks's conclusions, see Kenneth W. Noe, "Red String Scare: Civil War Southwest Virginia and the Heroes of America," *North Carolina Historical Review* 59 (1992): 301–22.

54. Theodore F. Davidson, "The Carolina Mountaineer: The Highest Type of American Character," in *First Annual Transactions of the Pen and Plate Club of Asheville, N.C.,* ed. Theodore F. Davidson (Asheville: Hackney and Mole, 1905), 84–85. For variations of this theme, see Spaulding, *Men of the Mountains,* 41–43; Humes, *Loyal Mountaineers,* 30–31; Caudill, *Night Comes to the Cumberlands,* 37–39; Waller, *Feud,* 30–31.

55. Quoted in Michael P. Johnson, *Toward a Patriarchal Society: The Secession of Georgia* (Baton Rouge: Louisiana State University Press, 1977), 50.

56. Circular by W. W. Avery and Marcus Erwin, quoted in Inscoe, *Mountain Masters,* 226; Richard O. Curry, *A House Divided: A Study of Statehood Politics and the Copperhead Movement in West Virginia* (Pittsburgh: University of Pittsburgh Press, 1964), chap. 9, esp. 91–92.

57. Drake, "Slavery and Antislavery in Appalachia," 28. For more extensive discussion of the slave trade in Appalachia, see Dunaway, "Put in Master's Pocket," and Noe, *Southwest Virginia's Railroad,* chap. 1.

58. G. W. Featherstonaugh, *Excursion through the Slave States* (New York: Harper and Brothers, 1844), 36–37, 46.

59. Joseph John Gurney, *A Journey in North America, Described in Familiar Letters to Amelia Opie* (Norwich, England: J. Fletcher, 1841), 53–54.

60. Sarah Gudger and Mary Barbour interviews in *The American Slave: A Composite Autobiography,* ed. George P. Rawick, vol. 14: *North Carolina Narratives* (Westport, Conn.: Greenwood Press, 1972), pt. 1, 354–55 (Gudger), 79 (Barbour). Aunt Sophia quoted in Drake, "Slavery and Antislavery in Appalachia," 27. For other examples of Appalachian ex-slave testimony and for the strongest case for cruelty and abuses inflicted on slaves in Appalachia, see Wilma A. Dunaway, *Slavery in the American Mountain South* and *The African-American Family in Slavery and Emancipation* (both Cambridge, England: Cambridge University Press, 2003).

61. Eric J. Olson, "Race Relations in Asheville, North Carolina: Three Incidents, 1868–1906," in *The Appalachian Experience: Proceedings of the 6th Annual Appalachian Studies Conference,* ed. Barry M. Buxton (Boone, N.C.: Appalachian Consortium Press, 1983), 153–56.

62. Edward L. Ayers, *Vengeance and Justice: Crime and Punishment in the Nineteenth-Century American South* (New York: Oxford University Press, 1984), 159–61.

63. William F. Holmes, "Moonshining and Collective Violence: Georgia, 1889–1895," *Journal of American History* 67 (December 1980): 589–611; W. Fitzhugh Brundage, *Lynching in the New South: Georgia and Virginia, 1880–1930* (Urbana: University of Illinois Press, 1993), chap. 5. See also Wilbur R. Miller, *Revenuers and Moonshiners: Enforcing Federal Liquor Law in the Mountain South, 1865–1900* (Chapel Hill: University of North Carolina Press, 1991), 52–53. It is perhaps noteworthy that the only black informant Miller cites as a victim of whitecappers was a Georgian.

64. George C. Wright, *Racial Violence in Kentucky, 1865–1940: Lynchings, Mob Rule, and "Legal Lynchings"* (Baton Rouge: Louisiana State University Press, 1990), chap. 2 (see particularly table 4, p. 73).

65. Robert P. Stuckert, "Racial Violence in Southern Appalachia, 1880–1940," *Appalachian Heritage* 20 (Spring 1992): 35–41.

66. Brundage, *Lynching in the New South,* chap. 4; and Brundage, "Racial Violence, Lynchings, and Modernization in the Mountain South," in Inscoe, *Appalachians and Race,* 302–16.

67. Charles Lanman, *Letters from the Alleghany Mountains* (New York: Putnam, 1849), 314; Olmsted, *Journey through the Back Country,* 226–27. It is worth noting that the mountain slaves to whom Gurney reacts are the first he encountered during his tour of the United States, whereas both Lanman and Olmsted moved into the southern highlands after extensive travel elsewhere in the South and thus had a basis for comparison with slave life that Gurney lacked.

68. Inscoe, *Mountain Masters,* chap. 5. Some reviewers of the book found this section less than convincing. See Shane White, "Feeling 'Awful Southern' or Slavery on the Periphery," *Reviews in American History* 18 (June 1990): 197–201; and reviews by Altina L. Waller, in *Register of the Kentucky Historical Society* 88 (1990): 346–48; John Schlotterbeck, in *Journal of Southern History* 57 (1991): 330–31; and Lynda Morgan, *American Historical Review* 96 (1991): 262–63. Much of Wilma Dunaway's work on slavery refutes these conclusions as well. It is admittedly a slippery point to prove, and the evidence must remain, by its nature, circumstantial and impressionistic.

69. Van Beck Hall, "The Politics of Appalachian Virginia, 1790–1830," in *Appalachian Frontiers: Settlement, Society, and Development in the Preindustrial Era,* ed. Robert D. Mitchell (Lexington: University Press of Kentucky, 1991), 184–86.

70. Gordon B. McKinney, "Southern Mountain Republicans and the Negro, 1865–1900," *Journal of Southern History* 41 (1975): 493–96.

71. Cimprich, "Slavery's End in East Tennessee," 84–85. Cimprich also indicated that antiblack sentiment among East Tennesseans did indeed intensify after emancipation, just as Eaton had complained.

72. Olson, "Race Relations in Asheville," 163–64.

73. J. Morgan Kousser, *The Shaping of Southern Politics: Suffrage Restriction and the Establishment of the One-Party South, 1880–1910* (New Haven: Yale University Press, 1974), 112, 224, 248, 264.

74. Fields, "Ideology and Race in American History," 144, 146. For further expansion of her arguments, see Fields, "Slavery, Race, and Ideology in the United States of America," *New Left Review* 181 (1990): 118. See also John B. Boles, "Cycles of Racism in Southern History," paper presented at conference, "Black and White Perspectives on the American South," September 1994, University of Georgia, Athens.

75. Fields, "Ideology and Race in American History," 155.

2

Between Bondage and Freedom

Confronting the Variables of Appalachian Slavery and Slaveholding

The historical scholarship on race relations in Southern Appalachia has expanded dramatically over the past couple of decades, and yet we still lack a comprehensive treatment of the subject. What has emerged instead, particularly in regard to the antebellum era, is a vast mosaic of stories that tell us a great many different things about slavery and slaveholders throughout the region. That case can be made by simply recounting some of those stories—in some cases, mere snippets of stories—of slaves and other African Americans at various times and locales in colonial and antebellum Appalachia.

In the early 1750s, a freed slave from Lancaster, Pennsylvania, settled along the western slopes of the Blue Ridge Mountains in Augusta County, Virginia and established himself as the only blacksmith to serve that rapidly populating frontier region. A Moravian missionary moving through the area was duly impressed by his encounter with this man in 1753, and in a diary entry, revealed much about him—that he was married to a Scottish woman, that his Pennsylvania background included familiarity with both the Quaker and Moravian faiths, and that he spoke as well as read both German and English. Only from other sources do we know that his name was Edward Tarr.

Tarr's blacksmith shop was well situated, right along the Great Wagon Road that carried so much traffic south. It soon became a local gathering spot, attracting regular convergences of other free blacks, of slaves, and even of whites of the "middlin' sort." But this success story proved relatively short-lived; by the following decade, the boisterous interracial gatherings led to complaints from certain white citizens that Tarr was a nuisance and his forge a disruption to the public order. The community demonstrated its disapproval in an odd way, though. In 1763, a court ordered the severed head of a slave executed for murder to be placed on a pike on the road just in front of Tarr's shop, even though it was fifty-some miles from where that slave's crime and execution had occurred. Soon thereafter, Tarr's wife Ann was brought before the county court on morals charges—the final straw that led Tarr to sell his land and his business at a loss and move to nearby Staunton, enough of an urban environment for him to assume a more low-key, perhaps anonymous, lifestyle.[1]

Farther west and several decades later, a young slave woman was punished when caught reading a book. In 1813, on a farm on the Kentucky side of the Tug River Valley (in present-day Lawrence County), an overseer came upon this slave, named D'lea, reading a religious tract and whipped her for it. Curiously, D'lea's literacy was shared by many of her fellow slaves, and both her owner and the overseer who punished her were fully aware of her skills. She spent most of her time at the plantation on the Virginia side of the Tug River, where her owner, Wilson Cary Nicholas, a former governor of the state, not only tolerated literate slaves, but in D'lea's case, seems to have capitalized on her so-called occupational literacy, which included some basic mathematical skills, in the management of his operation, specifically in the tallying of his hemp crop as it was bundled and shipped downriver. If D'lea had been on her home farm, she would likely have been spared any whipping. But Nicholas had sent her and about twenty other slaves to his second large holding across the river and the state line in order to hide them from a tax assessor making the rounds. With only this less tolerant overseer in authority at Nicholas's Kentucky farm, D'lea found herself the victim of either his resentment of her ability to read or some offense taken by the religious material he found her reading.[2]

1843. Newport, Tennessee. Abolitionist Ezekiel Birdseye, then based in this highland community on the state's eastern edge, attended the trial of a young slave man, Hannibal, accused of murdering his master. According to Birdseye, Hannibal had "been so frequently and cruelly scourged" at the hands of his owner that he was contemplating suicide. When his owner attacked him with a club as he was covering a coal pit, Hannibal struck back with the shovel he was holding, accidentally killing his master.

Hannibal's plight earned him a vigorous defense from two committed lawyers, who argued that their client was guilty of no more than manslaughter; they urged jury members to "regard him as a man, a fellow-man, entitled to all the justice that one of you are." They reminded the jury that no less than the supreme court of Tennessee had ruled that "when a master approached his slave with a dangerous weapon, the slave had a right to resist." The court itself was not unsympathetic to the abuse the defendant had suffered and to his striking back in self-defense. Nevertheless, the jury found Hannibal guilty of first-degree murder, and the judge—who Birdseye noted "is one of the most amiable men living, who has freed his own slaves, and whose opinion of slavery corresponds with ours"—was compelled to sentence him to death. In doing so, the judge "was himself so much overcome by his feelings that he found it difficult to conclude his sentence." Hannibal himself broke down in tears at that point, and Birdseye stated, "I should think that more than one half of the audience wept" upon hearing the sentence, which was carried out some two weeks later.[3]

A year later, in 1844, an extraordinary legal challenge by slaves protesting the current terms of their enslavement began to unfold in Clay County, Kentucky. This highland county in the southeastern corner of the state was the site of a thriving antebellum salt-mining industry, which, as elsewhere in Appalachia, resulted in a considerable concentration of slaves in an otherwise remote and impoverished mountain county. As part of their masterful analysis of the economic inequities and resulting culture of poverty in Clay County, Dwight Billings and Kathleen Blee have chronicled several disputes, legal and extralegal, between local slaveholders, and occasionally between slaveholder and slave.[4]

The murder of one of the county's most prominent slaveholders, Daniel Bates, set into motion a series of lawsuits by his slaves regarding both their past and future status.[5] Bates had been the subject of several disputes over the years, including an attempt on his life in 1840. Four years later, tensions between Bates and his brother-in-law, Abner Baker, over both business and marital matters led to a confrontation at Bates's salt furnace, in which Baker shot and killed him. Baker then claimed that Bates had "kept a band of lawless men and negroes about him," and worried that Bates had ordered his slaves to kill him.

There is no other evidence that Bates's slaves posed any threat to Baker or anyone else, but they did come into sharp focus with their master's murder for another reason: several of them chose to sue his estate for their freedom. Allison was the first slave to bring suit against Daniel's brother Stephen, in November 1844, a mere four months after Daniel's death. Her lawyer argued that their father, John Bates, had stipulated in his will that she be freed after eight years of being hired out, an operation overseen by the county sheriff's office. Although the case was initially dismissed, Allison and eight other slaves—Berry, Theophilus, Cuffee, Jane, Claiborne, Elsey, Alssysa, and Harriet (half of them women, significantly)—continued to press their case, ultimately resorting to the unusual tactic of suing for the value of their labor over the five years in which they considered themselves unlawfully enslaved, at rates ranging from $500 for Theophilus to $100 for Harriet. Remarkably, after nearly seven years of legal wrangling, the Kentucky Court of Appeals granted freedom to all slave plaintiffs in 1851, though it agreed to only a single cent in compensation for their many years of labor (which by then included the additional time during which their cases had wended their way to a resolution).[6]

A shift in scene to 1851 in the Silver Creek valley in Burke County on the eastern slopes of North Carolina's Blue Ridge Mountains. Robert McElrath, a local slaveholder, sent his son-in-law to California with four of his seventeen slaves in order to secure enough gold for him to pay off his debts. The slaves were young adult men except for "Uncle Jim," an elderly slave who had established himself as an expert place miner during the gold rush in Burke County's own South Mountains two decades earlier. McElrath's slaves were among hundreds from western North Carolina to be taken west to relive the glory days of

Burke County's brush with gold fever, but the owners of these slaves knew that whatever gains they made in terms of gold, they risked losing the very property they'd sent to procure it. In the free state that California had become in 1850, slaves' status as property was by no means secure, and many owners and guardians faced discipline problems as well as the refusal of slaves to leave California at the end of their westward ventures.[7]

The McElrath slaves apparently posed no such problems. Much of their cooperation and productivity may have lain in the fact that they were allowed one day a week to mine for themselves. But as their guardian accompanied them back home by the quickest route then available—by ship from Stockton to the isthmus of Panama and a week-long land crossing to another ship on the Caribbean side—a new opportunity presented itself. McElrath's son-in-law succumbed to malaria, and suddenly four slaves found themselves on their own carrying a substantial amount of gold—their own and their master's—on a ship bound for New York City. Yet, despite exposure in New York to abolitionists who urged them to remain there, the foursome eventually made their way back to Burke County and their master, where they were much extolled throughout the community for their fidelity and devotion to him.[8]

Sarah Gudger was 121 years old in 1937, when she was interviewed in Asheville by a local volunteer of the Federal Writers Project. Her story is as poignant as any told in that massive collection of ex-slave memories. Before she was emancipated in her late forties, Gudger was a slave on what she called a large plantation of the Hemphill family in the Swannanoa Valley east of Asheville. Her memories of bondage were of a grueling regimen of hard work conditions and heartbreaking family trauma. Her original master, Andy Hemphill, "was a good ole man, and the Missus she was good, too. She usta read de Bible t' us chillum afoah she pass away." Their deaths left Sarah and her fellow slaves in the hands of their son, William Hemphill, a much harsher taskmaster, under whom, she testified, "I nebbah knowed whut it was t' rest. I js wok all de time f'om mawnin' till late at night." Work included working in cornfields, chopping wood, washing clothes, and spinning until late into the night. She was whipped frequently and

50

never got much to eat. She had to endure long, harsh winters with inadequate clothing or bedcovers to withstand the cold.

Most striking in Gudger's testimony was the impact of "specalaters" on the local slave community. Although none of the slaves on her own plantation was ever sold away, those on William Hemphill's other plantation were—and apparently often. "Oh, dat wah a tebble time!" she recalled.

> All de slaves be in de field, plowin', hoein', singin' in de boilin' sun. Ole Marse he cum t'ru de field wif a man call de speculater. Dey walk round jes' lookin', jes lookin', All de da'kies know whut dis mean. Dey didn' dare look up, jes' wok right on. Den de specalater he see who he want. He talk to Ole Marse, den de claps de han'cuffs on him an' tak him away to de cotton country. Oh, dem was awful times! When de specalater was ready to go wif de slaves, effen dey was enny what din' wanta go, he thrash em, den tie em 'hind de waggin an' mek 'em run till dey fall on de groun', den he thrash em till dey say dey go 'thout no trubble. . . . When de da'kies wen' t' dinnah de old niggah mammy she say whar am sich-an-sich. None ob de othahs wanna tell huh. But when she see dem look down to de groun' she jes say: "De specalater, de specalater." Den de teahs roll down huh cheeks, cause mebbe it huh son o' husban' and she know she nebbah see 'em agin. Mebbe dey leaves babies t' home, mebbe jes' pappy an' mammy. Oh, mah Lawdy, my old Boss wah mean, but he nebbah sen' us to de cotton country.[9]

* * *

Sam and Nancy Williams make for one of the fullest and most compelling stories of individual slaves in the mountain South. Historian Charles Dew has reconstructed in much detail Sam's story, as he became and remained the chief forger in the extensive Buffalo Forge ironworks created by entrepreneur William Weaver in Rockbridge County, Virginia, in the late 1830s and operated through the rest of the antebellum era.

One of the more intriguing aspects of Sam's story is the fact that that both he and his wife, Nancy, established savings accounts at a bank in Lexington, nine miles north of Buffalo Forge. They each earned cash under a system of "overwork"—longer hours and work on Sundays and holidays—Sam through further work in the forge, and Nancy from housework and extra duties in Weaver's dairy operations, of which she was in charge. This added compensation was part of a system of positive incentives that Weaver applied not only for his enslaved workforce in his ironworks, but for his agricultural workers as well. For the Williamses, this overtime earned them cash payments of a mere fifty cents a day. Nonetheless, the pay accumulated enough through the 1840s and 1850s that the couple could buy sugar, molasses, and coffee to supplement their diet and also purchase cloth, decorative items, and substantial furniture for their home. Christmas presents from Sam to his wife included a silk handkerchief in 1841, a pair of buckskin gloves in 1849, and nine yards of silk in 1851.

The whole issue of a slave with a savings account came to a head in 1855, when a local free black cooper named Henry Nash refused to believe that a slave could have such an account and bet Sam Williams his watch that it wasn't so. The bet drew the attention of Weaver's nephew, who was also incredulous, until Weaver's lawyer confirmed that such was indeed the case, and that Sam had the right to withdraw funds from his account anytime without authorization from his owner or anyone else. Sam thus gained a second watch from that bet, after proving his claim by withdrawing his cash from the bank, showing it to Nash, and then redepositing it all.[10]

In 1842, the mayor of Greeneville, Tennessee, who was also a tailor and speculated in real estate, purchased his first two slaves, a brother and sister, both adolescents. His name was Andrew Johnson. The slaves' names were Dolly and Sam. As Johnson's political career advanced, on to Tennessee governor and U.S. senator, he acquired several other slaves. Though there are discrepancies in how many he ultimately owned, the total never seems to have been more than six or eight. Of those, Sam remained Johnson's favorite, so much so that the rest of his family chided him on how much he indulged Sam. Johnson's eldest daughter claimed that Sam did not belong to her father; rather, her father belonged to Sam. Sam's cockiness and often brash behavior elicited community disapproval as well as that of the Johnson family; on several occasions during Andrew's long absences from home, they threatened to sell Sam "down the river," though all knew there was little chance that such a threat would ever be acted upon.

Most resentful of Sam's favored status in his father's eyes was Charles Johnson, a ne'er-do-well and alcoholic who was fully aware of his father's disappointment in him. In January 1860, Charles wrote a letter to his father, then serving in the Senate in Washington, in which he revealed not only specific actions of Sam's that he found particularly offensive, but also his own frustrations that he himself had neither his own slaves nor any authority over his father's. Charles began by urging his father, once again, to sell Sam. "It does not suit him to stay in this country," he insisted, noting that "he is quite the independent gentleman." He informed the senator that Sam had defied an order from his mother (Andrew's wife Eliza) to go cut wood on her daughter's farm, stating that "he would 'be damed' if he wanted to cut wood there." Charles reported another spat between mistress and slave in which she accused him of not turning over the share of his earnings from hiring himself out to others in town; he responded that he was entitled to all income he derived from such work, and not merely half.

"I do not desire to own negroes," Charles assured his father, "but if I did, they should know their place or I would not have them about me. . . . It does seem that the more attention, the more kindness you show a negro, the less account he is; they seem to misconstrue it;—but after all, the negro to be of any value must be subjugated." Only the fewest of men, he asserted, "are fit to have neggroes; that is especially the case in E. Tennessee. The negro must have a Master; and those who use them severly seem to have the best slaves."[11]

Each of these stories raises as many questions as it answers. One of the most basic is the question of typicality in terms of the slave experience in Southern Appalachia. We see here slaves in four different states—some engaged primarily in agricultural labor; others in industrial enterprises. Some were part of relatively large slave communities; others part of much smaller holdings; one was a free black; others acted at times as if they were free. We see in their stories instances of great cruelty and inhumanity, as well as instances of kindness and tolerance. We see examples of repression, of violence, of bleak circumstances in which slaves were victimized and exploited in a variety of ways—some systemic to the institution and to the economy that it served in the highlands, some far more personal and vindictive—but we also see examples of opportunities within that system for slaves to become active agents in bettering their circumstances, even if only within the limited parameters dictated by both racism and bondage. So which of these varied situations are most representative of slavery in the mountain South? Does any one or more of these scenarios best reflect the nature of master-slave relationships within the region, thus rendering the rest flukes or anomalies?

I would suggest that all are equally valuable in understanding the multifaceted nature of Appalachian slavery, and—perhaps by extension—that throughout the American South. To begin with, each of the stories embodies ambiguities that blur any clear-cut lines as to the qualitative nature of slave life within the region; in almost all of these vignettes, we can find elements of *both*—opportunity and repression; benevolence and abuse; compassion and cruelty; tolerance and intolerance. In short, these stories point up the inherent contradictions in a system that was to a certain extent always subject to and driven by the foibles and even capriciousness of human nature on the part of both owners and slaves.

Take D'lea, for example, the literate young slave whipped for reading a religious tract. That her literacy enabled her to serve her master as an accountant of sorts, and perhaps in other managerial capacities, is extraordinary, particularly for a female slave. And yet, frontier historian Marilyn Davis-DeEulis used D'lea's story as one of several to illustrate a relatively high degree of literacy among slaves on both the Kentucky and Virginia sides of the Ohio Valley during slavery's formative years there. In applying her reading skills for something other than the utilitarian functions required by her master, however, D'lea suffered a whipping by a possibly insecure or even envious overseer, who was anything but appreciative of her intellect or religious conviction.

D'lea faced very different treatments by her owner and his overseer, a situation not at all uncommon in the plantation South. No less surprising perhaps are those several slaves subjected to differing treatments by different owners, even those who were members of the same family. Sarah Gudger bemoaned the death of her first master and mistress, under whom she felt she was treated well—and who had even provided her with some religious training; yet under their son, she and her fellow slaves faced far harsher working conditions, material deprivation, physical abuse, and emotional torment. Perhaps less explicably, the same man, William Hemphill, applied a double standard to slaves on different farms. Those slaves on his second plantation found themselves far more vulnerable and insecure, in that they were regularly subjected to the whims of speculators who bought them and sold them south; though fully able to describe that experience in wrenching terms, Gudger only knew of it secondhand; for somehow Hemphill never allowed slave sales to take place on the farm where she lived and worked.

The difference in generational attitudes toward slave property and the vulnerability of the slave trade appears again in Andrew Johnson's family. The indulgences of the future president led to what his son viewed as the totally unacceptable behavior of slave Sam, who was canny enough to take full advantage of Andrew's authority and protection to defy both Mrs. Johnson's and certainly their children's attempts to control him, and even expressed his dissatisfaction with the fact that he didn't have full rights to his earnings. As secure as Sam felt, though, it is apparent that the easy solution for slaveholders with temperamental or overly independent bondsmen was sale south —no idle threat, even in Greeneville, Tennessee, the heart of abolitionist Appalachia.

The legal battles waged by Daniel Bates's slaves suggest a very different set of cross-generational issues for slave owners. The failure of sons to live up to the final wishes of their father toward his bondsmen and women is not surprising. In collusion with local law authorities (the sheriff authorized and oversaw their continued hiring out), first Daniel and then Stephen sought the continued exploitation of men and women who should have been freed long before. Yet it was the slaves themselves, through local lawyers championing their interests with little expectation of monetary gain, who prevailed upon a legal system that they believed would and should protect their interests. Although it took nearly seven years for right to overcome might, these black men and women ultimately triumphed against powerful local interests—and overcame decades of legal and racial precedent—to win their freedom.

Edward Tarr's tale tells us much about the shifting sentiments toward African Americans at the community level over time and the vulnerability that often accompanied success on the part of black entrepreneurs or overly independent slaves. Tarr's blacksmith operation testified to the relative openness of early settlements in the remote back-country and the absence of the repressive infrastructure that would have precluded his achieving the same level of success in the more established and rigidly ordered Tidewater. But as the 1750s became the 1760s and 1770s, community norms evolved, and earlier forms of racial fluidity and tolerance gave way to more conventional forms of hierarchy and racial order. If the unruliness of Tarr's clientele was the excuse that led to ostracism and ultimately legal harassment and exile, the fact that his business proved so prosperous over the years and that many of those who frequented the site were both slaves and other free blacks must have bred communal resentment and discomfort among the growing white community. Tarr's experience took place on the colonial frontier, but it represents an all too familiar scenario of white discomfort with black economic success that would reappear in multiple other guises throughout the South from the antebellum years through the long and repressive era of Jim Crow.

And what are we to make of the McElrath slaves who were part of the California gold rush? It was certainly an unusual opportunity in and of itself, though one in which many Burke County and other western Carolina slaves participated. Some slaves did take advantage of their rights on free soil and remained in California, despite efforts by owner and guardians to force their return home. But many also came back to their homes in Burke County—often with little choice, and certainly few with the complete free agency with which the McElrath four returned. But for all of the self-congratulation their return sparked among the local slaveholding community—and the propaganda uses to which the story was put long afterward, the real motivation for their return home had little to do with fidelity to a benevolent owner. McElrath had shrewdly chosen four slaves who happened to be both husbands and fathers, and it was of course the love of family—parents, wives, and children—that ultimately brought them all home.

In Sam and Nancy Williams's story we again see both opportunity and its limitations. Their story is in some respects typical of many Appalachian slaves who found themselves exploited by grueling work in often dangerous circumstances in various antebellum extractive enterprises—coal, iron, and salt mines—and in the equally exploitative operations like Buffalo Forge that processed those raw materials. Yet by both temperament and talent, Sam Williams found himself in a leadership capacity of trust and responsibility that opened up prospects for material acquisition and a more comfortable life for his family. Even so, while he and his wife generated enough income to establish separate savings accounts, and to use those funds as they saw fit, they were still owned property and thus their options remained tightly circumscribed: they could not buy land, they could not travel, they could not move. All of their diligence and extra hours of hard work were ultimately applied to the furnishings of a house they neither owned nor could claim should their owner decide to sell them or merely to move them elsewhere.

Nor should we attribute any altruism to Sam and Nancy's owner. If the overwork system provided William Weaver's other slaves with similar opportunities to earn cash income, it does not mean that he was as an exceptionally benevolent master, but rather that he was an astute labor manager and businessman. His strategy obviously worked in his own self-interest: it provided him with a great deal of extra work, which in turn increased the profitability of his enterprise while raising the morale of a potentially unruly and inefficient workforce. That these were higher priorities than any goodwill toward those he owned becomes more apparent in light of the fact that Weaver on occasion resorted to more conventional forms of control and retribution: he sold to traders slaves whose behavior or attitude he found problematic, which meant separating spouses or parents from children.[12]

Finally, there is the tragedy of Hannibal in Newport, Tennessee. His story reflects the worst of slavery's abuses, the unrelenting physical—and most likely mental—cruelties that could drive a slave to suicide. The accident that led to the master's death also doomed the slave so determined to free himself from the reach of that master. And yet, while Hannibal's acquittal or even conviction on a reduced charge would have made for an even more extraordinary story, the most striking aspects in Ezekiel Birdseye's account of the case are the emotional reactions of both judge and courtroom observers, who obviously sympathized far more with the slave than with his master. (This story strikes me as perhaps the one most tied to a particular place. This area of East Tennessee—as Birdseye's activity there itself testifies—exhibited as much abolitionist, or at least ambivalent, sentiment toward slavery as any part of Southern Appalachia or the South; and yet even there, such sentiment failed to save a man from legally being hanged for an act of self-defense.)

Only at this most intimate level in which we see slaves and masters interacting as individuals within very particular settings and circumstances can we fully appreciate the contradictions and variables that so complicate the essence of the "peculiar institution" as it existed over the course of a century. As impressionistic and even fleeting as these snippets of reality may seem, we are attuned to the fact that they did not occur in a vacuum, either in time or in space. Each of the individuals in these stories, black and white, reflects larger entities—families, slave communities, slaveholding communities, both agricultural and industrial enterprises, government institutions, towns, and counties that comprised very particular locales in that vast geographical expanse we know as Southern Appalachia. Each of these incidents took place at particular moments in time as well, with the time period often integral to the ways in which these stories played out. From early frontier settlement to fully developed industrial era of the late antebellum period, chronology had much to do with the circumstances in which these African Americans found themselves, for better or for worse.

Lillian Smith, who wrote perhaps more passionately and perceptively about southern mores than any other white southerner, once observed of its racial order: "There is a structural, bony sameness through the region that can be called accurately 'the South'; but it is fleshed out in ten thousand different ways—ways often strikingly inconsistent with the 'beliefs' that seem inherent in the structure."[13] It seems that the vast and growing scholarship on slavery and race relations in Appalachia over the past couple of decades has in itself led us to new understandings of the inconsistencies that Smith notes. (She herself, incidentally, was a resident of Appalachia—Rabun County, Georgia—for most of her adult life.)

In generalizing about southern slavery, historians need to—and now easily can—take into account its existence in the mountain South. For far too long, its presence there was seen as a mere demographic distinction, and the simple fact that there were far fewer slaves and slaveholders in Appalachia than in the lowland South served as the be-all and end-all in explaining a regional "otherness" in terms of race. But what the rich and varied work of recent years suggests is that quantitative differences do not, in and of themselves, explain the qualitative differences in slavery. In lifting their eyes unto the hills, so to speak, historians will find not merely one new variable to challenge that "structural, bony sameness" to which Smith refers; they'll find multiple variables within and throughout the region, some of which confirm realities elsewhere in the American South, and some of which may be particular not just to Appalachia, but to even more specific settings within the region.

In an essay published in 1983, entitled "Slavery on the Edges of the Old South: or Do Exceptions Prove Rules?" British scholar Peter Parish suggested that the "deviants from the pattern of Southern slave society" can serve as valuable indicators of the strengths and weaknesses of the system as a whole—its flexibility, adaptability, potential for growth and development as well as for its inefficiencies and instabilities. Parish focuses on four exceptions to the acknowledged norm of plantation, agricultural slavery: slavery in cities, industrial slavery, the hiring out of slaves, and free blacks.

While the peripheries on which he concentrates are not geographical, and thus Appalachia does not factor into his analysis per se, it is interesting that three of his four categories are very much inherent in the way in which the institution manifested itself in the highland South, and are reflected in several of the stories told here—slave hiring, industrial slavery, and the free black experience. Thus it would be easy to extrapolate from Parish's thesis and make a case that Appalachia offers not merely one but multiple exceptions of its own. The "exceptions" noted here, if indeed they are that, do illuminate in subtle and perhaps not so subtle ways what Parish characterized as "many features of slavery and of Southern society generally—its racial attitudes and compromises, its internal pressures, its readiness sometimes to subordinate economic to social and racial priorities, its combination of inflexible rules and flexible application, and not least, the ability of slaves to exploit the weaknesses and loopholes of the system in their own interest."[14]

As such, Appalachia offers the student of American slavery something more than flukes, exceptions, or anomalies. By taking seriously and integrating into broader studies of race relations drawn from the mountain South, we can indeed come to appreciate the impact of geography, topography, demographics, and local and regional economies on the interactions of whites and blacks, slave or free. I would suggest again that there is much value in taking seriously the evidence we have of slavery at the most intimate and personal of levels—the stories of individuals, of families, of communities, from whatever sources and perspectives they come to us. Masters' records and correspondence; slaves' own memories and testimony; court transcripts and other legal documents; and outside observers with varying agendas—all remind us that perhaps the most ultimate variable in how the practice of slavery played out, regardless of its "structural, bony sameness," lay in human nature. This is where the continued fascination remains with the slave past, as with history in general, and where we as scholars are most likely to reach beyond our academic peers to a broader audience.

It is no surprise that the narratives of Frederick Douglass and Harriet Jacobs and other individual slaves have long been among the most vital and effective venues for understanding southern slavery. No doubt they continue to be assigned readings in high school and college classrooms more than any scholarly monograph because their stories so readily engage us in such vivid and emotional ways. Nor is it coincidental that with all the books that continue to be published on slavery even now, the two that generated the most excitement and attention in 2005—and those most likely to reach beyond a narrow academic audience—are Vincent Carretta's startlingly revisionist biography of Olaudah Equiano, and John Hope Franklin and Loren Schweninger's study of Sally Thomas, a Tennessee slave woman who achieved near freedom as a businesswoman and who, by very different means, worked to free her three sons.[15] As Franklin notes in the preface to this extraordinary saga of the Thomas family, the story "breaks nearly all the traditional stereotypes associated with such rational constructs as black/white and slave/free."[16]

One reads neither Equiano's nor Sally Thomas's stories for the typicality of their experiences, any more than one does Douglass's or Jacobs's narratives. It is, in fact, the extraordinary circumstances of each of these slave lives that make them so compelling—the fine lines walked between slavery and freedom and the dramatic situations in which they found themselves, the tragedies and occasional triumphs that were dictated as much by luck and happenchance as by their owners' dispositions and whims. The contradictions and complexities of African American life are fully apparent in each of these lives, and like many other such experiences, in Appalachia and throughout the South, they suggest that "the boundaries between slavery and freedom were always harsh and menacing but . . . sometimes more permeable and flexible than we imagine."[17]

Just as each of the stories told here suggests complex and sometimes ambivalent aspects of slave life in Appalachia, they also serve to remind us that Southern Appalachia has always been home to a far more complicated and diverse society and economy than once assumed. The vast explosion of scholarship on the region, particularly that focused on the nineteenth century, has made that point over and over again. Close examinations of Appalachia's slaves and slaveholders provide merely one more window into that complexity and diversity, as they challenge generalizations and stereotypes so long applied to both the region and to southern slavery. The editors of a 1995 essay collection noted of this new scholarship on nineteenth-century Appalachia: "None claim that the patterns described were necessarily unique to the southern highlands or were general to the whole mountain region."[18] And so it is with race relations in the region. No one scenario laid out here typifies the whole; nor are any of these types of incidents limited to highland contexts.

Slavery was an institution that, for all of its legal rigidities and clearly defined boundaries, often proved quite adaptable, malleable, and always subject to the idiosyncrasies of local demands and individual agendas. These variables are perhaps more evident in Appalachia than elsewhere. It was the one area (or certainly most extensive area) of the American South in which the vast majority of residents were neither slaves nor slaveholders, and where the institution, in order to be profitable, was forced to adjust to a range of settings and scenarios far removed from the plantation worlds of cotton, rice, or sugar.

This doesn't mean that the system in the mountains was any less harsh or cruel or exploitative than it was on those other areas.[19] Yet it does provide us an opportunity to view slaves as both victims and agents, and along with their masters, as individuals and in communities, in more intimate and nuanced terms that serve to inform our understanding not only of Appalachia as more than simply a periphery of the slaveholding South, but also of the strengths and weaknesses of the institution as it was adapted to this relatively atypical environment. In adding this "edge" of slavery, in Peter Parish's words, to the whole, we can indeed more fully appreciate not only the extent to which exceptions can prove rules, but also the possibility that what were once considered mere exceptions may not have been so exceptional after all.

Notes

1. J. Susanne Schramm Simmons, "Augusta County's Other Pioneers: The African American Presence in Frontier Augusta County," in *Diversity and Accommodation: Essays on the Cultural Composition of the Virginia Frontier,* ed. Michael J. Puglisi (Knoxville: University of Tennessee Press, 1997), 160–61, 163. Simmons drew on an unpublished paper by Turk McCleskey, "The Mystery of Edward Tarr," as the source of her treatment of him.

2. Marilyn Davis-DeEulis, "Slavery on the Margins of the Virginia Frontier: African American Literacy in Western Kanawha and Cabell Counties, 1795–1840," in Puglisi, *Diversity and Accommodation,* 194–99 passim.

3. Ezekiel Birdseye to *The Christian Freeman,* April 14, 1843, reprinted in Durwood Dunn, *An Abolitionist in the Appalachian South: Ezekiel Birdseye on Slavery, Capitalism, and Separate Statehood in East Tennessee, 1841–1846* (Knoxville: University of Tennessee Press, 1997), 252–54.

4. Dwight B. Billings and Kathleen M. Blee, *The Road to Poverty: The Making of Wealth and Hardship in Appalachia* (Cambridge, England: Cambridge University Press, 2000), chap. 3.

5. Billings and Blee provide a thorough account of the murder and Baker's trial in ibid., 124–31.

6. *Allison and others (of color) v. Stephen W. Bates; Theophilus, Jane, Cuffee, Claiborne, Elsey, Berry, Jr., and Assysa v. Stephen W. Bates,* Clay County, Ky., Circuit Court, 1844–1851. I am grateful to Dwight Billings for sharing transcriptions of these cases with me. Daniel Bates owned forty-four slaves at his death; his father, John, owned fifty-one. John Bates's will made various provisions for his slaves: he freed some, gave land to some, and stipulated that several—including the eight litigants in the case discussed here—serve eight years as hired labor and then be set free. Billings and Blee, *Road to Poverty,* 221.

7. John C. Inscoe, *Mountain Masters: Slavery and the Sectional Crisis in Western North Carolina* (Knoxville: University of Tennessee Press, 1989), 72–74.

8. Ibid., 73. The most extended version of this story is found in Thomas G. Walton, "Sketches of Pioneers in Burke County History," typescript (Thomas George Walton Papers, Southern Historical Collection, UNC), 10–11.

9. Sarah Gudger interview, May 5, 1937, in George P. Rawick, ed., *The American Slave: A Composite Autobiography,* vol. 14: *North Carolina Narratives, Part I* (Westport, Conn.: Greenwood Press, 1971), 350–58; quoted material on 352, 353, 354–55.

10. Charles B. Dew, "Sam Williams, Forgeman: The Life of an Industrial Slave at Buffalo Forge, Virginia," *Appalachians and Race: The Mountain South from Slavery to Segregation,* ed. John C. Inscoe (Lexington: University Press of Kentucky, 2001), 84–86. For a full discussion of the overwork system as practiced at Buffalo Forge, see Charles B. Dew, *Bond of Iron: Master and Slave at Buffalo Forge* (New York: W. W. Norton, 1994), 108–21.

11. Charles Johnson to Andrew Johnson, January 29, 1860, in Leroy P. Graf and Ralph W. Hoskins, eds., *The Papers of Andrew Johnson,* vol. 3: *1858–1860* (Knoxville: University of Tennessee Press, 1972), 404–5, quoted in David Warren Bowen, *Andrew Johnson and the Negro* (Knoxville: University of Tennessee Press, 1989). See pp. 51–54 for the fullest coverage of Johnson as slaveholder.

12. Dew, *Bond of Iron,* 108.

13. Lillian Smith, "Introduction" to Ely Green, *Ely: An Autobiography* (rept., Athens: University of Georgia Press, 1966), xxxi.

14. Peter Parish, "The Edges of Slavery in the Old South: Or, Do Exceptions Prove Rules?" *Slavery & Abolition* 4 (September 1983): 106–25, quotes on 108, 124.

15. Vincent Carretta, *Equiano, the African: Biography of a Self-Made Man* (Athens: University of Georgia Press, 2005); John Hope Franklin and Loren Schweninger, *In Search of the Promised Land: A Slave Family in the Old South* (New York: Oxford University Press, 2005).

16. Preface to Franklin and Schweninger, *In Search of the Promised Land*, xi.

17. Ibid., xii.

18. Dwight B. Billings, Mary Beth Pudup, and Altina L. Waller, eds., *Appalachia in the Making: The Mountain South in the Nineteenth Century* (Chapel Hill: University of North Carolina Press, 1995), 9–10.

19. Wilma A. Dunaway's *Slavery in the American Mountain South* and *The African-American Family in Slavery and Emancipation* (Cambridge, England: Cambridge University Press, 2003) provide the most unrelenting documentation of cruelty to and exploitation of Appalachian slaves.

3

Olmsted in Appalachia

A Connecticut Yankee Encounters Slavery in the Southern Highlands, 1854

Outside observers have provided among the richest primary sources for scholars of the antebellum South. Despite the stereotypical assumptions, florid prose, and regional and moral biases that characterize the majority of such travel accounts, their detailed descriptions of the people and places encountered have often been of great value to later chroniclers of slavery and the Old South.

Probably the most valuable of such accounts are three volumes of commentary on slavery and southern society written by Frederick Law Olmsted. These accounts are based on his fourteen months of travel throughout the South from 1852 to 1854.[1] Although it was his later career as a landscape architect, environmentalist, and urban planner for which Olmsted is most widely remembered, his much briefer stint as a journalist and social critic during the 1850s is equally significant. Because his mission to observe and report objectively on slavery and its effects on southern society was so precise, his route so extensive, and his observations so voluminous, historians from James Rhodes and U. B. Phillips to Kenneth Stampp and Eugene Genovese have made Olmsted's work the most cited and quoted of any contemporary source on the "peculiar institution." Yet relatively little attention has been paid to one of the most distinctive and uniquely revealing segments of Olmsted's southern tour: the summer month in 1854 in which he journeyed through the Southern Appalachians.

Born in Hartford, Connecticut, in 1822, the product of a comfortable New England upbringing and a Yale education, Olmsted seemed to have been imbued with a sense of wanderlust throughout his youth. After an extensive tour of Europe and the British Isles, which led to the 1852 publication of his first book, *Walks and Talks of an American Farmer in England*, Olmsted was commissioned by two New York newspapers to serve as a roving correspondent in the American South. That assignment led to a series of letters that appeared in the *New York Daily Times* and the *New York Daily Tribune* during and after his trip; the letters were then compiled and expanded into three volumes: *A Journey in the Seaboard Slave States* (1856), *A Journey through Texas* (1857), and *A Journey in the Back Country* (1860).[2]

Though Olmsted, like many of his fellow New Englanders, firmly opposed slavery, he was, early in the decade, almost as offended by the hyperbole and pious posturing of what he felt were overwrought and ill-informed abolitionists. He saw his southern assignment as an opportunity to provide a more objective appraisal of slavery based entirely on his firsthand observations. "Very little candid, truthful, and unprejudiced public discussion," he wrote, "has yet been had on the vexed subject of slavery." He maintained that the true nature of southern life, white and black, had thus far proved more impenetrable to insiders and thus subject to misconception than was true of most foreign countries.[3]

Once his trip was under way, Olmsted's concern was not so much the black labor system's cruelties and injustices to those enslaved. In fact, he found the physical treatment and quality of the slaves' lives to be somewhat better than he had anticipated. Rather it was the economic and cultural detriments that slavery inflicted on southern whites—slaveholders and nonslaveholders—that made up his most stinging indictment of the system. As a labor force, slavery proved grossly inefficient, due in part to too much indulgence on the part of owners and taskmasters. Olmsted concluded that, because of their lack of incentive and their inherent shortcomings as a race, slaves worked slowly and poorly. Even worse, they lowered the expectations for white labor output and locked southern agriculture into crude, backward methods that limited the progress and the productivity that characterized American farming elsewhere.[4]

A far more serious defect in Olmsted's eyes was the cultural and social stagnation that the peculiar institution imposed upon the South.

Slavery robbed the region's yeomen of any Calvinistic work ethic or of any incentive for self-improvement, material or otherwise. But what made Olmsted's commentary most original was that his descriptions of nonslaveholders—"unambitious, indolent, degraded and illiterate . . . a dead peasantry so far as they affect the industrial position of the South"—he found almost equally applicable to the ruling class.[5] Its black property inhibited intellectual activity or interests and perpetuated among the planter elite crude, primitive living conditions usually indicative only of frontier society.[6]

In the summer of 1854, toward the end of his second tour, that covering the "backcountry" or inland South, Olmsted moved into Appalachia. There he found exceptions to the deplorable conditions of the plantation South and evidence confirming his explanation for those conditions. From late June through late July, the Connecticut correspondent traveled through the hills of northern Alabama, passed briefly through Tennessee and Georgia, then moved through western North Carolina across the northeastern tip of Tennessee, and on into the Blue Ridge Mountains of Virginia. His itinerary included Chattanooga and the nearby copper-mining region of Polk County; the westernmost string of North Carolina county seats (Murphy, Waynesville, Asheville, Burnsville, and Bakersville); Elizabethton, Tennessee; and finally Abingdon and Lynchburg, Virginia.[7]

With the exception of the few substantial towns through which he passed, Olmsted's mountain route took him through areas with among the fewest slaves in the South. In 1850, the total slave population of the ten identifiable counties through which he passed was a little more than eight thousand—only 10 percent of the counties' total populations. Excluding Hamilton, Buncombe, and Washington counties, with their respective communities of Chattanooga, Asheville, and Abingdon, whose populations were larger, more affluent, and included a higher percentage of slaves, the remaining seven counties were home to a mere 2,446 slaves, who made up only 6.7 percent of the populace.[8]

While moving in and between these highland counties, Olmsted found much to confirm his general conclusions formed after observing other parts of the South. Though the impact of bondage on its black victims was a major concern of Olmsted's throughout his southern travels, he paid little attention to slaves themselves once he moved into the mountains. While he occasionally noted their presence in households or farms that he visited, he related only one specific encounter with a highland slave, a woman he observed while en route through a prosperous mountain valley. But neither her treatment nor her mental state interested him by then. In rounding up a herd of "uncommonly fine cattle," she forced the animals to leap over a four-foot fence rail rather than lower it, and she beat a pregnant heifer that failed to make the unreasonable jump. Such behavior confirmed to Olmsted his theory that "slavery breeds unfaithful, meritorious, inexact and non-persistent habits of working," habits that are inevitably passed on to white laborers as well, so that they become "even more indifferent than negroes to the interests of their employers."[9] Even though he maintained that the highlanders he observed were much more industrious than their lowland counterparts (no doubt due to the presence of far fewer slaves), this regrettable side effect of the system was nevertheless apparent in the mountains.

But Olmsted was also quick to note the much-improved temperaments of those in areas little touched by slavery, which he credited to the absence of black bondsmen and their owners. "Compared with the slaveholders," he generalized about the mountain residents he observed, "these people are more cheerful, more amiable, more sociable, and more liberal. Compared with the nonslaveholders of the slaveholding districts, they are also more hopeful, more ambitious, more intelligent, more provident, and more comfortable" (293). Even the material conditions of mountain life were, he claimed, an improvement over those of plantation society.

Olmsted wasted no time in drawing these conclusions. As he moved north into the Alabama hill country, he passed through a valley he described as having "thin, sandy soil, thickly populated by poor farmers." He added that "negroes are rare, but occasionally neat, new houses, with other improvements, show the increasing prosperity of the district" (220). The journalist would later go to great lengths to reinforce his case for the degenerative effects of slavery on the character and physical well-being of owners. He told of approaching a substantial log house with adjacent cabins for blacks, only to be told by its owner that he could afford to spare neither food nor fodder for Olmsted or his horse (233). A lengthy sequence on his visit with a Tennessee "squire" slightly farther along his route stressed the indolence and slovenly lifestyle exhibited by both his host and hostess. The squire slept late and did not change his clothes, and his wife spent most of her time smoking a pipe on the porch, leading their New England guest to exclaim incredulously, "Yet every thing betokened an opulent and prosperous farmer—rich land, extensive field crops, a number of negroes, and considerable herds of cattle and horses. He also had capital invested in mines and railroads, he told me" (236).

In his most clear-cut elaboration of this point, Olmsted described his accommodations on two consecutive nights near Elizabethton, Tennessee. One was the residence of a slaveholder; the other was not. Though similar in size and furnishings—"both houses were of the best class common in the region" (268)—and though the slaveholder was much the wealthier of the two, Olmsted maintained that he lived in much less comfort. His house was dirty, disorderly, and in need of repair; he and his wife were "very morose or sadly silent"; the household's white women were "very negligent and sluttish in their attire"; and the food was badly cooked and badly served by blacks (269). By contrast, Olmsted's next host, a nonslaveholder, lived in much neater, well-ordered, and comfortable quarters. The women were clean and well dressed, and everyone was "cheerful and kind." The food served was abundant and wholesome (the first Olmsted claimed to have had of that quality since Natchez, Mississippi, months earlier), and all work was carried on far more smoothly and conscientiously (269–70).

Though such convenient contrasts may strain credibility, the southern highlands provided the Connecticut Yankee with interesting variations to his theory that the negative effects of a slaveholding society extended well beyond its black victims. But it is his interviews with the region's inhabitants that serve as the most revealing and valuable aspects of his work, for his account gave voice to this ordinarily inarticulate and rarely quoted group. The testimony of these generally inaccessible southerners elicited by their northern guest serves as the most significant body of evidence regarding what has long been a baffling array of opinion, expert and otherwise, on racism in the mountains.

On no other aspect of Appalachian culture has opinion been so divided as on the question of how mountaineers regarded blacks. On the one hand are those who concluded that the lack of contact meant a lack of prejudice as well. Carter G. Woodson, an African American historian with West Virginia roots, was the first scholar—and still one of the few—to have dealt seriously with the subject of racial attitudes in the Southern Appalachians. He maintained that greater social harmony existed between the races there than elsewhere in the South. "There was more prejudice against the slaveholder than against the Negro," he wrote, and "with so many sympathizers with the oppressed in the back country, the South had much difficulty in holding the mountaineer in line to force upon the whole nation their policies," namely, the continuation of slavery. John C. Campbell agreed, stating that "large sections of the Highland South were in sympathy with the North on the Negro question." Far more recently, Loyal Jones, an Appalachian scholar and native western North Carolinian, asserted that the "Appalachians have not been saddled with the same prejudices about black people that people of the deep South have."[10] Such statements seem to credit mountain residents with a sort of moral superiority, as if being somewhat removed from the harsher realities of the institution enabled them to view it more objectively and to see the slaves' plight more sympathetically.

Other scholars have drawn from the "rugged individualism" and fierce independence associated with early mountain settlers the corollary that their love of freedom led them to repudiate the concept of human property. Those "true democrats" of Appalachia, according to one account, "cherish liberty as a priceless heritage. They would never hold slaves and we may almost say they will never be enslaved." An even more general assessment proposed that bondage and high altitudes were incompatible: "Freedom has always loved the air of mountains. Slavery, like malaria, desolated the alluvials of the globe. The skypiercing peaks of the continents are bulwarks against oppression."[11]

In stark contrast stand those who have posited that the lack of black contact by many white mountaineers resulted in an even more intense hostility toward blacks than that felt by whites in areas with more substantial black populations. This view owes much of its popularity to the oft-quoted statement of W. J. Cash in *The Mind of the South:* "The mountaineer has acquired a hatred and contempt for the Negro even more virulent than that of the common white of the lowlands; a dislike so rabid that it was worth a black man's life to venture into many mountain sections."[12] Some of the more secluded pockets of settlement in the southern highlands did have and continue to have reputations for their vehement opposition to a local black presence. A resident explaining the absence of blacks, free or slave, in the Rock Creek section of North Carolina's Mitchell County stated that "colored people have a well-founded belief that if they venture up there they might not come back alive."[13]

These extreme points of view suggest, at the very least, that the degree of racism among antebellum mountain residents ran the full gamut of opinion. But it should be noted that most of the statements quoted above come from twentieth-century sources and are largely conjectural as to how pre–Civil War highlanders would view a race with whom they had little or no contact. Thus Olmsted's testimony is particularly significant, in that it addresses these issues so directly.

Most of the mountain residents with whom Olmsted discussed the topic of slavery seem to have had equal contempt for slaves, their masters, and the system itself. Compared to their hatred of slavery in the lowland South, they had relatively few objections to the institution in their own area. One Tennessee mountaineer summed up the viewpoint held to varying degrees by almost all of those Olmsted interviewed. The journalist reported, "He'd always wished there had n't been any niggers here but he would n't think there was any better way of getting along with them than that they had" (239). One of Olmsted's hosts near Burnsville, North Carolina, stated, "Slavery is a great cuss . . . the greatest there is in these United States." But his explanation mentioned only the fact that it allowed eastern planters to dominate state government at the expense of westerners (259). Others expressed very real regional prejudices against the lowland society dominated by a slaveholding elite. Olmsted must have reveled in the chance to quote one mountain resident, whose objections to the system's moral effects on slaveholders and nonslaveholders alike echoed Olmsted's own: "He was afraid that there was many a man who had gone to the bad world, who wouldn't have gone there if he had n't had any slaves. He had been down in the nigger counties a good deal, and he had seen how it worked on the white people. It made the rich people, who owned the niggers, passionate, and proud and ugly, and it made the poor people mean" (263).

But despite their objections to the system, almost none of the highlanders that Olmsted encountered advocated abolition. The only exception was, significantly, a resident of East Tennessee, virtually the only section of the South with an ardent and well-developed anti-slavery movement.[14] This "man of superior standing" was a merchant and farmer near Elizabethton, whose home Olmsted described as "the pleasantest house I have yet seen in the mountain[s]" (262). Such praise from Olmsted should make it obvious that this man owned no slaves. Never missing an opportunity to belabor a point, Olmsted later noted that the slaveholding neighbors of this nonslaveholder had "houses and establishments . . . much poorer than his" (272).

This East Tennessean was far more outspoken than other high-land nonslaveholders about his disdain for the system and the blacks it embraced. Slaves "were horrid things," he said, insisting that he "would not take one to keep if it should be given to him." He main-tained that it "would be a great deal better for the country . . . if there was not a slave in it," and advocated sending all blacks to Liberia. Olmsted noted that this "colonizationist" even owned a copy of *Uncle Tom's Cabin* and said that he "thought well of its depiction of slavery and its message" (263–64). In reply to Olmsted's question as to whether most mountain residents felt as he did, the Tennessean replied, "Well, there's some thinks one way and some another, but there's hardly anyone here that do n't think slavery's a curse to our country, or who would n't be glad to get rid of it" (264).

But Olmsted found no one else in the highlands with as firm a com-mitment to ending the system. He was quick to dismiss similar anti-slavery rhetoric from three young men "of the poorest class" that he overtook on the road a day later. "Let the reader not be deceived by these expressions," he warned. "It is not slavery they detest; it is simply negro competition, and the monopoly of the opportunities to make money by negro owners, which they feel but dimly comprehend" (265).

The relative absence of slaves in the region defused any concern over the threat of black labor as competition. But the fear of a free black populace was very apparent among southern highlanders and accounted for much of their commitment to slavery. One mountain woman, on learning that Olmsted was from New York and that blacks there were all free, said "with disgust and indignation on her face" that "I would n't want to live where niggers are free, they are bad enough when they are slaves. . . . If they was to think themselves equal to we, I do n't think white folks could abide it—they're such vile saucy things" (237).

But even more often it was their belief in the rights of property owners that led most mountaineers to stop their condemnation of the institution short of advocating its abolition. To be deprived of one's possessions, human or otherwise, was an injustice with which they could and did identify. As one highland slave owner reminded his nonslaveholding neighbors, "If they can take our niggers away from us they can take our cows or hosses, and everything else we've got!"[15] Whatever distaste they may have felt for slavery or slaveholders, this argument was one in which most highland yeomen readily acquiesced. Even the seemingly subversive sentiments of the Tennessee "colonizationist" stopped short of infringing upon slaveholders' rights. He admitted, though reluctantly, that he "supposed it would not be right to take them away from those who had acquired property in them, without any remuneration" (263). As with most other southerners, the peculiar institution remained considerably less offensive to highlanders than did outside interference with either property rights or any other aspect of their own or other southerners' way of life.[16]

The backgrounds of the small mountain farmers Olmsted encountered also contributed to their attitudes toward black bondage. Some observers concluded that the region's poorer residents bore a strong grudge against slavery because their inability to compete with it as free laborers had forced them from their seaboard or piedmont homes up into the highlands. There, the argument followed, they were insulated from the system but quickly found themselves shut off as well from the economic opportunities that the outside world offered, thus adding to their resentment. As an early twentieth-century missionary to the mountains concluded, "The aristocratic slaveholder from his river-bottom plantation looked with scorn on the slaveless dweller among the hills; while the highlander repaid his scorn with

high disdain and even hate."[17] Similarly, another advocate of this thesis explained that southern highlanders "were penned up in the mountains because slavery shut out white labor and left them no market for
their skill and strength. . . . It denied those that looked down from
their mountain crags upon the realm of King Cotton a chance to expand, circulate, and mingle with the progressive elements at work
elsewhere in the republic."[18]

Whatever element of truth there was to those assumptions, Olmsted's interviews provide very real evidence that such displacement,
whether actual or imagined, was a source of Appalachians' animosity
toward the lowland planter class. But as his narrative also makes quite
apparent, an intense racism was far more widespread and deeply rooted in the cultural baggage that mountain settlers brought from the
lowlands. That racism in turn carried with it a basic belief in the institution of slavery, regardless of their feelings toward its most prosperous beneficiaries, the slaveholding elite."[19]

In light of the very slim body of evidence of such views from the
nineteenth century, much less the antebellum period, the sheer volume
of material provided by Olmsted's narrative regarding racial attitudes
among mountaineers makes it significant. Equally admirable is the
sensitivity with which he conveyed the variety of sentiments toward
slaves, slavery, and slaveholders that he witnessed along that route. But
one must be wary of accepting the comments of those he interviewed
as a thorough or accurate representation of overall regional attitudes.
One of the major attractions of the mountains to Olmsted, as he neared
completion of his second southern tour, was the contrast that they offered to the rest of the South. Mountain residents were, in effect, a
unique control group by which he could test his theories regarding the
impact of slavery on southern society; they made up virtually the only
group of southerners whose lives were relatively untouched by the institution. Thus his depiction of highland society became far more selective than was his itinerary in the region.

Olmsted visited several of the highlands' more bustling commercial hubs and population centers, such as Chattanooga, Asheville,
and Abingdon. These areas supported far larger populations, white
and black, and maintained many more vital links with other parts of
the South through trade and tourist networks than did the more re-

mote and primitive areas he also visited. The three counties in which these towns were located were home to 5,683 slaves in 1850. Not only did that make up an average of 13 percent of those counties' total populations—almost twice the average proportion of slaves in the seven other mountain counties that Olmsted visited—but these 5,600 slaves also accounted for more than two-thirds of the total slave populace in the ten-county area that Olmsted covered.[20]

The conclusions that Olmsted reached based on his observations of those larger and more prosperous highland communities are among his most astute and potentially significant. He noted, for example, that mountain masters were "chiefly professional men, shop-keepers, and men in office, who are also land owners" (226). He also concluded that "the direct moral evils of slavery are less—even less proportionately to the number of slaves," that the habits of those slaves "more resemble those of ordinary free laborers," and that they "exercise more responsibility, and both in soul and intellect they are more elevated" (226–27). The implications of such statements on the issue of master-slave relations are, at the very least, intriguing; yet Olmsted never elaborated on these generalizations or substantiated them with specific examples. He included no interviews with the benevolent and affluent slaveholding businessmen to whom he referred, nor did he indulge in detailed descriptions of their situations as he did so extensively for those more deprived, and deeply entrenched mountain residents.[21]

It would be another generation or more before the stereotypical image of the southern mountaineer in all his ignorance, isolation, and crudity emerged, so Olmsted could hardly be accused of giving in to such preconceived notions. Yet by limiting the bulk of his treatment to those he met who did fit that image, he certainly had much to do with laying the groundwork from which those stereotypes grew.

He made much of the ignorance of his mountain hosts, for example, particularly their misconceptions regarding slavery and the sectional crisis in which it was already embroiled. He recorded a conversation with the Tennessee "squire" regarding Irish laborers in New York. His slaveholding host assumed that they were imported from Ireland and purchased just as black labor from Africa had been. He was amazed to learn not only that New York had no slaves, but also that blacks there were free (236–37).

Slaves could become victims of their owners' ignorance, as was the case of a white couple with whom Olmsted spent a night. They thought that Virginia was a cotton-growing state to their south and had sold their three slaves south, largely because of the slaves' desire to be reunited with their mother in Virginia (240). He cited other instances in which highlanders thought coffee was grown in New York (262), confused the locations and proximity of Charleston, Texas, and New York (249–50), wondered if the Mexican War was over yet (266), and speculated about the nature of the "new country [of] Nebrasky," which one old woman "reckoned must be a powerful fine country, they'd taken so much trouble to get possession of it" (235).

But in recording mountaineers' vague and often highly distorted ideas about geography and politics, neither Olmsted's purpose nor his tone was as derogatory or as demeaning as those of later chroniclers of mountain life. His purpose was to demonstrate that mountain residents' statements regarding slavery and slaveholders were rarely thought out and were usually based on little beyond their own limited experience with blacks. Likewise, his descriptions of their crude living conditions and bleak lifestyles served a specific function in regard to his more general theories about slavery's impact on southern society. But there was an inherent contradiction in Olmsted's use of the southern highlands in substantiating his arguments. Olmsted blamed the deprivations of mountain life on the presence of slavery elsewhere and portrayed the highlanders as tragic, and perhaps innocent, victims of the institution. Yet, at the same time, a basic theme remained: mountain residents, free from so many of the shackles imposed upon those southerners with investments in or mere proximity to the system, were happier and better people than those less fortunate lowlanders.

Yet despite discrepancies, inconsistencies, and major omissions in his description and interpretation of racial and sectional attitudes among southern highlanders, the seventy or so pages that Olmsted devoted to the region in his *Journey in the Back Country* remain invaluable as a record of the most extended and substantive foray into an area neglected not only by contemporary travelers but also by historians of slavery and the antebellum era ever since. Much of the strength of Olmsted's overall commentary on the South lay in his determination to understand it at the grassroots level. The mere fact that he gave voice to the southern highlanders, one of the most inscrutable and misrepresented groups of antebellum Americans, is a remarkable indication of the extent to which he succeeded.

Notes

1. The fullest treatments of Olmsted's careers are Laura Wood Roper, *FLO: A Biography of Frederick Law Olmsted* (Baltimore: Johns Hopkins University Press, 1973); John Emerson Todd, *Frederick Law Olmsted* (Boston: Twayne Publishers, 1982); and Broadus Mitchell, *Frederick Law Olmsted: A Critic of the Old South* (Baltimore: Johns Hopkins University Press, 1924). The Mitchell book provides the best account of Olmsted's antebellum southern travels and writings, along with Charles E. Beveridge, introduction to *The Papers of Frederick Law Olmsted*, vol. 2: *Slavery and the South, 1852–1857* (Baltimore: Johns Hopkins University Press, 1981), 1–39.

2. Frederick Law Olmsted, *A Journey in the Seaboard Slave States* (New York: Dix and Edwards, 1856); Olmsted, *A Journey through Texas: or, a Saddle Trip on the Southwestern Frontier* (New York: Dix and Edwards, 1857); and Olmsted, *A Journey in the Back Country in the Winter of 1853–54* (New York: Mason Brothers, 1860). A condensed version of these three books was published in two volumes as *The Cotton Kingdom* (New York: Mason Brothers, 1861). On the circumstances that led to Olmsted's southern assignment and the subsequent publication of his work, see Beveridge, introduction, *Papers of Olmsted*, 9–35; and Mitchell, *Olmsted*, 47–53.

3. Olmsted, *Seaboard Slave States*, 176; Olmsted, *Back Country*, 103–4. See also Mitchell, *Olmsted*, 88–89.

4. Olmsted, *Seaboard Slave States*, 146–48; Olmsted, "The South," nos. 7 and 47, *New York Daily Times*, 17 March 1853, and 26 January 1854, in Beveridge, *Papers of Olmsted*, 2:103–10, 247–54; see also introduction, 13–15.

5. Beveridge, *Papers of Olmsted*, 2:252.

6. Todd, *Frederick Law Olmsted*, 57–58; Mitchell, *Olmsted*, chap. 2.

7. For Olmsted's schedule and route, see Beveridge, *Papers of Olmsted*, 2:309 (map) and 481–82 (itinerary).

8. The ten counties that can be identified along Olmsted's highland route are Hamilton, Polk, and Johnson counties in Tennessee; Cherokee, Macon, Haywood, Buncombe, Yancey, and Watauga counties in North Carolina; and Washington County in Virginia. County population figures are derived from Bureau of the Census, *Seventh Census of the United States, 1850* (Washington, D.C.: Robert Armstrong, 1853), table 1 for Virginia, North Carolina, and Tennessee, 256–57, 307–8, 573–74. For a discussion of the demographics of slavery in North Carolina's mountain counties, see John C. Inscoe, *Mountain Masters: Slavery and the Sectional Crisis in Western North Carolina* (Knoxville: University of Tennessee Press, 1989), chap. 3.

9. Olmsted, *Back Country,* 227. Subsequent quotations of material from *Back Country* are designated by page numbers within the text. Note the contrast in Olmsted's tone and interest regarding the treatment of slaves just six months earlier in "The South," no. 47, 24 Jan. 1854, in Beveridge, *Papers of Olmsted,* 2:247–52.

10. Carter G. Woodson, "Freedom and Slavery in Appalachian America," *Journal of Negro History* 1 (April 1916): 140, 149; John C. Campbell, *The Southern Highlander and His Homeland* (1929; rept., Lexington: University Press of Kentucky, 1969), 95; and Loyal Jones, "Appalachian Values," in *Voices from the Hills: Selected Readings of Southern Appalachia,* ed. Robert J. Higgs (New York: Unger, 1975), 512.

11. Julian Ralph, "Our Appalachian Americans," *Harper's* (June 1903): 37; and James W. Taylor, *Alleghania: A Geographical and Statistical Memoir* (St. Paul, Minn.: James Davenport, 1862), 1.

12. W. J. Cash, *The Mind of the South* (New York: Alfred J. Knopf, 1941), 219.

13. Muriel E. Sheppard, *Cabins in the Laurel* (Chapel Hill: University of North Carolina Press, 1935), 60.

14. Among the best discussions of antislavery sentiment in East Tennessee and its political repercussions are Oliver P. Temple, *East Tennessee and the Civil War* (1899; rept., Freeport, N.Y.: Books for Library Press, 1971); Mary Emily Robertson Campbell, *The Attitude of Tennesseans toward the Union, 1847–1861* (New York: Vantage, 1961); Vernon M. Queener, "East Tennessee Sentiment and the Secession Movement, November 1860–June 1861," *East Tennessee Historical Society Proceedings* 20 (1948): 64; E. Merton Coulter, *William C. Brownlow: Fighting Parson of the Southern Appalachians* (Chapel Hill: University of North Carolina Press, 1937); and Durwood Dunn, *An Abolitionist in the Appalachian South: Ezekiel Birdseye on Slavery, Capitalism, and Separate Statehood in East Tennessee, 1841–1846* (Knoxville: University of Tennessee Press, 1997).

15. Harry M. Caudill, *Night Comes to the Cumberlands: A Biography of a Depressed Region* (Boston: Little, Brown, 1962), 38.

16. For other evidence from Olmsted on the priority of property rights among mountaineers, see *Back Country,* 240.

17. Samuel T. Wilson, *The Southern Mountaineers* (New York: Little and Ives, 1914), 57. See also Campbell, *Southern Highlanders,* 94; and Edward J. Phifer, "Saga of a Burke County Family," *North Carolina Historical Review* 39 (Spring 1962): 145.

18. Ralph, "Our Appalachian Americans," 36.

19. Cratis D. Williams, "The Southern Mountaineer in Fact and Fiction" (Ph.D. diss., New York University, 1961), 379.

20. See note 8.

21. Olmsted did not have the letters of introduction during his backcountry trip that he had for much of the plantation South, where he utilized his own and his brother's various Yale acquaintances. For a fuller treatment of large slaveholders in the highlands and their relations with their slaves, see Inscoe, *Mountain Masters*, chaps. 3 and 4.

4

Mountain Masters as Confederate Opportunists

The Slave Trade in Western North Carolina, 1861–1865

On October 7, 1861, Colonel George Bower, the largest slaveholder in Ashe County, North Carolina, drowned. He was swept downstream when his two-horse carriage overturned as he attempted to ford the swollen Yadkin River at the start of a trip to Raleigh from his mountain home in the state's northwesternmost county. Two days later, Calvin Cowles, his friend and fellow slaveholder from nearby Wilkesboro, reported the tragedy in a letter to W. W. Holden in Raleigh. Cowles stated that Bower had been accompanied by a slave, who had urged him not to attempt the crossing given the force of the current. "The Carriage capsized and all went downstream," Cowles wrote, "except the Negro who fortunately escaped to tell the story. The alarm being given, 20 or 30 people went immediately through a drenching rain," where they searched in vain for the elderly colonel's body. In his account of the incident in the *North Carolina Standard* a week later, editor Holden shifted words just enough to imply a somewhat different scenario: that the "negro boy who was driving him made his escape."[1] While Holden may well have meant simply that he escaped his master's watery death, soon thereafter and ever since, the standard version of the incident has been that, as Ashe County's one history states, Bower drowned "while pursuing a runaway slave."[2]

It is tempting to speculate on whether or not Holden intentionally altered Cowles's version of the tragedy and on just how and why the slave became the cause of Bower's death rather than his attempted savior in the community's collective memory of the incident. Perhaps

80

in hindsight the ominous implications of that latter version proved too fitting to resist: that less than six months into the war, a powerful slaveholder had already fallen victim to his human property, with Bower's death an extreme portent perhaps of the fate of his counterparts throughout the South. Its implications are significant in the Carolina mountains alone, where the Bower drowning was part of a rather striking statistic: he was the first of four of the region's forty largest slaveholders who died violent deaths at or near their homes over the course of the war. Those losses were compounded by such numerous battlefield casualties among the sons of that elite that Zebulon Vance commented just after the war that in western North Carolina, "many old families are almost extinct in the male line."[3]

Yet if the war took an unusually heavy toll on the mountains' slaveholders, the institution itself suffered remarkably little in that particular region. Because of its insulation from any major military incursion until the war's waning months, the home-front experience in the Carolina highlands differed markedly from that elsewhere in the South, and even from that in other areas of Appalachia. Among the more striking and unexplored aspects of that experience is the continued stability and profitability of slavery for most of the war's duration. Despite a vast literature documenting the wide range of emancipation experiences among bondsmen and women throughout the Confederacy and border state South, little attention has been given to the impact of the war on the economics of slavery in those areas not in the path of liberating armies. Nor has the war's effect on the value of slave property or the dynamics of a slave trade been examined except as black labor was engaged directly in the Confederate war effort.[4]

The institution of slavery in the southern highlands exhibited a number of traits that distinguished it from plantation slavery elsewhere in the American South. Slaveholders made up only 10 percent of North Carolina's mountain population in 1860, and only 10 percent of the total were slaves. The limitations imposed on the region's agriculture by climate and terrain would have neither justified nor supported even this small labor force. Consequently, perhaps the most distinctive variation in the institution's highland manifestation was that its slaveholders were, as Frederick Law Olmsted accurately observed in 1854, "chiefly professional men, shop-keepers, and men in office who are also land owners, and give only divided attention to farming." As such, they utilized their slaves in various nonagricultural pursuits, from employment in their mercantile and hostelry operations to hiring them out for mining or construction projects. The flexibility inherent in slavery's adaptation to a highland economy kept it both viable and profitable for its beneficiaries, so much so that the number of mountain residents investing in slaves increased steadily over the course of the 1840s and 1850s.[5]

Given the growing value of their investments, it seems curious that mountain masters exhibited so little concern for the security of their black property holdings until late in the Confederacy's waning existence. The immediate prewar years had witnessed new fears across North Carolina of insurrectionary or subversive activity among its slave population, and a major thrust of the rhetoric during the secession crisis had been warnings of the effect of war on slavery's stability and indeed survival. A Raleigh newspaper editor expressed the concerns of many mountain residents as well when he noted in February 1861 that if armed conflict was to come, "the negroes will know, too, that the war is waged on their account," and they will "become restless and difficult to manage."[6]

Western Carolinians on both sides of the secession debate relied on racial fear tactics to make their case, outlining scenarios of upheaval aimed at slaveholding and nonslaveholding highlanders as well. Disunionist spokesmen W. W. Avery and Marcus Erwin printed a circular warning of the "terrible calamity of having three hundred thousand idle, vagabond free negroes turned loose on you with all the privileges of white men" if Republican coercion went unchallenged. Along the same lines but arguing in support of the Union, Asheville resident William Vance Brown pointed out that in case of war, slaves would suddenly become detrimental to southerners in that the North "can do awful damage & destruction by & through our slaves. Once arouse them to insurrection & they will carry murder, Rape & arson into the midst of our firesides."[7]

Yet despite such alarmism, there were few signs that mountain whites took seriously or even remembered such predictions once the war was under way. A significant factor in their lack of worry was the degree to which the institution's profitability continued to soar—or was perceived to soar—for most of the war's duration. While slavery had never been as demographically significant or economically central to southern highland society as it was elsewhere in the South, the latter antebellum years had proved very healthy ones for the slave trade in western North Carolina. Despite their relatively small numbers in the mountain counties, slave purchases during the 1850s resulted in a growth rate of the slave populace far exceeding that of the state as a whole.[8]

There is no indication that the vitality of this intraregional slave trade diminished as a result of secession and the war. Highland slaveholders were quick to finesse the new labor shortages the war imposed locally by hiring out their own slaves and serving as agents in renting or selling the slaves of others. The widespread practice of long- and short-term hirings of slaves had long been integral to the institution's viability in the southern highlands, and that flexibility allowed the region to adapt more effectively to wartime labor shortages than was true in other parts of the Confederacy.[9]

The Carolina highlands were on the receiving end of the considerable population mobility within the war-torn Confederacy, particularly the massive movements toward the interior by slaveholders and their slaves from vulnerable coastal regions stretching from tidewater Virginia through low country Georgia. Refugees, both black and white, poured into various North Carolina communities to avoid the disruptions and threats posed by the movement of armies elsewhere. Governor Zebulon Vance, himself a mountain native, viewed this shift with some alarm, complaining to Jefferson Davis in October 1862 that "thousands are flying from our Eastern Counties with their slaves to the centre & West to devour the very short crops and increase the prospect of starvation."[10]

Whereas many of those in flight found the western part of the state the most desirable area of retreat due to its relative stability and its distance from any major theater of war, highlanders themselves seemed to view the influx in a more positive light than did Vance, perhaps because of the caliber of those seeking refuge in their midst. Charlestonians and other South Carolina planters with summer homes in Flat Rock and Hendersonville often retreated there with much of their slave force—among them Confederate treasury secretary Christopher Memminger, Senator Thomas J. Semmes of New Orleans, Mary Chesnut, and assorted Middletons, Rhetts, and Lowndeses.[11] Late in 1863, the Confederacy's "fighting bishop," General Leonidas Polk, moved his family to Asheville for the duration of the war, after the fall of Nashville and then New Orleans, both of which his wife had called home, and the destruction of his daughter's Mississippi plantation. "Always thoughtful and provident," according to his daughter, Polk arranged for "some twenty excellent negro men & their families" to be brought up to join the family, while Mrs. Polk had other slaves of her own brought to Asheville from New Orleans.[12]

Even more common were efforts by lowland slaveholders to send their human property out of the reach of Union liberators or Confederate impressment officials. On the one hand, the demands for slave labor in constructing coastal fortifications made them ready targets of the latter. On the other, state officials were convinced that occupying Federal forces in the eastern part of the state were actively encouraging slaves to escape, prompting Governor Vance to issue a policy statement informing easterners that "it is the duty of all slaveowners immediately to remove their slaves able to bear arms." Vance's order was in response to more general instructions issued from the Confederate administration in Richmond in March 1863 that planters in coastal South Carolina, Georgia, and Florida were to withdraw their slaves into the interior "since they were liable to be lost at any moment." For South Carolinians in particular, western North Carolina was a viable site for such interior transfers.[13]

Even before such moves became official policy, mountain opportunists had reached out to eastern Carolina owners with tempting leasing or purchase offers. Nicholas W. Woodfin was the most aggressive in making this pitch. Along with other Asheville businessmen, he had actively sought hired slave labor in constructing the eagerly awaited Western North Carolina Railroad well before war seemed a possibility. With no intention of letting its progress lag once the conflict was under way, Woodfin continued to run advertisements for slave labor in newspapers across the state well into 1862. In December 1861, one such notice called for "100 able-bodied negroes," while another in March 1862 sought 50 more. He also used a more personal approach in offering his services as broker to slaveholding friends who sought safer havens for their slave property during the war. In May 1862, he wrote to former governor and Asheville native David L. Swain, then president of the University of North Carolina, with the following proposition: "Now upon the subject of your negroes. If you will send them up to this country I can yet hire them to advantage for the rest of the year. The men especially will command high prices, particularly before harvest commences. There is great demand for labor indeed. . . . It won't be as easy to place women & children, but it can be done."[14]

When, in early 1863, a Confederate rifle factory in Asheville faced labor shortages as military demands drained much of its original white male workforce, slaves became the logical and most accessible replacements. An advertisement for "ten negro men" in March was the first in a continuing effort by the armory's commander, Captain Benjamin Stone, to employ a biracial workforce in rifle production. His recruitment campaign for hired black labor also contributed to the influx of lowland slaves into the Asheville area.[15]

Calvin Cowles, the most energetic of Wilkes County's entrepreneurs, was fully aware of the financial opportunities made available by the new demand and was equally aggressive in seeking to bring new slave labor into the area, particularly through hiring contracts that allowed him to sublet those he had hired to his neighbors and relatives. His correspondence during the war's first two years is full of pleas to slaveholders in which he confirmed the rich opportunities such portable property offered in his own area. He informed a Mississippi business contact of the high demand particularly for adult males, then commanding annual rental rates of $125 or $150.[16]

By June 1862 Cowles complained that "hirelings cannot be had for money nor love," and asked his brother, then in eastern North Carolina, "Can't you catch me a Negro or two and send them up?" He intensified his search, asking particularly for blacksmiths or carpenters, but willing to consider any women and children that might be for hire. In 1863 he offered to rent at least one of the several farms among his vast landholdings to any refugees seeking to move from war-torn areas who could bring slaves with them. During one of his regular mercantile purchasing trips to Charleston and Savannah in April 1863, he sought to buy slaves as well. He reported to his wife that he had bought "Nancy," a forty-year-old "cook, washer, and house servant," for $805 at the slave mart in Charleston, but that he had had no luck in finding a "boy" of comparable worth.[17]

If outright purchases proved hard to come by, Cowles's efforts in the long-distance hiring of slaves seem to have paid off. Throughout the latter half of the war he corresponded with a variety of eastern North Carolina owners over the maintenance and welfare of their slaves then under his own care or of those whose labor he had in turn rented out. When his sister in Lenoir expressed concern over her financial situation in November 1862, Cowles urged her to hire out her slave Wash, noting that "prices rule high here, . . . [and] he ought to fetch you some money as his work is in demand."[18]

Woodfin and Cowles were by no means alone in these pursuits. Some highland residents saw the care and supervision of others' slaves as a service as well as a financial opportunity. Allen Davidson of Cherokee County, for example, wrote in February 1863 that he and other family members were willing to oblige relatives in middle Tennessee who wanted to send their slaves "up here this summer." "I would be glad if they'd do so," he wrote. "Uncle Harvy's folks would take some and us two or three [and] for a fair price board and clothe them."[19] But for most it was strictly business and it was through earlier business connections that such arrangements were made. Western Carolina merchants found their many antebellum contacts with South Carolina and Georgia markets to be effective conduits for moving slaves into the Carolina highlands for both short- and long-term usage, thus creating a vigorous regional market in which residents bought, sold, and traded slaves until the final three or four months of the war.

The effect of such activity was a considerable expansion of the mountain slave population. A Haywood County resident noted in May 1863 that the number of slaves in that county "has increased very rapidly since the war commenced." At least one Asheville resident was alarmed enough about the number of slaves being brought into Buncombe County from the coast that he informed Governor Vance, a fellow Buncombe native, in March 1863 that citizens there wanted more protection "from Negro Ravages." Two months earlier, a South Carolina–owned slave employed at the Asheville armory fell victim to local resentment at the increasing black presence in that community. A group of ruffians accosted the slave and, upon finding that he was wandering the streets without the proper "pass" from the armory, gave him a severe whipping.[20]

Yet despite the influx of new blacks into the region, the demand for their utilization and therefore the hiring rates they commanded also rose dramatically. In 1863 a Rutherford County owner hired six slaves for an annual fee of $618, almost twice as much as he had asked for their services two years earlier. Joseph Corpening, in Caldwell County, hired out four of his slaves, two men and two women, on annual contracts, and his accounts of such transactions show that they remained steady throughout the war years, despite dramatic increases in the rates charged. William, an adult male, earned Corpening a $28 annual fee in 1861. That rate doubled over each of the next two years to $47 in 1862 and $104 in 1863. By 1864, Corpening charged $510 for William's services and in January 1865, $525. Corpening's fees for the other male and one of the two women were fully comparable to those charged for William, so that a total of $113 collected in January 1861 for the four had grown by January 1864 to $1,165.[21] Such figures say as much or more about the dramatic depreciation of Confederate currency as they do about the increased value of slaves. But the perception was as important as the reality, and mountain residents interpreted these figures to mean slaves were an increasingly profitable investment, which in itself had much to do with the vitality of the slave market in the region.

Such activity was constant and involved sales as well as hirings, as numerous mountain masters took full advantage of new opportunities to both buy and sell black property. More often than not, such transactions were negotiated locally, but they were never confined to their own region. Just as Woodfin sought slaves for purchase in Charleston and Savannah, so he and others were very much aware of current prices in such major markets and the options for sale or purchase they continued to offer. In May 1863, Calvin Cowles advised his sister in the aftermath of the capture of her two unruly runaways: "Robert could have been sold in Charleston for $2500, but I presume

you allowed your philanthropy to influence you in marketing him—
he is with old friends. In Wash's case, I advise you that you put him
on the block in Richmond. . . . He has forfeited all claims on your
sympathy—get the most you can for him."[22]

The contrasting experiences of two highland families in the wartime slave trade illustrate the variety of scenarios in which these trends
could play themselves out. The extensive correspondence of the Lenoirs,
among the most established families and largest slaveholders in western
North Carolina, represents on the surface a very different approach to
their black property from that reflected in the letters of Alfred and
Mary Bell, a couple who used the opportunities the war provided to
break into the ranks of slaveholders for the first time. Yet behind the
actions of both Bells and Lenoirs lay some shared assumptions about
the future security and profitability of slavery in their region.

Colonel Thomas Lenoir, the eighty-year-old patriarch of Fort Defiance plantation in Caldwell County, died in March 1861 and left his
three sons and several sons-in-law to face the early months of the war
with the additional burden of settling his substantial estate, including
the distribution of his sixty-one slaves. Thomas, the colonel's eldest
son and namesake, was forty years old, and was persuaded by family
members not to submit to military service. He moved from Fort Defiance, however, and spent the war years at "the Den," a crude but vast
farm that was part of the family's extensive but remote highland holdings in Haywood County. Rufus, the youngest son, stayed at home to
manage the vast Caldwell County plantation, while Walter, two years
older than Rufus, was the only Lenoir to offer himself for Confederate military service.

The burdens of the war, compounded with that of their father's
estate, particularly his slave property, weighed heavily on the Lenoir
brothers. The lion's share of that burden fell upon Rufus, the sole
adult male remaining at Fort Defiance, but he never lacked long-
distance advice from Walter, wherever he was. While stationed at
Kinston, North Carolina, in April 1862, Walter lectured his younger
brother on investment opportunities for the more liquid part of his
inheritance. Pointing out that he was already a large landowner, further acquisition of real estate was not a very attractive option, and
Walter argued that most forms of personal property were also unrea-

sonably high priced at the time, though he knew they "must fall when public affairs again become settled by peace; and unless with a view to an early profit, [I] would not deem it prudent to invest largely in such property." But, Walter continued, "there are two kinds of personal property which form exceptions in this respect, negroes and cotton, both of which are depreciated in value, the first from political considerations & the peculiar character of the war waged by our powerful and unprincipled foe, & the other on account of the blockade." While there were risks in buying either, Walter reasoned from his eastern North Carolina vantage point that "for long investment and in a mere pecuniary point of view, I would prefer buying negroes or cotton near the point where they are in the greatest present danger & removing them to the mountains to any other investment in personal property."[23]

None of the three brothers embraced their new, vastly expanded slaveholdings with enthusiasm. But with the war under way, and their support of the Confederate cause nominal at least, they no longer invoked any ideological underpinnings to their distaste for their black property. They insisted instead—mainly to each other and to other family members—that it was the burdensome and often frustrating responsibilities to which they objected. While the colonel had instilled in his sons a paternalistic respect for slave family links, they were far quicker than he had been to sell much of their excess personnel. The pressure to do so was constant, a reflection of the wartime surge in market activity in the area. James Gwyn, an heir by virtue of his marriage to the colonel's daughter, recognized the potential and pressed his in-laws to make slaves as large a share of his portion of the estate as possible. He specifically asked for young slaves, an indication not only of his faith in the institution's future, but also of his awareness of the prices they commanded in an optimistic local market.[24]

When, in early 1863, the estate was settled and the division of slaves enacted, the Lenoir brothers moved quickly to convert sizable portions of that property into cash. Rather than carrying through with a public auction as they had advertised, they opted for private sales, and they seemed quite pleased with the prices their slaves brought. But Gwyn by then was a little more cautious than he had been a year and half earlier, due more to doubts about fluctuations in

Confederate currency than about the demand for slaves. "I have had several persons to see me to buy George and his family," he wrote in January, "but I have not sold them yet and I hardly think I will for a while at least, altho' I do not think I will keep them, but maybe they are as safe as the money I would get from them." Yet Gwyn was also adding to his holdings. He purchased several slaves from the estate of an elderly widow with no heirs, and he seemed to take great satisfaction in the fact that he acquired them "at two-thirds of traders prices as the will directed."[25]

In May 1863, Walter (who had returned home as an amputee several months earlier and had moved to Thomas's Haywood County farm) noted that the value of his slaves had doubled since their assessment at the time of his father's death. Gwyn had written to his brother-in-law Rufus from Wilkes County two months earlier that "there are many negro buyers in this part of the country. I dare say it is the same way with you & that you obtained large prices." Gwyn went on to complain about his failure to anticipate how rapidly prices were climbing and that he had succumbed too soon to market demands. He elaborated: "I had to sell one of Byram's and Betsey's children (Polly) which I disliked very much but she got too far along in the sleight of hand to keep; I only got $1250 for her—could now get $1800. I also sold Lark a few weeks ago, for $2000 which I then thought an exhorbitant price but it seems there is no telling what property will go for."[26]

Both the Lenoirs and Gwyn continued to make periodic sales— usually but not always in family groupings—throughout 1863 and into 1864. They never seem to have had trouble making such sales locally, to residents of Caldwell or neighboring counties. While they became more and more hesitant to accept Confederate currency as payment, they continued to express satisfaction with the profits accrued from such transactions.[27]

A very different story, but one equally indicative of the dynamic wartime slave trade in the Carolina mountains, is that of Alfred and Mary Bell in Macon County. Macon was far removed and in many respects very different from Caldwell and Wilkes counties—more deeply entrenched in the mountains and thus more remote, more sparsely settled, and newer than the plantation-scale farms held by several generations of the same family that characterized the fertile river valleys of the Blue Ridge's eastern foothills. Macon had only half as many slaves and a third as many slaveholders as Caldwell in 1860, yet the system there showed fully as much vigor and vitality as it did in the more affluent community of which the Lenoirs were a part.[28]

The Bells moved from north Georgia to Franklin, North Carolina, in 1860. Alfred, a dentist, had grown up in Macon County and returned to be near his father and other family members. He opened a dental practice and bought a small farm just outside of town. The young couple was not among the eleven slaveholders in the village, but like many of their nonslaveholding neighbors, they took advantage of both the white and black manpower sources available in the community. From their arrival until at least the end of 1862, they entrusted their farm to a white tenant and employed two slaves, Tom and Liza, both hired on an annual basis from the county's largest supplier, Dillard Love, whose ninety-five slaves made him western North Carolina's fifth largest slaveholder in 1860.[29]

After Alfred Bell's enlistment and departure from home at the head of his own Confederate company in November 1861, Mary continued to rely on the labor of their tenant and hired slaves. Yet they were more determined than ever to purchase slaves of their own. As a result of certain profitable investments, Mary's collection of back payments for her husband's dental services, and their share in Alf's family's jewelry business, the Bells were in the unusual position of having accumulated considerable capital early in the war, and like many young southern couples in earlier years, they saw slaves as a natural, indeed sound, investment. By December 1862, Alf was particularly eager to take such a step because he was nervous about the stability of the Confederate currency they were accumulating. "I don't think it good policy to keep money on hand," he wrote to Mary. "I want you to invest what you have in something, either for a negro or land." He trusted her judgment in choosing which, and thanked God he had a wife "who is not extravagant and is always trying to lay something up for the future."[30]

Slave trading was brisk in Macon County during the war's second year, and the Bells were very much interested in purchasing Martha, a cook, and her child from Dillard Love; other local residents also had considerable interest in the pair. Despite their interest and that of Martha herself in belonging to the Bells (she told Mary that she would "beg Mr. Love to sell her" to them), John Ingram, who had himself recently achieved slaveholding status with the purchase of four other bondsmen, beat the Bells in acquiring these two additional hands. Nor did they act on any of the other options they considered that fall. At some point in 1863, as payment for accumulated debts owed Alf, they came into possession of a female slave named Eve.

Their new bondswoman soon proved to be a nuisance to Mary Bell, and Alf assured her that there was no shortage of buyers in Franklin. With landholding becoming more of a priority for him, he suggested she trade Eve for one of several tracts of land he would like to have owned. In March 1864 he instructed her to try a neighbor's plot first, and "give any price for it that you think we can pay and live afterward." His final word on the subject: "I want the land bad." Then stationed in Alabama, his greatest distance yet from home, Alfred Bell's advice arrived too late; it crossed in the mail a letter from Mary Bell in which she announced: "Well, I believe I told you that you need not be surprised if [I] made a nigger trade. Well I have done it." What she had done, in fact, was to negotiate, with the help of Alf's brothers, the purchase of a slave family from Charleston. "I have swaped Eve for a man, woman, and child . . . and gave $1800 to boot," she explained.[31]

A Mr. Kilpatrick had purchased Trim, Aunt Patsy, and their daughter through a Charleston agent. Worried about his own mounting debts and recognizing that he had overextended himself with his new slave property, he agreed to let Mary Bell purchase them. In his own explanation of the transaction, Alf's brother assured him that his wife had pulled off a real bargain, and had gotten these slaves at far less than their current value in the mountain market. Mary provided rich detail in her descriptions of Trim, a thirty-five-year-old cooper who had made paint buckets in Charleston; his wife Patsy, forty years old and pregnant; and Rosa, their three-year-old daughter. Mary suggested that these were not the first low-country slaves who had been moved into her area when she wrote of Patsy: "She is like all the other south niggers—don't know much about the work as we do . . . but she is willing to try to learn to do anything." But she insisted: "I have told both [Trim and Patsy], that if they do not make my crib full of corn that I will sell them both in the fall for enough to fill it."[32]

Alf was obviously taken aback by the news of Mary's purchase. But comforted by his brother's insistence that the deal had indeed been a bargain, he stifled criticism of his wife, limiting his initial comments to: "I supose you will have negroes enough to make corn and rye this year. . . . Well, if they will suit you I am glad for the trade. I will try and pay the money." A week later he seemed even more resigned to his new status. "I hope we now can get along without having any thing to do with Love's negroes," he wrote. "I do crave to be independent and unbeholding to any body."[33]

While she took great satisfaction with her new status as slave owner, Mary Bell was not always content with the three individuals whose ownership endowed her with that position, particularly as Patsy's health kept her from being an effective worker. From the fall of 1864 on, Mary proposed to her husband further slave purchases either to supplement or to replace the family she owned. In particular, she had her eye on a slave couple, Betts and Alfred, whom she felt "would suit us as well as any we could get." She also learned that Mr. Kilpatrick, from whom she had purchased Trim, Patsy, and Rosa, was willing to buy back at least the father and daughter, though grudgingly admitting he would probably have to accept the sickly Patsy as well.[34]

Despite her urgency to take advantage of these opportunities, there is no indication that any such trade or purchase ever took place, since Alf's return home in February 1865 ended Mary's vivid record of their slaveholding experience. But the mere fact that within three months of the war's end such transactions were still taking place in the Franklin area suggests that slavery's death in the Carolina highlands came both suddenly and unexpectedly. It is tempting to pass judgment on Mary Bell's shortsightedness in making such risky investments in 1864, or to suggest that Alfred's preference for land over slaves suggests more foresight as to the latter's precarious future. Yet there is no evidence that he had any doubts as to either the Confederacy's ultimate victory or slavery's continued, and even safer, existence under that new regime. Had he had any qualms about the risks involved, he certainly would not have been so quick to encourage Mary in her pursuit of more slaves.

Nor were the Bells alone in such assumptions. That the vitality of the highland slave trade hinged on the ever-growing threats to black property elsewhere in the Confederacy never seems to have worried those in positions to take advantage of the bargain rates such situations generated. Even those selling slaves, like Kilpatrick, cannot be credited with any more prescience than those they sold to. It was, after all, at the end of 1864, with Lee's surrender less than four months away, that he indicated his willingness to buy back all three of the slaves he had earlier sold to the Bells.

Thus the Bells, more so than the Lenoirs but probably not unlike the majority of mountain slaveholders, were caught very much by surprise when all of their plans, maneuvers, and even skill in playing the slave market came to naught. That Mary Bell moved as readily and as enthusiastically into the ranks of slaveholders at the very point at which the institution was crumbling elsewhere suggests not only how healthy the market continued to be in the mountains during the war's final year, but also how few doubts either she or her community seemed to harbor about its continued viability and profitability.

In December 1864, Rufus Lenoir wrote Walter about the problems of troublesome slaves and noted that "unless I could feel more interest in the institution as a permanent one, I do not care to be troubled with dishonest ones." Yet in the same letter he acknowledged the high prices slaves still commanded as he contemplated the sale of his "young Venus." Only in February 1865 did the Lenoirs acknowledge the possibility that slavery's demise may have been eminent. In a family estate settlement involving the dispersal of slave property, a new conditional phrase accompanied the list of those slaves bequeathed to Walter: "provided that the events of the war do not result in the abolition of slavery or their removal from his control as owner."[35]

With the flurry of sales activity in early 1865, one might conclude that others sensed the system's doom as well, as they, like the Lenoirs and the Bells, continued to dispose of troublesome property. Only a week after the Lenoir document was drawn up, Mary Cowles in Caldwell County reported that her uncle had sold her slave Mike, "a scamp" and "a miserable drunkard" whom she was glad to be rid of at any price. Mike's reputation was too well known for him to command the asking price of $850 in Confederate currency at an auction, though a private sale was negotiated soon afterward. That same month Cowles's mother too was forced to sell a "mean negro" of her own, and while she too could not do so locally because of his reputation for thievery, she was able to sell him to a man near Charlotte.[36] Two months earlier in the same county, Rufus Patterson had recommended that his parents exercise the same option for two particularly troublesome slaves: sell them both. They were such troublemakers, Rufus wrote, that he felt sure his mother "would be decidedly happier if George & Rob are away."[37]

There is no indication that most such sales reflected owners' attempts to bail out of a doomed or even declining investment option; rather it was increasing discipline problems that seem to have instigated these sales, a trend that suggests a pervasive restlessness and even defiance among mountain slaves. Some owners sensed this shift in mood. "A general spirit of devilment is thro' the country," Rufus Patterson observed in December 1864. "I deem it best to be constantly on the lookout. Our negros need watching."[38] In hindsight, it seems odd that their masters and mistresses were not more sensitive in recognizing the increasing lack of complacency on the part of their slaves as symptomatic of the institution's imminent collapse. And yet there is little evidence that most drew any linkage between their personal problems with individual slaves and broader patterns of unrest or acknowledged the all too ominous reasons for this shift in behavior.

Alexander H. Jones of Hendersonville, one of the mountain region's most outspoken and influential Unionists, had expressed great impatience at secessionists' efforts to make slavery central to their arguments for leaving the Union. News of Lincoln's election, he wrote, were met with the howl of "nigger, nigger, nigger, as though the salvation of the whole world depended upon the negro and slavery."[39] Highlanders, like southerners elsewhere, did indeed make slavery's security a basic part of their rhetoric for or against secession, and with the war's end, the system's abolishment would prove its most revolutionary and long-lasting effect in that region as in most others. Yet ironically, once the war was under way and for much of its duration, slavery was among the aspects of the mountain economy and social structure that suffered least.

The disruptions and discipline problems slave owners faced remained, from their own perspectives, mere inconveniences; few interpreted such developments as ominous signs of the institution's collapse. The relative stability of the system, the increased demand for and market value of slave property, and its ever more crucial role in meeting the region's labor demands and agricultural productivity—all combined to create a false sense of optimism and complacency on the part of mountain masters. Such vitality was especially conspicuous in the midst of a region that, in many other ways, felt the full brunt of the conflict's destructive and disruptive forces. Such contradictions in the Confederacy's highland home fronts testify to the remarkable variation that characterized the peculiar institution throughout its hold on the American South. Even in its death throes, both the means and the rate at which slavery finally dissolved were subject to the particularities of local circumstances and the exigencies of war. For the mountains of North Carolina at least, that meant a final burst of profiteering and profits among slave owners oblivious to how sudden and complete their losses would be in the spring of 1865.

Notes

1. Calvin J. Cowles to W. W. Holden, October 9, 1861 (Calvin J. Cowles Papers, North Carolina Department of Archives and History, Raleigh [hereafter NCDAH]); *North Carolina Standard*, October 16, 1861.

2. Arthur L. Fletcher, *Ashe County: A History* (Jefferson, N.C.: Ashe County Research Association, 1963), 88; Ruth W. Shepherd, ed., *The Heritage of Ashe County, North Carolina* (Winston-Salem, N.C.: Hunter Printing, 1984), 96; John P. Arthur, *Western North Carolina: A History from 1730 to 1913* (Raleigh, N.C.: Edwards & Broughton, 1914), 165; and Martin Crawford, "Political Society in a Southern Mountain Community: Ashe County, North Carolina, 1850–1861," *Journal of Southern History* 55 (August 1989): 383. Crawford has noted elsewhere that some local accounts claim that both Bower and his black driver were in pursuit of yet another slave who had escaped when the accident occurred. The author thanks Crawford for clarifying aspects of this incident.

3. John W. Woodfin, one of Buncombe County's most prominent owners, was killed in a skirmish at Hot Springs, about thirty miles from his Asheville home, in October 1863. *Partisan Campaigns of Col. Lawrence M. Allen* (Raleigh: Edwards and Broughton, 1894), 14–15. W. W. Avery, the most politically prominent of Burke County's largest planter family, was wounded during a skirmish between the county militia and Kirk's raiders

and died at home soon afterward. Edward W. Phifer, "Saga of Burke County Family, Part III," *North Carolina Historical Review* 39 (Summer 1962): 314–15. Andrew Johnstone, one of the many Charleston elite who had moved with their slave forces into Henderson County, was murdered by bushwhackers who invaded his Flat Rock estate and shot him as he and his family sat at their dinner table. Eleanor Johnstone Coffin's account is in "The Murder of Andrew Johnstone, Esq.," July 13, 1864 typescript, Special Collections, University of Tennessee Library, Knoxville; see also Frank L. Fitzsimmons, *From the Banks of the Oklawaha* (Hendersonville, N.C.: Golden Glow, 1976), 121–25. Vance quoted from his letter to John Evans Brown in "Conditions Just After the War" [n.d.], excerpts published in *Confederate Veteran* 39 (June 1931): 215–17; he went on to detail the losses suffered by the Avery and Patton families.

4. On the increasing unprofitability of slavery during the war years, see James L. Roark, *Masters Without Slaves: Southern Planters in the Civil War and Reconstruction* (New York: W. W. Norton, 1977), 88–94. Among the best accounts of the new economic demands and opportunities for slave labor during the Civil War are Clarence L. Mohr, *On the Threshold of Freedom: Masters and Slaves in Civil War Georgia* (Athens: University of Georgia Press, 1986); Lynda J. Morgan, *Emancipation in Virginia's Tobacco Belt, 1850–1870* (Athens: University of Georgia Press, 1992), chap. 5; and Ira Berlin, Barbara J. Fields, Thavolia Glymph, and Joseph P. Reidy, eds., *Freedom: A Documentary History of Emancipation, 1861–1867*, Series I, Vol. I: *The Destruction of Slavery* (Cambridge, England: Cambridge University Press. 1985), chap. 9. None of the above refers to an active slave trade unrelated to Confederate military or industrial demands. The only references found to a more conventional trade in slaves during the war years are to areas outside the Confederacy, in Kentucky and Missouri. See Berlin et al., *Freedom*, 453, 494–95.

5. Various treatments of slavery in Appalachia include essays by Richard B. Drake, Charles B. Dew, Kenneth Noe, Wilma A. Dunaway, David Williams, and John E. Stealey III in *Appalachians and Race: The Mountain South from Slavery to Segregation*, ed. John C. Inscoe (Lexington: University Press of Kentucky, 2001); John C. Inscoe, *Mountain Masters: Slavery and the Sectional Crisis in Western North Carolina* (Knoxville: University of Tennessee Press, 1989); and two books by Wilma A. Dunaway, *Slavery in the American Mountain South* and *The African-American Family in Slavery and Emancipation* (Cambridge, England: Cambridge University Press, 2003). On Olmsted's commentary, see chap. 3 in this volume.

6. B. H. Nelson, "Some Aspects of Negro Life in North Carolina during the Civil War," *North Carolina Historical Review* 25 (April 1948): 145–47; quote from *North Carolina Standard*, February 5, 1861.

7. Avery and Erwin circular quoted in J. Carlyle Sitterson, *The Secession*

Movement in North Carolina (Chapel Hill: University of North Carolina Press, 1939), 220–21; William Vance Brown to John Evans Brown, April 15, 1861, Theodore Morrison Papers, Southern Historical Collection, University of North Carolina at Chapel Hill (hereafter cited as SHC).

8. The actual percentages of slaves in North Carolina's mountain counties varied greatly—from Burke County, with more than a quarter of its residents slaves in 1860, to Madison and Watauga counties, where slaves made up a mere 3.6 and 2 percent, respectively, of their 1860 populations. For demographic shifts and fluctuations in the profitability of slaves in the region before 1861, see Inscoe, *Mountain Masters*, 82–86.

9. See ibid., 76–81, 89–92, for a discussion of antebellum slave-hiring practices among western North Carolinians. For a broader study of slave hiring, see Jonathan D. Martin, *Divided Mastery: Slave Hiring in the American South* (Cambridge, Mass.: Harvard University Press, 2004).

10. Zebulon B. Vance to Jefferson Davis, October 25, 1862, in Frontis W. Johnston (ed.), *The Papers of Zebulon B. Vance,* Vol. I (Raleigh: NCDAH, 1963), 277.

11. Mary Elizabeth Massey, "Confederate Refugees in North Carolina," *North Carolina Historical Review* 40 (April 1963): 159–82, esp. 177–82; C. Vann Woodward (ed.), *Mary Chesnut's Civil War* (New Haven, Conn.: Yale University Press, 1981), 343, 422–24; and Henry C. Capers, *The Life and Times of C. G. Memminger* (Richmond, Va.: Everett Waddey, 1893), 370–71.

12. Katherine Polk Gale, "Life in the Southern Confederacy, 1861–1865," typescript, 18, SHC. On Mrs. Polk's Louisiana slaveholdings, see William M. Polk, *Leonidas Polk, Bishop and General,* 2 vols. (New York: Longmans, Green, 1915), 1:182–83.

13. Vance quoted in Nelson, "Some Aspects of Negro Life," 157. Confederate order quoted in Harvey Wish, "Slave Disloyalty under the Confederacy," *Journal of Negro History* 23 (October 1938): 442. On the movement of coastal slaves to inland and highland areas, see Nelson, "Some Aspects of Negro Life," 157–59; Morgan, *Emancipation in Virginia's Tobacco Belt,* 112–13; Mohr, *On the Threshold of Freedom,* chap. 4; Mohr, "Slavery and Class Tensions in Confederate Georgia," *Gulf Coast Historical Review* 4 (Spring 1989): 58–72; Wayne Durrill, *War of Another Kind: A Southern Community in the Great Rebellion* (New York: Oxford University Press, 1990), chap. 2; and Berlin et al., *Freedom,* 1:494–95, 772, 778–79.

14. N. W. Woodfin to David L. Swain, May 12, 1862 (Walter Clark Papers, NCDAH). For ads, see various issues of *Asheville News, North Carolina Standard,* and *State Journal* (Raleigh), December 1861 and March 1862.

15. Gordon B. McKinney, "Premature Industrialization in Appalachia: The Asheville Armory, 1862–1863," in *The Civil War in Appalachia,* ed.

Kenneth W. Noe and Shannon H. Wilson (Knoxville: University of Tennessee Press, 1997), 227–41.

16. Calvin J. Cowles to brother Andrew, March 5, 1862; Cowles to E. Foster, January 9, 1863, both in Letterpress Book K, Cowles Papers, NCDAH.

17. Cowles to brother Andrew, June 9, 25, July 8, 1862, January 30, 1863, ibid.; Cowles to his wife, April 5, 1863, Cowles Papers, SHC.

18. See, for example, Cowles's letters to slave owners in Hyde, Wake, and Pitt counties: D. C. Murray, September 10, October 10, 1863; to brother Andrew, September 15, 1863; to Rev. C. B. Reddick, February 25, April 6, 1865, to sister Mary, November 28, 1862, all Letterpress Book K, NCDAH.

19. A. T. Davidson to John Davidson, February 3, 1863, Davidson Family Papers, Atlanta Historical Society.

20. W. W. Lenoir to Joe Norwood, May 3, 1863, Lenoir Family Papers, SHC; William Pickens to Vance, March 2, 1863, Governor's Papers, NCDAH; McKinney, "Premature Industrialization in Appalachia," 234.

21. O. P. Gardner suit, Rutherford County Slave Records, NCDAH; Slave contracts, 1861–1865, Corpening Family Papers, Duke University. (There is no 1865 contract for the second woman.) John Cimprich provides the most comprehensive analysis of slave prices juxtaposed with inflation rates for 1861–1863 in *Slavery's End in Tennessee, 1861–1865* (Tuscaloosa: University of Alabama Press, 1985), 15–17. See also Nelson, "Some Aspects of Negro Life," 163–64.

22. Calvin to Mary Cowles, May 21, 1863, Letterpress Book K, Cowles Papers, NCDAH. See also bill of sale of Ashe County slave to Petersburg, Virginia, buyer, October 20, 1864, in Ashe County Slave Records, NCDAH.

23. W. W. [Walter] Lenoir to Rufus Lenoir, April 14, 1862, Lenoir Family Papers, SHC. For an insightful new study of Walter Lenoir and his family during this period, see William L. Barney, *The Making of a Confederate: Walter Lenoir's Civil War* (New York: Oxford University Press, 2007).

24. James Gwyn to Rufus Lenoir, May 15, 1861, Lenoir Family Papers, SHC.

25. W. W. Lenoir to Thomas I. Lenoir, February 25, 1863; James Gwyn to Rufus Lenoir, January 12, 1863, ibid.

26. W. W. Lenoir to Joseph Norwood, May 3, 1863; James Gwyn to Rufus Lenoir, February 9, 1863, ibid.

27. See, in addition to letters cited above, A. C. Hargrove to Thomas I. Lenoir, February 13, 1863; Thomas C. Norwood to Thomas Lenoir, March 9, 1863; W. W. Lenoir to Rufus Lenoir, August 17, 1863; and W. W. Lenoir to Aunt Sade, March 27, 1864, all ibid.

28. For slave population figures for these and other western North Caro-

lina counties, see Inscoe, *Mountain Masters,* tables 3.1 and 3.2, pp. 60–61, 84–85. On Macon County slaves, see also Jessie Sutton (ed.), *The Heritage of Macon County, North Carolina* (Winston-Salem: Hunter, 1987), 46–48.

29. The basic source for this discussion of the Bells is the correspondence between Alfred and Mary Bell in the Alfred W. Bell Papers, Duke University. For a fuller treatment of their situation, see chap. 7 in this volume, "Coping in Confederate Appalachia"; and "The 1864 Slave Purchases of Mary Bell: The Civil War's Empowerment of an Appalachian Woman: Mary Bell and Her 1864 Slave Purchases," in *Discovering the Women in Slavery: Emancipating Perspectives on the American Past,* ed. Patricia Morton (Athens: University of Georgia Press, 1996), 61–81.

30. Alfred to Mary Bell, December 9, 1862.

31. Ibid., March 17, 1864; Mary to Alfred Bell, March 11, 1864.

32. Mary to Alfred Bell, ibid. For the description of the sale by Alfred's brother Benjamin, see his letter of March 11, 1864.

33. Alfred to Mary Bell, March 31, April 8, 1864.

34. Mary to Alfred Bell, July 8, 17, November 24, 1864.

35. Rufus to Walter Lenoir, December 12, 1864; estate settlement, February 4, 1865, Lenoir Family Papers.

36. Mary Cowles to Calvin J. Cowles, February 9, 1865, Cowles Papers, NCDAH.

37. Rufus L. Patterson to his father, December 8, 1864, Jones and Patterson Family Papers, SHC.

38. Ibid.

39. Alexander H. Jones, *Knocking at the Door* (Washington, D.C.: McGill and Witherow, 1866), 9.

War

5

The Secession Crisis and Regional Self-Image

The Contrasting Cases of Western North Carolina and East Tennessee

No two adjacent regions of the upper South, and certainly none so much alike, reacted so differently to the secession crisis of 1860 and 1861 as did western North Carolina and East Tennessee. Despite similarities in topography, agricultural output, racial demography, and socioeconomic makeup, highlanders on either side of the border between the two states demonstrated sharp contrasts in their collective views regarding their commitment to the Union and to the South. No other part of what would become a Confederate state—except the northwestern counties of Virginia—resisted secession longer or with more vehemence than did the eastern third of Tennessee. Even after Tennessee passed its secession ordinance in June (the last state to do so), the vast majority of its mountain residents opposed casting their lot with the rest of the South, and even made a concerted effort to secede from their state in order to do so. No other part of the Confederacy supplied so many soldiers (more than 30,000) to the Union army, a contribution greater than that made by Rhode Island, Delaware, or Minnesota.

Just across their eastern border, North Carolina highlanders were far more divided among themselves as to the wisdom and merits of secession. But pro-secession arguments received as full a hearing there as they did anywhere in the upper South, and a substantial number of western Carolinians actively supported joining a new southern nation, starting with Lincoln's election in November 1860. A February 1861 referendum on a secession convention fully demonstrated the split among these westerners. But by May, the state's mountain coun-

103

ties were unanimous in their support of withdrawal from the Union and went on to provide the state's largest per capita number of volunteers to the Confederate army during the early months of the war. This chapter is an attempt both to characterize the nature of the differences in attitudes demonstrated by these two sets of southern highlanders, and to propose—if only tentatively—an explanation for those differences.

On the basis of their most quantifiable characteristics, one is struck far more by how much alike East Tennessee and western North Carolina were than by any marked differences. East Tennessee is generally defined as the state's thirty easternmost counties. It consists of three major mountain chains, the Cumberlands to the west and the Blue Ridge to the northeast and the Great Smokies to the southeast, separated by the broad valleys of the Tennessee and Holston rivers. Western North Carolina was never quite so specifically delineated, but it is defined here as what were in 1860 the state's fifteen westernmost counties, which for the most part make up a double tier of counties bordering Tennessee. This area also encompasses large parts of the Blue Ridge and Great Smoky mountains, along with all of the small but more rugged Black Mountain chain.

The vast majority of residents of both sections were small farmers with limited—but, by 1860, much improved—access to commercial markets beyond their region's bounds. No single cash crop dominated their agricultural output. Cotton was not conducive to either the terrain or the climate of the southern highlands, but corn, wheat, and other grains were grown in abundance, along with flax, tobacco, apples and peaches in more select areas within each section. Livestock proved to be the most marketable of mountain products, with many hogs and cattle and somewhat fewer sheep raised on both sides of the state line. Western Carolinians maintained an active trade with the plantation markets of South Carolina and Georgia, and its leaders eagerly pushed for railroad lines to link their part of the state with its eastern half and/or with those states to the south. By 1860, the Western North Carolina Railroad had almost reached Morganton, the most accessible of the region's commercial outlets, and construction was under way as far west as Asheville by the war's outbreak.

Internal improvements in East Tennessee had made a quantum

leap forward just a few years before the Civil War with the completion of the East Tennessee and Georgia Railroad in 1855 and the East Tennessee and Virginia line in 1858, which together cut through the heart of the Tennessee River valley and linked much of the region to markets both north and south via Bristol and Chattanooga. Both communities, along with Knoxville, the unofficial capital of the region, enjoyed significant growth spurts during the late 1850s as a result of these connections. Their North Carolina counterpart was Asheville, which had emerged much earlier as the vital and growing hub for much of the commerce and tourism that moved through the western part of the state. Thus on both sides of the mountains, Carolina and Tennessee highlanders maintained strong commercial ties with other parts of the South, and although the average farmer was only peripherally involved in the broader market economy, the growing prosperity of both regions very much reflected this expanding commercial activity.

Politically, both mountain sections had been bastions of Whig Party strength in their respective states until the party's demise in the mid-1850s, and both continued to mount stubborn resistance to the Democrats through the rest of the decade. Inhabitants of both regions felt victimized by intrastate sectional biases and neglect, and highlanders came to see themselves as beleaguered minorities whose rights and interests were either threatened or ignored by more powerful coalitions representing the central and far ends of their states.

Finally, and perhaps most important, the number and distribution of slaves within these adjacent sections were quite similar. According to 1860 census figures for Tennessee's thirty easternmost and North Carolina's fifteen westernmost counties, slaves made up only 12.5 percent and 10.2 percent of their respective populations. Though just over one-fourth (26.3 percent) of the population of Burke County, North Carolina, was enslaved, no other county in western North Carolina had more than a 19 percent slave population. In eight of the fifteen counties, slaves accounted for less than 5 percent of their residents. Knox County boasted the highest number of slaves per capita in East Tennessee, with 16.6 percent, and in fourteen of those counties, slaves made up less than 6 percent of the total. There were several areas in both mountain sections where slavery was nonexistent and whose residents had never seen a black person. Only one man in East Tennessee and two in western North Carolina owned more than a hundred slaves. About 83 and 85 percent (North Carolina and Tennessee, respectively) of slaveholders in 1860 owned fewer than ten slaves in 1850, compared with an average of 67 percent throughout the slaveholding South; less than 6 percent owned more than twenty, compared with 14 percent throughout the South.[1]

On the basis of these demographic, economic, and political characteristics, one would expect the highlanders of North Carolina and Tennessee to have reacted in much same way to the crisis thrust upon them in the winter and spring of 1860–1861. Yet sentiments in these adjacent sections were, as stated earlier, as different as any across the upper South. As late as the presidential election in November 1860, there was little indication of the divergent paths the two areas would take over the following months. John Bell, a Tennessean and the Constitutional Union candidate, carried about two-thirds of both states' mountain counties, but with only a 55 percent plurality in western North Carolina and 58 percent in East Tennessee over John Breckinridge, the Southern Democratic candidate. Debate in both sections, as elsewhere in the South, centered on which of the two candidates offered the greater deterrence to Lincoln's election and on whether the firm protection of southern rights (Democrats in support of Breckinridge) or the security of the Union (old Whigs supporting Bell) should be the higher priority at this preliminary phase of the crisis that all mountain residents hoped to avoid. Their preference for Bell, though by only slight margins, indicated relatively strong commitments to the Union, which at that point were not much greater than was true of the rest of their states as well.[2]

But soon after Lincoln's election and South Carolina's secession in December, the views of spokesmen from both highland regions began to take on slight but perceptible distinctions. Strong western Carolina voices urged that North Carolina join its southern sister in immediately withdrawing from the Union. U.S. Senator Thomas L. Clingman of Asheville joined with all three of the mountain districts' state senators, W. W. Avery, William Holland Thomas, and Marcus Erwin, in presenting a powerful case to their constituents as to the economic and military benefits not only of cutting ties with the Union, but of doing so without further delay. The majority of their fellow westerners, however, demonstrated far greater caution and embraced the "watch and wait" policy of so-called conditional Unionism, a stance based as much on the assurance that their options remained open and later action could be taken as needed. Zebulon B. Vance, then the region's congressman and most prominent Unionist, probably spoke for the majority of his constituents when he pointed out that "we have everything to gain and nothing on earth to lose by delay, but by too hasty action we make take a fatal step we can never retrace—may lose a heritage we can never recover."[3]

During the same period farther west, East Tennesseans were subject to a far more one-sided response to the crisis at hand. Their own U.S. senator, Andrew Johnson, along with Congressman Thomas A. R. Nelson and illustrious newspaper editor William G. "Parson" Brownlow, were among several spokesmen who were both quick and persistent in affirming their undying patriotism and loyalty to the Union, in denying the constitutional right of secession, and in warning of the dangers of the "slave oligarchy," under whose rule secession would bring them.[4]

Special elections held in February 1861 to determine whether or not to hold secession conventions in both states provide the first quantifiable indications we have of the differences emerging across state lines. On February 9, East Tennesseans resoundingly rejected the option of a convention, and thus any further consideration of their state leaving the Union. With a total vote in the region of more than 33,000 against and 7,500 for a convention, all but two of Tennessee's thirty mountain counties opposed it by substantial majorities.[5] Tennesseans rejoiced at the results, and Brownlow crowed in his Knoxville *Whig:* "There was never a party so disgracefully beaten in any State in the Union since the formation of the Government as this Disunion party is beaten in Tennessee! . . . Glorious old Tennessee has said at the ballot box that her interests are in the Union, and that *under the Stars and Stripes* the people will live."[6]

North Carolina's referendum on the same question took place less than three weeks later on February 28, and the voters of its mountain counties demonstrated far more mixed feelings than their neighbors to the west. By a slim majority (50.3 percent of the vote), the state as a whole rejected a call for a convention. Five of the fifteen mountain counties voted for a convention by margins of more than 60 percent. In three other counties, the electorate was almost evenly divided, and seven counties opposed a convention by heavy majorities.[7]

But these figures alone do not indicate the strength of Unionist sentiment in the region, for voters did not, in the end, equate a vote for a convention with a vote for secession. Many seem to have followed the lead of Zebulon Vance and other Unionists who opposed secession but felt that a convention would provide the most credible forum in which to do so. Thus the votes for a convention far exceeded those for secessionist candidates. Of the fifteen delegates elected from the mountain counties, all but one were Unionists.[8] The western electorate had clearly indicated that it was not yet ready to abandon the Union, but many voters (almost half) were not opposed the idea of a convention through which the state could make a firm defense of its rights either within or outside of the Union. By the same token, the majority of those delegates were clearly "conditional Unionists," whose commitment was to oppose immediate session but most of whom had publicly stated their opposition to coercion and their willingness to cast their lot with the Confederacy when and if further developments warranted it.[9]

That February 28 election reflected far more hesitancy and indecisiveness on the part of western Carolinians than was demonstrated by East Tennesseans earlier that month—or, for that matter, than was demonstrated by other North Carolinians on February 28. Union sentiment was far more intense and far less conditional in the "Quaker belt" counties of the piedmont than it was in the mountains.[10] It was only in response to events as clear-cut in their implications as the attack on Fort Sumter and President Lincoln's subsequent call for troops that the attitudes of western North Carolinians jelled and a decisive consensus of popular reaction emerged. For a number of reasons, they, like other North Carolinians, were becoming resigned to the inevitability of their state's secession, if not in favor of it, and to the idea of an ensuing war even before the pivotal events of mid-April 1861. Lincoln's call for 75,000 troops (including two North Carolina regiments) on April 15, followed by Virginia's secession two days later, ended all lingering doubts. Charles Manly's observation that "all are unanimous, even those who were loudest in denouncing secession are not hottest & loudest the other way" was as applicable to mountain residents as to those in any other part of the state.[11]

When North Carolina at last severed its ties with the Union on May 20, the vast majority of its western citizens approved of its action. The western counties elected pro-secession delegates across the board. (Only two Unionists even ran, and both were handily defeated.) Those elected joined with their counterparts across the state to vote unanimously to join the Confederacy.[12] With this response, as with those throughout every phase of the crisis, highland voters were very much in tune with the rest of the state and with much of the upper South.

The same cannot be said for East Tennessee, and it is through this period that the contrast between the two mountain regions becomes most striking. There, too, Unionists reacted with shock to Lincoln's call for troops. But those feelings were far more tempered by initial despair and uncertainty than by the blatant outrage that swept so much of the rest of the upper South. Some, such as "Parson" Brownlow, remained firm in their commitment to the Union. After having looked the matter "full in the face," he declared in his Knoxville newspaper that he was still for the "Stars and Stripes." He attempted to dismiss Lincoln's proclamation as merely a safeguard to protect Washington, D.C., and, as such, an act fully justifiable. Congressman Nelson denied that the war was one between North and South or between Lincoln and the South. It was, he maintained, "a war between the Constitution and those who have violated it."[13]

The consistency of their convictions, along with those of other Tennessee highland spokesmen, did much to overcome those mid-April blows to Unionist strength and organization. The delays that kept another referendum on secession from Tennessee voters until June 8 provided valuable time to revive an only briefly faltering following. Regional leaders were so successful in their efforts that by mid-May, secessionists faced such volatile hostility in much of the region that it became dangerous for them to speak publicly. Knoxville lawyer Oliver Temple recalled that "it was difficult to restrain the infuriated Union men from acts of violence against the disunionists. More than once, the leaders had to restrain them from marching into Knoxville in a body, and as they called it, 'clearing out the secessionists in the town.'"[14] In describing one of many Unionist rallies held during May and early June, Brownlow took great satisfaction in declaring that "great one-ness of purpose and more determined spirit we have never witnessed among any body of men." After another such rally, a group of citizens of Clinton informed fellow Tennesseans to their west that "there is no way under Heaven to get East Tennessee out of the Union! We don't intend to go, and so God help us, we won't!"[15]

Thus, while the state's popular referendum on June 8 merely con-firmed what already seemed to be a fait accompli in the western two thirds of the state, East Tennesseans continued to stand strong in their opposition to secession. Though Tennesseans as a whole voted them-selves out of the Union by a margin of more than two to one (105,000 for secession and 47,000 against), the results for the eastern third of the state were a complete reversal of those results, with support for the Union still at more than two to one (33,000 against secession and less than 15,000 for it).[16] These results clearly corroborated the Union-ist rhetoric that East Tennessee was indeed a distinctive region and demonstrated the extent to which it remained alienated from the rest of the state and the rest of the South.

The actions of mountain Unionists in Tennessee after June 8 made that point even more drastically. They were quick to argue that seces-sionist intimidation elsewhere in the state invalidated the election re-sults and that both secessionist governor Isham Harris and the state legislature had already made "illegal and unjustifiable" military ar-rangements with the Confederacy, even inviting the Confederate gov-ernment to make Nashville its capital.[17] Congressman Nelson, who had headed up the pre-election Unionist campaign and convention in the east, put into action the contingency plan discussed earlier. He called a convention to meet in Andrew Johnson's hometown of Greene-ville a little more than a week later to propose seceding from Tennes-see in order to remain in the Union. On June 17 that body, made up of 285 representatives of twenty-six counties, drew up a "Declaration of Grievances" against the state, which concluded: "We prefer to remain attached to the government of our fathers. The Constitution of the United States has done us no wrong. . . . We believe there is no cause for rebellion or cession on the part of the people of Tennessee."[18]

They submitted a petition to the legislature stating their intention of forming a separate state and asking its cooperation in allowing them to do so, after which they adjourned with plans to meet in Kinston later that month. Nothing further came of the effort, because Johnson felt pressured to leave the state and return to Washington, Brownlow was forced into hiding, and Nelson was captured by Confederate forces and taken to Richmond. From that point on, the status and fate of East Tennessee would be determined by military action; and yet the sentiments of its residents had remained clear and consistent for as long as they could be expressed.[19]

The big question all this raises, of course, is why two adjacent and such similar regions parted ways so dramatically as the secession crisis came to a head in the upper South. Much attention and analysis has been devoted to East Tennessee, due not only to the unusual intensity of its Unionism, but also to its military value as the largest predominantly loyal geographic area within the Confederacy (Lincoln saw it as a key to Union strategy early in the war), and to the fact that both the region and its political situation produced the next president of the United States. The standard explanations for its course have always been its small numbers of slaves and slaveholders, its sectional slights within the state, its strong Whig traditions, and the relative poverty it faced outside the Cotton Belt. All of these seem logical enough as causes for its Unionism until one considers them in juxtaposition with that far less fully explored situation in western North Carolina. That all the same factors were behind such different sentiments and consequences tends to undermine the significance of any of them as decisive in shaping the East Tennesseans' distinctive response to the secessionist crisis.

I propose that the crucial difference between antebellum East Tennessee and western North Carolina lay in their self-images—that is, how residents of each section perceived themselves and their region in relation to their respective states and to the South as a whole. Those differences, as demonstrated largely by the rhetoric and writings of those most influential public opinion shapers—their political leaders and journalists—are striking and go far toward explaining the contrasting actions each section took in the spring of 1861.

Many western Carolinians, for example, tended to view their part

of the state as a region on the rise. A number of spokesmen for highland North Carolina were quite active in promoting their economic
potential through an ever-increasing public appreciation for its distinctive land, mineral, forest, and climatic resources and conditions.
The French Broad River valley was one of several in the region described as among the nation's richest sections of agricultural abundance and diversity.[20] Other efforts at local boosterism stressed the
special qualities of terrain and growing season throughout the Carolina mountains, and a number of model farms were established by
both local landholders and seasonal residents that demonstrated the
rich possibilities of highland soil and climate. University of North
Carolina geologist Elisha Mitchell did much to publicize the mountains' potential for becoming "the New England of the South," and
Thomas Clingman, the district's congressman through the late 1840s
and much of the 1850s, vigorously promoted projects to develop his
region's production and marketability of dairy products, sheep, and
even wine.[21]

Contacts between the Carolina mountains and both the towns
and plantations of South Carolina and Georgia increased dramatically during the last two antebellum decades and took two very different forms. A demand for mountain products—from garden and
orchard produce to honey and molasses, indigenous herbs and roots,
and even bear and deer meat—created a healthy, if limited, participation in the market economy by ever-growing numbers of highland
farmers. All of this was overshadowed by the phenomenal livestock
trade, particularly in hogs and cattle, that every autumn moved south-
ward through the region's major valley arteries. Second, the reputation of certain highland areas as summer resorts, with their cool
climates, scenic beauty, and health-restoring mineral springs, led large
numbers of affluent planters, particularly Charlestonians, to migrate
to such communities as Flat Rock, Asheville, Hendersonville, and
Warm Springs for three to four months every year.[22]

These contacts, perhaps, had much to do with the remarkable
lack of animosity between the vast majority of nonslaveholding yeomen and the slaveholding elite within the region. But even more of a
factor was the fact that the west's most ardent champions of development and most influential commercial conduits to markets beyond

their own were also its largest slaveholders. With so much of the region's prosperity dependent on those efforts, local identities and loyalty overrode any class distinctions and did much to defuse potential resentment of mountain residents toward either slavery or slaveholders. Thus, far from anticipating a bleak future of poverty, isolation, or internal class dissension, western Carolinians and their leaders had ample reason for optimism on the eve of the Civil War, with a healthy and expanding economy mutually enjoyed by large and small farmers alike and based on what they recognized as their region's special endowments in natural resources, which in turn were noted and demanded by southerners elsewhere.

This awareness of regional attributes and strong southern ties was often emphasized in arguments put forward by highland secessionists, who predicted very beneficial effects on their section's status as a result of independence from the North. The inaccessibility of popular northern "watering holes" would send more planters from across the South to the Carolina highland resorts. Its geographic location and the fact that Flat Rock and Hendersonville were already the summer homes of several prominent southern officials, most notably Confederate Treasury Secretary Christopher G. Memminger, led some to speculate that the government itself might establish itself in the area. In this "mountain kingdom," wrote a Henderson County visitor, "it is contemplated to place the capital city of the Southern Confederacy, having its seat of government within 100 miles of the capitals of six other states."[23] William Holland Thomas, a leading secessionist from the state's southwestern corner, best summed up these aspirations: "The mountains of Western North Carolina would be the centre of the Confederacy," he pointed out, and as a result: "We shall then have one of the most prosperous countries in the world. It will become connected with every part of the South by railroad. It will then become the centre of manufacturing for the Southern market. The place where the Southern people will spend their money, educate their children and very probably make the laws for the nation."[24]

Ironically, East Tennessee shared many of the same attributes and advantages that Carolina highlanders so actively promoted and in which they took such pride. With its railroad already in place, its residents had even more reason to feel good about their present and future situation. And yet that region's leading spokesmen during the late antebellum period projected a very different image of their area and its people. Like western North Carolina, East Tennessee was by far the poorest section of its state, but its citizens seemed far more conscious of that fact than their neighbors to the east. As early as 1826, a Tennessee mountaineer stated what would become a theme echoed throughout his section when he lamented, "Our soil is poor in comparison with what is now called Middle Tennessee or in comparison with the Western District, and we have it not within our reach, as a people, to become rich."[25] Far from acknowledging those characteristics they shared with the rest of the state and the South (much less their dependence on them), Tennessee highlanders stressed their distinctiveness, even when it meant their inferiority. "We are a distinct and peculiar people," boasted one resident, "not to be confounded with other divisions in the state." Thomas Gray, a frequent visitor to the region, declared that East Tennesseans were "so attached to their mountains that they would rather live in poverty there than in wealth in cities or even in plains."[26]

Regional spokesmen often translated this long-nurtured inferiority complex into a virtue, so that highlanders came to take pride in the "humble" nature of their society and the egalitarian and independent spirit it reflected. One leading citizen declared that "East Tennessee is a better place to live [than] where there are temptations and opportunity to get wealth. . . . We are more moral and religious and less absorbed in the business and cares of the world than the people of west Tennessee or any cotton country."[27] None pursued this theme more effectively than Andrew Johnson. He parlayed his own modest beginnings into a major political asset, and he achieved impressive success as a Democrat among a predominantly Whig electorate by presenting himself in the Jacksonian mold of a champion of the common man and an opponent of elitism or privilege in any form. Although he played down class distinctions within his own region (he was, after all, a slaveholder himself by 1860), Johnson effectively utilized the regional inferiority sensed by his mountain constituents to augment their antagonism and distrust of the planter aristocracy that controlled so much of the rest of the South. This identity became so firmly entrenched among East Tennesseans that when applied to the secession question, longtime partisan opponents of Johnson, such as Parson Brownlow and Thomas Nelson, were quick to adapt his themes to their pro-Union cause. Johnson equated secessionism with anti-egalitarianism and claimed that the disunionists' true intention was to enact the very scenario most feared by his freedom-loving listeners: "to form an independent government in the South as far removed from the people as they can get it."[28]

Brownlow proclaimed, "Johnson is right!" and elaborated: "We can never live in a Southern Confederacy and be made hewers of wood and drawers of water for a set of aristocrats and overbearing tyrants. . . . We have no interest in common with the Cotton States. We are a grain-growing and stock-raising people, and we can conduct a cheap government, inhabiting the Switzerland of America."[29] Oliver Temple later wrote of these months: "The overpowering influence of slavery, the fear of falling under the condemnation of the mighty oligarchy of slaveholders, to some extent paralyzed the minds of men" in East Tennessee.[30]

It is important to note that this fear of slaveholding power did not grow out of an abhorrence of the system itself, a conclusion that might logically be drawn since East Tennessee had been the site of the South's most fully developed antislavery movement. Probably as a result of an early influx of Methodists and Quakers into the area from Pennsylvania and Ohio, abolitionist activity flourished there during the first third of the nineteenth century. The nation's first manumission societies and its earliest abolitionist newspaper were established there in 1815 and 1819, respectively. But their impact on Unionism several decades later seems only indirect. While antislavery rhetoric undoubtedly fanned the flames of class resentment among mountaineers against the planter aristocracy, a rampant racism among these highlanders led very few to support their cause. By 1860, Unionist leaders were sensitive to charges that they opposed black bondage, and most were empathetic in maintaining that they fully supported the institution.[31]

One of the major arguments embraced by Andrew Johnson and other Unionist leaders was that slavery's future was far more secure within the Union where it enjoyed constitutional protection than it would be outside the Union and without that protection. They were quick to condemn abolitionists as well as southern fire-eaters for having brought about the needless crisis at hand. Brownlow wrote, "My contempt for the Abolitionists of the North is only equaled by my hatred of the Disunionists of the South." In Philadelphia, he engaged in a much-publicized five-day debate with an abolitionist and utilized the by then sharply defined proslavery ideology to the fullest.[32] And yet there were those for whom slavery's survival was not the top priority to be considered in the debate over secession. Temple may well have spoken for more of his fellow East Tennesseans when he said just before the June 8 election: "If we had to choose between the government on one side without slavery, and a broken and dissevered government with slavery, I would say unhesitatingly, 'Let slavery perish and the Union survive.'"[33]

Certainly intersectional rivalries did much to embitter the eastern third of Tennessee against the rest of the state. Though often politically aligned with the Whig stronghold at the opposite end of the state against the Democratic middle on national issues, highlanders felt resentment and alienation toward legislatures and governors who they believed imposed excessive taxation on them and yet consistently overlooked them in the appropriation of state funds for railroad and river improvements bestowed on other parts of the state.[34] East Tennessee was the earliest settled and oldest part of the state. Knoxville had been designated as the state's first capital when it entered the Union in 1796, but as early as 1812, the legislature voted to move it west to its fast-emerging rival, Nashville. This move was in itself a real setback in terms of the region's political influence and stature, the first indication of the region's diminishing role as a mere "outlying province," as Thomas Nelson once called it. That loss of political clout was a reflection of economic and demographic drainage from East Tennessee as well. J. G. M. Ramsey of Knoxville bemoaned that outmigration, but he admitted that he had considered moving west himself, for the "insulated position of East Tennessee made farming there, even with the greatest industry and strict frugality, so unproductive and unremunerating," thus prompting "a constant emigration of the industrious and enterprising . . . to sections of the country having greater commercial facilities." He, like many fellow East Tennesseans, found it particularly frustrating, and even demeaning, to see so much of the wealth, influence, and power pass over their more historically entrenched region into the more recently settled areas to the west.[35]

This was a situation far different from that in western North Carolina, and one could argue that this difference in itself had much to do with the conflicting self-images projected by the two sections. North Carolina's mountains were the last part of the state to be settled and remained the most undeveloped section of a much older and more fully established colony and state. Thus, whereas western Carolinians were at the same level of underdog status in relation to other sections of their state as East Tennesseans, the former still managed to see themselves as "up and coming" or catching up; whereas many of the latter were left with the impression of having been passed over and left behind.

These frustrations, along with East Tennesseans' self-perceived distinctiveness as a region, led to a serious campaign in 1841 and 1842 to withdraw from the rest of the state and form a separate state (to be called Franklin, a reminder of the aborted attempt by an earlier generation to break away from North Carolina in the 1780s). Spurred by a legislative rebuff of internal improvements promised to the region, several counties produced resolutions in support of independent statehood. A young Brownlow, then based in Jonesborough, led the charge, declaring Nashville to be "a seat of Dictation" and that "we have long enough been 'hewers of wood and drawers of water' in the hands of Middle Tennesseans."[36] This proposal actually passed the state legislature's upper house before it was crushed in the lower. Despite having made significant gains in internal improvements by the time of the secession crisis, the memories and resentment of earlier slights remained strong, so that East Tennesseans had few qualms in attempting, on June 17, 1861, a move they had made twice before— seceding from the state of which they were then a part.

The mountain residents of North Carolina had also been engaged in serious east–west sectional battles with an "eastern oligarchy" that controlled, and even monopolized, the state government in Raleigh. Intense battles over broadened suffrage and ad valorem taxation were waged between the two halves of the state in the late 1840s and 1850s, as were ongoing disputes over discrepancies in state allotments for internal improvements, just as in Tennessee. Yet, interestingly enough, these differences among North Carolinians left almost no permanent scars that carried into the secession crisis. Far from alienating them from their fellow Tar Heels to the east, mountain residents demonstrated a strong identity with and loyalty to their state throughout the crisis, and they based much of their discussion for or against secession on its effect on the state as a whole.[37] In fact, it seems likely that the intrastate sectional rivalry over the previous decades actually contributed to secessionist sentiment in the mountains.

It is here that Thomas Clingman emerges as a key figure. His first efforts as a politician were in championing western interests in the state legislature in the early 1840s. He then went on to Congress and in the 1850s became an even more outspoken champion of slavery and southern rights. As such, he embraced the dual themes that dominated late antebellum politics for his constituents. In two very different spheres of sectional tension, as westerners within the state and as southerners within the nation, they were made increasingly aware of themselves, with Clingman's guidance, as an abused minority whose rights and interests were threatened by government power on two fronts, federal and state, controlled respectively by northerners and easterners whose interests conflicted with their own. Thus he could exhort them in 1849 to tell the eastern-dominated legislature in Raleigh: "if they want white slaves they must look for them elsewhere than in the Western reserve," and a year later, warn congressmen from the North that "if you intend to degrade and utterly ruin the South, then we will resist. We do not love you, people of the North, well enough to become your slaves."[38]

Clingman was among the first to recognize the striking parallels between the wrongs, or perceived wrongs, inflicted on his constituents from powers in both Raleigh and Washington, and throughout his congressional career he made the most of the emotional and political potential of those dual threats. Nourished by his constant harangues on behalf of their interests, western Carolinians' consciousness of themselves as oppressed westerners was easily translated into an equally strong consciousness of themselves as oppressed southerners, and the two roles continued to reinforce and complement each other throughout the 1850s.[39]

There was no such blatantly pro-southern, secessionist voice comparable to Thomas Clingman's in East Tennessee. By the same token, Unionism never enjoyed nearly as full-bodied or consistent a hearing in western North Carolina as Andrew Johnson, Parson Brownlow, and others provided in East Tennessee. This is not to say that these individuals and their differences alone determined the course their constituents and/or readers took when faced with the ominous choices before them as the nation split in two. Rather, the key to their success as popular and influential spokesmen for their fellow mountaineers lay in their ability to recognize, verbalize, and ultimately exploit preexisting insecurities, prejudices, sources of pride, and self-perceptions, which they in turn translated into appropriate and effective ideological rhetoric for the crisis at hand. A number of recent studies stress the significance of community pressures in bringing about conformity on this vital issue.[40] It was indeed a major factor on both sides of the North Carolina–Tennessee border, and one that had much to do with the influence these spokesmen were able to exert in consolidating and mobilizing those they led.

These two regional underdogs of Southern Appalachia had much in common, but their inhabitants' sense of who they were, where they were from, where they were headed, and how they fit into larger wholes were quite different. It was those distinctions and the way in which they were spotlighted and exploited by their respective leaders that provide much—though by no means all—of the answer as to why the courses of North Carolina and Tennessee highlanders diverged so sharply in their attitudes toward secession in the spring of 1861.

Notes

1. Eighth Census of the United States, 1860; Population and Slave Schedules for Tennessee and North Carolina. For a broader overview of the racial demographics of Appalachia, see William H. Turner, "The Demography of Black Appalachia: Past and Present," *Blacks in Appalachia,* ed. Edward J. Cabbell and William H. Turner (Lexington, 1985).

2. Computed from W. Dean Burnham, *Presidential Ballots, 1836–1892* (Baltimore, 1955), 648–68; and R.D.W. Connor, ed., *A Manual for North Carolina* (Raleigh, 1913). See also Marguerite Bartlett Hamer, "The Presidential Campaign of 1860 in Tennessee," *East Tennessee Historical Society's Publications* 3 (January 1931): 3–22 (hereafter cited as ETHSP).

3. Zebulon B. Vance to William Dickson, December 11, 1860, *The Papers of Zebulon Baird Vance,* Vol. I: *1843–1862,* ed. Frontis W. Johnston, (Raleigh, 1963), 72.

4. As the most prominent Whig leaders in the region, Nelson and Brownlow were longtime political adversaries of Johnson until their Unionist commitments made them strong allies during the secession crisis. Thomas B. Alexander, "Strange Bedfellows: The Interlocking Careers of T.A.R. Nelson, Andrew Johnson, and W.G. Parson Brownlow," ETHSP 24 (1952): 68–91; and Oliver P. Temple, *East Tennessee and the Civil War* (1899; rept., Freeport, N.Y., 1971), 189–90; Other treatments of the three men's relationship include Steve Humphrey, *"That D—d Brownlow": Being a Malicious Description of Fighting Parson William Gannaway Brownlow* (Boone, N.C., 1978), 206–7; Royal F. Conklin, "The Public Speaking Career of William Gannaway (Parson) Brownlow" (Ph.D. diss., Ohio University, 1967), 128–37; and Thomas B. Alexander, *Thomas A. R. Nelson of East Tennessee* (Nashville, 1956), 76–83.

5. Nashville *Banner,* February 22, 1861, cited in Vernon M. Queener, "East Tennessee Sentiment and the Secession Movement, November 1860–June 1861," *ETHSP* 20 (1948): 64–65; and Mary Emily Robertson Campbell, *The Attitude of Tennesseans toward the Union, 1847–1861* (New York, 1961), appendix C, 288. For more recent analyses of the secession crisis in East Tennessee, see Noel C. Fisher, *War at Every Door: Partisan Politics and Guerrilla Violence in East Tennessee, 1860–1869* (Chapel Hill, 1997), chap. 2; W. Todd Groce, *Mountain Rebels: East Tennessee Confederates and the Civil War, 1860–1870* (Knoxville, 1999), chap. 2; and Robert Tracy McKenzie, *Lincolnites and Rebels: A Divided Town* [Knoxville] *in the American Civil War* (New York, 2006), chap. 3.

6. Knoxville *Whig,* February 16, 1861. Emphasis in original.

7. Computed from Connor, *North Carolina Manual,* 1013–15; and Mark Kruman, *Parties and Politics in North Carolina, 1836–1865* (Baton Rouge, 1983), table 31, 276–78. See also John C. Inscoe, *Mountain Masters: Slavery and the Sectional Crisis in Western North Carolina* (Knoxville, 1989), 243–47, table 9.2, and map 7, 242; and Daniel W. Crofts, *Reluctant Confederates: Upper South Unionists in the Secession Crisis* (Chapel Hill, 1989), 144–52.

8. Clarke M. Avery of Burke County was the only secessionist candidate elected. The most thorough and accurate compilation of the February election results is found in Kruman, *Parties and Politics,* table 31, 276–78. See also J. Carlyle Sitterson, *The Secession Movement in North Carolina* (Chapel Hill, 1939). In Sitterson's analysis of those results, he lists three secessionist delegates elected from the west, but for Jackson and Haywood counties, T. D. Bryson and William Hicks, respectively, were more cautiously

Unionist than openly secessionist. Raleigh *Register,* February 23, March 6, 9, 1861.

9. Sitterson, *Secession in North Carolina,* 219; Inscoe, *Mountain Masters,* 231–37. Of the ten delegates whose views at this time are know, all were conditional rather than unconditional Unionists. Only the views of the delegates of Ashe, Alleghany, Wilkes, and Watauga counties cannot be ascertained, though Sitterson labels them unconditional Unionists.

10. See Kruman, *Parties and Politics,* 211–13; Sitterson, *Secession Movement in North Carolina,* 195; and William T. Auman, "Neighbor against Neighbor: The Inner Civil War in the Randolph County Area of Confederate North Carolina," *North Carolina Historical Review* 61 (January 1984): 59–92.

11. Charles Manly to David L. Swain, April 22, 1861, David Lowry Swain Papers, North Carolina Department of Archives and History, Raleigh.

12. Inscoe, *Mountain Masters,* 248–55; Sitterson, *Secession Movement in North Carolina,* 210–14.

13. Knoxville *Whig,* April 27, 1861; E. Merton Coulter, *William G. Brownlow: Fighting Parson of the Southern Appalachians* (Chapel Hill, 1937), 149–51; and Alexander, *Thomas A. R. Nelson,* 82.

14. Temple, *East Tennessee and the Civil War,* 196.

15. Knoxville *Whig,* June 8, 1861; D. K. Young et al. to W. B. Campbell, June 3, 1861, cited in Alexander, *Thomas A. R. Nelson,* 82. For a more nuanced analysis of the long-term strength of East Tennessee Unionism, see Robert Tracy McKenzie, "Prudent Silence and Strict Neutrality: The Parameters of Unionism in Parson Brownlow's Knoxville, 1860–1863," in *Enemies of the Country: New Perspectives on Unionists in the Civil War South,* ed. John C. Inscoe and Robert C. Kenzer (Athens, Ga., 2001), 73–96.

16. Temple, *East Tennessee and the Civil War,* 199–200.

17. Ibid.

18. "Proceedings of the East Tennessee Convention, Greeneville, June 17, 1861," cited in J. Reuben Sheeler, "The Development of Unionism in East Tennessee, *Journal of Negro History* 29 (April 1944): 182–84. The best accounts of that meeting are found in Temple, *East Tennessee and the Civil War,* chap. 11; Campbell, *Attitude of Tennesseans,* 207–10; Thomas W. Humes, *The Loyal Mountaineers of Tennessee* (Knoxville, 1888), 102–19; and Fisher, *War at Every Door,* 37–40.

19. Temple, *East Tennessee and the Civil War,* chap. 11; Fisher, *War at Every Door,* 38–42.

20. William W. Malet, *An Errand in the South in the Summer of 1822* (London, 1863), 236; and "Picturesque America: On the French Broad River, North Carolina," *Appleton's Journal* (December 7, 1870): 737. For similar descriptions of western North Carolina, see Inscoe, *Mountain Masters,*

chap. 1; and various entries in Kevin E. O'Donnell and Helen Hollingsworth, eds., *Seekers of Scenery: Travel Writing from Southern Appalachia, 1840–1900* (Knoxville, 2004).

21. Elisha Mitchell to his wife, Maria, July 20, 1828, Elisha Mitchell Papers, Southern Historical Collection, UNC–Chapel Hill; Thomas L. Clingman, *Selections from the Speeches and Writings of Hon. Thomas L. Clingman* (Raleigh, 1877), 113–15.

22. See Wilma Dykeman, *The French Broad* (New York, 1955), 137–51; John C. Inscoe, "Diversity and Vitality in Antebellum Mountain Society: The Towns of Western North Carolina," in Sam Gray, ed., *The Many Faces of Appalachia* (Boone, N.C., 1984).

23. Malet, *Errand to the South*, 248.

24. William Holland Thomas to his wife, January 1 and June 17, 1861, William Holland Thomas Papers, Duke University.

25. Samuel C. Williams, ed., "Journal of Events of David Anderson Deaderick," *ETHSP* 8 (1936): 130.

26. Queener, "East Tennessee Sentiment," 72; Temple, *East Tennessee and the Civil War*, 76.

27. Williams, "Journal of David Deaderick," 130.

28. Quoted in Crofts, *Reluctant Confederates*, 158. In addition to Crofts, other assessments of Johnson's Unionist views include Ralph W. Haskins, "Andrew Johnson and the Preservation of the Union," *ETHSP* 33 (1961): 43–59; and introduction, Leroy P. Graf and Ralph W. Haskins, eds., *The Papers of Andrew Johnson*, Vol. 4: *1860–1861* (Knoxville, 1976), xix–xxxiv.

29. Knoxville *Whig*, January 26, 1861.

30. Temple, *East Tennessee and the Civil War*, 180–81.

31. Discussion of antebellum mountain attitudes toward slavery and race include Carter G. Woodson, "Freedom and Slavery in Appalachian America," *Journal of Negro History* 1 (April 1916); Richard Drake, "Slavery and Antislavery in Appalachia," *Appalachian Heritage* 14 (Winter 1986): 583–601; and several other essays in Inscoe, ed., *Appalachians and Race*; and "Race and Racism in Nineteenth-Century Appalachia," chap. 1 in this volume. On abolitionist sentiment in East Tennessee, see Asa Earl Martin, "The Anti-Slavery Societies of Tennessee," *Tennessee Historical Magazine* 1 (1915): 261–81; and Durwood Dunn, *An Abolitionist in the Appalachian South: Ezekiel Birdseye on Slavery, Capitalism, and Separate Statehood in East Tennessee, 1841–1846* (Knoxville, 1997).

32. Vernon M. Queener, "William G. Brownlow as an Editor," *ETHSP* 4 (1932): 80; and McKenzie, "Prudent Silence and Strict Neutrality," 81–82. The best account of the Philadelphia debate is found in Coulter, *William G. Brownlow*, 97–109. The intensity of Brownlow's commitment to slavery, though, varied according to the local, regional, or national base of the audience to whom he spoke or for whom he wrote.

33. Temple, *East Tennessee and the Civil War,* 196–97.

34. On sectionally divisive issues within the state, see Thomas P. Abernathy, *From Frontier to Plantation in Tennessee: A Study in Frontier Democracy* (1932; rept., Tuscaloosa, Ala., 1967); and Paul H. Bergeron, *Antebellum Politics in Tennessee* (Lexington, Ky., 1982).

35. William B. Hesseltine, ed., *Dr. J.G.M. Ramsey: Autobiography and Letters* (1954; rept., Knoxville, 2002), 17–18; Robert Tracy McKenzie, "Wealth and Income: The Preindustrial Structure of East Tennessee in 1860," *Appalachian Journal* 21 (1994): 260–79.

36. Jonesborough *Whig,* December 8, 1841, quoted in McKenzie, *Lincolnites and Rebels,* 18.

37. On East–West sectional rivalry in North Carolina, see Thomas E. Jeffrey, "Internal Improvements and Political Parties in Antebellum North Carolina, 1836–1860," *North Carolina Historical Review* 55 (April 1978); Kruman, *Parties and Politics;* Guion G. Johnson, *Ante-Bellum North Carolina: A Social History* (Chapel Hill, 1937); and Inscoe, *Mountain Masters,* chaps. 6 and 7.

38. Thomas L. Clingman, "Address to the Freemen of the First Congressional District of North Carolina on the Recent Senatorial Election, December 18, 1848" (Washington, D.C., 1849), 15; Clingman, "In Defense of the South against the Aggressive Movement of the North, Delivered in the House of Representatives, January 22, 1850," in *Speeches and Writings,* 252. The latter speech was made within the context of the growing sectional controversy of California's entry into the Union as a free state.

39. For an expanded treatment of these ideas, see John C. Inscoe, "Thomas Clingman, Mountain Whiggery, and the Southern Cause," *Civil War History* 33 (March 1987). For other treatments of Clingman's views on secession and southern rights, see Thomas E. Jeffrey, "'Thunder from the Mountains': Thomas Lanier Clingman and the End of Whig Supremacy in North Carolina," *North Carolina Historical Review* 56 (October 1979); Marc W. Kruman, "Thomas L. Clingman and the Whig Party: A Reconsideration," *North Carolina Historical Review* 61 (January 1987). See also Jeffrey, *Thomas L. Clingman: Fireeater from the Carolina Mountains* (Athens, Ga., 1999), chaps. 5 and 6.

40. See, for example, Croft, *Reluctant Confederates,* chap. 1; Robert C. Kenzer, *Kinship and Neighborhood in a Southern Community: Orange County, North Carolina, 1849–1881* (Knoxville, 1987); Martin Crawford, *Ashe County's Civil War: Community and Society in the Appalachian South* (Charlottesville, Va., 2001); Ralph Mann, "Mountain, Land, and Kin Networks: Burkes Garden, Virginia, in the 1840s and 1850s," *Journal of Southern History* 50 (August 1992): 411–34; and Jonathan D. Sarris, *A Separate Civil War: Communities in Conflict in the Mountain South* (Charlottesville, Va., 2005).

6

Highland Households Divided

Familial Deceptions, Diversions, and Divisions in Southern Appalachia's Inner Civil War

co-authored by Gordon B. McKinney

Late in 1863 Madison Drake, a Union captain from Wisconsin, escaped from a Confederate prison in Salisbury, North Carolina, and made his way with a group of fellow fugitives into the state's mountains toward the safety of Union-occupied East Tennessee. In a published account of that journey, he described an encounter he and his party had in Caldwell County, on the eastern slopes of the Blue Ridge. As they approached a small mountain homestead seeking food and directions, Captain Drake and his companions encountered a "vixen" of a woman who immediately recognized them as Yankee fugitives and gave them an impassioned tongue-lashing. Spewing her hatred of them and threatening to turn them in to local authorities, she assured them that they would hang from the same tree on which an earlier Northern fugitive had met his demise, and that she would gladly help carry out the execution.

Yet all hope of aid from this household was not lost, for the crippled husband of this "vixen" sat on the stoop and listened passively "while his spouse was declaiming against us so virulently." When she concluded her tirade, he winked at the men and, hobbling off the stoop, motioned for them to follow him. At a safe distance from the house, this "happy or unhappy husband," as Drake called him, married only six weeks, confided that he sympathized with their cause. He informed them that he had served in the Confederate army until he had been wounded and discharged. Two of his brothers, also Con-

124

federates, had been captured in battle, had "taken the oath," and were doing good business in the North. He was determined to do likewise and saw Drake and his companions as a means for his own escape. He "resolved to befriend" the fugitives and proposed guiding them across the mountains to Union lines if they would return with other forces and take him prisoner, thus allowing him to escape both impending conscription and his shrewish bride. Their conference was cut short by his wife's appearance, which sent the fugitives scurrying on their way, abandoning the "kind-hearted but unfortunate" husband to her supervision.[1]

Drake's story reveals three basic features of wartime loyalties in the mountain South: first, that it often took a very fluid form, the crippled husband having changed sides at least once since the war's outbreak; second, that the divisions between Union and Confederate loyalties were often localized, splitting not only communities and neighborhoods, but even families and households; and finally, that such divisions, and the tensions they generated, often meant some level of deception among family or household members.

If this particular scenario, of a husband concealing his sentiments from his wife, seems an extreme one, it was not unique. It is one of several documented accounts of Appalachian households in which family members—husbands and wives or parents and children—were divided in their loyalties to the northern or southern cause, and in which at least one party felt the need to keep his or her feelings concealed from those with whom they lived. This was part of a phenomenon Michael Fellman, in his study of the Civil War in Missouri, termed "survival lying." Individuals and families who lived in areas sharply divided and wracked by guerrilla warfare were often forced to practice extensive deception and role playing to protect themselves and their households. "Loyalty was not the safest and most common presentation of self during this guerrilla war," Fellman noted. "Prevarication was. Frankness and directness led to destruction more often than did reticence and withdrawal."[2]

Such was certainly true of Southern Appalachia as well. Within the Confederacy, no region experienced more of such internal upheaval, and thus the need for deception and role-playing than did the mountain South. With fewer slaves and more tenuous ties to the market economy, many—but by no means all—highlanders in North Carolina, Tennessee, Virginia, and Georgia found themselves increasingly alienated from the rest of their states as the sectional crisis unfolded. Some expressed vehement opposition to secession and remained firmly committed to the Union cause, either openly or more subversively, long after the war was under way. Many others resigned themselves to what they saw as the inevitability of the new nation into which they were forced by the vast majority of nonmountain residents who dominated their states, but they did so only halfheartedly. A North Carolina woman probably spoke for many as she bemoaned that new reality: "The Union is gone and all these things follow it. . . . How quietly we drifted into such an awful night into the darkness, the lowering clouds, the howling winds, and the ghostly light of our former glory."[3]

Those political and ideological divisions, and the emotional baggage that accompanied them, were already established, if often still fluid, as the secession crisis played out—and they were exacerbated by the war that followed. A stronger political base and more effective leadership kept Unionist sentiment far more viable among East Tennesseans than among western North Carolinians, who quickly capitulated to the Confederate cause after the attack on Fort Sumter, though pockets of Unionist strength continued to exist there, just as Confederate enclaves emerged across the state line in the Tennessee mountains.[4] Thus many households and/or individuals quickly acquired minority status locally as either Confederate or Union sympathizers, depending upon the predominant sentiments of the communities of which they were a part. Some Appalachian families were made more vulnerable by the instability caused by the military and political power struggles that wracked certain highland regions. Such was particularly true of East Tennessee, where Confederate control over a hostile civilian majority during the war's first half capitulated to Union forces from mid-1863 on. The brutal harshness of early Rebel occupation policies led to equally harsh retaliation and vindictiveness, as once-oppressed Unionists became the oppressors of their disunionist neighbors and kinsmen.

From such divisions the war degenerated into a harrowing guerrilla conflict in much of the mountain South. As a Georgia Unionist escaping northward during the war noted as he moved into the Smoky Mountains, "I knew that we were now approaching the border country where some were Secessionists and others Union people, and with each step we took our danger from bushwhackers and scouts increased. . . . All showed me that we were gradually getting into the bloody ground of western North Carolina and East Tennessee, where neighbor fought with neighbor and brother slew brother."[5] In so volatile and uncertain an atmosphere, questions of allegiance and commitment were never far from the surface.

The scholarship on the Civil War in Appalachia is growing by leaps and bounds, and those same issues of identity and divided loyalties now preoccupy historians as much as they did those we study.[6] Although we know much about how highland Unionists fared as minorities and majorities in the context of region, of community, and even of neighborhood, we have not yet explored in any substantive way the extent to which divided loyalties penetrated that most intimate of social institutions: the family. These familial divisions— between spouses and between generations—highlight at the most basic level the uncertainties and fluctuations of ideological commitments among southern highlanders. In examining the variety of motives and influences that pushed families into such awkward and on occasion destructive circumstances, we hope to reveal even more about the multifaceted nature of loyalty and patriotism and how they shaped the localized dynamics of family and kinship structure during this most divisive of American wars.

First, a look at several other examples of such household divisions. An Indiana officer who led a group of escapees from Camp Sorghum in Columbia, South Carolina, toward Union lines in Tennessee crossed paths with three sisters from the Hollinger family in Flat Rock, North Carolina. The fugitives presented themselves as Confederate troops in what they knew to be a predominantly pro-southern neighborhood.[7] Only after the oldest, and boldest, of the three young women (who ranged in age from sixteen to twenty-four) vehemently denounced the men, the South, and the cause for which they were fighting, did the Indianans reveal their true colors. Once the Hollinger sisters were convinced that they were indeed Federal soldiers, they generously offered them aid. Over the next three days they fed the fugitives, provided them concealed shelter, and procured a guide to lead them across the mountains into Tennessee, as they had already done for other Union fugitives.

But the sisters too were engaged in survival lying, for as they explained to the men in their care, two of them were married to Confederate soldiers. They also sought to shield their parents from their activities and refused to let the men in their charge approach their house. Although both parents were equally strong Unionists, the family lived as tenants on the summer estate of the Charlestonian Christopher Memminger, secretary of the Confederate treasury. The daughters believed that the less their father knew of their caretaking efforts for Union soldiers, the safer his position would be, both within this Henderson County community and on Memminger's estate. Thus, in effect, these daughters and wives conducted an Underground Railroad operation for Northern troops and sympathizers without the knowledge of either their parents or their husbands, though the reasons for concealing their activity from them differed.[8]

Despite the predominance of Unionist sentiment among Tennessee's highlanders, strong pockets of Confederate sympathy forced some Unionists there to engage in surreptitious activity, often at considerable risk, to oppose the cause for which other family members fought. Jeannette Mabry of Knox County was married to a rather errant Confederate soldier whose family held strong southern sentiments; yet she remained "unflinchingly true to the Union," and her actions as an informant and as a caretaker of Union soldiers and their families made her legendary among participants of a guerrilla war that devastated Tennessee's Smoky Mountains. Mabry made herself an indispensable contact for Union guides operating in and around Knoxville. No guide, it was said, considered his mission complete unless he stopped to trade intelligence with her. Her relative affluence and social position and the variety of charitable acts she undertook on behalf of refugees and indigents made her a particularly visible figure, and even an inspiration to other Unionists in the area. Oliver Temple, among her most ardent admirers, later wrote of her impact in his decidedly partisan account of the war in East Tennessee: "Around the camp-fires in Kentucky, and in other distant fields where duty called them, no name left behind was uttered more frequently by the exiles, nor with a tenderer or more sincere invocation of a blessing on it, than that of Jeannette Laurimer Mabry."[9] Yet neither Temple nor the other accounts mention what her heroic actions meant to her Confederate husband or in-laws.

Another group of Federal fugitives encountered such deception across generations—a Unionist mother who kept her subversive activity secret from her Confederate son. While fleeing across the remote wilderness of southwestern North Carolina, West Virginian Michael Egan and two companions made contact with Henry Grant, a "fire-tried Unionist." Grant, wrote Egan, wanted to "relieve our distress and give us the shelter of his hospitable roof at once, but there is a slight obstacle in the way—there is an armed rebel soldier in the house." This young Confederate was a neighbor, home on leave, and the dilemma was resolved only when Grant confided in the soldier's widowed mother, who lived in the adjoining house. To their surprise, they found that "she had no real sympathy with the Southern cause," despite the fact that her only son was fighting for it. She agreed to take the Union refugees under her roof, concealing both their presence and their identities from her son.[10]

Not all such ideological splits between spouses involved deception at that most intimate level; in some cases, deceiving others involved a partner's complicity. In the poignant case of a North Carolina highlander, related in a memoir he titled *The Adventures of a Conscript*, W. H. "Buck" Younce revealed the high price he paid romantically for his initial refusal to resort to survival lying. As a committed Unionist in a predominantly Confederate neighborhood in Ashe County, Younce lay low during the war's first year. Only as the pressures of conscription loomed large in the fall of 1862 did he move with others across the state line into Tennessee, a mere six miles from his home, in order to enlist in a Union company. In so doing, he passed by the home of his fiancée, Edith Carroll, and despite the advice of his two companions, Younce separated from them to spend the first night of his trek at the Carroll home.

Younce, a mere twenty years old at the time, was fully aware that the Carrolls, including Edith, the youngest of three daughters, were committed Confederates, even though they were among the few families so inclined in this northeastern corner of Tennessee. On earlier visits, according to Younce, Edith had "used all the persuasive powers at her command to influence me to volunteer in the Confederate army, but I always met her arguments with my side of the question, and her influence proved to no avail." Edith was surprised to see Buck on this particular night, and despite his efforts to obscure his reason for being in her neighborhood, she reached the correct conclusion and protested vehemently: "Oh, no; it can't be possible that you are fleeing for refuge! You can not only be turning your back upon your own country in the darkest hour of our peril, but by this act blasting every hope for an honorable and useful life in the future." Seeking to shame her young beau, Edith ended her speech by proclaiming: "O, if I were only a man, how I would teach you a lesson in patriotism by shouldering my musket and marching to the front!"

Buck responded with an equally impassioned denunciation of "the wicked and unjust cause" she represented and insisted that "the Government to which you refer so eloquently is not my country. . . . I cannot and will not fight for a government that seeks to enslave me and whose cornerstone is slavery." Edith resigned herself to the firm resolve of her betrothed, with a final speech assuring him of her personal loyalty to him. "It grieves me," she said, "that you have determined on this course, but I assure you that, come what may, not a word or deed of mine shall ever do you harm. I will shield and protect you so far as it is in my power to do so."

Alas, such assurances from his hostess proved worthless, when only minutes later a home guard force from Ashe County, having been alerted by some witness (Edith's father, perhaps?) to Younce's presence there, arrived at the house, where they were admitted by Mr. Carroll, who turned Buck over to them. In a dramatic confrontation with his Confederate captors, Edith tearfully inquired about his fate, which led the leader of the group, a Mr. Long, to recognize the reason for Buck's presence in this pro-southern household. "You are insane, or perhaps worse, in love," he accused Buck. "I do not know which: but I do know you are not in love with your country." The young prisoner, still defiant, responded: "Yes, sire, I am in love with Liberty."

Buck's captors escorted him back to North Carolina and into the Ashe County jail. A day later, an influential friend and Confederate captain approached Younce and offered the option of volunteering for service in his company, rather than face conscription or imprisonment as a deserter. Reluctantly, Younce agreed to do so and marched off to fight with fifty other recruits the next day.

"I was the hero of the occasion," he later wrote. "There was more rejoicing over one sinner that repented than over ninety and nine that went not astray." But, he continued, "They could not read my thoughts. My purposes were the same, and I believed that I would find refuge under the flag of my country someday," which he did indeed before the year was out.

This lapse into survival lying proved all too temporary and failed to serve Buck Younce's romantic interests, if indeed Edith Carroll ever heard of his celebrated conversion. These two young lovers were separated by their very different senses of patriotism and a father who proved far less willing than did his daughter to tolerate those differences. Only at the end of Younce's memoir does Edith's name appear again. Writing in 1901, he informed his readers that she had married another man just after the war's end and was the mother of a grown family. "I have never seen her," he concluded, "since that midnight parting before mentioned"; he made no mention at all of a wife or family of his own.[11]

In some cases the tensions caused by these more open divisions within families led to violent consequences. The murder of a prominent Confederate in northwestern North Carolina was the result, in part, of a family squabble resulting from a marriage that linked two families on opposite sides. Late in the spring of 1864, in the North Fork community, which straddled Watauga and Ashe counties, Isaac Wilson was plowing a field on his farm while home on furlough when he was shot and killed by members of the Potter family, into which his niece had married. Tensions between the Confederate Wilsons and the Unionist Potters had escalated as a result of the marriage that had made them in-laws, with particular resentment on the part of the bride's family. As part of the local home guard, other Wilsons had been among those who had executed Jack Potter, the groom's father, several months earlier, and in feudlike retaliation other Potter men and their "bushwhacking" accomplices, lying in ambush in woods surrounding Isaac Wilson's farm, fired upon and killed their in-law, the community's most prominent Confederate soldier.[12]

Another death resulting at least in part from divided allegiances within a Greeneville, Tennessee, household, had even greater historical significance. Because the victim in that case was the Rebel raider and Confederate general John Hunt Morgan, the family in whose home he spent his last night alive remains the most famous, or perhaps infamous, divided house in the mountain South. Greeneville was a major Unionist stronghold and the home of Andrew Johnson, but Morgan knew and often stayed with the town's most notable pro-southern hostess, Catherine Williams. Williams, the widow of a physician, had two sons in Confederate service and a third who was a Federal officer. It may have been Morgan's misfortune that the wife of that third son, herself an ardent Unionist, was living with her mother-in-law when he and his staff took up quarters there on September 4, 1864.

Although historians disagree about the subsequent course of events, circumstantial evidence at the time suggested, and popular opinion quickly assumed, that Lucy Williams, the "Yankee" daughter-in-law, slipped away from the house as soon as she knew Morgan would be staying there and alerted Union forces about fifteen miles away. Early the next morning those troops surrounded the Williams house and killed Morgan as he tried to escape through a nearby vineyard. Lucy herself adamantly maintained her innocence in the affair, but her denials were suspect, given that her continued residence with her mother-in-law probably depended on how convincing she was in establishing her innocence in the events that brought such notoriety to that house and its residents. It is revealing that the presumption of her complicity in Morgan's death, as detested and feared as he was by most Greeneville residents, led to Lucy's own social ostracism in this Unionist community. She was soon forced to move to Knoxville and later was divorced from Catherine Williams's Unionist son. Rather than being hailed as a heroine by her Unionist compatriots, Lucy Williams was shunned for betraying both a house guest and the mother-in-law under whose roof she lived.[13]

Women's roles in these divided households were not always as active or subversive agents. In at least one highland household, a mother served merely as peacemaker between her Union and Confederate sons. A folk history of Tennessee's Smoky Mountains includes the story of Nancy Ghormley's family in Chilhowee. Visits home by two of her sons, one serving the South as Tennessee's provost-marshal, the other as a Confederate recruiting officer, were interrupted when three other sons and two grandsons, all wearing Union blue, also returned home. As the two groups encountered each other in the front yard, "talk became spirited," and "hands rested on sword hilts." At that point Nancy Ghormley took matters into her own hands by walking outside, announcing that dinner was ready, and instructing her off-spring: "Gentlemen, leave your guns and swords in the yard and come in to dinner. You are all my children." The fact that the story ends there implies that these were boys who listened to their mother.[14]

Each of the divided households described above was an anomaly. No patterns emerge from this varied array of stories to suggest that such familial tensions were integral parts of the social upheavals that wracked the mountain South from 1861 to 1865. In fact, each of these cases flies in the face of what was perhaps the most obvious and universally agreed upon factor in Appalachia's war within a war—the remarkable extent of kinship solidarity in terms of wartime loyalties. If the strength of family bonds has long been recognized as a pre-dominant characteristic of southern society, it has been an even more conspicuous facet of Appalachia's image. From early stereotyping of the clannishness and even inbreeding of southern highlanders to the myths and realities of the infamous feuds to sociological analyses of the 1960s and 1970s, family ties for better or worse have been central components in Americans' perceptions of "this strange land and peculiar people."[15]

The recent scholarship on the Civil War in the southern highlands has also acknowledged the centrality of family bonds. Historians recognize—and debate—a number of determinants of loyalties of mountaineers: socioeconomic and slaveholding status, political partisanship, spatial patterns of settlement and market accessibility, migratory patterns and duration of residence, even religious affiliations. But of all the variables that help explain such allegiances, almost all scholars of the region seem to agree that the most immediate and consistent determinant of one's Unionist or Confederate identity lay in the allegiance of one's family.

Community studies make this point particularly well. Phillip Palu-dan's book on the Shelton Laurel massacre in Madison County, North

Carolina; Durwood Dunn's on Cades Cove, Tennessee; Martin Crawford's on the war in Ashe County, North Carolina; Altina Waller's on the Hatfield-McCoy feud in the Tug Valley of Kentucky and West Virginia; Tracy McKenzie's on Knoxville, Tennessee; Jonathan Sarris's on two north Georgia counties; and Ralph Mann's on Sandy Basin and Burkes Garden, Virginia—all find kin networks to have been central in explaining the loyalty or disloyalty of individuals or households within neighborhoods or communities.[16] In the most detailed reconstruction of such localized loyalties, Mann contends that the residents of Sandy Basin looked back at the Civil War "as a war of family against family, or more precisely, family group against family group," and that within neighborhoods that included "a wide range of individual personalities and convictions . . . ultimately kin pressure promoted family group solidarity on matters concerning the war."[17]

So how does one account for these splits within some highland households? No single explanation can account for the various situations described here. For several, though, the very fact of family solidarity serves to explain such divisions rather than contradict them. The ideological differences between married couples more often than not resulted from the differing loyalties of the two families from which they came. It is telling that so many of these households were newly constructed and so many couples newlyweds; one of the most revealing such instances related here is that of the marriage that never took place because of such divisions. The star-crossed, and state line–crossing, lovers Buck Younce and Edith Carroll each adhered to the ideological stance of their parents, even though the Younce family's Unionism and the Carrolls' pro-Confederate stance were minority positions in their respective communities.

Although such differences prevented Buck and Edith from becoming husband and wife, other marriages across similar lines did take place. The Caldwell County "vixen" and her crippled groom, whose story opened this essay, were only just married when he sought to make his escape from her and the Confederate war effort. The Hollinger sisters in Flat Rock adhered to the antislaveholding sentiments of their parents, into whose home they returned, rather than to the Confederate stance of their absent husbands. And the assassination of

Isaac Wilson stemmed in part from resentment of his niece's marriage on the part of her Unionist in-laws.

The sheer tentativeness and fluidity of sentiment in areas characterized by partisan confusion may account for some of the differences among family members. Such wavering was evident from the war's beginning and became even more pronounced as the brutality and hardship of the conflict, or mere war-weariness, set in. In May 1861, in the midst of a Confederate rally in Wilkes County, North Carolina, until that time the area's acknowledged Union stronghold, an observer described the dramatic shift in the community's sentiments but noted the superficial nature of the change: "The people seem nearly united in the Cause of the South," wrote James Gwyn, "but I think if an influential man had got up and espoused the other side, he would have had a good many to join them."[18] Oliver Temple, the earliest chronicler of East Tennessee Unionism, also recognized local pressures as determinants of how individuals formed their allegiances. "Sympathy with friends and kindred," he wrote, "became the bond that united the South. Tens of thousands of men who had no heart for secession, did have heart for their neighbors and kindred. This almost universal fellowship and sympathy drew men together in behalf of a cause which one-half of them disapproved."[19]

It has taken a novelist to pinpoint an even more basic reason that young mountain men at least initially cast their lot with the new southern nation within which they found themselves. In *Cold Mountain*, his celebrated epic of the war in the Carolina highlands, Charles Frazier suggests that baser instincts shaped those decisions. In reflecting on the reasons men go to war, and this war in particular, his central character, Inman, concludes that it was "change" or "the promise of it that made up the war frenzy in the early days. The powerful draw of new faces, new places, new lives. And new laws whereby you might kill all you wanted and not be jailed but decorated." Frazier elaborated: "Men talked of war as if they committed it to preserve what they had and what they believed. But Inman guessed that it was boredom with the repetition of the daily rounds that had made them take up weapons. . . . War took a man out of that circle of regular life and made a season of its own, not much dependent on anything else. He had not been immune to its pull."[20] If indeed it was the novelty of the experience that led highlanders to enlist, such sentiments were no doubt among the first to be abandoned as the war dragged on and the novelty quickly wore off.

The superficial and often fickle nature of those loyalties was fast becoming apparent by early 1862. Increasing desertion rates and other forms of disaffection began to expose what another highlander observed, that many who had sworn allegiance to the Confederacy did so "only from the teeth out."[21] Such shallow commitments may well have led one family member to abandon the cause for which others in the household continued to fight. Desertion was merely one indication of many highlanders' war-weariness and lack of enthusiasm for the cause they had fought for. While hardships at home often lured men back home, sometimes such desertion came sooner than wives or other family members found honorable or acceptable. Thus the crippled husband ready to accompany Madison Drake and company out of the South completely stemmed from war-weariness in battle, while his bride remained staunchly committed to the southern cause that he, unknown to her, had abandoned. By the same token, those men facing more traditional military situations away from home were not subject to the same demoralizing home front hardships, deprivations, or upheaval that made spouses, elderly parents, or younger siblings more susceptible to fluctuations in their loyalties and commitments to the war. The mother who agreed to shelter Michael Egan and his companions had undergone a thorough change of heart that her Confederate son, still in uniform, had not.

Equally significant, guerrilla warfare forced full families into a level of participation that more traditional warfare never did. In the process gender roles were blurred or even reversed. Women sometimes found themselves taking far more active, even dominant, roles in protecting their men or defending their property; they also found opportunities to provide military and other intelligence, to aid fugitives and refugees, and on occasion to betray enemies. In the fullest treatment of the subject, Michael Fellman wrote of Missouri's "inside war": "Disintegration, demoralization, and perverse adaptation engulfed women's behavior and self conceptions as it assaulted the family and undermined male-female and female-female . . . relationships.

Like male civilians in a guerrilla war theater, women were both victims and actors."[22]

Such was certainly the case in Southern Appalachia as well. Both soldiers and civilians recognized the clout women wielded in waging the unconventional warfare in the mountains. Given the circumstances that later led to the death of his commander, there is a certain irony in the fact that it was one of John Hunt Morgan's officers who observed of East Tennesseans: "Did I stay long in this country, I should fear losing that respect and regard for the female sex, which I have been raised to have—here they unsex themselves, and by their conduct, lose all claim to be respected and regarded as ladies. . . . Was I in authority here, I should treat them as men."[23]

For some mountain women, the responsibilities such localized warfare thrust upon them in their husbands' absence instilled an independence of spirit that led them to form loyalties different from those of the men who had left them. Or if other factors may have led to their differing loyalties, the new assertiveness either forced upon or granted to them led women to express their sentiments in visible or vocal ways. Although many engaged in survival lying for very practical reasons even within their own households, others spoke out or even lashed out, becoming like the "talking heroine" that a Winchester, Virginia, woman admiringly labeled a neighbor.[24] Given the volatility of local feelings and the levels of violence across gender lines, to speak one's convictions was often very risky. Other women—such as Jeannette Mabry, Lucy Williams, and the Hollinger sisters—did much more than talk. Through their actions in support of the Union and Federal troops, they actually shaped to varying degrees the dynamics of the conflict in their area.

Either articulating or acting upon their convictions, particularly when they differed from those of other family members, these women demonstrated another significant facet of their experience: they were not apolitical. The wives, mothers, and daughters in most of the households depicted in this essay not only made their views known to at least one observer, through whom they entered the historical record. They also took distinctive stands, adhered with great conviction to one cause or the other, and exhibited a strong sense of duty that sometimes put them and their households at considerable risk. It is telling that of all the examples cited here, only one woman ever took a neutral stand—Nancy Ghormley in her efforts to keep the peace among her sons at the dinner table.

Finally, one must acknowledge what is missing from most of these stories: how these household divisions were ultimately resolved. Although we have used the word "tensions" in describing these relationships, in most cases we have no direct evidence of that tension between spouses or between parents and children. This is in part because of the deception that prevented any open confrontation between family members, and in part, because family members were separated from each other, most often with a husband engaged in military service far from home. But what repercussions were there when the war ended, when these couples and other family members were reunited? Did love conquer all, and the joy of reunion override differing allegiances that by then would have been rendered irrelevant? Did survival lying perhaps extend through those reunions, with the hope that a lack of knowledge of a spouse's activities would allow a marriage to survive? The few answers we have from the couples we have dealt with here are not encouraging. The betrothal of a Unionist and his Confederate fiancée was broken as a result of these divisions. And in at least one instance, that of Lucy Williams, divorce resulted from her all too fateful betrayal against the Confederacy, or at least the notoriety attached to the assumption of betrayal. In the case of the Unionist cripple and his Confederate bride, one sees a marriage with very low odds of weathering the war-imposed tensions it would have had to endure. But we have no way of knowing the levels of deception, of forgiveness, or of affection that may have kept other marriages and households intact despite the tensions that had divided them during the war years.

A somewhat different scenario of household division is offered as a conclusion. If the practical necessities sometimes forced the survival lying of spouses, parents, and children, such duplicitous dual loyalties could, on occasion, provide unexpected benefits for those forced into such situations. Napoleon Banner and G. W. Dugger of Banner Elk, North Carolina, sent five sons between them into Union regiments in Tennessee but were themselves "detailed" by Confederate authorities to employment at the ironworks in nearby Cranberry. Such entanglements secured their safety, as Dugger's son Shepherd later explained: "The Yankees passed over Napoleon for working for the South because he had three sons . . . in the Federal army, and the Homeguard let him off for being a Union man because he was hammering iron for the Confederacy." The elder Dugger was spared for the same reasons. "Thus," Shepherd Dugger summarized, "father and Napoleon sat on the top of a four-pointed barbed wire fence that divided the two armies, and so well did they balance themselves that they sat there four years and never got their hide split."[25]

Many Appalachian families found themselves perched precariously atop a barbed-wire fence during those four years of war. Some managed to maintain their balance better than others. In many parts of the southern highlands, Unionists could not afford to flaunt openly their allegiance to what remained a minority cause and an enemy force for the region at large. The sheer variety of ways in which they maintained dual identities and the reasons they chose to do so—ranging from conscientious and ideological to opportunistic and mercenary— testify both to the variables in human nature and to the vacillations in loyalties and commitments toward the war and the fluidity with which they exerted themselves. For the most part, family bonds provided a vital resource in southern highlanders' attempts to survive the multiple pressures—social, economic, military—the conflict imposed on the region. Yet the fact that, at least on occasion, such pressures forced families to fall on opposite sides of that conflict, often in deceptive or subversive ways, adds to our appreciation of the momentous local impact of this most uncivil of wars on that part of the South in which the bonds of kinship and family otherwise proved most durable.

Notes

1. J. Madison Drake, *Fast and Loose in Dixie* (New York: Authors' Publishing, 1880), 140–41.

2. Michael Fellman, *Inside War: Guerrilla Conflict in Missouri during the Civil War* (New York: Oxford University Press, 1989), 48–49.

3. Gordon B. McKinney, *Southern Mountain Republicans, 1865–1900: Politics and the Appalachian Community* (Chapel Hill: University of North Carolina Press, 1978), 19.

4. The literature on East Tennessee Unionism is vast. Among the most recent assessments of sentiments there during the secession crisis are Jona-

than M. Atkins, *Parties, Politics, and the Sectional Conflict in Tennessee, 1832–1861* (Knoxville: University of Tennessee Press, 1997), chap. 8; Noel C. Fisher, *War at Every Door: Partisan Politics and Guerrilla Violence in East Tennessee, 1860–1869* (Chapel Hill: University of North Carolina Press, 1997), chap. 2; Peter Wallenstein, "'Helping to Save the Union': The Social Origins, Wartime Experiences, and Military Impact of White Union Troops from East Tennessee," and W. Todd Groce, "The Social Origins of East Tennessee's Confederate Leadership," both in *The Civil War in Appalachia: Collected Essays,* ed. Kenneth W. Noe and Shannon Wilson (Knoxville: University of Tennessee Press, 1997); and Robert Tracy McKenzie's essay in *Enemies of the Country: New Perspectives on Unionists in the Civil War South,* ed. John C. Inscoe and Robert C. Kenzer (Athens: University of Georgia Press, 2001). On the minority Confederate presence in that region, see W. Todd Groce, *Mountain Rebels: East Tennessee Confederates and the Civil War, 1860–1870* (Knoxville: University of Tennessee Press, 1999); Daniel E. Sutherland, ed., *A Very Violent Rebel: The Civil War Diary of Ellen Renshaw House* (Knoxville: University of Tennessee Press, 1996); and Robert Tracy McKenzie, *Lincolnites and Rebels: A Divided Town in the American Civil War* [Knoxville] (New York: Oxford University Press, 2006).

On secession sentiment in western North Carolina, see John C. Inscoe, *Mountain Masters: Slavery and the Sectional Crisis in Western North Carolina* (Knoxville: University of Tennessee Press, 1989), chaps. 8 and 9. For a comparison of the two regions, see "The Secession Crisis and Regional Self-Image," the previous chapter in this volume.

5. W. H. Parkins, *How I Escaped* (New York: Home Publishing, 1889), 114–15.

6. In addition to other work cited throughout these notes, the first four essays in Noe and Wilson's *Civil War in Appalachia* focus specifically on this issue. The eleven essays in that volume reflect the extent and range of current scholarship on the war in the highland South, as do several essays in Daniel E. Sutherland, ed., *Guerrillas, Unionists, and Violence on the Confederate Home Front* (Fayetteville: University of Arkansas Press, 1999); and several in Inscoe and Kenzer, *Enemies of the Country.*

7. The fugitive narratives of Union soldiers or escaped prisoners provide rich and underutilized sources on the war and its impact on the areas through which they moved. For an analysis of those moving through the Southern Appalachians, see chap. 8, "Moving through Deserter Country," in this volume.

8. J. V. Hadley, *Seven Months a Prisoner* (New York: Charles Scribner's Sons, 898), 180–86. In the final paragraph of his memoir, Hadley stated that in the summer of 1897, he returned to North Carolina and visited the Hollinger sisters, "and found them all alive—all married and happy in their mountain homes, with large families about them" (258).

9. Oliver P. Temple, *East Tennessee and the Civil War* (1899; rept., Freeport, N.Y.: Books for Libraries Press, 1971), 426–27. For other references to Jeannette Mabry, see Georgia Lee Tatum, *Disloyalty in the Confederacy* (Chapel Hill: University of North Carolina Press, 1934), 151; Paul A. Whelan, "Unconventional Warfare in East Tennessee, 1862–1865" (master's thesis, University of Tennessee, 1963), 139; and William A. Stasser, "'A Terrible Calamity Has Befallen Us': Unionist Women in Civil War East Tennessee," *Journal of East Tennessee History* 71 (1999): 74. On the questionable Confederate status of Jeannette's husband, George Mabry, and the much stronger credentials of his brother, Joseph, see McKenzie, *Lincolnites and Rebels*, 131–34.

10. Michael Egan, *The Flying Gray-Haired Yank; or, The Adventures of a Volunteer* (Marietta, Ohio: Edgewood Press, 1888), 325–28. On the strains that generational differences within households often put on mothers and wives, see Gordon B. McKinney, "Women's Role in Civil War Western North Carolina," *North Carolina Historical Review* 69 (January 1992): 52–53, 55.

11. W. H. Younce, *The Adventures of a Conscript* (Cincinnati: Editor Publishing, 1910), 5–16, 105. For a discussion of the authenticity of Younce's memoir, see Martin Crawford, *Ashe County's Civil War: Community and Society in the Mountain South* (Charlottesville: University Press of Virginia, 2001).

12. The fullest and clearest account of this tangled affair, interpreted as an example of the power of family solidarity in the face of divided allegiances, is found in chap. 5 of Crawford, *Ashe County's Civil War*. See also the memoir of Isaac Wilson's son, and commentary on it in *Appalachian Journal* 34 (Fall 2006), and "Guerrilla War and Remembrance," chap. 15 in this volume. For an earlier, far less complete version of Isaac Wilson's murder, see John Preston Arthur, *A History of Watauga County, North Carolina, with Sketches of Prominent Families* (Richmond, Va.: Everett Waddey, 1915), 170–71. The same book includes a detailed account of another, similar set of tensions that led to a violent break between Keith Blalock and his stepfather and stepbrothers (163–64).

13. The most detailed accounts of Morgan's death and Lucy Williams's role in the incident are Cecelia Fletcher Holland, *Morgan and His Raiders: A Biography of the Confederate General* (New York: Macmillan, 1942), 339–48; and James A. Ramage, *Rebel Raider: The Life of John Hunt Morgan* (Lexington: University Press of Kentucky, 1986), 232–40. For a more recent historiographical discussion of the incident, see Fisher, *War at Every Door*, appendix B, "Union Informants and the Death of John Hunt Morgan," 186–87.

14. Alberta and Carson Brewer, *Valley So Wild: A Folk History* (Knoxville: East Tennessee Historical Society, 1975), 170.

15. A mere sampling of the literature on Appalachian families and kinship includes John C. Campbell, *The Southern Mountaineer and His Homeland* (New York: Russell Sage Foundation, 1921); Patricia D. Beaver, *Rural Community in the Appalachian South* (Lexington: University Press of Kentucky, 1986); Jack E. Weller, *Yesterday's People: Life in Contemporary Appalachia* (Lexington: University Press of Kentucky, 1965); *We're All Kin: A Cultural Study of a Mountain Community* (Knoxville: University of Tennessee Press, 1981); Dwight B. Billings and Kathleen M. Blee, *The Road to Poverty: The Making of Wealth and Hardship in Appalachia* (New York: Cambridge University Press, 1999); and many of the works cited in the following notes.

16. Phillip S. Paludan, *Victims: A True Story of the Civil War* (Knoxville: University of Tennessee Press, 1981); Durwood Dunn, *Cades Cove: The Life and Death of a Southern Mountain Community, 1818–1937* (Knoxville: University of Tennessee Press, 1988), chap. 5; Altina L. Waller, *Feud: Hatfields, McCoys, and Social Change in Appalachia, 1860–1900* (Chapel Hill: University of North Carolina Press, 1988), 29–33; Ralph Mann, "Family Group, Family Migration, and the Civil War in the Sandy Basin of Virginia," *Appalachian Journal* 19 (Summer 1992): 374–93; Mann, "Guerrilla Warfare and Gender Roles: Sandy Basin, Virginia, as a Test Case," *Journal of the Appalachian Studies Association* 5 (1993): 59–66; Martin Crawford, "Confederate Volunteering and Enlistment in Ashe County, North Carolina," *Civil War History* 37 (March 1991): 29–50, and "The Dynamics of Mountain Unionism: Federal Volunteers of Ashe County, North Carolina," in *Civil War in Appalachia,* ed. Noe and Wilson, 55–77; Jonathan D. Sarris, "Anatomy of an Atrocity: The Madden Branch Massacre and Guerrilla Warfare in North Georgia, 1862–1865," *Georgia Historical Quarterly* 77 (Winter 1993): 679–710; Sarris, "An Execution in Lumpkin County: Localized Loyalties in North Georgia's Civil War," in *Civil War in Appalachia,* ed. Noe and Wilson, 131–57; and Robert Tracy McKenzie, "Prudent Silence and Strict Neutrality: The Parameters of Unionism in Parson Brownlow's Knoxville, 1860–1863," in *Enemies of the Country,* ed. Inscoe and Kenzer, 73–96. See also John W. Shaffer, "Loyalties in Conflict: Union and Confederate Sentiment in Barbour County," *West Virginia History* 50 (1991): 109–28.

The fullest account of divided families elsewhere in the nation is by Amy Murrell Taylor, in *The Divided Family in Civil War America* (Chapel Hill: University of North Carolina Press, 2005), which focuses on the border states of both the Union and the Confederacy.

17. Mann, "Family Group, Family Migrations," 374, 385.

18. James Gwyn to Rufus T. Lenoir, May 2, 1861, Lenoir Family Papers, Southern Historical Collection, University of North Carolina, Chapel Hill. For more on the tentativeness of Unionist sentiment, see John C. Inscoe and Gordon B. McKinney, *The Heart of Confederate Appalachia: Western*

North Carolina in the Civil War (Chapel Hill: University of North Carolina Press, 2000), chap. 4.

19. Oliver P. Temple, *Notable Men of Tennessee from 1833 to 1875: Their Times and Their Contemporaries* (New York: Cosmopolitan Press, 1912), 243.

20. Charles Frazier, *Cold Mountain* (New York: Atlantic Monthly Press, 1997), 218.

21. Quoted in Paludan, *Victims,* 64.

22. Fellman, *Inside War,* 193. Fellman's chapter 5 is devoted to women's roles in Missouri's guerrilla war. On the role of women in Appalachia's Civil War, see McKinney, "Women's Role"; Dunn, *Cades Cove,* chap. 5, esp. 135–38; Mann, "Guerrilla Warfare and Gender Roles," 59–67; "Coping in Confederate Appalachia," the next chapter in this volume; David H. McGee, "'Home and Friends': Kinship, Community, and the Role of Elite Women in Caldwell County during the Civil War," *North Carolina Historical Review* 74 (October 1997): 363–88; and Stasser, "A Terrible Calamity."

23. G. W. Hunt to John Hunt Morgan, November 26, 1864, quoted in Fisher, *War at Every Door,* 117.

24. Quoted in Drew Gilpin Faust, *Mothers of Invention: Women of the Slaveholding South in the American Civil War* (Chapel Hill: University of North Carolina Press, 1996), 200.

25. Shepherd M. Dugger, *War Trails of the Blue Ridge* (Blue Ridge, N.C.: n.p., 1932), 204–5.

7

Coping in Confederate Appalachia

Portrait of a Mountain Woman and Her Community at War

Late in the summer of 1863, an anonymous "Voice from Cherokee County" wrote a letter to the *North Carolina Standard* in Raleigh, bemoaning the oppressive impact of Confederate policy on the state's mountain region. He paid tribute to those highlanders he maintained were most victimized by the hardships—its women, that "class of beings entitled to the deepest sympathy of the Confederate government . . . the wives, children, mothers, sisters, and widows" left behind by those fighting for the southern cause. This voice from the state's westernmost county went on to extol "the thousand instances of women's patriotism, in resigning without a murmur the being in whom her affections centered, to all the horrors of war, and after her husband's departure, uncomplainingly assume all the duties of the sterner sex; accompanied by her little brood, labor from mom to night in the cornfield, or wield the axe to fell the sturdy oak."[1] The glorification of Confederate womanhood was obviously well under way by the war's midpoint and was pervasive enough to have reached what was among the remotest parts of the Confederacy and of the Carolina highlands.

Among those "thousand instances" so glorified by the chivalric Cherokee County resident was Mary Bell in adjacent Macon County. She did indeed spend much of the war laboring in the cornfield, chopping wood, and caring for a growing "little brood." But she did not do so "uncomplainingly" or "without a murmur," and most assuredly, she did not do so from any patriotic sentiments toward the Confederacy or sense of duty to the southern cause.

This essay is an examination of Mary Bell's Civil War experience.

Her husband left home in November 1861, and, except for intermittent visits and an extended stay in 1863, was gone until February 1865. Throughout that period, Mary wrote lengthy letters at frequent intervals that provide the basis for reconstructing in considerable detail the impact of the war on her, her family, and her community.[2] At one level, her account serves as a case study of the plight of Appalachian women on the Confederate home front; at the same time, it provides another variable to the growing collection of individual experiences through which historians are coming to new understandings of how the Civil War shaped the status and role of southern women and how those women, in turn, affected the war effort.

In *Womenfolks,* her 1983 paean to her southern distaff ancestry, Shirley Abbott maintained, with tongue somewhat in cheek, that "the fortitude of upper-class southern women during the Civil War is one of the sacrosanct themes in the mythology of the region: great-granny defying those blue-coated sons-of-bitches under the portico, just after she had personally buried the silver and put down a small mutiny among the field hands. . . . The backwoods women (lacking any such melodramatic props) had little to be heroic about."[3] That view may well have reflected not only popular perceptions but also the focus of scholarly scrutiny at the time. The latter at least has changed substantially in the intervening years, thanks to significant work dealing with the ways in which southern women at all socioeconomic levels and in various parts of the Confederacy coped with the crisis.[4] Even for Appalachian women, who would certainly qualify under Abbott's categorization of those whose efforts were so unappreciated, such neglect is being remedied as historians of the region are providing new insights into the dynamics of highland home fronts from a variety of angles.[5]

Thus Mary Bell's version of the war years does not so much fill a void as it corroborates, amplifies, and personalizes the conclusions drawn by other studies of wartime women at community, regional, or national levels, while at the same time offering some unexpected variations on a number of those conclusions. Bell's vivid descriptions and often outspoken assessments of both her own problems at home and those of her neighbors provide a unique perspective on a mountain community caught in a war from which, in some respects, it was snugly insulated, yet that in other respects intruded daily into the lives of its residents. Bell's letters also portray a woman who grew over the course of those years without her husband. Though not always conscious of the direction or degree of that change, she left in her letters a rich chronicle of the adjustments in her life and in her attitudes from 1861 to 1865 that allows historians to trace the course of her personal development in the midst of crisis.

Mary Bell was twenty-six years old when she moved with her husband to his North Carolina hometown only a year before the Civil War broke out. Little is known of the early life of either husband or wife. A native of Rome, Georgia, Mary married Alfred Bell in 1856 and moved with him three years later to the mountain community of Clayton in Georgia's northeastern corner, where Alfred's older brother was a physician. Alfred himself was a dentist and went into practice with his brother for about a year, when he decided to return to Franklin, North Carolina, just thirty miles north of Clayton, where his father, Benjamin W. Bell, among the community's founding fathers and the county's first sheriff, lived and operated a jewelry and clock-making business.[6] The Alfred Bell family, which then included two young daughters, bought a house in the village and a nearby farm. Alfred quickly established a thriving dental practice and took an active role in his father's enterprise as well. The farm he turned over to a tenant and hired slaves, whose activities he closely supervised.[7]

Franklin was a small community of fewer than 150 residents in 1860, when the Bells made it their home. The seat of Macon County, Franklin was also the county's only village, serving the commercial and governmental needs of its more than six thousand inhabitants. Situated in the Little Tennessee River valley on the edge of the Great Smoky Mountains about seventy miles southwest of Asheville, Franklin was built on the site of what had once been a sacred Cherokee village and was settled by whites only after the area was wrenched from that tribe in the 1830s. In some respects it remained a frontier community throughout the antebellum period. The few travelers who reached that remote southwest corner of North Carolina commented on the physical beauty and fertile setting but noted too the only partial appearance of civilization. British geologist George Featherstonaugh, moving through the area in the early 1840s, wrote of

Franklin: "What a dreadful state of things! Here was a village, more beautifully situated . . . that might become an earthly Paradise, if education, religion, and manners prevailed. . . . But I could not learn that there was a man of education in the place disposed to set an example of the value of sobriety to the community." Some progress may have been made by the time Charles Lanman journeyed through the area five years later, for his comment, after encountering a few leading citizens, was that, "like all the intelligent people of this county, [they were] very polite and well informed." He went on to describe the village as "romantically situated on the Little Tennessee . . . surrounded with mountains and as quiet and pretty a hamlet as I have yet seen among the Alleghanies."[8]

In 1860, Macon County was extremely rural, even by Appalachian standards, with Franklin the only place that bears some semblance to a concentrated community. Like most mountain holdings, Macon's 632 farms were relatively small; almost 60 percent had less than fifty acres and only 12 percent had more than a hundred acres. The diversity of the farms' output was also typical. Corn was the basic commodity, but it was supplemented by a variety of grains, as well as apples and peaches (the majority of which were distilled into their more potent liquid form). Sixty-two slaveholders (6.5 percent of the household heads) and 519 slaves (8.6 percent of the population) lived in Macon County in 1860, both totals higher than those of adjacent counties. Only two men owned more than twenty slaves; one of them, Dillard Love, a member of one of western North Carolina's oldest and most influential families, owned seventy-one.[9]

During the secession crisis, feeling in the county was strongly divided as to whether or when North Carolina should withdraw from the Union. But unionism never gained the firm foothold there that it did in other parts of the Carolina highlands, and Macon County residents rallied to the Confederate cause as soon as the opportunity presented itself. Soon after the war broke out, Franklin became a recruiting center for Confederate troops, and Macon County, like the rest of the southwestern counties, quickly fulfilled its initial enlistment quota as called by Governor John Ellis.[10] Alfred Bell delayed in joining that surge. Only in the fall of 1861 did he raise a company of Macon County volunteers and, as their captain, lead them to Asheville, where as part of North Carolina's 39th Regiment they spent three cold and frustrating months awaiting assignment to active duty. "We are very willing," he assured his wife at the end of January, 1862, "to leave this Buncombe War & goe to Jeff Davises War."[11]

Two days after he left home in November 1861, the correspondence between Alfred and Mary Bell was under way, and her new roles as wife, manager, and local citizen began to take shape. Among the most striking of those roles, as reflected in her early letters, was her very active interest in Captain Bell's military affairs. She was never shy about expressing her views or dispensing advice as to how he should conduct himself in his relationships with his officers and fellow soldiers or in commenting on the military affairs of other local residents. In her first letter, Mary reported to Alf that two Macon County men who she felt should have gone into his company were thinking of organizing their own instead. She expressed contempt for such unrealistic ambitions and for those of another acquaintance who had stayed home "to attend to his business," waiting to enlist until he could do so as captain of his own company. "I am in hopes he will not get into your regiment," she wrote, "unless he would volunteer & risk his chances" regarding officership.[12]

Mary continued to provide regular reports of the comings and goings of her husband's volunteers and of other Macon County men who had or had not enlisted, along with her speculation as to their motives for doing so. On several occasions she told him of efforts to retrieve his men and others who either temporarily or permanently abused furlough privileges. Because his company remained so close to home for so long, keeping the men in camp and committed to the cause proved difficult. By the end of January, Bell was referring to some in his company as "traitors and deserters" and inquiring of his wife as to their whereabouts.[13]

One of those, Tom McDowell, fled south into Georgia to avoid arrest. Mary reported that McDowell's wife blamed Bell for his fugitive status and that "she would rather see him die than see him go into your company." Mary feared that Mrs. McDowell and others "were making up rumors against" Bell, presumably for his role in the attempt to reclaim his troops. Those rumors were the first hint of military tensions growing out of the discontent of fellow residents. Mary was quick to dismiss the worth of those elusive charges, advising Alf that he should tell Tom McDowell what she had heard another wife tell her defecting husband: that he "was a disgrace to the Southern Confederacy and Jeff Davis would blush to own him." "If I were you," Mary mused, "I would blush to have such a man as Tom in my company. If you were to ever get in a close place he would be certain to stump his toe and fall down. The yankees would get him and great would be the loss."[14]

Mary was just as resentful of wives who had not yet had to make the same sacrifice she was making. In March 1862, she admitted that for herself and a neighbor, "our daily prayer is that a draft will come and take every married man that can leave home as well as our husbands could. It makes us very mad to see other women enjoying themselves with their husbands and ours gone." A month later she repeated in even stronger terms her discontent at the inequality of local sacrifice as she saw it: "Whilst some are made to mourn all the days of their lives on account of some dear one who has died whilst fighting for their country, others will be glorying in the wealth they have made by staying at home and speculating while the war was going on and other poor wretches were fighting for them."[15]

It is quite apparent, however, that Mary's resentment of those not serving the cause militarily or otherwise had little to do with her own commitment to the Confederacy. As early as March 5, 1862, she urged Alf not to reenlist when given the option. Only the week before, he and his company had been sent to East Tennessee, already the site of considerable activity as what amounted to a Confederate occupation force sought to control a large and unruly Unionist populace. That move, along with the arrival of the first of many corpses to be returned to Franklin, may have inspired sudden concern in the young Mrs. Bell for her husband's safety. "I do not care what inducements is held out," she insisted, "you must not enlist." Nor did she hide her very personal reasons for such a request: "I hope for my sake you not think of doing it for I am a poor miserable wretch without you—the world is dark and dreary and everything is a blank without the presence and cheering smiles and devoted love of my dear husband."[16]

Mary laid blame for this bleak situation squarely at the feet of one man and more than once cursed him for the misery he had inflicted upon her. "I believe we have a just God, and that sooner or later Abraham Lincoln will meet with his just rewards. I may be called heartless and wicked, and doubtless am, but it does one good to think that a retribution awaits such tyrants as old Abe."[17] But such hatred of Lincoln did not necessarily entail any patriotism for the new nation created in response to his election. Mary's apathy toward the Confederate cause was apparent from her earliest letters. Never did she profess any patriotic sense of duty as a motive or reason for pride in her activities and considerable achievements during the course of the war. Indeed, on more than one occasion she showed as much contempt for Confederate policies and efforts as she did for the Union cause and its most localized manifestation, the detested "Tories."

In her first letter to Alf, Mary wrote of some dresses she was having made and asked him if he could obtain needed materials more cheaply in Asheville than she could get them in Franklin. "I do not ask the Yankees any odds if I can get thread and dye stuffs. . . . I see no sense in relying on things that are made entirely in the South." The following May she was somewhat derisive in describing the efforts of local women who, at the request of Governor Ellis's wife, were "getting up a subscription here to make a gunboat for the defense of North Carolina." "Don't you think it is too late to think about making gunboats?" she asked Alf. She contributed only fifty cents to the cause, and her daughters gave twenty-five cents that "their grandpa gave them to throw in." She claimed she "told the girls I had sent all [to] the gunboat I thought I ought to send, that I would be willing to subscribe a good deal more if I had you at home."[18]

By April 1862, Mary could take some satisfaction in the fact that a Confederate conscription act had passed, but she was realistic—or cynical—enough to predict that it "will take some who ought to go as well as some who really are excusable, whilst some will be left behind still who ought to go." She was quick to agree with her husband that the proposed age span of eighteen to thirty-five should have been extended, for, she observed, "there are men here at 45 just as able and who have just as much right to go as men at 35." Ultimately, her interest in any conscription policy was how it would affect her beloved Alf, and she was not particularly optimistic, fearing that "it will also hold on some who are already gone that ought to have the privilege of coming home a while if they wish too."[19]

Like many wives, Mary Bell expressed grave concern about her husband's moral character. Her letters to him admonished him on his sobriety ("Mashburn says that he got drunk while he was gone with you, I am afraid that you had it on the road and by so doing gave him encouragement to drink"); urged him to take up religion ("My earnest prayer is that you will prepare yourself for a better life"); and questioned various vices of which she had heard rumors, especially infidelity ("Reports are that you, Capt. Bell, a man in whom evry one had the utmost confidence as being a true devoted and virtuous husband, could play cards, drink whiskey, and ____ as many women as any man in camps and by so doing had won the love and respect of nearly evry man in the regiment . . . I should think that if by such acts I had to gain the love of men, I should consider it dearly").[20]

Strikingly, the pervasiveness of alcoholism filled her letters and homilies. As even outside observers had noted of Franklin and other mountain villages, alcohol abuse was very much in evidence among the citizens well before the war, and the strains of the crisis merely aggravated the situation.[21] Mary commented frequently on the drunkenness of local soldiers on leave. When Bell had sent men back home to round up deserters, she reported, "in place of going sober as they ought to have done, they had to have whiskey and get drunk." She particularly resented the fact that they had drawn her younger brother Dee into their company. He got "drunk with the rest of them & has been drinking ever since." She hoped that Alf could persuade Dee to go to war "as the best thing that can be done for him." Nor was she alone in seeing the therapeutic value of military service for alcoholic menfolk. She told Alf of an acquaintance whose public and reckless displays of drunkenness had made his wife so "perfectly miserable" that "I think she would be glad for him to join the army hoping it will do him some good."[22]

But where Mary's advice and wifely wisdom proved most needed —though there is little indication that Alf listened—was in her counsel on a series of disciplinary actions that stemmed from the mutual dislike of Bell and his commanding officer, David Coleman. That situation, which took most of the war to play itself out, is revealing not only in regard to Alfred Bell's problems and his wife's insights into them, but also for its indication of the active if long-distant roles wives could play in company politics and military relationships.

Soon after Bell's regiment moved to East Tennessee, it reorganized and elected new officers. Much to Alf's chagrin, David Coleman, a well-connected Asheville businessman and legislator who had served as the regiment's colonel since its formation, was reelected to that position.[23] Captain Bell conveyed his bitter disappointment to Mary, who knew her husband's hot temper and independent streak better than anyone else, sensed problems arising from his resentment, and urged him "not to be too hasty" in any decision he made about leaving the regiment for another. "Remember," she cautioned, "you are all fighting for the same cause and there ought not to be any tumult or strife among you." Perhaps unconsciously, she even adopted Lincoln's biblical epigram to make her point. "A house divided against itself," she concluded, "cannot stand."[24]

Mary's fears were confirmed when, in June 1862, her husband initiated and circulated a petition among his fellow officers calling for Coleman's resignation as colonel on the grounds that he spent far too much time drunk and was reluctant to lead his men—or allow others to do so—into battle. Coleman responded by promptly arresting Bell and four other officers, suspending their commands, and threatening them with courts-martial. Mary showed greater concern over Alf's fate than he did because much of her information on her husband's behavior came from other wives in Franklin. She urged moderation, writing Alf that "I do not want you to be satisfied with men who do not do their duty, but I do not want you to get prejudiced and think everything they do is wrong. Perhaps you are prejudiced against Coleman," she gently suggested. "It is rumored here that you have been, or are about to be, reduced in rank for some hand you took in the election. Has anything happened that could start such a rumor?" Alf refused to take the situation seriously and remained cocky, claiming that he welcomed a court-martial because it would accomplish his ultimate goal, "an investigation of the facts as they are." He reported that "our prayers is peace or a battle that our rongs may be avenged . . . nobody scared thoe."[25]

Mary's letters during that period were far more consumed with Alf's predicament than his own were, and she mustered a variety of tones in responding to it. In the same letter she could boost his ego ("I do not want to make you vain, but the news got back home that you are the most popular captain in the regiment"); gently humor him ("You must not get too saucy and get into mischief . . . if you do and I find it out I will request Coleman to put you to digging up stumps"); offer serious advice ("Please be calm and do nothing in your difficulties that you can be reproached with. I do not think you will do anything wrong if you will govern your temper"); and even rationalize the situation from her own perspective ("I feel almost in hopes that you will be cashiered and then your men cannot blame you . . . as I have a use for you at home").[26] Only rarely was she explicit in laying out her worst fears: "I am in dread continually for fear that you will in a mad fit do something you ought not to do. I hope for my sake and the sake of your little children that you will be willing to take more than you would otherwise do." That was not the first time she reminded him of his growing family: "You must not forget that you have a darling babe at home that you have never seen."[27]

Though the situation seems to have abated with no real resolution by the end of the summer, Alf's problems with his colonel continued. He had to write Mary in September, "I am againe under arest againe not by myself." Coleman had ordered the arrest of all officers for "not marching our companys in line." Bell dismissed the trumped-up charge as more indicative of the disturbed commander's state of mind than of Bell's own behavior. "He is drunk all the time," he claimed. "The boys pray for a fight."[28]

The ongoing divisiveness within this western Carolina regiment was apparently a major topic of discussion among the women of Franklin. Sooner or later many sided with either Coleman or Bell, most likely reflecting the biases of husbands who served with both. Yet even women whose husbands were not associated with the regiment had opinions on the matter. Mary Bell reported a visit from Lizzie Woodfin, the wife of the community's only physician, who thus was still at home. She assured Mary that she was "as bitter against Coleman as any of us." Mary had doubts about her sincerity, however. Earlier Mary had written of a public spat between Mrs. Woodfin and a Mrs. Copeland, and now she feared that the former would hear that "I had written to camp about her quarrel" and "will probably not like it if she hears it."[29]

The role of wives at home proved even more central to a later episode in the ongoing feud. In March 1864, with his regiment still intact and stationed near Pollard, Alabama, Bell wrote Mary that once more Colonel Coleman had arrested him. The charges this time, said Alf, related to "my neglegince of my dutys assigned me in western N.C. and absents without leave all for spite." The charges originated from local reports that during an extended mission in Macon and surrounding counties the previous fall to round up deserters and gather new recruits, Bell had built a house, practiced dentistry, and (in connection with his father's business) made jewelry. His service record summed up the charges as "alleged speculation." The sources of these accusations, Bell informed his wife, "were my good lady friends at home who have been writing their husbands." He blamed their maliciousness on regimental politics: "all caused by my being the Sen. Capt. and the Office of Maj. to fill and others more desirous of promotion than I." Salena Reid seems to have been the primary culprit, and Bell saw in her action, among other things, a lack of gratitude that serves as yet another indication of the interdependency the war forced upon the mountain community. She "ought to remember my father hailed wood for her when her own father would not do it and my wife loned her money when she needed it. Such ungrateful women I have no use for."[30]

Mary too, of course, deplored the new trouble Mrs. Reid had apparently brought upon her husband; she seemed particularly bothered by the fact that as a result of correspondence home from Bell's fellow soldiers, the story "is going evry where here." "The first time I see that good lady friend of yours I shall tell her of it good," she ranted but then, deferring to Alf's judgment, added, "unless you say for me not to." Although John Reid and his wife insisted to Mary that they were not the source of the reports of Bell's activities at home and earnestly sought to make amends, Mary's opinion of them softened only when the bright side of her husband's latest arrest and confinement became apparent: it kept him out of harm's way during the Atlanta campaign in which his regiment was by midsummer fully engaged.

Both Bells took satisfaction too in the fact that Reid never was promoted to captain, "as that was his sole object to get me out of the way."[31]

The involvement of Mary Bell and other wives in their husbands' military affairs resulted in part from the small close-knit community from which they came and the fact that so many of that community's residents served together in the same unit during the course of the war. Tensions, disputes, or rivalries that may have had prewar roots carried over from home to camp and from camp back home. As the Bell situation demonstrates, the behavior of wives and other family members could and often did exacerbate such tensions, if only through the very effective and all-important conduit of correspondence to and from the field. That power of the pen in linking home and battlefront gave gossip or hearsay added force in shaping the relationships, ambitions, and rivalries among soldiers from the same area who served together.[32]

If the closeness of Mary Bell's mountain community proved a sore point in her husband's ongoing problems in his regiment, it also had much to do with her success in coping with the hardships of the war years. Far more than many in her situation, she succeeded in making the best of the hard realities she faced. Equally significant, perhaps, was the fact that she was fully aware of her achievements and viewed them with great satisfaction.

Mary Bell was unlike the many southern women who began the war as determined and duty-bound partners in the Confederate war effort, only to be worn down by frustration, weariness, and self-pity that led to anger or indifference toward that very cause. As already demonstrated, she never professed a commitment to anything more than herself and her family, which perhaps explains why her bitterness and anger were vented so early during her husband's Confederate service. Yet as the war progressed, the tone of her letters suggests that her continued efforts to cope with home-front hardships without her husband made her an increasingly independent and self-confident woman who almost thrived on meeting the various challenges thrown her way.

In addition to caring for her growing family—she bore two children and lost one during the war (thus spending more than a third of the war pregnant)—Mary took on new responsibilities in Alfred's absence as manager of their farm and as fiscal agent for his dental practice and other business interests. Alf's early letters to her gave her detailed instructions for dealing with a variety of financial concerns, from negotiating with hired hands or (in the case of slaves) with their owners, to collecting debts owed him, paying his own debts, and authorizing new loans, most often to men in his company or their wives. During the same period, Mary's letters to him were full of questions that reflected her unfamiliarity and uncertainty in fulfilling those new responsibilities.

Mary reported in April 1862 that Alf's brother had proposed a swap of some property but that she declined what was most likely an advantageous bargain. She stated: "I was afraid to do it for fear I might get cheated" by her own brother-in-law and "for fear it might not prove good and you would not like it." Later that month, she informed Alf that a note he held on a debt owed him was not in their money box and reluctantly confessed that their young daughters had somehow removed it, used it for drawing paper, and misplaced it.[33]

Otherwise Mary's reports indicated dutiful adherence to his instructions and demonstrated little initiative or judgment in so doing. It was also obvious that she took little pleasure in those duties. Yet her success quickly boosted her self-confidence and earned her the respect of other Franklin residents, male and female. By the summer of 1862, she had begun to exercise her own discretion in making loans to Captain Bell's men, which she reported to him so that he might collect from the men when they returned to camp and were paid. She wrote in August that "as usual I had to loan some of your men some money." After laying out the particulars—in that case, five-dollar loans to three different men and the mother of another—she wrote, "I hope I did nothing wrong." Her rationalization for such generosity—"I seem to have their good will as well as their Capt. and I thought perhaps I had better keep it by being good to them"—is yet another indication of how conscious she was of the impact wives at home could have on their husbands' interests in camp.[34]

Shortly thereafter, however, Mary began to express misgivings about Alf's generosity. She confided to him her fear "that in your dislike to do anything that appears stingy or niggardly, you would allow yourself to become a looser." After a gentle warning that he not over-extend himself with handouts merely to assure his popularity among his troops, she concluded, "Please don't think your little wife is medling with things that don't concern her dearest, or if you do, try to excuse her."[35]

Mary grew more and more self-assured in conducting other types of business as well. She was especially proud of her skill in bartering, which as the war went on became an increasing but never exclusive means of doing business locally. She became more adept and confident in handling transactions that were often complex, sometimes involving a variety of currencies as well as produce. In one typical report, she described a series of barters she negotiated in April 1864. Those transactions also revealed the community's interdependence and the degree to which Mary Bell had made herself an integral part of an intricate local trade network:

> John McConnel has paid me five bushels [of corn] and says that I will have to wait until he goes south after corn before he can pay me any more. Mr. Lores Ell owes me 4 bushels of Apples which he promised to bring this week but has not done it yet. Alfred and Simeon still owes the 4 bushels they have not brought any corn yet. Alfred sent me two hams which I credited on the old account which leaves him $1.64 in debt. Albert has only paid 1¼ bushels which leaves him in debt 3¾ bushels, Joe 2½ bushels, Arther 1 bushel, Adie McConnell 1½ bushels.

She continued in the same letter to explain her attempts to get payment for corn sold on credit to a neighboring woman, payment of which was to include dried fruit; her unsuccessful attempts to obtain straw from people who still owed her for corn; and another neighbor's payment of a past debt in freshly milled wheat.[36] By December she had swapped milk cows with Amanda Cunningham and, in a deal in which she took particular pride, traded a calf to Benny Dobson for his pregnant sow. "I want to raise my own meat," she wrote Alf, and two men told her "they would have give two such calves for such a hog" as the one she acquired. One of them, Mary boasted, "says I can cheat."[37]

Her role in the Bells' jewelry business also provided Mary with experience that made her a shrewd businesswoman. In December

1864 she informed her husband with great satisfaction that she had charged a soldier twenty dollars, which he willingly paid, for the repair of his watch. She explained that she had arrived at the fee based on what she believed was the current equivalent of two bushels of corn, apparently a standard for such a service for much of the war. When she asked her father-in-law the next day whether that charge had been reasonable, he replied that he would have asked for a mere dollar and "sorter opened his eyes wide" at her minor windfall in acquiring twenty times that amount. "So you see," she concluded to Alf, "I did not learn to cheat from either of my dadies, it must have been from my husband!"[38]

The grain, produce, and other goods accumulated through Mary's increasingly aggressive bargaining skills were supplemented by other goods Alf was able to supply from the various locales in which he served. Mary constantly sought such opportunities and asked him to obtain and send her a variety of goods, including thread and "dye stuffs" from Asheville and nails and tallow candles from Knoxville (which Mary had noted in a newspaper were cheaper than any available in Franklin).[39] By 1864 she was even being supplied with rice— "as cheap food as we can buy"—from acquaintances coming from South Carolina. Meanwhile, Alf sent shoes from Atlanta for her children and slaves.[40]

As for her responsibilities in agricultural production, Mary never lacked for male workers on her farm a mile or so from town or on her garden plot in town; nor did she ever lack for male advice. Hired day labor and tenants made up a substantial part of the southern highlands' agricultural workforce, and in the early months of Alf's absence, a tenant and a hired slave continued to work different sections of the Bell farm under Mary's close supervision.[41] Though on occasion she referred to Bill Batey, the white tenant, as an overseer, there is no indication that he had any supervisory authority over Tom, the hired slave. Alf's father and brother, both Franklin residents, were also regular sources of support, advice, and—on occasion—manpower. Mary's father-in-law stayed with her and the children sometimes, and she spent a good bit of time at his house. In November 1861, Mary wrote to Alf in the first of what would be for her a typical letter combining reporting and inquiry: "Your father is shucking corn tonight. Tom is done sewing your wheat, he did not sew any rye for you, did you want him to sew some?"[42]

Other local men were available for short-term hire or volunteered their services or equipment. In April 1862, for instance, Mary wrote: "I got Charles to work for me one day and have got everything that I wanted planted now. I paid him in irish potatoes." When she was "quite busy" helping to get her corn shelled, a neighbor "found out we were shelling and loaned us his sheller so we got it shelled out pretty quick." Whereas she was firmly in control of her own garden plot, her early reports on farming operations indicated a detachment and uncertainty of what was happening there. In the same letter cited above, she admitted that "I have not found out whether Batey has sowed your cloverseed or not but I guess he has. Pa [Alf's father] is going to let me have some flax seed and some sugarcane seed." She went on to say that she planned to plant both "in this lot here," an indication that she did not entirely trust the more distant operation out of town or its overseers.[43]

Perhaps because of that lack of full confidence in Tom or Batey, Mary constantly plied her husband with questions regarding their activities. "Had I better get Bill Batey to haul your lumber?" she asked in June 1862. "He seems to be a pretty good hand to wagon. I told Pa to inquire if it was ready. I can get Dan to cut my wood, how much did you give Jule's negro to cut by the month? Dan wanted to charge me 75 cts a month." She found these new responsibilities burdensome and after such reports to Alf usually concluded by stating, "I should like so much for you to come home." At one point, she wrote out of utter exhaustion: "I wish I could be both man and woman until this war ends."[44]

Alf was always quick to respond to her letters with extensive and often specific instructions and advice, detailing the timetable and procedure for what and when to plant, much of which she was to pass on to her "overseers." When she complained of Batey's uselessness after their apple crops had been converted into liquid form—"I do not think he will do much while his brandy lasts"—Alf told Mary to tell his tenant that "if he turns his attention to drinking and is letting the place and things go to rack I shall not let him stay. . . . Tell him he must divide the brandy with me. You must lock it up in the stove for me."[45]

In January 1862, Mary reported "a big scrape up in town." The slaves of a Mr. McCay had stolen around 600 pounds of meat and sold it to slaves on neighboring farms. McCay apparently whipped his slaves into a confession that revealed a wide variety of co-conspirators in the operation, including at least one of the Bells' hired slaves and their overseer, Tom. Alf responded by instructing his wife to guard their smokehouse closely (which she had already informed him she was doing) and to "have a clasp and staples and lock it with the best padlocks that we have."[46]

By the end of that first summer on her own, Mary demonstrated considerably more knowledge of what was transpiring on both their own and other farms. On August 29, 1862, she began a letter practically gushing with farm statistics:

> Father has had his thrashing done this week and had only 54 bushels of wheat. Jesse Guffee had 31. You had 4 ½ of your own and 5 from Wm. Guffee. You have 16 ½ bushels of very good rye. . . . I would like to know what land you want rented for that and who to. Pa says we should plant more rye. Grain is very high and can hardly be bought. There is a great cry for seed of both wheat and rye. Wheat is bringing $4.00 in Haywood [County]. Two bushels of your rye will have to go for thrashing and about ⅔ of a bushel of wheat. . . .

She continued in the same vein for another paragraph. Yet she still deferred to her husband's opinion on dispensation of their crop and reported that Mr. Batey too was "very anxious for you to come home."[47]

Very little correspondence exists between the Bells in 1863, in part because Alf spent much of the year at or near home. In 1864, as a more regular exchange of letters resumed, one can detect a subtle role reversal in the Bells' correspondence. Mary conveyed a new assurance in her reports of her activity and decision making in both financial and agricultural matters. More often than not, Alf, not Mary, asked the questions. At times he had to remind her merely to keep him abreast of the farm's progress. At other times he barraged her with questions that reveal the range of her agricultural responsibilities:

> how is your wheat and rye doing. what ground have you in corn, is the oats any account. is your clover doing good . . . is there any apples or

peaches. is your horses poore. who does your blacksmithing. you can have those old Sythes fixed up so they will [be ready] for your harvest . . . is your potatoes any account. have you any lettice and onions. Have you old rye enough for coffee, do you get any milk. how does your cowes look. is the pasture good. has your foot got well. what hurt it. have you plenty to eate.[48]

Alf fully realized how much Mary had developed as a farmer and resigned himself to her newfound independence in that role. "As for your farming operations," he told her, "I have nothing to say nor advice to give. Besides if I had, Caty [his nickname for Mary] takes no advice but acts for herself and on her own judgement."[49] Her letters did indeed contain mere reports, often only casual references, on what she had done or decisions she had made regarding all aspects of the farm, from planting and harvesting to storage and marketing. Particularly revealing is the extent to which she described the operation in first-person singular: "I think I will have a clover patch by next year"; "my horses are fatter than any of my neighbors work horses"; "I like my darkies better I believe than I did at first."[50]

While Mary still complained about the burden she bore, she seemed to do so with far less rancor than had been the case two years earlier. "I have almost overdone myself this week," she informed Alf in April 1864, "spinning, coloring blue, and making soap. I have been gardening some today too." She later mused that "you have three broke down women on your place [his sister and a slave were the other two]. I believe I am the stoutest one and I am almost give out. We can all eat hearty and that is all you can brag on." She took pride in how hard she worked, and on occasion she openly acknowledged her achievement: "I do not want to boast any but I think you can say now that you have a wife that does not eat any idle bread although she can eat a good deal when she can get it." But her spirits remained high because of her sense of accomplishment. In July she was exuberant over how well the farm was going: "I felt so good that evrything went right with me I do not think any person could have made me mad for two or three days if they had of spit in my face."[51]

Mary's references to her father-in-law and other men on whom she had depended at home were less and less frequent, as were her pleas, so desperate throughout 1862, for her husband's return. She continued to express her love for Alf and was at times eloquent in how much she missed him; yet her calls for his return often seemed perfunctory. In February 1864 she ended a letter with a rather matter-of-fact question: "Are you going to reenlist or what are you going to do? Get out if you can honorably." Perhaps most revealing, she began a letter in June by exclaiming, "O! Would that you were here today." But the reason behind her urgent desire for her husband's presence at that point was not, as it had been in the past, to pass onto him the work and responsibilities that were then hers alone, but rather, as her next sentence indicated: "I would take you over the farm and show you our prospect for a crop."[52]

Even the threat of that scenario most feared by those on the home front—attack by enemy forces—hardly shook Mary's newly gained confidence. In early February 1864, 250 men of the First Wisconsin Cavalry moved across the Tennessee border into southwestern North Carolina and got as far as Macon County before turning back.[53] Though the party was never closer than twenty miles from Franklin, the residents panicked at this first real threat of enemy incursion into their area. By the time Mary reported the incident to Alf, the excitement had waned and fears subsided. But she was smug in mocking her fellow townspeople for the panic to which she apparently never succumbed. "I guess you have heard," she said, "of the great yankee and tory raid we had or at least expected to have. . . . It was the most ridiculous thing I ever heard of. I think evry man in Macon Co., except those that were too old to get away, skidadled—home guards, preachers, doctors and all, except Cousin William Roane and he ventured far enough to find out that they were not coming." She was no more sympathetic toward the frightened women left behind by Franklin's male population as she described the two or three days in which they had had to endure the prospect of "fine times during yankee holadays." In a somewhat scornful tone, she detailed a variety of mishaps other women encountered in their efforts to hide their valuables and livestock and safeguard their homes, much of which comes across as little more than slapstick in her irreverent retelling of various incidents.[54]

Alf's response was just as lighthearted. He had heard newspaper accounts of the raid before he received Mary's letter but waited until he had read her version before commenting, "We are glad to hear that the people at home had all excaped the yankees so well by flying to the mountains and staying there untill the women and children ran the yankees back." He later commented that "the home guards of Macon should have a flag presented to them by the ladies for their galantry."[55]

It was only a month after that scare that Mary Bell's confidence in her business and farm-management skills culminated in the achievement in which she took most pride and satisfaction: her purchase of a slave family. With no trepidation of either long- or short-term risks in such an investment and no sense at all that she and Alf might well have become among the last Americans ever to achieve slaveholding status, Mary, with the help of Alf's brother, negotiated the purchase of three slaves. In so doing, she achieved what had been a major goal since the war began.

The Bells had discussed the purchase of one or more slaves on several occasions, and as the value of Confederate currency became increasingly questionable, Alf urged Mary to convert their accumulating cash into property of some sort. In December 1862, he declared: "I don't think it good policy to keep money on hand. I want you to invest what you have in something, either for a negro or land." She chose the former. The fact that Alf entrusted his wife to undertake so momentous a transaction indicates how much he respected her growing business acumen. In effect he gave her free rein in terms of whom or what she purchased and how much she paid. "I want you not to ask me anything about it," he told her. "Its enough for you to know that I want you to buy it. . . . I have a wife, and I thank god for it, who is not extravagant and [is] always trying to lay something up for the future."[56]

Mary backed off from making such a purchase at that time, but late in the summer of 1863, while Alf was at home, they accepted a teenage slave girl, Eve, as payment for a long-held note owed Alf. Within several months, after Alf had returned to his regiment in Georgia, she negotiated a deal that involved trading Eve along with a cash payment in order to acquire a slave family of three, recently brought into the area from Charleston. The details of this transaction are not related here. Rather, Mary's purchase and subsequent relationship with this new slave force, which comes to dominate her correspondence with Alf through the rest of the war, are chronicled in chapter 4 in this volume, where it is set within the context of other wartime slave sales and purchases.[57]

In many respects, Mary Bell's acquisition and management of her labor force—hired and purchased, white and black—provide the most dramatic reflection of how the war allowed her to mature and to assert a sense of independence she probably would never have known otherwise. Just as the war imposed new challenges and responsibilities on her, it also provided her with new opportunities, of which she took full advantage. Hunger, poverty, and material deprivation were never among the hardships she faced. Her husband's comfortable financial situation and his position in the community helped to shield her, but Mary's skillful management of their resources in his absence also contributed substantially to her well-being. The relative lack of deprivation made Mary Bell's wartime experience quite different from that of many other women in the same region, on whom the war's impact was far more destructive, physically, emotionally, and materially.[58]

Yet her achievement was hardly unique or even unusual among Confederate women. In her general description of the plight of southern womanhood at war, Anne Firer Scott laid out the essence of the Bells' experience with almost uncanny precision. "Husbands hurrying off to the army," Scott stated, "sent back all kinds of instructions about the planting, harvesting, and marketing of crops, the management of slaves, the education of children, the budgeting of money, the collecting of old debts, and every other aspect of their business, apparently in perfect confidence that their wives would somehow cope. The women, in their turn, were polite about asking advice and begged for guidance, while carrying on as if they had always been planters, business managers, overseers of slaves, and decision makers."[59]

Yet Mary Elizabeth Massey noted in the opening sentence of her book *Bonnet Brigades* that "had every woman and girl of the 1860s described the ways in which she was affected by the Civil War, no two accounts would have been alike."[60] It is the particularities of Mary Bell's experience and the context in which it took place that make her letters worth such close scrutiny. Whereas there was much that was typical about her response to the war, her individuality also bears examination. She was never subjected to the brutal and destructive forces that victimized so many Appalachian women as a result of the peculiar nature of the war waged in that region.[61] And unlike thousands of her counterparts, Mary Bell never offered her services to a military hospital or went to work in a factory; she was never part of any women's voluntary association or patriotic activity to support the men and boys in gray or the cause for which they fought; she never participated in a bread riot; and she never signed a petition or wrote letters on her own behalf or Alf's to President Jefferson Davis or Governor Zebulon B. Vance.[62] For the most part, she coped with the war in very private terms and reacted to it through purely personal means.

Mary's almost total self-absorption is among the most striking aspects of the self-portrait her letters provide; from beginning to end, her own and her family's well-being were her only priorities. She did not fit the pattern of the many women throughout the South and in western North Carolina who were initially caught up in the spirit of the war and the meaning of the Confederate cause, only later to be disillusioned and embittered by the increasing hardships that cause imposed on them, whose deteriorating willpower became a major impetus to massive desertions and much-weakened morale among Confederate fighting men. Mary was bitter and cynical about the war from the beginning and thumbed her nose at the patriotism of other Franklin women. If she ever consciously encouraged her husband's abandoning the military to return home, it was during his first few months away. Though she genuinely missed him throughout the war's duration, she was far more self-secure and her need for him far less acute during its final year.

Drew Gilpin Faust has noted the number of southern women who yearned to be men so that they might make themselves useful to the Confederacy. Mary Bell was among those expressing her desire for what Faust calls "a magical personal deliverance from gender restraints."[63] Yet when Mary proclaimed, "I wish I could be both man and woman," she had in mind nothing as magnanimous as contributing to the war effort; she simply yearned for the strength to keep her farm, family, and finances afloat for the duration. She was certainly not alone in her firm adherence to those limited and localized goals; if anything distinguished Mary Bell's efforts, it would probably be the degree to which she succeeded in managing all three and the tremendous satisfaction she took in doing so.

Yet she could not have done it on her own. Her success was very much the result of community interdependence, as reflected by the reciprocal nature of her relationship with fellow Franklin residents that emerges as a dominant theme in her letters. Despite her self-absorption, Mary relied heavily on her neighbors, just as they often called upon her for aid of various sorts. The war's demands forced new levels of cooperation and interaction on that mountain community as it did many others. Despite Mary's cynicism toward the "cause" and her disdain for many of those in whose midst she lived, she used them and was used by them.

Perhaps what most distinguishes Mary Bell's experience as Appalachian in nature is the sense of community that it so vividly conveys. Gordon McKinney maintains that it was the disintegration of community structure and economy that so victimized many western North Carolina women and placed them at the forefront of the bitter and often destructive divisiveness that plagued much of the southern highland populace.[64] But the conditions that rendered other communities dysfunctional do not seem to have been as acute in Franklin. While Mary Bell's descriptions suggest that the potential for internal disorder was present, the Macon County seat also enjoyed a variety of circumstances that insulated it from the worst ravages of the war and enabled it to weather the crisis far better than other mountain communities.

The flexibility of local trade patterns and labor arrangements that characterized the antebellum economy of much of the southern highlands proved a tremendous asset to the Bells and other Macon County residents in adapting to the new demands imposed by the war. Faced with manpower shortages as acute as those elsewhere in the South, families with the financial wherewithal, such as the Bells, turned to long-established practices of long- and short-term slave hirings and tenant employment. The great diversity of highland agricultural production allowed for a degree of local self-sufficiency that sheltered the community from the deprivation such a crisis might, and often did, impose in the cotton South.

Franklin's physical remoteness shielded it from much of the military movement that disrupted so many southern lives and households. Even the brutal and destructive bushwhacking that plagued so many sections of the southern highlands was never a serious threat to that particular corner of Appalachian North Carolina.[65] Yet Franklin was never so inaccessible that constant contact with its men in the field or access to goods and services well beyond the local supplies was ever denied those of its residents with the means to acquire them.

Perhaps the most significant factor in Franklin's avoidance of internal collapse or upheaval was that political sentiments there were never as divided as they were in East Tennessee or other sections of the Carolina highlands. Though in neighboring Cherokee County, Unionists and deserters threatened Confederate wives and Confederate raiders harassed the wife of a prominent Unionist, unionism never achieved a stronghold in the state's southwestern corner; nor do Franklin residents (perhaps buffered by Cherokee County from spillover of Tennessee's Unionist influence) ever seem to have engaged in such confrontations.[66] The tensions and disagreements that arose between the Bells and fellow residents were limited to petty jealousies or personality conflicts that never split the community to the extent that more basic disagreements over commitment to the Union or to the Confederacy would have. Thus local animosities were never a threat nor a barrier to the mutual dependency on which Franklin residents came to rely so heavily, animosities that could well have negated the advantages their insulation and self-sufficiency provided.[67]

Unfortunately, Alf's return home in February 1865 brought the Bells' vivid record of their wartime lives to a sudden halt. One can only guess what long-term effects Mary's "emancipation" had on her marriage, her household, or her place in the community. Nor can one know how either spouse reacted to the loss of their newly acquired slave property; how much of a role Mary continued to play in Alf's business affairs or farm management; or to what extent Confederate defeat and its subsequent burdens demoralized her or punctured her steadily growing self-esteem. From an 1890s perspective, John Andrew Rice wrote that "in 1860 the South became a matriarchy." If Mary's wartime role does not fully support such hyperbole, Rice's subsequent analysis seems a remarkably apt description of the Bells' situation: "The men went away from home to other battlefields, leaving the women free to manage farm and plantation directly, without their bungling hindrance; when they returned, those who had escaped heroic death . . . found their surrogates in complete and competent charge and liking it."[68] That being very much what Alfred Bell returned home to in February 1865, it is hard to imagine that his household ever reverted to the full patriarchy it had been before he marched off to war.

Notes

1. *North Carolina Standard* (Raleigh), August 19, 1863.

2. The Bell correspondence is found in the Alfred W. Bell Papers, Special Collections Department, Duke University Library, Durham, N.C.

3. Shirley Abbott, *Womenfolks: Growing Up Down South* (New Haven: Ticknor and Fields, 1983), 62.

4. George C. Rable, *Civil Wars: Women and the Crisis of Southern Nationalism* (Urbana: University of Illinois Press, 1989); Drew Gilpin Faust, *Mothers of Invention: Women of the Slaveholding South in the American Civil War* (Chapel Hill: University of North Carolina Press, 1996); Catherine Clinton, *Tara Revisited: Women, War, and the Plantation Legend* (New York: Abbeville Press, 1995); Jean Friedman, *The Enclosed Garden: Women and Community in the Evangelical South, 1830–1900* (Chapel Hill: University of North Carolina Press, 1985), chap. 5; Michael Fellman, *Inside War: The Guerrilla Conflict in Missouri during the American Civil War* (New York: Oxford University Press, 1989), chap. 5.

Some of the best works on those issues focus on North Carolina women, including Paul D. Escott, *Many Excellent People: Power and Privilege in North Carolina, 1850–1900* (Chapel Hill: University of North Carolina Press, 1985), chap. 3, esp. 63–67; Victoria Bynum, *Unruly Women: The Politics of Social and Sexual Control in the Old South* (Chapel Hill: University of North Carolina Press, 1992), chaps. 5 and 6; and Jane Turner Censer, *The Reconstruction of Southern White Womanhood, 1865–1895* (Baton Rouge: Louisiana State University Press, 2003), which focuses on North Carolina and Virginia women.

5. Gordon B. McKinney, "Women's Role in Civil War Western North Carolina," *North Carolina Historical Review* 69 (January 1992): 37–56; Phillip Shaw Paludan, *Victims: A True Story of the Civil War* (Knoxville: University of Tennessee Press, 1981); Ralph Mann, "Guerrilla Warfare and Gender Roles: Sandy Basin, Virginia, as Case Study," *Journal of the Appalachian Studies Association* 5 (1993): 59–66; and Mann, "Family Group, Family Migration, and the Civil War in the Sandy Basin of Virginia," *Appalachian Journal* 19 (Summer 1992): 374–93.

For more general recent work on Appalachian women during the nineteenth century, see Milton Ready, "Forgotten Sisters: Mountain Women in the South," in *Southern Appalachia and the South: A Region within a Re-*

gion, ed. John C. Inscoe, vol. 3 of *Journal of the Appalachian Studies* Association (1991): 61–67; Sally W. Maggard, "Class and Gender," in *The Impact of Institutions in Appalachia*, ed. Jim Lloyd and Anne G. Campbell (Boone, N.C.: Appalachian Consortium Press, 1986); Margaret Ripley Wolfe, "Waiting for the Millennium, Remembering the Past: Appalachian Women in Time and Place," in *Women of the American South: A Multicultural Reader*, ed. Christie Anne Farnham (New York: New York University Press, 1997), 165–88; Mary K. Anglin, "Errors at the Margins: Rediscovering the Women of Antebellum Western North Carolina," in *Appalachia in the Making: The Mountain South in the Nineteenth Century*, ed. Dwight B. Billings, Mary Beth Pudup, and Altina Waller (Chapel Hill: University of North Carolina Press, 1996); and "Talking Heroines," chap. 9 in this volume.

6. Lawrence E. Wood, *Mountain Memories* (Franklin, N.C.: privately published, n.d.), 75.

7. Information on the Bells' antebellum life was gleaned from the inventory description, Bell Papers.

8. George W. Featherstonaugh, *A Canoe Voyage up the Minnay Sotor . . .*, 2 vols. (London: R. Bentley, 1847), 1:281; Charles Lanman, *Letters from the Alleghany Mountains* (New York: G. P. Putnam, 1849), 81. For other nineteenth-century observations of Franklin and Macon County, see A. R. Newsome (ed.), "The A. S. Merrimon Journal, 1853–1854," *North Carolina Historical Review* 8 (July 1931): 313–14; Myron H. Avery and Kenneth S. Boardman (eds.), "Arnold Guyot's Notes on the Geography of the Mountain District of Western North Carolina," *North Carolina Historical Review* 15 (July 1938): 282–83; and Wilbur G. Zeigler and Ben S. Grosscup, *The Heart of the Alleghanies; or, Western North Carolina* (Raleigh: Alfred Williams, 1883), 82–83. For recent but impressionistic histories of the county, see Wood, *Mountain Memories,* and Jessie Sutton (ed.), *The Heritage of Macon County* (Winston-Salem: Hunter Publishing, 1987).

9. For Macon County statistics on population, landholdings, agricultural output, and slaveholdings in 1850 and 1860 in relation to other western North Carolina counties, see John C. Inscoe, *Mountain Masters, Slavery, and the Sectional Crisis in Western North Carolina* (Knoxville: University of Tennessee Press, 1989), tables 1.1, 1.2, 1.3, 3.2, and appendix. For general accounts of Macon County before and during the Civil War, see special issue of the *Franklin Press,* June 26, 1925; and Sutton, *Heritage of Macon County,* 43–51.

10. On early recruiting efforts in southwestern North Carolina, see Vernon H. Crow, *Storm in the Mountains: Thomas's Confederate Legion of Cherokee Indians and Mountaineers* (Cherokee, N.C.: Press of the Museum of the Cherokee Indian, 1982), 10–15; and John C. Inscoe and Gordon B. McKinney, *The Heart of Confederate Appalachia: Western North Carolina*

in the Civil War (Chapel Hill: University of North Carolina Press, 2001), chap. 3.

11. Alfred to Mary Bell, January 30, 1862, Bell Papers. All subsequent references to correspondence refer to this collection. On January 30, 1862, the *Asheville News* noted that "Coleman's Battalion is here and eager to meet the enemies of their country. . . . They are tired of listless inaction and would hail with joy the order to march." For a history of the 39th Regiment and Bell's service record, see Louis H. Manarin and Weymouth T. Jordan Jr., (eds.), *North Carolina Troops, 1861–1865: A Roster* (Raleigh: Division of Archives and History, 1985), 10:104–9, 120.

12. Mary to Alfred Bell, November 13, 1861.

13. Alfred to Mary Bell, January 30, 1862. See her letters of November 13, 1861, and January 30, 1862.

14. Mary to Alfred Bell, February 10, 1862.

15. Ibid., March 5, April 28, 1862.

16. Ibid., March 5, 1862. She expressed similar sentiments in letters of April 4 and June 13, 1862. In her March 5 letter, she noted that one victim had died of measles, while another had been one of the men who wanted to lead his own company.

17. Ibid., June 20, 1862.

18. Ibid., November 13, 1861, May 22, 1862. In the spring of 1862, North Carolina women organized a statewide fundraising campaign to construct wooden gunboats in Washington and Wilmington, North Carolina, to protect the coast from Union attack.

19. Ibid., April 28, May 22, 1862. The act, calling for the first draft in American history, was passed on April 16, 1862. In September the age of eligible draftees was raised to forty-five, and in February 1864 it was extended again to cover men from ages seventeen to fifty. See Emory M. Thomas, *The Confederate Nation: 1861–1865* (New York: Harper and Row, 1979), 152–55, 260–61, for a thorough account of Confederate conscription.

20. Mary to Alfred Bell, January 20, March 5, August 26, 1862. Mary's reference to Alf's encounters with prostitution was a legitimate concern as long as he was in East Tennessee. A Confederate major stationed near Knoxville wrote of that region in 1863: "Female virtue if it ever existed in this Country seems now almost a perfect wreck. Prostitutes are thickly crowded through mountain & valley in hamlet & city." Quoted in Bell I. Wiley, *Confederate Women* (Westport, Conn.: Greenwood Press, 1975), 162.

21. See George Featherstonaugh's comment on Franklin earlier in this chapter. Franklin was not alone in its reputation for the insobriety of its citizenry. Augustus S. Merriman wrote in 1854 of Jewel Hill in nearby Madison County: "I do not know of any rival for this place in regard to drunkenness, ignorance, superstition, and the most brutal debauchery." Newsome, "A. S. Merriman Journal," 319. See Bruce E. Stewart, "Select Men of Sober

and Industrious Habits: Alcohol Reform and Social Conflict in Antebellum Appalachia," *Journal of Southern History* 73 (May 2007): 289–322.

22. Mary to Alfred Bell, January 30, 1862. See also her letters of June 28 and August 26, 1862, and his letter of September 18, 1862.

23. Coleman, a nephew of David L. Swain, was an ambitious and accomplished young man, who seems to have been well liked and respected by most others. There appears to be no other evidence of the problems that Alfred Bell cites with his leadership or deportment. For sketches on Coleman, see F. A. Sondley, *A History of Buncombe County, North Carolina,* 2 vols. (Asheville: Advocate Printing, 1930), 11, 768–69; John Preston Arthur, *Western North Carolina: A History from 1730 to 1913* (Raleigh: Edwards and Broughton, 1914), 403–4; and Frontis W. Johnston (ed.), *The Papers of Zebulon Baird Vance* (Raleigh: Division of Archives and History, 1963), 1:19n. For a vivid contemporary description of Coleman, see Newsome, "A. S. Merrimon Journal," 310. The most thorough treatment of Coleman's Civil War career is found in David C. Bailey, *Farewell to Valor: A Salute to the Brothers Coleman . . . of Asheville Days Remembered* (Asheville: Hexagon, 1977). Despite a detailed treatment of Coleman's leadership of the 39th North Carolina, Bailey makes no mention of Alfred Bell or the dissension in his company.

24. Mary to Alfred Bell, May 29, 1862.

25. Alfred to Mary Bell, June 18, July 6, 1862; Mary to Alfred Bell, June 28, 1862.

26. Mary to Alfred Bell, July 20, 1862.

27. Ibid., July 27, 1862.

28. Alfred to Mary Bell, September 1, 1862.

29. Mary to Alfred Bell, July 27, 1862.

30. Alfred to Mary Bell, March 31, April 8, 1864. Salena Reid was the wife of Lieutenant John Reid, who headed the other Macon County company of Coleman's regiment. The author is grateful to Richard Melvin for information about these and other individuals in Franklin with whom the Bells interacted.

31. Mary to Alfred Bell, April 22, June 5, 17, 1864.

32. On the localistic nature of Union military companies and their linkage to communities, see Reid Mitchell, "The Northern Soldier and His Community," in *Toward a Social History of the American Civil War: Exploratory Essays,* ed. Maris Vinovskis (Cambridge, England: Cambridge University Press, 1990), 78–92. On the impact of such community-composed units on desertion rates among North Carolinians, see Peter S. Bearman, "Desertion as Localism: Army Unit Solidarity and Group Norms in the U.S. Civil War," *Social Forces* 70 (December 1991): 321–42.

33. Mary to Alfred Bell, April 4, 28, 1862.

34. Ibid., August 26, 1862.

35. Ibid., August 29, 1862.

36. Ibid., April 15, 1864.

37. Ibid., December 16, 1864.

38. Ibid.

39. Ibid., November 13, 1861, June 28, 1862.

40. Ibid., June 18, 1864; Alfred to Mary Bell, June 28, 1864.

41. Recent studies have made it increasingly apparent that tenantry made up a significant part of the antebellum agricultural workforce in the southern highlands. See Frederick A. Bode and Donald E. Ginter, *Farm Tenancy and the Census in Antebellum Georgia* (Athens: University of Georgia Press, 1986), 116–17, table 6.1, p. 131 [for north Georgia mountains]; Wilma A. Dunaway, *The First American Frontier: Transition to Capitalism in Southern Appalachia, 1700–1860* (Chapel Hill: University of North Carolina Press, 1996); Joseph D. Reid Jr., "Antebellum Southern Rental Contracts," *Explorations in Economic History* 13 (January 1976): 69–83 [for Haywood County, North Carolina]; and Tyler Blethen and Curtis Wood, "The Pioneer Experience to 1851," in *The History of Jackson County, North Carolina,* ed. Max R. Williams (Sylva, N.C.: Jackson County Historical Association, 1987), 83–95.

42. Mary to Alfred Bell, November 13, 1861.

43. Ibid., April 5, 1862.

44. Ibid., June 13, May 22, 1862. Mary referred to Julius T. Siler, who lived across the street from the Bells, and whose family was among Macon County's largest slaveholders. Siler's wife, May, was David Coleman's sister.

45. Ibid., August 26, 1862; Alfred to Mary Bell, September 18, 1862.

46. Mary to Alfred Bell, January 30, 1862; Alfred to Mary Bell, February 8, 1862.

47. Mary to Alfred Bell, August 26, 29, 1862.

48. Alfred to Mary Bell, June [n.d.], 1864.

49. Ibid., April 10, 1864.

50. Mary to Alfred Bell, July 8, 1864.

51. Ibid., April 22, July 8, 1864. For context on the traditional roles of women as farmers, see Elizabeth Fox-Genovese, "Women in Agriculture during the Nineteenth Century," in *Agriculture and National Development: Views on the Nineteenth Century,* ed. Lou Ferleger (Ames: Iowa State University, 1990): 267–301.

52. Mary to Alfred Bell, February 19, 1864, June 5, 1864.

53. Crow, *Storm in the Mountains,* 59. The most detailed account of this and earlier raids into adjacent Cherokee County appears in Margaret Walker Freel, *Our Heritage: The People of Cherokee County, North Carolina, 1540–1955* (Asheville: Miller Printing, 1956), 225–31. The only such incident reported in Macon County is an "unconfirmed story" of a Union man traveling through the county on his way to East Tennessee who was killed,

beheaded, and buried between Franklin and Highlands. Sutton, *Heritage of Macon County,* 46.

54. Mary to Alfred Bell, February 19, 1864.

55. Alfred to Mary Bell, March 17, 1864.

56. Ibid., December 9, 1862.

57. For a fuller account of Mary Bell and her slaves, see John C. Inscoe, "The 1864 Slave Purchases of Mary Bell: The Civil War's Empowerment of an Appalachian Woman," in *Discovering the Women in Slavery: Emancipating Perspective on the American Past,* ed. Patricia Morton (Athens: University of Georgia Press, 1996), 61–81.

58. Gordon B. McKinney, "Women's Role in Civil War Western North Carolina," *North Carolina Historical Review* 69 (January 1992): 69–82; and Inscoe and McKinney, *Heart of Confederate Appalachia,* chap. 8.

59. Anne Firor Scott, *The Southern Lady: From Pedestal to Politics, 1830–1930* (Chicago: University of Chicago Press, 1970), 82.

60. Mary Elizabeth Massey, *Bonnet Brigades* (New York: Alfred A. Knopf, 1966), ix.

61. Both Gordon McKinney and Ralph Mann provide richly documented accounts of the brutalization of women by the guerrilla warfare, military raids, bushwhackers, and deserters that plagued southern highlanders. McKinney, "Women's Role in Civil War Western North Carolina," 43–46; Mann, "Guerrilla Warfare and Gender Roles." For accounts of women in similar circumstances in Missouri, see Fellman, *Inside War,* chap. 5.

62. Perhaps because he was a western Carolinian himself, scores of mountain women wrote to Governor Vance during the war. Much of Gordon McKinney's analysis of highland women is based on their letters to him. There is little evidence that women's aid societies or charitable associations were ever formed in the state west of Buncombe County. McKinney, "Women's Role in Civil War Western North Carolina," 54.

63. Drew Gilpin Faust, "Altars of Sacrifice: Confederate Women and the Narratives of War," *Journal of American History* 76 (March 1990): 1206–7.

64. McKinney, "Women's Role in Civil War Western North Carolina."

65. Although Confederate colonel W. W. Stringfield of Thomas's legion had used Franklin as the base for his defensive patrols during the latter part of the war, the closest military action to Franklin was the war's final skirmish in North Carolina, which took place forty miles away in Waynesville on May 6, 1865. Arthur, *Western North Carolina,* 602–21, and Crow, *Storm in the Mountains,* 136–37.

66. Inscoe and McKinney, *Heart of Confederate North Carolina,* chap. 5; Freel, *Our Heritage,* 225–31.

67. Examples of mountain communities torn apart by ideological differences include Shelton Laurel in Madison County, North Carolina, and Cades Cove, Tennessee. For analysis of how destructive an impact such divi-

sions had on community life, see Paludan, *Victims;* and Dunn, *Cades Cove,* chap. 5. See also Kenneth W. Noe, "Red String Scare: Civil War Southwest Virginia and the Heroes of America," *North Carolina Historical Review* 69 (July 1992): 301–22; and Mann, "Family Group, Family Migration, and the Civil War in the Sandy Basin of Virginia," 374–93.

68. John Andrew Rice, *I Came out of the Eighteenth Century* (New York: Harper and Brothers, 1942), 116–17, quoted in Scott, *Southern Lady,* 100.

8

"Moving through Deserter Country"

Fugitive Accounts of Southern Appalachia's Inner Civil War

Outside observers have been vital to both our understanding and our misunderstanding of Appalachian society. Particularly valuable as source material on the southern highlands in the nineteenth century, their works range from the amply descriptive antebellum travel accounts of Caroline Gilman, James Buckingham, and Frederick Law Olmsted, through the local-color fiction and nonfiction of the post–Civil War popular press, to the more socially conscious tracts of missionaries, social workers, and journalists in the latter part of the century. While all these works have been and remain essential to scholars seeking to understand preindustrial mountain life, all too often they have been sources of the many stereotypes, misconceptions, and distortions to which this region, more than almost any other in the country, has been subjected.

Among the most overlooked of regional commentaries by outside observers are those documenting one of the chapters most crucial in the Southern Appalachian experience (as of course it was for the South and the nation as a whole), the Civil War.[1] No other epoch in our history has elicited written records from so vast a number of participants. Edmund Wilson, in the introduction to his *Patriotic Gore*, asked, "Has there ever been another historical crisis of the magnitude of 1861–1865 in which so many people were so articulate?" Or, as Louis Masur more recently stated, "The Civil War was a written war," one in which hundreds of participants and observers "struggled to capture the texture of the extraordinary and the everyday."[2]

Among the vast literature that indeed did capture the texture of

175

the extraordinary and the everyday is a considerable body of prison narratives. The most scholarly authority on the subject, William Hesseltine, noted in 1935 that the Library of Congress catalog listed almost three hundred titles of published reminiscences or personal narratives by former prisoners, most of them Union soldiers in Confederate prisons.[3] Remarkably, almost a fourth of those works were by men who escaped from such prisons and whose narratives cover their post-prison experiences as fugitives. Among these, I have located twenty-five accounts by Union soldiers whose escape routes led them through the southern Appalachian Mountains.

Published as early as 1863 and as late as 1915, these books and articles are often sensationalistic in nature and melodramatic in tone. Their titles reflect their various approaches, which range from the stark minimalism of W. H. Parkins's *How I Escaped,* Alonzo Cooper's *In and Out of Rebel Prisons,* and John Ennis's *Adventures in Rebeldom* to J. Madison Drake's *Fast and Loose in Dixie*—which bears a typical mid-nineteenth-century subtitle that doubles as a synopsis: *An Unprejudiced Narrative of Personal Experience as a Prisoner of War . . . With An Account of a Desperate Leap from a Moving Train of Cars. A Weary Tramp of Forty-five Days through Swamps and Mountains. Places and People Visited. Etc., Etc.*—and Junius Browne's *Four Years in Secessia: Adventures Within and Beyond the Union Lines: Embracing a Great Variety of Facts, Incidents, and Romance of the War, Including . . .* six more lines of subtitle. The literary merit of these works, like their scope and format, varies considerably, reflecting in part the very different types of experiences their authors had as soldiers, as prisoners, and as fugitives.

Yet the narratives of those whose escape routes took them through Southern Appalachia share a great deal. In crossing what was unknown and perilous territory for most, these fugitive-authors observed and experienced the region in ways quite different from those of the more casual antebellum travelers or the late nineteenth-century mission workers and journalists. Union escapees found themselves in the highlands not by choice but by necessity. For many, the risk of capture or death was all too immediate, and their treks through this treacherous terrain were as surreptitious as they could make them. Their judgments of the people and situations they encountered often were matters of life and death. Miscalculating the lay of the land or the loyalties of those upon it could—and on occasion did—prove fatal for these men, whose survival depended on knowing which residents they could trust and which they should avoid. As literature, their writings often are seriously flawed and amateurish; yet, because these men proved so astute in their perceptions of the country through which they traveled, their accounts, taken together, provide an unusually detailed and full-bodied portrait of a section of the Confederacy that suffered as much turmoil, devastation, and deprivation as any area of the South not overrun by Union armies.

Of the twenty-five fugitives whose narratives are considered here, just over half escaped from Camp Sorghum, a Confederate prison for Union officers in Columbia, South Carolina; most of the rest broke out of a similar facility in Salisbury, North Carolina. Two narratives involve groups of Federal soldiers who fled from a tobacco warehouse-turned-prison in Danville, Virginia. By 1864, all three of these makeshift prisons were vastly overcrowded; in both structure and manpower, security was grossly inadequate, and escapes were commonplace. The Columbia site was so poorly guarded that 373 of the 1,200 officers incarcerated there escaped before the prison was abandoned for more secure quarters.[4]

For escapees from these three prisons, the mountains of North Carolina, Virginia, and Georgia offered the most obvious escape routes, if only because they had to be crossed in order to reach East Tennessee and eastern Kentucky beyond, the most accessible areas with predominantly Unionist populations. By the latter half of the war, the Tennessee highlands were occupied by Union forces and thus offered even more reliable sanctuary. In addition, the rugged, sparsely settled terrain en route to those Unionist strongholds offered good hiding places, remote roads, and a populace sufficiently sympathetic to lend support and assistance along the way. In North Carolina's highlands, there developed a network among the pro-Union minority that one "passenger," a New York cavalry captain, described as "an underground railway, as systematic and as well arranged as that which existed in Ohio before the war." It served two purposes, he wrote: "first to protect or secrete loyal North Carolinians who wished to avoid the rigid conscription of the south; and second, to aid in the escape of such Yankee prisoners as might choose that precarious route to freedom."[5]

Thus, a variety of circumstances made Southern Appalachia a haven for refugees of all sorts—those Ella Lonn once (oddly ignoring the escaped prisoner faction) described as "marauders, bummers, strolling vagabonds, negroes, rebel deserters, Union deserters, all bent on committing outrages."[6] These elements, combined with the divisive character of local sentiment, created an unusually volatile environment, which turned the war into an intensely localized guerrilla campaign fueled by personal animosities, vandalism, and other atrocities that had little bearing on military strategy or even ideological commitment beyond regional or community concerns.

The prison escape narratives provide an abundance of detail and insight into the dynamics of this inner war. This chapter focuses specifically on how their authors treated the three groups of mountain residents with whom they had the most direct contact, and who thus emerge as the dominant and most sharply etched characters: Unionists, women, and blacks. Because it was those segments of the mountain populace upon whom the success of their escapes and their chances of survival hinged, the fugitive writers, not surprisingly, portrayed all three in the most sympathetic, admiring, and often idealized terms. Despite the obvious bias apparent in these accounts, however, the graphic detail, expansive coverage, and relative consistency of the portrayals of southern highlanders in these twenty-five works make them valuable and generally credible source materials. No other contemporary coverage of the Civil War in Southern Appalachia portrays as vast a spectrum of the population as vividly or with as much complexity and nuance as do these works.

Among the more elusive aspects of the war in the highland South are the extent and nature of Unionist sentiment in the region. These aspects, too, have been among those most subjected to myth and distortion since the conflict ended. While the fugitive narratives are no more helpful than those of later scholars in explaining why certain highlanders pledged allegiance to either the Union or the Confederacy, they do provide a great deal of descriptive detail and generous commentary on the many individuals and groups the fugitives encountered. Like so many other treatments of the subject, their narratives often exaggerated the extent of Unionist sentiment in the region or tended to see the populaces of all highland locales as committed to the Union.

A New York officer, moving westward after escaping from Salisbury, stated that western North Carolina "was to the full as loyal as West Virginia."[7] Such an assessment is a distortion and, in part, may typify attempts by many of these authors, particularly those publishing their work during or just after the war, to stress to northern readers the diversity of southern views, the strength of pro-Union loyalties in some parts of the South, and the deteriorating support for the Confederate government among southern civilians.

Such misconceptions were sufficiently widespread that some escapees actually entered highland areas with a false—and dangerous—sense of security about the prevalence of Unionist sentiment, only to have this complacency shaken once they encountered a very different reality. During his 1864 escape from Columbia en route to Knoxville, Major Charles Mattocks of Maine stated in his journal that, in crossing into North Carolina, "our Rubicon is passed. . . . We now feel highly encouraged and think we have accomplished the most dangerous portion of our journey. Visions optimistic begin to loom up." His optimism proved premature, though; he and several companions were captured ten days later by Rebel scouts deep in the Smoky Mountains, just a mile and a half from the Tennessee state line.[8]

A Salisbury escapee noted, as he and his fellow fugitives entered western North Carolina, "We experienced little trouble in finding 'friends,' for they were everywhere." Soon thereafter, they were startled to find themselves face to face with a local Confederate officer, who charged them with being "d—n Yankees." The prisoners panicked, but the officer quickly alleviated their fear by informing them that, as the father of three sons killed in battle and another dying of fever in a Delaware prison, he had lost all interest in the war. He allowed the Union men to proceed unharmed, but, once out of his sight, they raced away, still unsure of his intentions or truthfulness. They agreed that "hereafter we must be more careful, and not act on the hypothesis that every person we meet is devoted to the Union, even though he is a *North* Carolinian."[9]

It is hardly surprising that these authors so often romanticized the heroism and self-sacrifice of the resident Unionists they encountered. J. Madison Drake met "hundreds of this class" in Caldwell County, North Carolina, along with many of their "boon companions, the lyers-out." "In all my wanderings," Drake wrote, "I had never seen a more intelligent or determined people. Mingling with them, as I did for weeks, I thought of the brave defenders of the Tyrol, of the hardy Waldenses, fighting and dying among the hills for dear Liberty's sake." Although many had been comfortable farmers before the war, during the conflict their loyalties had reduced them to poverty and ruin, he claimed, and forced them to abandon everything—their homes and their families—to go into hiding, all "because of their devotion to the Government."[10]

A Wisconsin colonel, fleeing through the mountains of north Georgia in hopes of reaching Sherman's army, confirmed this description, noting that "with few exceptions, these were rough, unlettered men . . . but generous, hospitable, brave, and Union men to the core; men who would suffer privations, and death itself, rather than array themselves in strife against the Stars and Stripes, the emblem of the country they loved. . . . Uneducated though they were, under their homespun jackets beat hearts pure as gold, and stout as oaks."[11]

For some, such praise was a bit more forced and required some rationalization. In a chapter on "Union Bushwhackers," Junius Browne acknowledged that these southern allies were hardly passive victims of Confederate harassment. He admitted that they often took the offensive and that their aggression, like that of their Confederate oppressors, "was treacherous, coldly calculating, brutal." Yet, he wrote, "I cannot find it in my heart to blame many of the men who resort to it in the mountainous regions of North Carolina and Tennessee." He explained their transformation: "They were quiet, peaceable, industrious, loyal; opposed to the doctrine of Secession, and all its attendant heresies; the natural antagonists of the Slaveholders; lovers of the Union for the Union's sake, and regarded as an enemy whoever would seek its destruction. . . . Domestic by nature and habits, they were unwilling to quit their firesides and the few acres that had been their World. They would rather die than surrender all they valued in life. Yet they could not stay at home." After describing the harassment to which they had been subjected by their neighbors and by Home Guard troops, Browne concluded, "It is not difficult to conceive how a few months of such experience would transform a man from an enduring saint to an aggressive demon."[12]

Albert Richardson, a *New York Tribune* correspondent (and Browne's companion in many of their southern exploits), was perhaps the worst offender in patronizing the "Union mountaineers" he met. "Theirs was a very blind and unreasoning loyalty, much like the disloyalty of some enthusiastic Rebels. . . . They had little education; but when they began to talk about the Union their eyes lighted wonderfully, and sometimes they grew really eloquent. . . . They regarded every Rebel as necessarily an unmitigated scoundrel, and every Loyalist, particularly every native-born Yankee, almost as an angel from heaven." Richardson perhaps strains readers' credibility most in asserting the mountaineers' great affection for the North. "How earnestly they questioned us about the North!" he wrote. "How they longed to escape thither! To them, indeed, it was the Promised Land."[13]

The more Unionists Richardson encountered in moving westward toward Tennessee, the more noble they became. He much belabored the extent of their suffering: "Almost every loyal family had given to the Cause some of its nearest and dearest. We were told so frequently —'My father was killed in those woods;' or 'The guerrillas shot my brother in that ravine'—that, finally, these tragedies made little impression upon us." Later on, after listening to a woman along the Blue Ridge relate stories of her family's trials and tribulations, Richardson waxed poetic: "The history of almost every Union family was full of romance. Each unstoried mountain stream had its incidents of daring, of sagacity, and of faithfulness; and almost every green hill had been bathed in that scarlet dew from which ever springs the richest and ripest fruit."[14]

Despite the exaggeration and sentimentality that infects much of this work, the fugitive accounts offer some of the most thorough assessments we have of both the extent of Unionist sentiment in the mountains and the varying degrees of commitment associated with it. Even though Unionists are the central and most vividly portrayed figures in these narratives, their authors make it quite clear that they were very much a minority in most parts of the southern highlands. Although some areas of north Georgia and western North Carolina were known as strongholds of Unionist sentiment (one fugitive, for instance, noted that Wilkes County, North Carolina, had acquired a reputation among the rebels as "the old United States"),[15] there never was a highland area where local Unionists felt safe or comfortable among their neighbors, or where the fugitives themselves felt that they were not in enemy territory until they crossed the state line into Tennessee.

In traveling through the Georgia mountains, John Azor Kellogg of Wisconsin was surprised to see "three or four men at work digging sweet potatoes—*each man with a musket strapped to his back.*" He went on to compare the situation with that of the early pioneers, who "were compelled to defend themselves against the North American savages in a war prosecuted without regard to the laws governing civilized nations." "But this," he continued, "was in the interior of Georgia, one of the older States, in the noon-tide of the nineteenth century. These men were not warring with savages, but with their fellow men of the same race, with their neighbors, their former friends and acquaintances."[16]

Most fugitives quickly recognized and acknowledged the distinctions between the truer Unionists and the disaffected "outliers" who had deserted from the Confederate army or were hiding in the hills to elude conscription officers. Although usually sympathetic to the position forced by Confederate authorities upon these more localized refugees, they demonstrated less compassion for them than for the more "noble" and consistent Unionist stalwarts. Some softened their judgments of individual deserters and other outliers by stressing instead what wavering loyalties or even cowardice indicated about the Confederate cause and its power to sustain the type of devotion the Union inspired.

After encountering a group of young men "lying out" along the North Carolina–Virginia border, Richardson noted that they included both deserters from the Army of Northern Virginia and individuals evading conscription. At least one of their number admitted to having "foolishly acquiesced in the Revolution because at first it seemed certain to succeed, and he wished to save his property . . . now he heartily repented." Such men, Richardson concluded, were an index of the change that recently (as of December 1863) had come over Confederate sympathizers in that area, and suggested only a superficial commitment to either cause.[17]

On a number of occasions, the Union escapees found themselves dependent upon these deserters, sharing their mountain hideouts and their limited resources, benefiting from their wilderness survival skills and their guidance through the troublesome terrain. In such cases, their gratitude overshadowed any contempt the authors might have felt for the less than ideologically pure motives that brought them together. Madison Drake noted the irony in such circumstances: "Here we were, four Yankee officers, in the heart of the enemy's country, in a mountain fastness, surrounded by some of the men whom we had encountered in battle's stern array at Bull Run, Roanoke, Newbern, Fredericksburg, and on other ensanguined fields, who now were keeping watch and ward over our lives, which they regarded as precious in their sight—willing to shed their blood in our defense."[18]

Among the more striking aspects of these mountain-based narratives is the extent to which fugitives encountered slaves throughout the region. While such contacts with blacks were frequent and to be expected among escaped prisoners moving through other parts of the South, the fact that such contacts were equally prevalent in highland areas seems unusual, given the much smaller slave population in the highland South. Yet blacks seemed to be everywhere. Only one of these twenty-five descriptions of Appalachian escape routes notes a scarcity of slaves. In moving into the mountains of northeastern Georgia, a New York lieutenant bemoaned the fact that "the people in that section were generally very poor, and owned no negroes. We missed the assistance of the slaves very much."[19] Almost all other narratives relate incidents in which black residents aided their efforts in the mountains.

There are a number of explanations for what at least was perceived as little difference in racial demographics between lowland and highland escape routes. One is simply that these fugitives were intent on finding slaves and sought them out wherever possible. Another is that the black populace of Confederate Appalachia swelled greatly as lowland slaveholders in areas vulnerable to Union interference sent their human property—under various arrangements of hire, sale, or temporary guardianship—to the seemingly safer environment of the remote highlands.[20]

Slaves often guided fugitives through the rugged and treacherous mountains as they moved through the Carolinas or north Georgia toward Knoxville. Many opened their homes to these men, sometimes hiding them for days at a time and feeding them generously. Others provided passersby with clothing, foodstuffs, or other supplies (more often than not, their masters' property) or offered medical care if needed. To a number of fugitives, slaves' information on the political persuasions of residents of their area was the most valuable service they offered. Slaves usually were well aware of which white residents were Unionists and therefore useful to those making inquiries, and which were not. Upon encountering a lone white Unionist, to whose mountain cabin he had been directed by helpful slaves west of Greenville, South Carolina, a Rhode Island fugitive was exasperated with "this most ignorant man I had ever met, black or white." While the hermit expressed his willingness to help, the soldier wrote that he was too ignorant to do so and that "we could do better with the negroes" in terms of information and advice.[21]

John Kellogg found that what he called the slave "telegraph line" in Georgia's northeastern highlands was equally useful in reporting on military activity within the region. From slaves near Carnesville, his party learned at what points Sherman's occupation forces still held strong between Atlanta and Chattanooga, and used that information to plan the route to take in maneuvering through the northern part of the state. "We also obtained from them accurate knowledge of Sherman's troops only five days previous; and this, too, a hundred and fifty miles from the scene of action." So impressed was Kellogg with the informational services they provided that he wrote that, in his opinion, "they were, as a class, better informed of passing events and had a better idea of questions involved in the struggle between North and South, than the majority of that class known as the 'poor white' of the South."[22]

Of course it was not only in the highland South that slaves proved to be such valuable collaborators. They engaged in such subversive activity wherever opportunity arose throughout the Confederate South. Most escaped prisoners already had benefited from collusion with friendly blacks long before they moved into mountain regions, and those experiences had taught them to seek out black allies once there. A group of six escaped prisoners, in flight to West Virginia from a Danville, Virginia, prison, were forced to abandon one of their number in a "crippled and almost helpless condition" during the harsh winter of 1864, leaving him alone "in a bleak mountain country" of the Virginia Blue Ridge. In speculating upon his chances for successful escape, one of his former companions remarked that his only "difficulty . . . will be in avoiding Rebel citizens and finding a true Union friend to care for him for a few days." To this another in the company replied, "He must have nothing to do with any body but a negro, or he's a goner."[23]

Charles Mattocks of Maine and a fellow fugitive found themselves lost in the Carolina highlands in late 1864 and noted in his journal, "We must find some friendly negro tomorrow or live on raw corn until we do." In an entry two days later, he stated, "There are plenty of farm houses in sight in the valleys here, but no signs of the wealthy planters as in South Carolina. No darkies in sight." When they finally did encounter slaves working in a cornfield in the French Broad River valley, they approached them with confidence, drawing on a lesson obviously learned from earlier experiences in plantation country. "We have seldom ventured to ask food from house servants as they are not generally so Yankee-ized as the field hands," Mattocks explained. "Being generally well-fed, well clothed and perhaps petted by their masters, many of them come to look up[on] slavery as an advantage to them, while their less fortunate brethren and sisters who labor in the fields from daylight till dark do not become quite so favorably impressed with the institution."[24]

Albert Richardson practically gushed over the African Americans he encountered in western North Carolina. "By this time," he wrote, "we had learned that every black face was a friendly face. So far as fidelity was concerned, we felt just as safe among the negroes as if in our Northern homes. Male or female, old or young, intelligent or simple, we were fully assured they would never betray us." It was not simply kindness toward strangers that motivated the hospitality and aid bestowed by highland blacks, slave or free. Recipients of those kindnesses were convinced that it was the cause for which they had fought that determined the extent of black assistance. As Richardson saw it, "They were always ready to help anybody opposed to the Rebels. Union refugees, Confederate deserters, escaped prisoners—all received from them the same prompt and invariable kindness. But let a Rebel soldier . . . apply to them, and he would find but cold kindness."[25] Junius Browne was more eloquent in describing black partisanship as he witnessed it: "The magic word 'Yankee' opened all our hearts, and elicited the loftiest virtues. They were ignorant, oppressed, enslaved; but they always cherished a simple and beautiful faith in the cause of the Union and its ultimate triumph."[26]

In some cases, the slaves encountered by escaped prisoners were on the run themselves, a factor that made not only for sympathy but also for empathy on the part of some fugitive-authors. On more than one occasion, soldiers who had found shelter in slave cabins shared those tight quarters with escaped slaves, or "travelers," as blacks called runaways.[27] In some cases, slaves begged to accompany the fugitives as they moved toward Union lines and freedom. Such requests elicited mixed reactions from whites who suddenly found themselves asked to help those from whom they had received such vital assistance.

William Burson met five slave men in Wilkes County, North Carolina, who asked if they could accompany him to East Tennessee. After hiding out for several days under the care and protection of these slaves, Burson and his party were joined by local Confederate deserters. He asked their advice about taking the black men with him. One of the deserters assured him that "they were all good fellows and belonged to rebel masters whom they would be glad to see robbed of their slaves" but warned him about the added risks in his own escape if he were accompanied by runaway slaves. Their presence probably would assure that all would be hanged if captured. This frightened Burson's companions, who urged him to abandon the idea, but Burson reiterated his own resolve to contribute in this small way to the emancipation process, maintaining that "to anybody who had treated me as well as the negroes had, I would do all in my power to assist them out of bondage." His commitment remained firm, but upon receiving a warning of impending arrest by the Home Guards and hence needing to make a quicker retreat from the area than he had anticipated, Burson "informed the darkies of our danger. 'Well, well,' they said, 'nebber mind us, massa, we'll come arter awhile.'" They never appear again in Burson's aptly titled narrative, *A Race for Liberty*. [28]

Michael Egan found it more difficult to shake off unwanted black company. In moving into the Carolina highlands, Egan, a Union captain from West Virginia, met two young slave men who had decided to make a "joint effort to escape into the Union lines" and asked Egan if they could join him. Egan resisted their pleadings, stating that, even though he "fully appreciate[d] the sad predicament of the unfortunate negros . . . I could not allow my sympathies to jeopardize my own safety." "Whatever chance of life they might have owing to their commercial value," he reasoned, "I could expect none" as a presumed smuggler of slave property, "an unpardonable offense in the South." Egan bid the two black youths good-bye and "spurted ahead," only to find "to my surprise and annoyance they still follow close on my heels, making prodigious efforts to keep me in sight." He finally resigned himself to accepting the company of these "persistent darkies" but stuck with them only until they heard "the sickening sounds of the barbarous Siberian hounds" of their master, at which point he abandoned them to their fates.[29]

The courage and generosity exhibited by some slaves led their white beneficiaries to reassess their own racist assumptions. Alonzo Cooper, a New York cavalryman captured in 1864 by local Home Guards and imprisoned in Asheville's flimsy jail, was ashamed of the way his companions treated a fellow black prisoner. A local slave who shared a cell with several Union captives paid a heavy price for his attempt to aid them. In accord with a preconceived plan of escape, this "large, powerful negro" seized the guard and held him, while his white cellmates took his keys and made their exit. Intimidated by the threats of another guard, the "cowards" retreated back to their cell. Assuming that the slave alone had instigated the attack that allowed the white prisoners to escape, the guard ordered that he be given a hundred lashes.[30]

In his postbellum account of the incident, Cooper expressed genuine revulsion at the slave's punishment. He claimed to be "astonished to find such brutality among those who professed civilization," calling it "the most sickening transaction I ever witnessed." He was particularly offended by the complacency with which the southern jailers carried out this "exhibition of fiendish cruelty." Only after witnessing it, Cooper claimed, was he "ready to believe that the system of human slavery was capable of developing total depravity into the hearts of slave holders." He was almost as harsh in passing judgment on his own companions' role in the incident. "The poor ignorant black man's only fault," he wrote, "had been his confidence in the courage of his white associates. . . . If anyone should be punished it should be those whose lack of sense had got this poor fellow into a scrape and then like cowards basely deserted him."[31]

More positive encounters with African Americans inspired similar abolitionist sentiments. Richardson was taken in by "a peculiarly intelligent mulatto woman" he encountered near Wilkesboro, North Carolina. After an hour's conversation with this slave wife (who also was forced to be the mistress of her master), he concluded: "Using language with rare propriety, she impressed me as one who would willingly give up life for her unfortunate race. With culture and opportunity, she would have been an intellectual and social power in any circle." Inspired by this and other contacts with highland blacks, Richardson extolled the race as a whole and expressed his optimism for their prospects, once emancipated: "Some one has said that it needs three generations to make a gentleman. Heaven only knows how many generations are required to make a freeman! But we have been accustomed to consider this perfect trustworthiness, this complete loyalty of friends, a distinctively Saxon trait. The very rare degree to which the negroes have manifested it, is an augury of brightest hope and promise for their future. It is a faint indication of what they may one day become, with Justice, Time, and Opportunity."[32]

John Kellogg prided himself on the liberalization of his attitude toward blacks, declaring of those who had aided his escape efforts: "Those men and women who succored us in our great peril are my friends, and will be met and treated as such, wherever found, though their skins be darker, and their hair curl tighter than my own." After extolling their generosity toward him, he avowed, "May my right hand wither and my tongue cleave to the roof of my mouth, when I forget to be grateful to that people, or fail to advocate their cause, when their cause is just!"[33]

Massachusetts Lieutenant James Gilmore's manuscript account of his escape from Richmond's Libby Prison and his subsequent flight through the mountains of Virginia was so filled with stories extolling the character and courage of the blacks who aided him that abolitionist Edmund Kirke acquired it and published it in 1866. "It gave me," Kirke proclaimed in an introduction to the volume, "my first vivid idea of the present disposition and feelings of the Southern negroes." He informed Gilmore's brother, who had delivered the manuscript to him, that it should be published, "for it tells what the North does not as yet fully realize—the fact that in the very heart of the South are four millions of people—of strong, able-bodied, true-hearted people—whose loyalty led them, while the heel of the 'chivalry' was on their necks, and a halter dangling before their eyes, to give their last crust, and their only suit of Sunday homespun, to the fleeing fugitive, simply because he wore the livery and fought the battles of the Union."[34]

In her recent study of the impact of the Civil War on Victorian Americans, Anne Rose notes that few of those who wrote of their wartime experiences mentioned blacks, free or slave. Even those who became involved in legislative or social efforts to aid freedmen after the war had little to say about their own encounters with them during the war.[35] If that was indeed the case, the fugitive narratives are even more distinctive in their forthright and detailed descriptions of their interactions with highland slaves. In aiding, guiding, and confiding in the Union refugees who moved into their midst, these mountain blacks contributed more to their own cause and ultimately were more indebted to the fugitives they helped than they ever could have suspected at the time. They had no way of knowing that their good deeds would be commemorated in print, or that such testimony on their behalf might serve to win northern sympathies and respect, as the nation wrestled with the issue of black status and benefits after the war.[36]

Of all of the mountain residents observed by these fugitives, however, their most profuse adulation was reserved for the white women they encountered. Wives and mothers were often left at home alone, as the men of their households were engaged in military service, had become casualties of such service, or were avoiding it, often by hiding in caves and forests near their homes. Fugitives seem to have approached women with less trepidation than they did men, especially when the loyalties of those with whom they were forced into contact were in doubt. Michael Fellman has written of women caught up in the guerrilla warfare that characterized the Civil War in Missouri: "Disintegration, demoralization, and perverse adaptation engulfed women's behavior and self-conceptions as it assaulted the family and undermined male-female and female-female . . . relationships." Women, as both victims and actors, "were compelled to participate, which they did with varying degrees of enthusiasm, fear, and rage."[37]

Such an assessment is equally applicable to the women of Appalachia, and the escaped prisoner narrators depicted that full range of responses among the women they encountered. While most accounts of the plight of Appalachian women during the war have stressed their victimization, these fugitive narratives suggest that just as often they, like Fellman's Missouri women, were assertive and effective participants in local conflicts. Although they never neglected, and often movingly conveyed, the sacrifices and hardships endured by highland women during the war, the fugitive narrators were even more impressed with the strength, resourcefulness, and courage of the women—both Unionist and Confederate—they encountered. No doubt because the Federal fugitives so were often the recipients of their aid, Unionist women were among the figures most celebrated in these narratives. More significant, perhaps, these works demonstrate the extent to which such women played key roles in the subversive activity that undermined Confederate strength in the region, often in surprisingly militant and physically aggressive ways.

Women were among the most outspoken partisans in the region, and the fugitives never resisted the temptation to quote their tough talk expressing devotion to the cause. A "voluble, hatchet-faced, tireless woman" in Cashiers, North Carolina, hosted a group of refugees who "listened in amused wonder to the tongue of this seemingly untamed virago, who . . . cursed, in her high-pitched tones, for a pack of fools the men who had brought on the war."[38] Aunt Becky, an elderly woman in Henderson County, North Carolina, was quoted by another fugitive as having said, "I ain't afraid of those rebels. I tell them, 'you may hang old Aunt Becky if you want to, but with the last breath I draw I will shout, Hurrah for the Union!'"[39]

A young girl who guarded the entrance to beleaguered Cades Cove in Tennessee's Smoky Mountains, using a horn to warn her community of approaching danger, told a Massachusetts fugitive that she would tell anyone attempting to take her horn to go to hell. The reply of this young "sentinel," he claimed, "was rather a surprise to me as I had always had a great respect for women, but had met only the kind that used soft words." Yet he obviously admired her and understood the situation that induced such manly language, noting that the soft-spoken women he had known up to that point "had not been on the 'battle line,' so to speak," and had lived in pleasant homes and surroundings.[40]

In some instances, such defiance conveyed vindictive intent. In an 1887 memoir, Frank Wilkeson, a Union private who had served at an Alabama refugee camp for southern Unionist civilians, wrote of the Appalachian women who had sought safe haven there. They were determined that the Confederate neighbors from whom they had fled should pay for their actions. "I heard them repeat over and over to their children the names of men which they were never to forget, and whom they were to kill when they had sufficient strength to hold a rifle," he recalled. "These women, who have been driven from their homes by the most savage warfare our country had been cursed with . . . impressed me as living wholly to revenge their wrongs."[41]

An intriguing dimension of many of these descriptions of highland women lies in two features that, in terms of Victorian values, seem contradictory. While fully documenting the ways in which these women assumed the roles of protector, provider, and guardian of their homes, their families, and often their husbands, the fugitives spared no romantic cliché or florid Victorian flight of prose in describing the femininity and sexual allure of these hearty belligerents in skirts.

Under the chapter heading "A Noble Woman," for example, J. Madison Drake recounted an incident in which a woman discovered him and his companions as they hid in a ravine near her remote cabin. "She was a typical woman of the North Carolina mountains," Drake wrote. "No shadow of fear manifested itself in her somewhat masculine features, as she boldly advanced toward us." Mrs. Estes, as he later learned to call her, demanded that the Union prowlers identify themselves and offered them food if they could assure her that they were not in the area to round up deserters. "You must not use any deceit [or] you will be shot down where you stand. A dozen true rifles are now levelled on you, and if I raise my hand you will fall dead at my feet. . . . If you turn out to be spies, seeking the life of my husband and his friends, you will rue the day you ventured into this wild." Drake concluded, "We had never met before such a woman . . . certainly the bravest of her sex."[42]

Once Drake and his companions had affirmed their northern identities and assured Mrs. Estes that they posed no danger to her deserter husband, she became a kind and generous ally. Her hospitality proved boundless; once ensconced as a comfortable, well-fed guest in her cabin, Drake focused less on her masculine features and fearless demeanor, remarking instead that "she looked quite handsome now, having combed her hair smoothly down her ruddy cheeks, and with her comely form robed in a green dress . . . and a gracious smile, worthy of a queen."[43]

Other physically enticing women proved equally hardened to the realities of the conflict encroaching upon their remote highland homes. Along the Nolichucky River in western North Carolina, William Parkins, a fugitive from South Carolina, was taken in by a Unionist sympathizer known as "Old Yank" and his daughters, described by Parkins as "three comely, bright-eyed, lithe but buxom mountain maidens." In relating the harassment he had endured at the hands of Confederates as a result of his nickname and well-known sympathies, Old Yank told Parkins that, in response to one attempt to force him into service, "I just reached 'round the door and pulled out my Henry rifle, an' my gals understood it an' got their double-barreled shotguns, an' I just told them boys I had lived too long in the mountains to be scared that way, an' if they . . . laid hands on an ole man like me they'd never do it agin, fur my gals had the bead on 'em."[44]

Junius Browne wrote of "A Nameless Heroine" in East Tennessee, who, though only sixteen or seventeen years old, "had assisted many true men out of awkward predicaments and dangerous situations, and had shown herself willing at all times to aid them." Working closely with that most notorious of mountain Unionist guides, Daniel Ellis, "she had often arisen at night when she obtained intelligence of importance, and communicated it to loyalists some miles distant, preventing their capture or murder by the enemy." Browne, obviously quite taken with this teenager's courage and capabilities, devoted several pages of his book to recounting her exploits in much detail. Clearly, he was much taken with her demeanor, noting that she was "decidedly fair, intelligent, of graceful figure, and possessed of that indispensable requisite to an agreeable woman—a sweet voice." He confessed to gazing at her "as she sat there, calm, smiling, comely, with the warm blood of youth flushing in her cheek, under the flood of mellow moonlight that bathed all the landscape in poetic softness and picturesque beauty."[45] While such descriptions likely reflect the natural proclivities of military males too long denied female companionship, it is obvious that much of the attraction had to do with more substantive and less sexual qualities.

Fugitives' interest in the women they encountered often lay in their independent and often outspoken views regarding the war and their courage in expressing those views. Soon after moving into North Carolina after an escape from Columbia's Camp Sorghum, Captain J. V. Hadley and a group of fellow fugitives approached three young women in Flat Rock, in Henderson County, taking the opportunity "to investigate the Union sentiment in the mountains." The men identified themselves as Confederate soldiers and were surprised to receive a stern lecture from one of the girls, who blamed the men for bringing on the war. Her tirade serves as one of the few explicit declarations of mountain Unionists' opposition to the Confederate cause. "For a few niggers," she charged the soldiers, "you've driven this country to war, and force men into the army to fight for you who don't want to go, and you've got the whole country in such a plight that there's nothing going on but huntin' and killin' . . . all the time."[46] Pleased with the girl's response and impressed with her courage in confronting what she thought were enemy soldiers, Hadley and his companions revealed their true allegiances to her and her sisters, and received aid and shelter from them.[47]

Drew Gilpin Faust has noted the number of southern women who expressed a yearning to be men during the course of the Civil War. While none of the women encountered and quoted here ever articulated a wish for what Faust calls "a magical personal deliverance from gender restraints," many demonstrated to the Union fugitives whom they aided just how capable they were of crossing the lines of traditional gender roles to meet the new demands the war imposed on them.[48] Of equal significance, though, is the degree to which the fugitives admired and celebrated the manly virtues and masculine role-playing—the practical and ideological independence, the assertiveness, and even the militancy—of the Union women whom they encountered, particularly when these women were serving the fugitives' interests and needs so well.

How, then, are we to assess the value of this "subgenre" of Civil War literature as a commentary on Southern Appalachian society? In contrast to most depictions of mountaineers during the nineteenth century, these accounts present appraisals of their subjects that are far more positive than most. Northern fugitive soldiers brought fewer preconceptions and prejudices concerning southern mountain life into the region. Their intent at the time was neither to observe, nor comment upon, nor improve what they found. In the midst of a war in which their lives were very much at stake, the escaped prisoners characterized mountaineers in terms of their behaviors and attitudes, noting the extent to which both served to alleviate their own predicaments. Their status as hunted men was crucial to their powers of observation and criteria for assessment.

Other Union soldiers who moved through Appalachia had far different reactions to the highlanders with whom they had to interact. Southwestern Virginia was inundated with Federal troops intermittently throughout the war, with major incursions into the region in late 1861 and early 1864. Kenneth Noe has analyzed the letters, diaries, and regimental histories produced by those soldiers and finds their characterizations of the highland populace they observed "by far some of most degrading depictions of mountain people ever penned." They dismissed their subjects in much harsher terms than did those who moved through the same area before the war. Typical of the former commentaries is that of Rutherford B. Hayes, who served in the area with the 23rd Ohio Volunteer Infantry in 1861 and 1862. "What a good-for-nothing people the mass of these western Virginians are!" he wrote, going on to refer to them as "unenterprising, lazy, narrow, listless and ignorant, members of a helpless and harmless race."[49]

Nor were Union troops as tolerant or as generous as the fugitives toward the blacks or white women with whom they came in contact in moving through the Confederacy. In his study of the behavior and attitudes of Sherman's troops, Joseph Glatthaar found that, while attitudes toward the many slaves and former slaves with whom the troops came in contact varied greatly, they harbored a great deal of resentment toward blacks and often mistreated them. An Ohio captain confirmed that "the silly prejudice of color is as deeply rooted among northern as among southern men. Very many of our soldiers have as yet no idea of treating this oppressed race with justice."[50]

In his book on Federal soldiers' experiences and perceptions of the war, Reid Mitchell, in a chapter entitled "She-Devils," noted the extent to which northern troops condemned southern women for their savagery, their treachery, and the "irrational zeal" with which they supported the rebellion and drove their men to do likewise. Such contempt for these women, whom many Federals saw as the most determined and even dangerous of Rebels, cast them as little more than prostitutes or "loose women" devoid of the virtues characteristic of northern womanhood.[51]

In all such cases, both in and outside Appalachia, invading or occupying forces were fully secure and in control of their situations. No doubt, they rarely were intimate with, or particularly dependent upon, those into whose communities they had intruded. One wonders whether Hayes and his comrades would have been so contemptuous of those remote Virginia highlanders had they been forced to move through the same territory as escaped prisoners. By the same token, one wonders how differently the men of Sherman's army of liberation would have reacted toward slaves and slavery had they, as prisoners on the run in enemy territory, found the aid of those slaves vital to their survival. Ironically, too, the qualities that Union troops found so contemptible in Confederate "she-devils"—their toughness and stubborn resolve—were the very ones that the fugitives, grateful to their female allies, celebrated in their descriptions of those women. The physical allure of these highland heroines seems to have been directly correlated with their ideological correctness. An Illinois private's observation from East Tennessee—"There is some good looking girls down heare, union girls that is"—is a blatant example of the interplay of sexual and political biases conveyed with only slightly more subtlety in many of the fugitive narratives.[52]

Dependence and gratitude tend to breed tolerance and open-mindedness. No other travelers through Southern Appalachia ever were so dependent upon the highlanders they met or had as much reason for gratitude toward them as did these escaped prisoners of war. The aid they received, the kindnesses bestowed upon them, and the collusion with those of like loyalties assured the safe passage, and even saved the lives, of many Union fugitives; hence they were predisposed to portray those responsible in a generous light. As a result, mountain Unionists appear as men of intelligence, courage, and steady resolve; their wives as both "angels of mercy" and strong, determined, and capable fighters; and mountain slaves as intelligent, cunning, defiant, and patriotic allies.

But such impressions, if they registered at all, proved fleeting in the national mindset. William Hesseltine, in assessing the propagandistic purposes of the prison narratives, maintained that their authors wrote of the atrocities they endured in southern prisons in order to assure the South's punishment during Reconstruction, and to keep alive public resentment of Rebel cruelties. "No group in America furnished more gore for the bloody shirt," Hesseltine claimed, "than ex–prisoners of war."[53] Such motives may also have inspired the neo-abolitionist tone of several of the narratives.

The prison passages of these works, along with others, served as effective antisouthern propaganda; curiously, though, the post-prison sections dealt with here had little or no influence in shaping more positive perceptions of the one group of southerners they consistently portrayed in a favorable light—those in Appalachia during this very period in which a national consciousness of the region was emerging —but in very different terms. The literary and socially conscious "discovery"—or, as Allen Batteau terms it, the "invention"—of Appalachia by northerners in the late nineteenth century served "to provide American society with colorful characters for its fiction, perfect innocents for its philanthropy, and an undeveloped wilderness in which to prove its pioneering blood."[54] It took demeaning and distorted imagery to do so. By the 1870s and 1880s, just as many of the fugitive narratives were being published, other accounts were also emerging, portraying Appalachia as "a strange land and peculiar people."[55] In such accounts, southern mountaineers emerged as depraved and semi-barbaric people, notable for their moonshining, feuding, and inbreeding, as well as for their poverty and ignorance.

At the same time, a more uplifting aspect of Appalachian myth-making also was under way: the creation of "Holy Appalachia."[56] Much of the appeal to those discovering the region in the latter half of the nineteenth century was its apparent ethnic purity, its whiteness. Historian James Klotter has reasoned that rampant racism and other barriers thwarted philanthropic impulses toward southern freedmen during Reconstruction. Those impulses then were transferred to another group of southerners perceived as equally needy and perhaps more deserving—the mountaineers who were, in the words of a turn-of-the-century ethnographer, the "purest Anglo-Saxon stock in all the United States."[57]

Other northerners, intent upon sectional reconciliation with the South, found its highlanders' wartime loyalty—that "union column thrust deep into the heart of the Confederacy"—vital to its mission of bringing the country together. They were quick to exploit a corollary of Appalachia's image as a solid bastion of Unionism by suggesting that this lack of support for the Confederacy was due to highlanders' opposition to slavery. According to one lofty assertion, Appalachians "cherish liberty as a priceless heritage. They would never hold slaves and we may almost say they will never be enslaved."[58]

The fugitive prison narratives could not be used to buttress such views of the highland South. Their depiction of regular and constant contact between slaves and free blacks throughout the mountains clashed with the image of Appalachia as both a slaveless region and a racially pure populace. By the same token, those who championed Appalachians' unwavering commitment to the Union would have found these narratives questionable sources of validation. While mountain Unionists emerge as the heroes and heroines of the fugitive accounts, they also make quite apparent their minority status within their region; their heroism stems from the fact that they were forced to cope within an ideologically hostile environment.

In short, there seems to have been little place in the rapidly evolving imagery of postbellum Appalachia for the more complex and nuanced narratives of the Civil War fugitives. Not only did these accounts undermine the stereotypes of a primitive, violent, and depraved people; they also showed a populace more diverse in terms of race, political ideology, and socioeconomic circumstances than the dictates of regional stereotyping and image making could bear. While these narratives contradict—and might have provided useful correctives for—much of the simplistic condescension with which the region was being perceived after the war, there is no evidence that they were ever put to such use.[59] One can speculate that, upon close scrutiny, such sources proved less useful because their complexities, contradictions, and variables would have diluted the simplicity of the myth that, when the war came, "Appalachian America clave to the old flag."[60]

The very depth and credibility of those narratives, in effect, diminished their polemical value during an era in which less ambivalent and multilayered messages were in vogue. Yet their very rich and often powerful portraits of Appalachians—along with the sheer volume of material they contain—have encouraged recent historians of the war and of the region to utilize the narratives in challenging the very mythology that was created at the same time when they, too, were being produced and read.

Notes

1. Three of the most comprehensive treatments of the nineteenth-century literature on Appalachia make no mention of the Civil War fugitive narratives. They are Cratis D. Williams, "The Southern Mountaineer in Fact and Fiction" (Ph.D. diss., New York University, 1961); Henry D. Shapiro, *Appalachia on Our Mind: The Southern Mountains and Mountaineers in the American Consciousness, 1870–1920* (Chapel Hill: University of North Carolina Press, 1978); and Allen W. Batteau, *The Invention of Appalachia* (Tucson: University of Arizona Press, 1990).

2. Edmund Wilson, *Patriotic Gore: Studies in the Literature of the American Civil War* (New York: Farrar, Straus, and Giroux, 1962), ix; Louis P. Masur, *"The Real War Will Never Get in the Books": Selections from Writers during the Civil War* (New York: Oxford University Press, 1993), iv. For other treatments of the Civil War as conveyed in memoir and autobiography, see Daniel Aaron, *The Unwritten War: American Writers and the Civil War* (New York: Knopf, 1973); and Anne C. Rose, *Victorian America and the Civil War* (Cambridge, England: Cambridge University Press, 1992), chap. 6. On the high literacy rate of Civil War soldiers, see James M. McPher-

son, *What They Fought For, 1861–1865* (Baton Rouge: Louisiana State University Press, 1994), 1, 4–6.

3. William B. Hesseltine, "The Propaganda Literature of Confederate Prisons," *Journal of Southern History* 1 (Feb. 1935): 56. In the bibliography of Hesseltine's earlier *Civil War Prisons: A Study in War Psychology* (Columbus: Ohio State University Press, 1930), 261–80, he lists 212 such works—148 books, 55 articles, and 9 nineteenth-century accounts of others' experiences.

4. Hesseltine, *Civil War Prisons,* 165–67; see also Hesseltine, "The Underground Railroad from Confederate Prisons to East Tennessee," *East Tennessee Historical Society's Publications* 2 (1930): 55–69.

5. James W. Savage, "The Loyal Element of North Carolina during the War," a pamphlet (Omaha, Neb.: privately published, 1886), 4. For other accounts of this network, see William Burson, *A Race for Liberty; or, My Capture, My Imprisonment, and My Escape* (Wellsville, Ohio: W. G. Foster, 1867), 80; Hesseltine, "Underground Railroad"; Paul A. Whelan, "Unconventional Warfare in East Tennessee, 1861–1865" (master's thesis, University of Tennessee, 1963), chap. 5; and Arnold Ritt, "The Escape of Federal Prisoners through East Tennessee, 1861–1865" (master's thesis, University of Tennessee, 1965).

6. Ella Lonn, *Desertion during the Civil War* (New York: Century, 1928), 200–201.

7. Savage, *Loyal Element of North Carolina,* 4. Savage cites a Captain Hock of the 12th New York Cavalry as the source of this information.

8. Philip N. Racine, ed., *"Unspoiled Heart": The Journal of Charles Mattocks of the 17th Maine* (Knoxville: University of Tennessee Press, 1994), 236–37, 246–47.

9. J. Madison Drake, *Fast and Loose in Dixie* (New York: the author, 1880), 177, 117–18.

10. Ibid., 178.

11. John Azor Kellogg, *Capture and Escape: A Narrative of Army and Prison Life,* Original Papers, no. 2 (Madison: Wisconsin Historical Commission, 1908), 165.

12. Junius Henri Browne, *Four Years in Secessia: Adventures Within and Beyond the Union Lines* (Hartford, Conn.: O. D. Case, 1865), 351–52.

13. Albert D. Richardson, *The Secret Service, the Field, the Dungeon, and the Escape* (Hartford, Conn.: American, 1865), 458.

14. Ibid., 470, 473.

15. Ibid., 451.

16. Kellogg, *Capture and Escape,* 165–66. Emphasis in original.

17. Ibid., 459.

18. Drake, *Fast and Loose in Dixie,* 160.

19. A. O. Abbott, *Prison Life in the South: At Richmond, Macon, Sa-*

vannah, Charleston, Columbia, Charlotte, Raleigh, Goldsborough, and Andersonville during the Years 1864 and 1865 (New York: Harper and Bros., 1865), 236.

20. For a fuller account of such transactions, see chap. 4 in this volume, "Mountain Masters as Confederate Opportunists."

21. James M. Fales, *The Prison Life of James M. Fales,* ed. George N. Bliss (Providence, R.I.: N. Bangs, Williams, 1882), 55–56.

22. Kellogg, *Capture and Escape,* 147, 149.

23. William H. Newlin, *An Account of the Escape of Six Federal Soldiers from Prison at Danville, Va.: Their Travels by Night through the Enemy's Country to the Union Pickets at Gauley Bridge, West Virginia, in the Winter of 1863–64,* rev. ed. (Cincinnati, Ohio: Western Methodist Book Concern, 1886), 54, 56.

24. Racine, ed., *"Unspoiled Heart,"* 237–39.

25. Richardson, *Secret Service,* 444–45.

26. Browne, *Four Years in Secessia,* 368.

27. See Charles O. Hunt, "Our Escape from Camp Sorghum," in *War Papers Read before the Commandery of the State of Maine, Military Order of the Loyal Legion of the United States* (Portland, Me.: Thurston Press, 1898), 1:96.

28. Burson, *Race for Liberty,* 79–82.

29. Michael Egan, *The Flying Gray-Haired Yank; or, The Adventures of a Volunteer* (Marietta, Ohio: Edgewood, 1888), 279–82. See also W. H. Parkins, *How I Escaped,* ed. Archibald C. Gunter (New York: Home, 1889), 118, for an account of a similar incident.

30. Alonzo Cooper, *In and Out of Rebel Prisons* (Oswego, N.Y.: R. J. Oliphant, 1889), 188–97.

31. Ibid., 197–98.

32. Richardson, *Secret Service,* 444–45.

33. Kellogg, *Capture and Escape,* 148.

34. James R. Gilmore, *Adrift in Dixie; or, A Yankee Officer among the Rebels* (New York: Carleton, 1866), 11–12. (Edmund Kirke's name appears on the title page of the book and the author's name does not. The author is identified by two different names elsewhere—as Gilmore in the copyright citation, and as Henry L. Estabrooks in Kirke's introduction.)

35. Rose, *Victorian America,* 242–44.

36. Nina Silber, *The Romance of Reunion: Northerners and the South, 1865–1900* (Chapel Hill: University of North Carolina Press, 1993), discusses factors contributing to beneficent impulses of northern whites toward southern blacks after the war. Interestingly, Silber includes analyses of northern attitudes toward both blacks and mountaineers in a single chapter (chap. 5, "Of Minstrels and Mountaineers: The Whitewashed Road to Reunion," 124–58), but within the chapter makes no attempt at linking the two.

37. Michael Fellman, *Inside War: The Guerrilla Conflict in Missouri during the American Civil War* (New York: Oxford University Press, 1989), 193.

38. W. H. Shelton, "A Hard Road to Travel Out of Dixie," *Century Magazine* 40 (Oct. 1890): 937.

39. Hunt, "Our Escape from Camp Sorghum," 113.

40. Charles G. Davis, "Army Life and Prison Experiences of Major Charles G. Davis," undated typescript, in Special Collections, University of Tennessee Library, Knoxville, quoted in Durwood Dunn, *Cades Cove: The Life and Death of a Southern Mountain Community* (Knoxville: University of Tennessee Press, 1988), 137–38.

41. Frank Wilkeson, *Recollections of a Private Soldier* (New York: Putnam, 1889), 232–33, quoted in Philip Shaw Paludan, *Victims: A True Story of the Civil War* (Knoxville: University of Tennessee Press, 1981), 23.

42. Drake, *Fast and Loose in Dixie,* 148–50.

43. Ibid., 152.

44. Parkins, *How I Escaped,* 116–17. Parkins calls this book a novel, but it varies only slightly from his autobiographical narrative, "Between Two Flags; or, The Story of the War by a Refugee," and his 1885 typescript in the William H. Parkins Papers, Atlanta History Center.

45. Browne, *Four Years in Secessia,* 421–23. Daniel Ellis identifies this "nameless heroine" as Melvina Stephens, the daughter of a "good Union man" at Kelly's Gap, Tennessee. See Daniel Ellis, *Thrilling Adventures of Daniel Ellis, the Great Union Guide of East Tennessee for a Period of Nearly Four Years during the Great Southern Rebellion* (New York: Harper and Brothers, 1867), 357–58.

46. J. V. Hadley, *Seven Months a Prisoner* (New York: Charles Scribner's Sons, 1898), 180–81.

47. For a more extended version of these sisters' story, and for a discussion of other outspoken women whose loyalties often contradicted those of their husbands or parents, see chap. 6 in this volume, "Highland Households Divided."

48. Drew Gilpin Faust, "On the Altars of Sacrifice: Confederate Women and the Narratives of War," *Journal of American History* 76 (March 1990): 1200–1228, quotation on 1206–7. For treatments of similar demands and the responses to them by Confederate women in Appalachia, see Gordon B. McKinney, "Women's Role in Civil War North Carolina," *North Carolina Historical Review* 69 (January 1992): 37–56; Ralph Mann, "Guerrilla Warfare and Gender Roles: Sandy Basin, Virginia, as a Test Case," *Journal of the Appalachian Studies Association* 5 (1993): 59–68; and chap. 7 in this volume, "Coping in Confederate Appalachia."

49. Kenneth W. Noe, "'Appalachia's' Civil War Genesis: Southwest Virginia as Depicted by Northern and European Writers, 1825–1865," *West*

Virginia History 50 (1991): 102; and Noe, "Exterminating Savages: The Union Army and Mountain Guerrillas in Southern West Virginia, 1861–1862," in Noe and Wilson, eds., *Civil War in Appalachia*, 104–30.

50. Quoted in Joseph T. Glatthaar, *The March to the Sea and Beyond: Sherman's Troops in the Savannah and Carolina Campaigns* (New York: New York University Press, 1985), 55–56. James McPherson, *What They Fought For*, 58–67, documents considerably more variety in Union soldiers' attitudes toward southern blacks, noting that sentiment opposing emancipation was based on "a mixture of racism, conservatism and partisan politics," while support for emancipation among northern troops was the result more of pragmatic than of altruistic motives.

51. Reid Mitchell, *The Vacant Chair: The Northern Soldier Leaves Home* (New York: Oxford University Press, 1993), chap. 6. For other treatments of Union soldiers' interactions with southern women, see George C. Rabie, *Civil Wars: Women and the Crisis of Southern Nationalism* (Urbana: University of Illinois Press, 1989), chap. 8; Nina Silber, "Intemperate Men, Spiteful Women, and Jefferson Davis," in *Divided Houses: Gender and the Civil War*, ed. Catherine Clinton and Nina Silber (New York: Oxford University Press, 1992), 283–305; Charles Royster, *The Destructive War: William Tecumseh Sherman, Stonewall Jackson, and the Americans* (New York: Knopf, 1991), 86–87; and Glatthaar, *March to the Sea*, 71–76.

52. Mitchell, *Vacant Chair*, 98, using this quotation, notes a correlation among virtue, prettiness, and a pro-Union stance in Federal perceptions of southern women. Quotation from Albertus A. Dunham and Charles LaForrest Dunah, *Through the South with a Union Soldier*, ed. Arthur H. DeRosier Jr. (Johnson City, Tenn.: East Tennessee State University Research Council, 1969), 48.

53. Hesseltine, "Propaganda Literature of Confederate Prisons," 64–65.

54. Batteau, *Invention of Appalachia*, 1.

55. This term was coined by Will Wallace Harvey in "A Strange Land and a Peculiar People," *Lippincott's Magazine* 12 (October 1873): 429–38.

56. Batteau applies this term to Berea College President William G. Frost, a "latter-day abolitionist" whose turn-of-the-century chronicles of mountain life made him one of the era's most influential image makers. Batteau, *Invention of Appalachia*, 74–78.

57. James C. Klotter, "The Black South and White Appalachia," *Journal of American History* 66 (March 1980): 832–49; Ellen Churchill Semple, "The Anglo-Saxons of the Kentucky Mountains: A Study in Anthropogeography," *Bulletin of the American Geographical Society* 42 (August 1910): 566. See also Silber, *Romance of Reunion*, 143–52.

58. William G. Frost, "Our Contemporary Ancestors in the Southern Mountains," *Atlantic Monthly* 83 (March 1899): 314.

59. Among the proponents of the myth of Unionist Appalachia were

Frost, "Our Contemporary Ancestors," 311–19; Julian Ralph, *Dixie; or, Southern Scenes and Sketches* (New York: Harper and Brothers, 1896); and Samuel T. Wilson, *The Southern Mountaineers* (New York: J. J. Little and Ives, 1914). Scholarly analyses of these and other works include Shapiro, *Appalachia on Our Mind*, 87–90; Batteau, *Invention of Appalachia*, 77–79; Klotter, "Black South and White Appalachia"; Silber, *Romance of Reunion*, 143–52; Kenneth W. Noe, "Toward the Myth of Unionist Appalachia, 1865–1883," *Journal of the Appalachian Studies Association* 6 (1994): 73–80; and chap. 12 in this volume, "A Northern Wedge Thrust into the Heart of the Confederacy."

60. Quotation from Frost, "Our Contemporary Ancestors," 314.

9

"Talking Heroines"

Elite Mountain Women as Chroniclers of Stoneman's Raid, April 1865

By the fall of 1865, Cornelia Phillips Spencer was already at work on a book that would be published the following year entitled *The Last Ninety Days of the War in North Carolina.* The Chapel Hill widow took on this task at the suggestion of David Lowery Swain, former governor of the state and longtime president of the University of North Carolina. She originally conceived of—and contracted for—her narrative as a series of articles in *The Watchman,* a new journal established by a UNC professor at war's end to promote sectional reconciliation. The "unexpected favor" with which readers received the series led Spencer to expand her narrative and reissue it in book form.[1]

While she acknowledged in her opening pages that it would be long before the "history of the late war can be soberly and impartially written," Spencer said she recognized that future historians would need to have evidence from private sources in order to do so, noting that "history has no more invaluable and irrefragable witnesses for the truth than are to be found in the journals, memoranda, and private correspondence of the prominent and influential men who either acted in, or were compelled to remain quiet observers of the events of their day."[2]

In this statement, Spencer revealed both class and gendered biases common to her era and long afterward as to who made history and whose perspectives were worthwhile in capturing and preserving it—"prominent and influential men." She was diligent in her attempts to obtain from such sources their own memories, correspondence, and other records in order to construct her account of the conflict's waning days in her home state. Her own prominence in the university town—a professor's daughter and close friend and confidante of Swain—gave her entrée to a number of connections who provided her with considerable materials, including former governors Zebulon B. Vance and William A. Graham and state Supreme Court justice Thomas Ruffin. Not surprisingly, Spencer did not seem to have actively sought such input from women around the state, though their voices occasionally made their way into her narrative.

A major part of Spencer's book—three full chapters—chronicles General George Stoneman's raid through western North Carolina in April 1865, a mission one later historian described as "a knife thrust into the virtually undefended back of the South."[3] As in the rest of her book, the female perspective on that traumatic culmination of the war in the southern highlands appears only fleetingly. Yet what has made this raid so striking to historians is the unusual number—and fullness—of accounts written by women who lived along Stoneman's route and experienced encounters with his troops. Like an outspoken woman in Winchester, Virginia, who verbally challenged disruptive Union troops and was called by an admiring neighbor "one of the talking heroines," a number of these Appalachian women in North Carolina also confronted the enemy at their doorsteps and demonstrated real courage and resolve in doing so.[4] But the trait shared by all of them was the impulse to record their experiences in vivid and often heartfelt terms.

Several of these accounts are extended diary or journal entries; some are long, descriptive letters written in the moment or just afterward; and others are memoirs, which may or may not have been meant for publication, composed well after the fact. Of those preserved and accessible to us today, these narratives, taken together, provide fresh insights into the ways the elite women of the Carolina highlands experienced this incursion that so threatened their homes and their families and how they chose to convey their observations, feelings, and actions in written form.[5] In "talking" with a pen about what they had endured, these women not only provide us with alternative perspectives on the war's latter days than those provided by the "prominent and influential" men on whom Cornelia Spencer depended for her book; they also reveal much about class and racial tensions, for which Stoneman's Raid proved a catalyst, and about the considerable void that separated the region's elite from their less fortunate neighbors and fellow highlanders.[6]

The women who left such vivid written records of their encounters with Stoneman were (with one exception) natives of western North Carolina and were fully part of the local elites that dominated the county seats or their rural environs. Their families had been among the first to settle in these towns and fertile valleys. While not plantation mistresses, they probably had more in common with such women of the lowland South than they did with most women in their own region, those situated on more isolated highland homesteads in more remote parts of the mountains, those far more vulnerable to the fierce guerrilla warfare and bushwhacker harassment that had plagued those outlying areas for much of the war's duration.

Most of those "talking heroines" were members of slaveholding families who owned between four and forty-two slaves in 1860.[7] Their husbands and/or fathers held extensive farmlands but were just as likely to be lawyers or merchants, or engaged in other business or professional endeavors. Whereas these women endured some wartime tribulations—the absence of husbands and other men in Confederate service, shortages of various foodstuffs and household goods—they had been relatively insulated from the violence and abuse of enemy armies or mobs. Perhaps because they remained out of harm's way until the war's final month, these women remained committed to the Confederate cause and portrayed themselves in their narratives as true southerners.

In hindsight, it seems rather remarkable that most of these women remained so oblivious to such attacks and other upheavals. In 1862, soon after moving to the French Broad Valley of Buncombe County from her family's Mississippi plantation, Katherine Polk Gale commented on her new home: "Peace & plenty ruled everywhere. The country was so shut in from the world, it seemed almost impossible for the desolations of war to reach the happy homes along the route." Much of her account of the war years in Asheville dwells on the hospitality she enjoyed and the friendships she made among "the many charming, cultivated people" there. "Though we knew in Asheville, the war was going on relentlessly," she wrote, "there was nothing in our surroundings to suggest it, as we were so far removed from everything connected with it."[8]

A number of these women, situated as they were in county seats or in the broad valleys along the eastern slopes of the Blue Ridge, expressed similar degrees of complacency in terms of their own comfort and safety for much of the war's duration. Most were part of close kinship or neighborhood networks that provided both social interaction with other women of their own class and a mutual support system that allowed them to weather both material and emotional burdens the war imposed. Emma L. Rankin in McDowell County spoke for many of her peers when she wrote, "Up to the winter of '64–'65 our experience of the trials of the war was confined to the anxiety about friends in the army, and the privations which were lightly esteemed and cheerfully borne, hoping always for a joyful end. True we were far from blockade goods, but what cared we. . . . We had thought it highly improbable that a blue-coat would ever be seen in our secluded region."[9] As late as February 1865, Ella Harper, Rankin's sister-in-law in Lenoir, acknowledged to her husband their good fortune in being "exempt from the severe forms of trial incident to this dreadful war."[10]

Such impressions could hardly have differed more from those of far less privileged and far more vulnerable women elsewhere in the region. As Katherine Gale was enjoying a pleasant social life in Asheville, women in adjacent Madison County were being whipped and hanged by their fingers by Union troops seeking information about their husbands' whereabouts. The guerrilla warfare that wracked the more remote parts of both the Blue Ridge and Smoky mountains made many women both active agents and likely targets of the ruthless violence and deliberate cruelties it spawned.[11] For other poor women, crop failure, the disruption of access to market goods, and the destruction or theft of livestock, foodstuffs, or other property vital to their welfare meant that starvation posed the greatest challenge they faced during the war years. Much of that desperation comes through in the letters of such women, often barely literate, to Governor Zebulon Vance, himself a native of the region, and thus assumed by many in the mountains to be a sympathetic resource for alleviating their problems.[12]

There is little evidence that the elite women felt much sympathy for their more beleaguered neighbors' suffering. Class distinctions were never far from the surface in their commentary on those from whom they so distanced themselves. Mary Bell, of Franklin, North Carolina, for instance, expressed her disdain for less fortunate men and women who faced a Union raid in the northwestern part of her own county. "It was the most ridiculous thing I ever heard of," she wrote to her husband, Alfred. "I think evry man in Macon Co., except those that were too old to get away skidadled." She was no more sympathetic toward the frightened women left behind, as she described the two or three days in which they had had to endure the prospect of "fine times during yankee holadays." In a somewhat scornful tone, she detailed a variety of mishaps other women encountered in their efforts to hide their valuables and livestock and to safeguard their homes, much of which comes across as little more than slapstick in her irreverent retelling of various incidents.[13]

In Wilkes County, Lizzie Lenoir, a member of one of that area's oldest and most prominent families, conveyed nothing but contempt for women who raided granaries in nearby Jonesville in January 1865. This was the last of several "bread riots" instigated by groups of women throughout the Confederacy, who were driven to mob action by food shortages and their frustration at local officials' failure to respond in any equitable way. Like most others, this effort failed, much to Lenoir's satisfaction. Somewhat bemusedly, she informed her aunt of a "band of *women,* armed with axes" who converged in wagons on a granary and demanded its ground corn. "There was only one man in the place," she wrote, "and he (Leonidas like) stood in the door of the house and bid defiance to the crowd. You know women generally want to carry their point, and it was with great difficulty that our hero could withstand them. They were happily thrown into confusion by an old drunk man coming up with a huge *brush* in his hand, striking their horses with it, causing them to run away with their wagons, and some of *them* in it." She concluded smugly, "They didn't get any of the corn."[14]

Neither of these women showed any sympathy, much less empathy, for the desperate plight of the wives and mothers driven to such drastic measures. Only with Stoneman's Raid three months later did the region's female elite face the same sort of trauma themselves. Their complacency came to an abrupt end thanks to a New York general and the six thousand cavalrymen he led in wreaking havoc on their towns, villages, and valleys in April 1865. Major General George Stoneman, a West Point graduate, headed up the district of East Tennessee early in 1865 when General Ulysses S. Grant ordered him to lead a cavalry raid into the interior of South Carolina, "visiting a portion of the state which will not be reached by Sherman's forces," including Columbia. His orders were to destroy railroads and other military resources, and then to move to Salisbury, North Carolina, the site of a major Confederate prison, on his way back to East Tennessee, and liberate its Union prisoners. Grant also saw Stoneman's mission as a diversionary tactic, drawing away from Sherman's path at least some of the Confederate forces that would otherwise challenge his march northward.[15]

Owing to a series of delays, Sherman had already taken Columbia and had moved on into North Carolina by the time Stoneman was ready to move. His mission was thus scaled back to a raid on the Salisbury prison, with the destruction of property and military resources a secondary goal as his troops moved through the North Carolina mountains, thus preventing either General Robert E. Lee's army in Virginia or General Joseph E. Johnston's around Raleigh from making a westward retreat through North Carolina.

On March 28, Stoneman crossed the state line into North Carolina with his six thousand horsemen, nearly all the available cavalrymen then in East Tennessee. While most of these troops were units from Pennsylvania, Michigan, Ohio, and Kentucky, a sizable number of "home Yankees" were along as well, many of them Carolina highlanders recruited into Union service. They first attacked and ransacked the small town of Boone, whose residents the approaching raiders caught fully by surprise. From there they moved east out of the mountains and through foothill communities until they reached their ultimate destination of Salisbury on April 12, where they destroyed vast supply depots, public buildings, cotton mills and tanneries, a foundry, and the prison—although Confederate authorities had moved its few remaining occupants to Charlotte a month before. From Salisbury, Stoneman's forces split: two brigades, under Brigadier General Alvan C. Gillem, headed directly west again, attacking similar targets in several towns as they moved toward Asheville, like Salisbury a community that Union forces targeted because of its role as a center of Confederate activity. Colonel William Palmer led a third brigade south toward Lincolnton and Charlotte before turning west toward Asheville. Stoneman himself, having achieved the primary goal of the raid in Salisbury's destruction, returned to Tennessee, taking with him nearly a thousand prisoners, mostly home guardsmen and Confederate veterans who had returned home, either injured or ill.

The destruction of Boone set a pattern of disruption and property damage that the Union forces continued to inflict on other towns along their route—though with significant variations. The degree of damage done depended in part on how local citizens responded to the raid. Thus Winston and Salem, then two separate towns, escaped harm when the mayor and a contingent of leading citizens greeted the invading force on the outskirts of town waving white handkerchiefs. At the other extreme, Morganton citizens sought to ambush Stoneman's men as they moved west from Salisbury—and paid a heavy price for their resistance. In reaction to such local aggression, the most intense home defense they had faced on this mission, the Federal troops were allowed to engage in wholesale plundering of the nearly deserted town and harassment of the few remaining residents—mainly women—on a scale not yet authorized. Likewise, Asheville, simply by its well-recognized role as the region's center of Confederate activity, faced the final and most brutal attack by Stoneman's men. The unexpectedness of an incursion on this scale caught many, if not most, residents there off guard. Part of their shock came from the fact that this attack came two days after an armistice had been reached by General Gillem and the Confederate commander, General James G. Martin, on April 26.

One of the more striking aspects of the encounters between these Union forces and the elite women whose homes and property they threatened was the willingness of many of the women to play the role of "talking heroines," that is, to personally confront either Stoneman himself or another of his officers either as supplicants or in defiance. Emma Rankin of Lenoir, who tutored Colonel Logan Carson's children at his Pleasant Gardens farm in nearby McDowell County, was quick to challenge "an impudent lieutenant" who asked her where the horses had been hidden. When he refused to believe her reply that the slaves had hidden them, noting that he was from Kentucky and knew as much about blacks as she did, "I told him that if he was a Kentuckian he ought to be ashamed of being in that band of marauders." After more of his insolence, Rankin wrote, he left in search of the horses, assuring her that they would find the horses, that "Yankees never fail in search."[16]

Rankin, like others, also reported kindnesses from individual soldiers. When a Union cavalryman strayed from his passing company and galloped up to the door and asked to see Miss Rankin, she said, "If his Satanic majesty had called for me, I could scarcely have been more astonished." He told her that he had guarded her father's house in Lenoir from the vandals that often followed in their wake and was delivering to her a letter from her father, as he had promised to do. He assured her that "Lenoir was not injured by us at all," though she claimed she knew that they had "eaten up the meager supplies which the village afforded, if nothing more."[17]

The detail with which these women recounted such exchanges suggests that they took real satisfaction in their own boldness in confronting the enemy invaders. In Lenoir, one of the towns taken early by Stoneman's raiders, General Gillem confronted Callie Hagler and "impertinently" said to her: "I know you are a rebel from the way you move—Ain't you a Rebel?" She replied by asking him if he had ever heard the story of the tailor's wife and the scissors. When he said he had, she said, "Then I am a rebel as high as I can reach" and wrote that her answer seemed to amuse him. Yet on another occasion soon afterward, Gillem was not so amused. Hagler recalled, "While denouncing the cruelties of the Confederates to their prisoners, he became very angry at [me] for venturing to suggest that the Federal authorities might have saved them all the alleged suffering by exchanging and taking them North where provisions were plenty."[18]

That such women could actually debate such issues with the enemy invading their towns and homes suggests a certain affinity, based on mutual class consciousness, between Union officers and local elites who sensed each other as socioeconomic equals. Many of these women recognized and appreciated the distinction between well-bred

Union officers and the more uncouth soldiers under their command. Mary Taylor Brown, who lived on the outskirts of Asheville, defended her socializing with General Gillem and other Union officers. "When I come in contact with a *gentleman*," she wrote, "I respect him as a gentleman, no matter if he does not agree in sentiment with me. I think some of the people of Asheville make themselves appear very ridiculous in their scornful manners toward the Federals."[19]

Such respect was often mutual. Colonel Palmer, one of Stoneman's commanders, confirmed his own sensitivity to such bonds. He later wrote of the leading citizens of Wilkes County's Happy Valley community, saying that he respected their leadership and the extent to which their neighbors looked up to them. He singled out one of those for particular praise, describing him as "one of the finest specimens of a country gentlemen that I have ever met. . . . Although he was a rebel, [he] belonged to the Free-Masonry of Gentlemen, and before I knew it I found myself regretting every bushel of corn that we fed, and sympathizing for every one of his fence rails that we were compelled to burn. . . . He was a man of fine feelings, had always been generous and kind to his poor neighbors, who were chiefly loyal, and was spoken of in the highest terms." Palmer concluded, "We frequently meet such gentlemen in our marches, and always make it a point to leave them as far as possible unmolested so that they may remain to teach nobility by example to the communities in which they live."[20]

Those residents fortunate enough to have been the beneficiaries of this partiality toward "country-gentlemen" were, of course, relieved to be spared, and some seemed a little smug in taking credit for the exemptions they were well aware that many in the region had not enjoyed. After seeing that her town escaped any severe repercussions from yet a second visit from the invading Yankees, Laura Norwood declared, "I was proud of the way Lenoir acted—all stuck together and the Yankees said they liked us better than any people they had met." Lest that observation imply any undue consorting with the enemy, Norwood added with equal pride that they claimed "it was the d—est little rebel town they ever saw."[21]

But such appreciation for southern noblesse oblige and class hierarchy did not extend to the rank and file of Stoneman's troops, and it certainly did not save all of the western Carolina elite from the pillaging and harassment. Nor were all officers as sympathetic as some were. "Much depended on the personal character and disposition of the commanding officer of these detachments," Cornelia Spencer wrote. "If he happened to be a gentleman, the people were spared as much as possible; if he were simply a brute dressed in a little brief authority, every needless injury was inflicted, accompanied with true underbred insolence and malice."[22] The term "underbred" suggests the extent to which class distinctions underlie these judgments, just as insolent and malicious behavior marked men as common and unschooled in the deference they should have shown their social superiors, even if they were southerners.

Gillem and his men were among those most resented for their ruthless disregard for women in particular. Callie Hagler of Lenoir, mentioned earlier, paid dearly for confronting him. She had "naturally supposed that his presence would protect her person and property" and that of her daughter and her niece, who lived nearby. But according to a local informant, "On the contrary, his proximity seemed to give license to great pillage and outrage, for they suffered more than any one else in the village." The home of Hagler's daughter was "pillaged from top to bottom," as soldiers broke open barrels of sorghum and poured it over a large supply of wheat and over the floors of the house. They destroyed furniture and crockery, and "what was not broken was defiled in a manner so disgusting as to be unfit for use." When Hagler went to Gillem and asked him to control his men, he turned his back on her, stating simply, "Well, there are bad men in all crowds."[23]

Verena Chapman, the wife of a Presbyterian minister in Hendersonville, had an equally negative experience with Gillem's contingent. When she wrote a year later to Cornelia Spencer, her anger at the treatment inflicted on her and others in the area was still palpable—largely because they were victimized after the armistice had been signed. "Not supposing for a moment that even these faithless, dishonourable, Constitution-breaking vandals would be utterly regardless of the law of nations," Mrs. Chapman vented, "as to proceed in the face of a known truce to overrun and destroy the region through which they were passing." Nothing in their treatment toward highland residents had changed as a result of this truce. "All the way from Rutherfordton," she claimed, "they had swept the country of negroes, horses, and carriages, clothing, and supplies of every kind." (The very items she listed suggest that it was not the poor whose violation she resented.) Not only did such theft continue as they moved from Hendersonville to Asheville, but when "some delicate high-bred ladies followed them to their encampment to endeavour to regain their horses and carriages, they were treated by the yankee officers with great indignity and disrespect."[24]

This effrontery earned the Federal troops her long-sustained contempt. As late as May 1866, Chapman continued to defy the efforts of her reverend husband to moderate her resentment and see some redeeming features in the reunited nation brought about by the war's end. "Please tell me," she implored Cornelia Spencer, "if it wouldn't be just as sinful to 'pray' for *these* 'enemies' as for the Devil?" Over the past year, she confided, she had never dared to pray the passage of the Lord's Prayer that reads, "Forgive me my trespasses as I forgive those who trespass against me." "I know that I am wicked—and those wretches have made me so," she concluded, "but I cannot be a hypocrite."[25]

Even during the war itself, few other mountain women expressed bitterness this intense over the Yankee invaders, even when they were victims of their vandalism. In fact, for many, such treatment by Stoneman's troops proved less troublesome, and certainly less frightening, than the actions of the so-called rear guard, those roving bands of bushwhackers, deserters, and other local malcontents whose aggressions were unleashed by the Union troops' presence. In the wake of Stoneman's march, such groups were emboldened to take action of their own. As soon as the Federals left Lenoir, Joseph Norwood described his relief at how little damage the troops had inflicted on the town but wrote of a still-gnawing worry: "We have been under constant apprehension about tory—or robber raids, and I have been serving on guard at town every third night. . . . We are in danger constantly." Indeed, local raiders did attack the vulnerable town, ransacking houses and threatening the women who were forced to watch the plunder. According to one account, "The ladies were firm in resisting their demands and they left without doing much mischief."[26]

In Morganton, where the Federal troops, then under Gillem's

command, were allowed to engage in their most wholesale plundering yet, it was women from the nearby South Mountains who moved down to the Burke County seat to add to the chaos. According to a local source, they "swarmed our streets proclaiming their 'jubilee' and rejoicing that the Yankees had arrived. . . . Thus these dishonest traitorous hordes, of our own beautiful mountain clime, conspired and leagued with the Yankees, urging them on in the work of plunder, and wholesale theft which was carried on during Monday, Tuesday, and a part of Wednesday."[27]

Among the most vividly described of such attacks was that inflicted on Robert C. Pearson's home in the western part of Burke County. Pearson, a prominent banker and railroad official, was not home at the time, but a member of his household left an account that clearly revealed her class and cultural biases. In language far more derogatory than any used to describe Stoneman's men, she called the vandals, both men and women, "lazy and disloyal elements that inhabit our 'South Mountains' around the town of Morganton, that class of people . . . an ignorant, illiterate, uncultivated set, untrue in every respect, false to their God and traitors to their country." She went on to describe their actions: "When the 'rear guard,' the nine robbers, entered the house to plunder and pilfer, their women followed in, to reap their share of the spoils. . . . The mountain women were laden with everything they could carry, such as clothing, bedding, even dishes, and such." With contemptuous amusement, she described the reaction of an "old hag" when the mob discovered a wine cellar of sorts and distributed bottles of champagne among themselves. The sound of the cork popping from the first bottle they opened led to a panic. The old woman fled, declaring "it was pizen, put there to kill them for nobody had ever seen liquor pop that way."[28]

In light of these flagrant attacks by the poor in their midst, elite women often assumed the Yankee invaders to be the lesser threat and even approached officers with whom they sensed some rapport, asking for protection from either further abuse from those under their command, or from the even more unruly native rabble. Ella Harper noted in her diary on April 15, "At sunset the Yanks rushed in on us. We obtained a guard about our house after they came in, and fared better than some others."[29]

215

At Pleasant Gardens, Emma Rankin called on a "young lieutenant . . . who looked more like a gentleman than any of them I had seen
. . . and asked him if he could not stay and guard us while a negro
regiment that was just coming in sight was passing. He politely ac-
ceded to my request, and orderd a big black negro in an officer's uniform, who was just going into the back door, back to the lines." She
concluded that story declaring: "Oh! How horrid those negroes
looked in that blue uniform; and how the air was filled with oaths!
But that was characteristic of their white comrades also." Lieutenant
Davis warned her that "stragglers who followed the raid, and belonged to no command, were the worst, and . . . we would probably
be more annoyed than we had been before." He regretted that he
could stay no longer to protect her and the Carsons, but he said that
she should tell the stragglers that he, the officer of the day, had just
left and "threaten them with him." They were indeed soon beset by
"a half dozen men dashing up the creek, whooping and yelling and
cursing, and as drunk as they could be," who tormented the family
for several hours and demanded all jewelry and watches in the house
before eventually moving on.[30]

The most dramatic instance of the class-based differences between
the threat posed by local rowdies and Yankee invaders was recorded
by Mary Taylor Brown in an extraordinary letter she wrote to her
stepson in Australia. Brown, who lived with her husband, W. Vance
Brown, on the road between Hendersonville and Asheville, vividly recounted her terror when faced with the local marauders unleashed by
the approach of Stoneman's raiders on Sunday night, April 23:

> Squads of armed ruffians were coming in and plundering and cursing
> all night long while I was the only one to encounter them in the house
> and Pa was the only one to contend with them at the stables, barn,
> corn crib and smoke house, where they robbed us of every thing but a
> little hay and few pieces of bacon. . . . My soul stood trembling within
> me lest some demon would lay violent hands upon my person and I
> might be deprived the use of the firearm I had concealed to use in self
> defense. . . . But, thank God my prayers were heard and I escaped un-
> touched, tho' a thousand curses were hurled into my face and I was
> called a thousand times "a damned lying rebel."[31]

If the trauma Mary Brown endured on Sunday night was not untypical of what many western North Carolina women faced at the time, the events of the following day certainly were.

It was on that Monday, and at a site not far from the Brown farm, that General Gillem met James G. Martin, his Confederate counterpart based in Asheville and a West Point classmate, and reached a truce. Vance Brown invited Gillem and several of his staff to stay with him and Mary, which resulted in an extraordinary scene of sectional reconciliation. "Little indeed was the sum of all we had to offer for the repasts of our invited guests," Mary Brown wrote, "but the best of our little we gave as unto friends, tho' there were all our foes." Following dinner, "The officers and men enjoyed their pipes and laughed and talked in gay good humor, feeling quite at home among such friendly rebels. . . . Maria [her stepdaughter] played and sang some of her Rebel airs and the gentlemen sang some of their Union songs. Genl. Gillem had his band come up and play some beautiful old Union pieces." In a rather understated assessment of the evening, Mrs. Brown concluded that "Monday night quite a different scene was presented from the one on Sunday."[32]

That gathering must have seemed to those involved a very intimate expression of the war's end. But it was not to be. Mississippi refugee Katherine Polk Gale, who lived in Asheville, picked up where Mary Brown's narrative ended to describe an even more curious turn of events over the next few days. On Tuesday, April 25, Gillem's troops marched through Asheville in an orderly and nonthreatening manner, and local residents breathed a sigh of relief, having heard of how differently they moved through other towns along their route. On Wednesday morning, Gale recalled, "We all felt very secure" as the troops continued to move on westward toward Tennessee, "having strictly regarded the rights of property." But she quickly added, "That was in the morning of an ever memorable day."[33]

Late that afternoon, the Union forces took Asheville residents completely by surprise when they turned back on the city in an undisciplined spree of looting and ransacking. Katherine Gale was on a quiet walk with friends, during which they were "discussing the affairs of the day & congratulating ourselves on its peaceful termination," when suddenly they heard galloping horses and clanking sabers. They "turned to see the meaning of it all; a troop of Yankee

Cavalry in hot pursuit of three women. Pistols were fired in quick succession." Thus began two harrowing days during which Katherine and other women were chased through the streets, harassed by various groups of "ruffians," had their houses searched and looted, and in many cases, witnessed their men (in Katherine's case, her uncle) arrested and carried away by "these wretches."[34] Not even Fayetteville, destroyed by Sherman's troops two months earlier, had "suffered more severely by pillage," according to Cornelia Spencer in her narrative. "The Tenth and Eleventh Michigan regiments certainly won for themselves in Asheville a reputaton that should damn them to everlasting fame."[35]

Another Asheville resident, Sarah Bailey Cain, left a harrowing account of a gang of "villainous looking men" who rushed into her parents' home, ransacked it, beat her father and then fired shots at him when he attempted to keep them from stealing, and carried her brother, a Confederate officer, away under arrest, along with all jewelry and much bacon. ("Watches," she wrote, "seemed to be their favorite loot," and she related several instances of physical force against acquaintances, both women and men, in order to get them.) On Friday, April 28, as the prisoners—more than thirty local men and officers, including General Martin—were to be led off to Tennessee, Sarah went with her father, a prominent judge, to the town's center to bid farewell to her brother, one of the prisoners. "We passed through an immense crowd of a few citizens, a great many privates, and insolent negroes in U.S. uniforms," she wrote. "One of these negroes called out to my father, 'How do you like this, old man?'" As a result of that incident alone, she stated, "I have loathed the uniform ever since." In moving quickly to find her brother, Sarah walked under a U.S. flag that the troops had suspended from the Eagle Hotel out over the street. She was later reprimanded by other women who had walked around the square to avoid passing under what they still viewed as an enemy's emblem.[36]

The ransacking of Asheville marked the end of Stoneman's Raid. That it concluded on such an unexpectedly hostile and destructive note, particularly given that news of the war's end elsewhere had already reached the region, cast a pall over many residents and compelled the area's elite women to describe it so emotionally on paper.

The fullest accounts we have of the highs and lows of those turbulent few days all come from women who witnessed or experienced them firsthand. For some, like Verena Chapman and Sarah Bailey Cain, their bitterness was still very much in evidence well after the war's end. For others, such resentment waned more quickly, but not without similar expressions of defiance.

As dreaded as the incursion of Union troops was, for some of the more affluent women whose homes they violated there was another enemy more dreaded—those in whose midst they lived. The threats they posed suggest the complexities of the region's divided loyalties and the extent to which class identity shaped both the security and insecurities of the more affluent western Carolinians and their sustained commitment toward the Confederacy in its waning days. In this part of Appalachia, such divisions were not as clearly determined by class—wealthy Confederates and poor Unionists—as the stories here may indicate. Yet they do depict the additional tensions and pressures that both class and gender brought to bear on home-front hardships in the southern highlands and on the war's legacy for the region.

That written legacy in itself suggests another distinction that pervades much of this historical record—that, as elsewhere, it was largely shaped by the region's literate elite. But why did women, in particular, feel so compelled to tell their stories? Whether recorded in journals, letters, or memoirs, these were for the most part sustained narratives of considerable length in which these women recorded not only the many incidents of their own experiences and those of their neighbors and other acquaintances, but also their feelings then and later. Some were matter-of-fact accounts, rather objective in tone; others reflected the writers' lingering, passionate resentment of the Union invaders and made their emotional responses integral in shaping their memories into narrative form.

Most of the women cited here were already writing regularly—in letters, diaries, or journals—about their wartime experiences. So it was not Stoneman's Raid alone that inspired them to put pen to paper. Yet the raid was, for most of these women—indeed, for most residents of western North Carolina—the most traumatic and memorable event in a war that, until its final month, had kept major armies and military incursion at bay. Had they not been in the path of Stoneman and his troops, their wartime experience and how they interpreted it afterward would have been far different, and perhaps far less pronounced.

Whereas some did so more consciously than others, these women used their narratives—particularly in describing this traumatic incursion they faced at war's end—to articulate for themselves and for others their own roles in the conflict and those of other women, and to rationalize their efforts, their sacrifices, and the ultimate failure of the cause and the nation for which both were made. Only a few weeks after the war's traumatic conclusion in Buncombe County, Mary Taylor Brown wrote: "I will boldly say, I am a Southern woman! and have battled for her rights. . . . To defend the South, love prompted me to action and an undying confidence that she was right carried me onward through fire and blood." Yet, she concluded, "Now that in God's providence slavery is abolished and the state again brought into union and under the same government, I cordially respond from my heart, All is well!"[37]

By the same token, Katherine Polk Gale philosophized not only about the meaning of the war's end for herself and other women, but about the role they would play in coping with defeat as well. "The consciousness of having tried to preserve home & fireside, therefore having done that which they conceived to be right, sustained the sorrow-stricken hearts throughout the whole Southland," she wrote. "The women will again do their part in bearing bravely whatever the future has in store for them and will prove themselves to be worthy mothers, wives & daughters of the brave soldiers who have so manfully borne the horrors of the four years war."[38]

The luxury of privilege allowed these women to see and to commemorate themselves and their peers in such ennobling terms. These "talking heroines" saw themselves as vital to the defense of their households and region and took great pride afterward in having performed their roles well. As much as any other factor, that self-satisfaction probably drove their impulse to write at such length about their experiences. It probably never occurred to them that poorer mountain women—that "ignorant, illiterate, uncultivated set" for whom they had shown such disdain—might have interpreted the conflict, its impact, and their roles in it in very different terms.

Notes

1. Cornelia Phillips Spencer, *The Last Ninety Days of the War in North Carolina* (New York: Watchman Publishing Co., 1866), preface. For the circumstances surrounding the book's authorship and publication, see Phillips Russell, *The Woman Who Rang the Bell: The Story of Cornelia Phillips Spencer* (Chapel Hill: University of North Carolina Press, 1949), chap. 9; and Sarah E. Gardner, *Blood and Irony: Southern White Women's Narratives of the Civil War, 1861–1937* (Chapel Hill: University of North Carolina Press, 2004), 49–52.

2. Spencer, *Last Ninety Days of the War,* 14–15.

3. Ina W. Van Noppen, *Stoneman's Last Raid* (Raleigh: North Carolina State Archives, 1961), 112. This is the fullest scholarly account of the raid in recent times. It appeared first as a series of articles in the *North Carolina Historical Review* (4 issues, 1961); and subsequently, like Cornelia Spencer's narrative, in book form.

4. Quoted in Drew Gilpin Faust, *Mothers of Invention: Women of the Slaveholding South in the American Civil War* (Chapel Hill: University of North Carolina Press, 1996), 200.

5. It is probably coincidental that the fullest account of Stoneman's Raid, besides Mrs. Spencer's narrative, is also by a woman, Ina W. Van Noppen, cited in note 3.

6. There are a variety of other themes, in addition to class, that the writings of these women could also support, on which I do not focus in this essay. They all discuss the loss of their slaves with various degrees of anger, disdain, and relief. Several of them note the violation of domestic space and the invasion of privacy by Stoneman's men, a theme Lisa Tendrich Frank has found central in her study of Southern women's reactions to Sherman's troops. See her paper "'I Am a Southern Woman': Patriotic Femininity in the Invaded South, 1864–1865," delivered at Southern Historical Association meeting, Baltimore, November 2002. And one could use these writings to examine the psychological means by which these women rationalized Confederate defeat, as Jean V. Berlin has done in "Did Confederate Women Lose the War?" in *The Collapse of the Confederacy,* ed. Mark Grimsley and Brooks D. Simpson (Lincoln: University of Nebraska Press, 2002)—or to explore the gender ideologies of both southern women and Union troops as reflected in their encounters, as Jacqueline Glass Campbell does in *When Sherman Marched North from the Sea: Resistance on the Confederate Home Front* (Chapel Hill: University of North Carolina Press, 2003).

7. For a list of major slaveholders and their holdings in the region in 1860, see John C. Inscoe, *Mountain Masters: Slavery and the Sectional Crisis in Western North Carolina* (Knoxville: University of Tennessee Press, 1989), appendix 1, 265–66.

8. Katherine Polk Gale, "Recollections of Life in the Southern Confederacy, 1861–1865," typescript, in Leonidas Polk Papers, Southern Historical Collection, University of North Carolina, Chapel Hill (hereafter cited as SHC), 14, 17.

9. Miss E. L. Rankin, "Stoneman's Raid," an 1885 essay reprinted in a pamphlet titled *In Memoriam: Emma Lydia Rankin*, privately published on the occasion of her death in 1908, North Carolina Collection, University of North Carolina, Chapel Hill, 18–19, 20.

10. Ella Harper to George W. F. Harper, February 2, 1865, George W. F. Harper Papers, SHC, quoted in David H. McGee, "'Home and Friends': Kinship, Community, and Elite Women in Caldwell County, North Carolina, during the Civil War," *North Carolina Historical Review* 74 (October 1997): 386. McGee's article focuses on the mutual support system these women developed over the course of the war.

11. Philip Shaw Paludan, *Victims: A True Story of the Civil War* (Knoxville: University of Tennessee Press, 1981), 96; James O. Hall, "The Shelton Laurel Massacre: Murder in the North Carolina Mountains," *Blue & Gray* (February 1991): 23; and John C. Inscoe and Gordon B. McKinney, *The Heart of Confederate Appalachia: The Civil War in Western North Carolina* (Chapel Hill: University of North Carolina Press, 2000), 194–95. See "Unionists in the Attic," chap. 13 in this volume, for another perspective on the Shelton Laurel massacre. To learn more about other violence and cruelty committed against women in the region, see Margaret Walker Freel, *Unto the Hills* (Andrews, N.C.: privately printed, 1976), 129–61, on such incidents in Cherokee County, N.C.; William R. Trotter, *Bushwhackers: The Mountains,* vol. 2: *The Civil War in North Carolina* (Greensboro, N.C.: Signal Research, 1988), 188–200; and Keith Bohannon, "'They Had Determined to Root Us Out': Dual Memoirs by a Unionist Couple in Blue Ridge Georgia," in *Enemies of the Country: New Perspectives on Unionists in the Civil War South,* ed. John C. Inscoe and Robert C. Kenzer (Athens: University of Georgia Press, 2001), 97–120.

12. The best account of these women, drawn largely from their letters to Governor Vance, is Gordon B. McKinney's "Women's Role in Civil War Western North Carolina," *North Carolina Historical Review* 69 (January 1992): 37–56. See also Inscoe and McKinney, *Heart of Confederate Appalachia,* chap. 8; and Inscoe, "Mountain Women, Mountain War," *Appalachian Journal* 31 (Spring/Summer 2004): 343–48 (part of a roundtable discussion of the historical realities of the film *Cold Mountain*).

13. Mary to Alfred Bell, February 19, 1864, in Alfred W. Bell Papers, Special Collections, Duke University Library. For a full account of Mary Bell's wartime experience, see "Coping in Confederate Appalachia," chap. 7 in this volume.

14. Lizzie Lenoir to Sarah J. ["Sade"] Lenoir, January 22, 1865, Lenoir Family Papers, SHC. On other such raids, see Inscoe and McKinney, *Heart of Confederate Appalachia*, 197–98; Paul D. Escott, "The Moral Economy of the Crowd in Confederate North Carolina," *Maryland Historian* 13 (Summer 1982): 1–17; and Teresa Crisp Williams and David Williams, "'The Women Rising': Cotton, Class, and Confederate Georgia's Rioting Women," *Georgia Historical Quarterly* 86 (Spring 2002): 49–83.

15. Van Noppen, *Stoneman's Last Raid*, 4–5. For briefer accounts of the raid, see Inscoe and McKinney, *Heart of Confederate Appalachia*, 243–58; and Trotter, *Bushwhackers*, part 5. It is curious how little attention is paid to Stoneman's Raid in broader histories of the war. It rates no mention at all, for instance, in three recent treatments of the war's end: Grimsley and Simpson, *Collapse of the Confederacy*; Jay Winik, *April 1865: The Month That Saved America* (New York: HarperCollins, 2001); or William C. Davis, *An Honorable Defeat: The Last Days of the Confederate Government* (New York: Harcourt, 2001).

16. Rankin, "Stoneman's Raid," 26–27.

17. Ibid., 29.

18. R. L. Beall to Cornelia Phillips Spencer, August 1866, Cornelia Phillips Spencer Papers, SHC.

19. Mary Taylor Brown to John Evans Brown, June 20, 1865, W. Vance Brown Papers, SHC.

20. Quoted in Thomas Felix Hickerson, ed., *Echoes of Happy Valley: Letters and Diaries, Family Life in the South, Civil War History* (Durham, N.C.: privately printed, 1962), 105. These class-based responses by Southern women to Union troops are analyzed in Faust, *Mothers of Invention*, chap. 9; and Stephen V. Ash, *When the Yankees Came: Conflict and Chaos in the Occupied South, 1861–1865* (Chapel Hill: University of North Carolina Press, 1995), 19–20, 42–44. On the reaction of Union troops to Southern women, see Reid Mitchell, *The Vacant Chair: The Northern Soldier Leaves Home* (New York: Oxford University Press, 1993), chap. 6, "She Devils."

21. Laura Norwood to Walter Gwyn, April 25, 1865, James Gwyn Papers, SHC.

22. Spencer, *Last Ninety Days of the War*, 196.

23. Robert L. Beall to Cornelia Spencer, August 1866, Spencer Papers, SHC.

24. Verena Chapman to Cornelia Phillips Spencer, May 8, 1866, ibid.

25. Ibid. Of this letter, Spencer informed Zebulon Vance: "Mrs. Chapman sent me a 16-page letter! She is certainly a smart woman & very *womanish* (High praise, I know!)." Cornelia Phillips Spencer to Zebulon B. Vance, August 24, 1866, Spencer Papers, SHC.

26. Joseph C. Norwood to Walter W. Lenoir, April 2, 1865, in Hickerson, *Echoes of Happy Valley,* 104; Ella Harper diary, April 17, 1865, George W. F. Harper Papers, SHC. Final quote from R. L. Beall to Cornelia Phillips Spencer, August 1866, Spencer Papers, SHC.

27. Robert L. Beall, "Notes on Stoneman's Raid in Burke County and the Town of Morganton" (1866), manuscript in Spencer Papers, SHC.

28. Ibid.

29. Ella Harper diary, April 15, 1865, George W. F. Harper Papers, SHC.

30. Rankin, "Stoneman's Raid," 29–31.

31. Mary Taylor Brown to John Evans Brown, June 20, 1865, W. Vance Brown Papers, SHC.

32. Ibid.

33. Gale, "Life in the Southern Confederacy," 50.

34. Ibid., 52. Historians offer various explanations for this sudden reversal of policy by the Union forces, all of which rest in part on the fact that Gillem gave up command to others and proceeded to Nashville, where the first postwar session of the Tennessee legislature was convening. See Spencer, *Last Ninety Days of the War,* 232; Van Noppen, *Stoneman's Raid,* 89–90; John G. Barrett, *The Civil War in North Carolina* (Chapel Hill: University of North Carolina Press, 1963), 363–65; and Inscoe and McKinney, *Heart of Confederate Appalachia,* 255–57.

35. Spencer, *Last Ninety Days of the War,* 231–32.

36. Sarah Jane Bailey Cain, "The Last Days of the War in Asheville, N.C.," typescript, John Lancaster Bailey Papers, SHC, 35–36.

37. Mary Taylor Brown to John Evans Brown, June 20, 1865, W. Vance Brown Papers, SHC.

38. Gale, "Life in the Southern Confederacy," 57.

Remembrance

.

10

The Racial "Innocence" of Appalachia

William Faulkner and the Mountain South

Yoknapatawpha County, Mississippi, is a long way from Southern Appalachia, and William Faulkner has never been noted as a chronicler of the mountain experience. But in at least two instances he did write of southern mountaineers, and in both he emphasized their isolation from the rest of the South, and in particular, from its black populace. In an early and little-known short story, "Mountain Victory," and in what is arguably his finest novel—*Absalom, Absalom!*—Faulkner related the initial encounters of nineteenth-century highlanders with African Americans. In "Mountain Victory" it is a black man who intrudes upon an Appalachian family's home. In *Absalom, Absalom!* it is a mountaineer who leaves his native environment and discovers in its lowland setting the peculiarities of the "peculiar institution." The differences in these situations are considerable, and yet it is the similarities that are more revealing—for both scenarios involve white mountaineers traumatized by their first interracial confrontations and the drastic actions to which they are driven as a result.

Probably no other American novelist has left us with as rich a body of work dealing with the subtleties, complexities, and ambiguities of southern race relations as has William Faulkner. According to Joel Williamson in his 1993 study of Faulkner as a southern historian, "race was central, integral, and vital." This was particularly true of Faulkner's fiction of the 1930s, works that "remain probably the ultimate indictment not merely of the injustices of the racial establishment in the South in and after slavery, but in its capacity for the often subtle, always brutal reduction of humanity, both black and white."[1]

Faulkner's two attempts to apply these themes to the mountain South indicate that he was intrigued by what he believed to be probably the only group of white southerners never to have known blacks and whose lives had been untouched by the basic biracial character of the rest of the South. In applying this "brutal reduction of humanity" to mountaineers suddenly exposed to members of a second race, Faulkner provided some not so subtle insights into the anomaly of what he perceived as the racial "innocence" of Southern Appalachia. This chapter explores how Mississippi's greatest writer dealt with that anomaly in his fiction and of the array of early twentieth-century sources from which he drew his assumptions of the racial dynamics of this southern region, a region so different from his own.

"Mountain Victory" first appeared in the *Saturday Evening Post* in December 1932 and was included two years later in Faulkner's first short story collection.[2] It is the story of a Confederate major, Saucier Weddel, who returns at the Civil War's end to his Mississippi plantation from service in Virginia. Accompanied by Jubal, his black body servant, he approaches the cabin of a Tennessee mountain family and asks to spend the night. The rest of the story addresses the mixed reactions of the five-member family to the two strangers: the fanatical hatred of the eldest son, Vatch, a Unionist veteran who bitterly resents both "rebels" and "nigras"; his unnamed sister's strong sexual attraction to this refined uniformed officer; the awe of his young brother Hule; and the wary distance and more muted hostility maintained by both parents. When his sister's lust hardens Vatch's resolve to murder both of the unwanted guests, his father warns them to leave immediately. But Weddel, though probably aware that a delay could cost him his life, refuses to leave until his black companion (temporarily immobilized by potent mountain corn whiskey) can go with him. When the two finally attempt a hasty retreat off the mountain the next morning, Vatch and his father ambush and kill them as well as young Hule, who is caught in their range of fire as he makes a last desperate effort to save his new hero.

Despite the story's intriguing premise and literary merit (Irving Howe called it "Faulkner's best piece of writing about the Civil War"),[3] "Mountain Victory" has been all but overlooked by most critics. The few attempts at analysis have recognized as major themes either the clash between lifestyles of the plantation aristocrat and the poor white mountaineer;[4] the contrasting loyalties between family members and between master and servant;[5] or the most obvious source of tensions between the Tennesseans and their visitors, their opposing sympathies toward the Union and the Confederacy.[6]

But a more subtle and perhaps more important catalyst for the ensuing tragedy is the Tennesseans' racial hostility toward their guests. Faulkner portrayed the highlanders' unfamiliarity with blacks by describing how Jubal's appearance makes them think of primates. They see him as "a creature a little larger than a large monkey" and "crouched like an ape in the blue Union army overcoat." The family's initial dismay as they watch the two men approach—they stare as if they have seen "an apparition"—takes on new meaning when, well into the narrative, it becomes apparent that they think Major Weddel is a black man, too. When Vatch calls him "you damn nigra," Weddel recognizes the real source of the Union sympathizer's hostility. "So it's my face and not my uniform," he replies. "And you fought four years to free us, I understand." The sister broaches the question directly to his servant, whose disdain for what he calls "deseyer igntunt mountain trash" is heightened by such an assumption. "Who? Him? A nigger? Marse Soshay Weddel?" Jubal exclaims. "It's caze yawl aint never been nowhere. Aint never seed nothing. Living up here on a nekkid hill whar you cant even see smoke. Him a nigger? I wish his maw could hear you say dat."[7]

It is only when the father confronts Weddel about his racial make-up that the source of the confusion is revealed. Weddel explains that his father was part French and part Choctaw Indian, which accounts for his own appearance, described by Faulkner as "a half Gallic half Mongol face thin and worn like a bronze casting."[8] Compounding the mountain family's confusion about Weddel's race is his kind treatment of his black servant. Because Jubal is ill, the major allows him, his companion and protector since childhood, to ride his horse and to wear his coat.[9] This close relationship between master and former slave, along with a certain "uppitiness" on the part of the latter, adds to the family's suspicions of Weddel's racial identity and their distaste *over not only* the presence of both men but the connection between them. Their lingering uncertainty becomes a crucial factor in sealing the pair's tragic fate because of the daughter's lust for the Mississippi soldier, who may have black blood. The possibility of a biracial union proves to be as strict a taboo for these mountain men as for most other southerners and thus provides the added impetus for their deadly ambush. Ultimately, though, it is Faulkner's penetrating and subtle depiction of the variety of responses to these outsiders—from revulsion to attraction, from fascination to contempt, all stemming from their unfamiliarity with either blacks or interracial relationships—that forms the heart of the story and the most basic explanation for its violent denouement.

In *Absalom, Absalom!* published four years later in 1936, Faulkner perpetuated and expanded these themes of highland racism, but with interesting variations. In this second version of the clash between cultures, it is the mountaineer who becomes the outsider. Only late in the novel does Faulkner reveal the background of his protagonist, Mississippi planter Thomas Sutpen, and the incident that sets the novel's plot in motion. Sutpen was born in 1808 in the mountains of what would much later become West Virginia. When he was ten, his mother died and his father, for reasons never fully ascertained, took him and his sisters back to resettle in Tidewater Virginia, near the mouth of the James River. "The whole passel of them . . . slid back down out of the mountains, skating in a kind of accelerating and sloven and inert coherence like a useless collection of flotsam on a flooded river." The narrative at this point is subtly transferred to Sutpen's young eyes, and his uninitiated impressions of plantation life are among Faulkner's most perceptive passages. The account begins with the statement that "Sutpen's trouble was innocence."[10] While much of his naïveté can be ascribed to his youth, Faulkner quickly makes it apparent in his fullest description anywhere of Southern Appalachian society that young Sutpen represents a regional innocence as well:

> He was born where what few other people he knew lived in log cabins with children like the one he was born in—men and grown boys who hunted or lay before the fire on the floor while the women and older girls stepped back and forth across them to reach the fire to cook, where the only colored people were Indians and you only looked down at them over your rifle sights. . . . Where he lived the land belonged to anybody and everybody and . . . only a crazy man would go to the

trouble to take or even want more than he could eat or swap for pow-
der or whiskey. . . . So he didn't even know there was a country all divided and fixed and neat because of what color their skins happened to
be and what they happened to own, and where a certain few men not
only had the power of life and death and barter and sale over others,
but they had living men to perform the endless repetitive personal offices . . . that all men have had to do for themselves since time began.
. . . So he had hardly heard of such a world until he fell into it.[11]

While perpetuating the standard stereotypes of a slovenly primitive
lifestyle, Faulkner stressed even more the egalitarian, nonmaterialis-
tic, almost utopian communal nature of mountain life. In describing
this undeveloped, idyllic society, he imbued it with a moral superiority over the more sophisticated and "civilized" caste system of the
plantation South. The image of the family sliding down out of the
mountains suggests not only a geographical descent but a social, economic, and moral backsliding as well. Faulkner clearly implied that
the critical factor in making the journey that Melvin Backman has
called "the unhappy transition from frontier independence to sharecropping subservience" is the black presence in the flatlands and the
racism inherent in that new social setting.[12] Thus it is the awakening
of such feelings in Sutpen on which this episode centers and which
makes it, in turn, central to the novel's meaning.

Faulkner described the first black man seen by these mountain
children as "a huge bull of a nigger . . . his mouth loud with laughing
and full of teeth like tombstones" as he carries their inebriated father
out of a tavern "over his shoulder like a sack of meal." Soon afterward, his sister is nearly run over by a carriage driven by a "nigger
coachman in a plug hat shouting 'Hoo dar, gal! Git outen de way
dar!'" In observing this new and foreign landscape and in finally settling with his family in a cabin on the edge of a plantation "where
regiments of niggers with white men watching them planted and
raised things that he had never heard of," young Thomas Sutpen
learns the difference "not only between white men and black ones,
but . . . between white men and white men" as well. That awareness
fully registers in a personal sense only about two years later when
Sutpen delivers a message from his father to the plantation owner on
whose land they live. Knocking on the mansion's front door, he is met

by a house servant who, without even hearing the purpose of his errand, instructs him to use only the back door. That reprimand by a man he describes as a "monkey nigger" with a "balloon face"—in terminology reminiscent of "Mountain Victory"—sends the boy running from the house in shock and confusion.[13]

This rebuff becomes a traumatic turning point for Sutpen, as he at once discovers his innocence and loses it. For it is at this instant that he is first made conscious of his own status within this newly discovered racist and class-distinctive world. "He had never thought about his own hair or clothes or anyone else's hair or clothes until he saw that monkey nigger, who through no doing of his own happened to have had the felicity of being housebred in Richmond maybe, looking . . . at them." His shame at the slave's contempt for his patched jeans and lack of shoes leads the boy to the further humiliating realization that the plantation owner, "the rich man (not the nigger) must have been seeing them all the time—as cattle, creatures heavy and without grace, brutely evacuated into a world without hope or purpose for them, who would in turn spawn with brutish and vicious prolixity."[14]

Out of his humiliation and his sense of helplessness to retaliate for the insult inflicted on him, Sutpen, only thirteen or fourteen years old, resolves that in order to live with himself and to challenge the superiority of the planter class and those they own, "you have got to have what they have that made them do what the man did. You got to have land and niggers and a fine house to combat them with."[15] With that goal firmly implanted in his mind, he leaves the cabin and his family in the middle of the night, never to see them again. He somehow manages to get to the West Indies and eventually to Mississippi, where he begins his rise to wealth and power as a planter, a course that ultimately leads to his own and his children's tragic downfall, brought on by miscegenation, interracial marriage, and murder.

Thus, in two very different contexts, Faulkner portrayed the innocence of the southern mountaineer confronting the biracial character of the rest of the South along with the bewilderment and hostility toward a heretofore unknown entity—a black man. In both cases that contact leads to traumatic overreactions of significant consequence. For a writer whose work was constantly attuned to the variations and complexities of race relations in the South, it is easy to see why the premise explored in these two works so intrigued Faulkner. And one can readily trace the sources of his interest and information regarding the southern highlands, a region he would not see firsthand for many years to come.

Faulkner's own family traced its roots back to late eighteenth- and early nineteenth-century residents of Haywood County, North Carolina, which at that time covered much of the area from Asheville to the Tennessee border. His great-great-grandfather, Joseph Falkner, was born and raised in western North Carolina just after the Revolutionary War, his father having moved there from South Carolina during that conflict.[16] Joseph married Caroline Word of Surry County, and in 1825 they began a westward trek to Missouri. They got only as far as Knoxville when she delivered William Clark Falkner, whose first name his literary great-grandson would bear. That migratory pattern from the Carolinas to the frontier wilds of the Old Southwest, of which his own family was a part, provided the basis for the backgrounds of his fictional families, the Sartorises and the Compsons, as well as Calvin Burden, and of course, Thomas Sutpen, despite the latter's more circuitous route via Tidewater Virginia and Haiti.[17]

Much more immediate influences on the highland depictions of "Mountain Victory" and *Absalom, Absalom!* were literary sources. An Irvin S. Cobb story, relating the ambush and murder of a homeward-bound Confederate veteran by Tennessee mountaineers, provided the bare bones for Faulkner's short story.[18] But the theme of both of Faulkner's works—racism made all the more virulent by mountain innocence—seems to have been shaped as much by three fictional works on Southern Appalachia inscribed by Faulkner and added to his library in September 1932, just a month before he submitted "Mountain Victory" to the *Saturday Evening Post.* They were Emmett Gowen's *Mountain Born* and Grace Lumpkin's *To Make My Bread,* two recently published novels, and George Washington Harris's 1867 classic collection of stories and sketches, *Sut Lovingood,* the tone of which is set by its subtitle, *Yarns Spun by a "Nat'ral Born Durn'd Fool" Warped and Wove for Public Wear.*[19]

Faulkner once listed *Sut Lovingood* as one of his favorite literary creations, and it remained one of the select volumes that he kept most accessible throughout his life in a bookcase next to his bed.[20] Though race relations remained peripheral to Harris's tales of East Tennessee, blacks were on occasion subjects of the racist derision typical of nineteenth-century regional humorists. There are casual references as well to the contempt mountaineers had for blacks as part of the outside world. Harris wrote of one particularly colorful but stereotypical backwoods moonshiner: "He hates a circuit rider, a nigger, and a shot-gun—loves a woman, old sledge [a card game], and sin in eny shape."[21]

More pervasive in Harris's "yarns" is the sense of that unstructured and carefree society that Faulkner envisioned. Lovingood's philosophy of life sounds strikingly like Faulkner's description of Sutpen's birthplace: "Men were made a-purpus jus' to eat, drink, an' fur stayin' awake in the early part of the nites: an wimen were made to cook the vittles, mix the spirits, an' help the men do the stayin' awake. That's all, an' nothin' more, unless it's fur the wimen to raise the devil atwix meals, an' knot socks atwix drams, an' the men to play short cards, swap hosses with fools, and fite fur exercise, at odd spells."[22] Faulkner seems to have extracted much of that description for his own use, but he dropped the satiric disdain in which Harris wrapped it. In his romanticized twentieth-century interpretation, mountain "innocence" is taken far more seriously and treated with considerably more respect than Harris, a native East Tennessean, could ever muster for it.

More in tune with Faulkner's tone is Emmett Gowen's *Mountain Born*. Despite its focus on feuding Tennessee families, Gowen assigned much the same sense of virtue and purity to mountain society, which he has a New York executive and homesick highland expatriate describe as "beautiful and Arcadian." Its residents, he wrote, "can't read, but their hearts are full of poetry and their heads full of fine thought."[23] But of these three works it is Grace Lumpkin's proletariat novel, *To Make Our Bread,* that provided Faulkner with the most basic inspiration for the Thomas Sutpen story. Like Faulkner, Lumpkin focused on a mountain family who moves out of the hills and finds its innocence shattered when faced with the hard realities of a racist and class-conscious society in the flatlands. Driven from their home in the South Mountains of North Carolina by encroaching lumber companies around the turn of the century, the McClures are forced to settle in a piedmont industrial community (modeled on Gastonia, North Carolina), where they eventually become involved with the labor unrest in its textile mills in the 1920s.

Their initial interracial contacts are only incidental to Lumpkin's themes, but she conveyed both the curiosity and surprise of the mother and daughter and the contemptuous avoidance of the former's elderly father when they first see black children on entering a mill town. "They're niggers," he informs the women. "White and black don't mix." The McClure women's reactions bring to mind Faulkner's description of the Sutpen girls who, along with "the other white women of their kind," have a "certain flat level silent way . . . of looking at niggers, not with fear or dread but with a kind of speculative antagonism." Even more incidental, but possibly an influence on Faulkner's short story, is the elderly McClure's reference, in relating his experiences in the Civil War, to a "rich man's son" who serves in the army with a slave to care for him, who stays on even after he knows he is free.[24]

Although Faulkner once stated that he "never read any history,"[25] he wrote these stories in the wake of a number of historical treatments of Southern Appalachia that contributed greatly to the popular image of the region as all white. From the 1890s on, a variety of published works contributed to the dual assumptions upon which Faulkner based these two works—the absence of blacks in the mountains and the strong animosity mountain residents felt toward them. In 1897, a journalist wrote admiringly of the north Georgia mountains, "Nowhere will be found purer Anglo-Saxon blood." In 1901, an ethnogeographer echoed these sentiments for another part of the region. Kentucky mountaineers have not only kept foreign elements at bay; they have "still more effectively . . . excluded the Negro. This region is as free of them as northern Vermont."[26]

As for hostility toward blacks, East Tennessee seems to have generated more commentary than other parts of the mountain South, perhaps because of the lengthier Union occupation it endured during and after the Civil War. In a seminal and widely used document collection on Reconstruction first published in 1906, Walter Fleming included several passages illustrating the irony of the fact that the

South's most ardent Unionists were also among its most intense racists. From northern journalist J. T. Trowbridge's observations in 1865, Fleming singled out the quote "East Tennesseans, though opposed to slavery and secession, do not like niggers." He also drew from congressional testimony of Freedman's Bureau officials in 1866 the statement "It is a melancholy fact that among the bitterest opponents of the Negro in Tennessee are the intensely radical loyalists of the mountain district—the men who have been in our armies."[27] Whether or not Faulkner ever read these specific passages, the same concept—that mountain Unionists could also be rabid racists—comes through so clearly in "Mountain Victory" that it seems hardly coincidental that he set his story in East Tennessee.

By far the most popular treatments of the region, Horace Kephart's *Our Southern Highlanders* (1913 and 1922) and John C. Campbell's *The Southern Highlander and His Homeland* (1921), were still in wide circulation in the early 1930s. Their pronouncements on the racism and racial demographics of the mountain South represent a culmination of contemporary thought on highlanders' attitudes, past and present, and were perhaps the most accessible of nonfictional corroborative sources for Faulkner's interpretation of the antebellum mountaineer at the time he was writing.

Kephart noted that "the mountains proper are free not only of foreigners but from negroes as well." In many mountain settlements, "negroes are not allowed to tarry," he wrote, explaining that the mountaineers' dislike of blacks is simply an instinctive racial antipathy, coupled with a contempt for anyone who submits to servile conditions.[28] Campbell echoed these conclusions. While acknowledging variations in racial demographics and attitudes in the region, he stressed that even in his own time there were mountain counties "without a single Negro inhabitant and where it was unpleasant if not unsafe for him to go." He told of a terrified child who beheld a black man for the first time and called him a "no-tail bear."[29]

Such examples are certainly exceptional, but it is in such instances that perception most deviates from reality. Though there were certainly pockets of extreme isolation and alienation throughout the southern highlands, the depictions of racial "innocence" were far too simplistic, romanticized, and exaggerated a notion to apply to the region and its people as a whole. The black presence in many parts of Southern Appalachia was considerable, and slaveholding was by no means as foreign to much of the area as Faulkner and his sources implied.

Only within the past decade and a half have historians and sociologists fully embraced the reality of an African American presence in the southern highlands, particularly for the antebellum period. We know that slavery existed in every county in Southern Appalachia in 1860, and despite considerable shifts in the region's racial demographics after the Civil War, there was never a point at which an all-white population characterized the region.[30] We now have a variety of local and regional studies on the impact of both the presence and the multiple functions of slaves throughout Appalachia. We have also recognized and documented the class distinctions created because of the presence of those slaves, and the considerable economic and political influence wielded by those mountain masters who owned them.[31]

Countering the idea of racial hostility among mountain residents are indications that many opposed slavery on humanitarian grounds, that those who owned slaves treated them more leniently, that there were several strongholds of abolitionism in East Tennessee and Kentucky, and that the highlands served on occasion as safe havens for slaves escaping oppression and cruelty elsewhere. The rampant Unionism of much of the region during the Civil War and the Republicanism afterward also led more distant observers to equate such sentiments with racial liberalism.[32]

While those trends too were as much perception as reality, Faulkner never showed any interest in these alternative facets of highland race relations. It was the darker side of the white Appalachian mindset—their latent but volatile racism—that most intrigued him. His application of the term "innocence" to his fictional highlanders did not imply any benign sentiments or lack of prejudice toward blacks simply because they were unknown entities; rather, it suggested only an ignorance of African Americans and of the multitiered society their presence imposed on the rest of the South.

Yet it wasn't even that innocence or the single-race vacuum in which it was bred that most inspired Faulkner's treatment of the mountain South. In both "Mountain Victory" and *Absalom, Absalom!* it was the challenges to that innocence from which problems arose and plots emerged. Once exposed to the reality of that second race, mountaineers experienced what Joel Williamson termed a "brutal reduction of humanity." For the Tennessee hosts of Major Weddel and for the Sutpen family who "slid back down" out of the Virginia highlands into Tidewater plantation society, first-time interactions with blacks ended in tragedy. Faulkner's genius is most evident in his ability in these cases to portray his highlanders as both victims and perpetrators of their respective tragedies. Not only did men and boys lose their innocence; they found their humanity brutally reduced as well.

Faulkner owed much to current literary and historical treatments of the Appalachians in his depiction of an exclusively white society unencumbered by the stratification and oppression of the plantation South and yet as racially prejudiced as, if not more than, almost any other segment of the South. The basis for this assumption had been alive and kicking for more than a century by the time it drew Faulkner's attention, and it was by no means on the wane when he discovered it. Five years after the publication of *Absalom, Absalom!* W. J. Cash gave it even more widespread credence when, in *The Mind of the South,* he concluded, like Kephart, Campbell, and Faulkner: "Though there were few slaves in the mountains, [the mountaineer] had acquired a hatred and contempt for the Negro even more virulent than that of the common white of the lowlands, a dislike so rabid that it was worth a black man's life to venture into many mountain sections."[33]

One cannot say whether Faulkner's work was among those that helped shape Cash's views. But even if not a direct influence on Cash, Faulkner's depictions of the racial innocence of the mountain South would ensure the viability of such assumptions for years to come. Because Faulkner reached such a vast readership, he gave the views of his sources—the mountain chroniclers—far greater and longer-lasting exposure than they would probably have otherwise enjoyed. As with many of the myths of southern history, the very adaptation by William Faulkner of this concept of Appalachian racism infused it with new levels of meaning, dramatic force, and even credibility.

Notes

1. Joel Williamson, *William Faulkner and Southern History* (New York: Oxford University Press, 1993), 7.

2. William Faulkner, "Mountain Victory," *Saturday Evening Post,* Dec. 3, 1932; later reprinted in Faulkner, *Doctor Martino and Other Stories* (New York: H. Smith and R. Hass, 1934).

3. Irving Howe, *William Faulkner: A Critical Study* (Chicago: University of Chicago Press, 1975), 264.

4. Ibid.

5. Dorothy Tuck, *Crowell's Handbook of Faulkner* (New York: Crowell, 1964), 171.

6. Philip Momberger, "A Critical Study of Faulkner's Early Sketches and Collected Stories" (Ph.D. diss., Johns Hopkins University, 1970), 244–50. Momberger's is the most thorough analysis of "Mountain Victory."

7. William Faulkner, "Mountain Victory," *Collected Stories* (1950; rept., New York: Random House, 1977), 746, 753, 747, 751, 763, 756.

8. Ibid., 762. Weddel's background is established in another Faulkner short story, "Lo!" in *Collected Stories,* 381–403.

9. Faulkner may well have based the relationship between Weddel and Jubal on that between his own great-grandfather, Colonel William Clark Falkner, and his body servant, Nate. For full accounts of Colonel Falkner's Civil War career, see Joseph Blotner, *Faulkner: A Biography,* vol. 1 (New York: Random House, 1974), 20–32; Williamson, *Faulkner and Southern History,* chap. 2; and Daniel J. Singal, *William Faulkner: The Making of a Modernist* (Chapel Hill: University of North Carolina Press, 1997), 22–27.

10. William Faulkner, *Absalom, Absalom!* (1936; reprint, New York: Random House, 1951), 223, 220. Sutpen's past is reconstructed by Quentin Compson and his Harvard roommate, based on Compson's grandfather's version of what Sutpen had told him. For an analysis of Thomas Sutpen as a mountaineer, see Lynn Dickerson, "Thomas Sutpen: Mountain Stereotype in *Absalom, Absalom!" Appalachian Heritage* 12 (Spring 1984): 73–78.

11. Faulkner, *Absalom, Absalom!* 221–22.

12. Melvin Backman, *Faulkner: The Major Years: A Critical Study* (Bloomington: Indiana University Press, 1966), 98.

13. Faulkner, *Absalom, Absalom!* 225, 231, 226–27, 232.

14. Ibid., 232, 235.

15. Ibid., 238.

16. Blotner, *Faulkner,* vol. 1, 8–9. See also his genealogical chart in vol. 2, 222–23. The family's name was spelled without a "u" until the author himself added it. For his explanation of the new spelling, see *William Faulkner: A Biographical and Reference Guide,* ed. Leland H. Cox (Detroit: Gale Research Co., 1982), 4.

17. William Faulkner, *Sartoris* (1929; rept., New York: Random House, 1956), 9; *The Sound and the Fury* (1929; rept., New York: Random House, 1966), 404; *Light in August* (1932; rept., New York: Random House, 1967), 228.

18. Howe, *William Faulkner,* 264.

19. Joseph Blotner, *William Faulkner's Library: A Catalogue* (Charlottesville: University Press of Virginia, 1964), 34–36, 41. See also Dickerson, "Thomas Sutpen," 74. Though all three books have inscriptions in Faulkner's handwriting dated September 1932, this did not necessarily mean that he had only then acquired these volumes. His copy of *Sut Lovingood* was one his grandfather had owned long before. Milton Rickels, *George Washington Harris* (New York: Twayne Publishers, 1965), 128.

20. Jean Stein, "William Faulkner: An Interview," in *William Faulkner: Three Decades of Criticism,* ed. Frederick J. Hoffman and Olga W. Vickery (East Lansing: Michigan State University Press, 1951–1960), 79; Rickels, *George Washington Harris,* 128. Indeed, one wonders if Faulkner derived the name *Sutpen* from Lovingood's first name.

21. George W. Harris, "The Knob Dance: A Tennessee Frolic," in *High Times and Hard Times: Sketches and Tales by George Washington Harris,* ed. M. Thomas Inge (Nashville: Vanderbilt University Press, 1967), 46.

22. Quoted in F. O. Matthiessen, *American Renaissance: Art and Expression in the Age of Emerson and Whitman* (New York: Oxford University Press, 1941), 642.

23. Emmett Gowen, *Mountain Born* (Indianapolis: Bobbs-Merrill, 1932), 235–36.

24. Grace Lumpkin, *To Make My Bread* (New York: Macauley, 1932), 144–45, 230, 86.

25. Robert Cantwell, "The Faulkners: Recollections of a Gifted Family," in *William Faulkner,* ed. Hoffman and Vickory, 57.

26. William Brewer, "Moonshining in Georgia," *Cosmopolitan* 23 (June 1897): 132, cited in Nina Silber, *The Romance of Reunion: Northerners and the South, 1865–1900* (Chapel Hill: University of North Carolina Press, 1993), 144; Ellen Churchill Semple, "The Anglo-Saxons of the Kentucky Mountains: A Study in Anthropogeography," in *Appalachian Images in Folk and Popular Culture,* ed. W. K. McNeil, 2nd ed. (Knoxville: University of Tennessee Press, 1995), 151. For a fuller discussion of this issue, see "Race and Racism in Nineteenth-Century Appalachia," chap. 1 in this volume.

27. Walter Lynwood Fleming, *A Documentary History of Reconstruction,* vol. 1 (Cleveland: A. H. Clark, 1906–1907), 81–82.

28. Horace Kephart, *Our Southern Highlanders* (New York: Outing, 1913), 453–54.

29. John C. Campbell, *The Southern Highlander and His Homeland* (New York: Russell Sage, 1921), 94–95.

30. On the racial demographics of Appalachia, see Robert P. Stuckert, "Black Population of the Southern Appalachian Mountains," *Phylon* 48 (June 1987): 141–51; and James B. Murphy, "Slavery and Freedom in Ap-

palachia: Kentucky as a Demographic Study," *Register of the Kentucky Historical Society* 80 (1982): 151–69.

31. See, for example, Richard B. Drake, "Slavery and Antislavery in Appalachia," *Appalachian Heritage* 14 (Winter 1986): 25–33; John C. Inscoe, *Mountain Masters: Slavery and the Sectional Crisis in Western North Carolina* (Knoxville: University of Tennessee, 1989); Kenneth W. Noe, *Southwest Virginia's Railroad: Modernization and the Sectional Crisis* (Urbana: University of Illinois Press, 1994); Robert Tracey McKenzie, "Wealth Income: The Preindustrial Structure of East Tennessee," *Appalachian Journal* 21 (Spring 1994): 260–79; Mary Beth Pudup, "Social Class and Economic Development in Southeastern Kentucky, 1820–1880," in *Appalachian Frontiers: Settlement, Society, and Development in the Preindustrial Era*, ed. Robert D. Mitchell (Lexington: University Press of Kentucky, 1991), 235–60; and Martin Crawford, "Political Society in a Southern Mountain Community: Ashe County, North Carolina, 1850–1860," *Journal of Southern History* 55 (August 1989): 373–90.

The breadth of scholarship on race in Appalachia is reflected in two essay collections: William H. Turner and Edward J. Cabbell, eds., *Blacks in Appalachia* (Lexington: University Press of Kentucky, 1985); and John C. Inscoe, ed., *Appalachians and Race: The Mountain South from Slavery to Segregation* (Lexington: University Press of Kentucky, 2001).

32. Recent explorations of these views include Turner and Cabbell, *Blacks in Appalachia*, 21, 201; Drake, "Slavery and Antislavery in Appalachia"; Inscoe, *Mountain Masters*, chap. 5; "Race and Racism in Nineteenth-Century Appalachia" (chap. 1 in this volume); David W. Bowen, *Andrew Johnson and the Negro* (Knoxville: University of Tennessee Press, 1989), 15–16; Kenneth W. Noe, "Toward the Myth of Unionist Appalachia, 1865–1883," in *Journal of the Appalachian Studies Association* 6 (1994): 73–80; and Durwood Dunn, *An Abolitionist in the Appalachian South: Ezekiel Birdseye on Slavery, Capitalism, and Separate Statehood in East Tennessee, 1841–1846* (Knoxville: University of Tennessee Press, 1997).

33. W. J. Cash, *The Mind of the South* (New York: Alfred A. Knopf, 1941), 219.

11

A Fugitive Slave in Frontier Appalachia

The Journey of August King *on Film*

In Jerry Williamson's book *Hillbillyland*, the most comprehensive study so far of Hollywood's depiction of the mountain South, there is no mention of black people. In Thomas Cripps's *Slow Fade to Black,* the most thorough treatment of African Americans on film, there is no mention of Appalachia. Neither exclusion is at all surprising, nor is there any reason to expect such coverage in either case. The two subjects—race relations and Southern Appalachia—did not intersect to any significant degree in popular culture, in literature, or on film,[1] until 1996, with the release of a remarkable movie that focuses on the nature of slavery and race relations in a highland setting.

The Journey of August King is an exceptional film in several respects. First, it is easily among the most serious and historically accurate depictions of the mountain South ever. Second, aside from assorted sagas of Daniel Boone or Davy Crockett, it is the only film firmly set within antebellum Appalachia. Finally, it is one of the most sensitive and sophisticated portraits of slavery and antislavery sentiment ever produced by Hollywood, and it stands alone as perhaps the only examination of slavery on film that is not placed within a usually generic and stereotypical lowland plantation setting.

The credit for these distinctions, of course, lies not with Hollywood producers alone. First and foremost, it is Asheville native John Ehle's 1971 novel that provides the basis for the film; Ehle himself adapted the book to film.[2] An Asheville native, Ehle has had a literary career consisting, in part, of a vast fictional output. Of eleven novels to date, seven are deeply researched reflections on the historical experience of western North Carolina's settlement and subsequent development. His fiction, which ranges chronologically from the late eighteenth century through the post–World War II era, breaks through regional stereotypes in bold and substantive ways. According to his friend Borden Mace, one of the film's associate producers, "John has revealed a greater truth and accuracy about Southern Appalachian life than many historians and sociologists," an assessment with which few critics would take issue.[3]

This is particularly true of Ehle's seventh novel, *The Journey of August King,* simply because he even approached the subject of slavery in a highland setting. The book, which Ehle has translated to the screen with commendable fidelity, confronts in both subtle and not so subtle ways themes that historians have only far more recently tackled in regard to the mountain South.[4] It not only explores the ways in which slaveholding, racism, abolitionist sentiment, and class distinctions played out in a highland setting; it also conveys the realities of isolationism and connectedness, of subsistence and market economies in this still formative society early in the nineteenth century. And all of this is reflected through a deceptively simple escape story.

While returning home from a semiannual weeklong trip to a bustling market, identified in the book as Old Fort, North Carolina, August King, a recently widowed farmer, discovers in hiding an escaped teenage slave girl named Annalees. After fleeting encounters with her, King reluctantly befriends the starving, footsore, and desperate young woman. Over the course of the next three days of trekking back to his farm in a remote cove community, he conceals her with great difficulty, shunning acquaintances and sacrificing his own newly acquired stock and supplies in order to protect her from her ruthless master and the fearsome search party her owner has hired to find her. In the process, King also falls in love.

Though certainly uncharacteristic of commercial Hollywood production values, the love story between King and Annalees remains, as it was in Ehle's novel, underplayed and ultimately unconsummated. Yet the attraction between these two characters is very real and effectively conveyed by actors Jason Patric and Thandie Newton. (Newton had already scored on-screen as Thomas Jefferson's Sally Hemings, the most compelling character in the otherwise disappointing

Merchant–Ivory production *Jefferson in Paris*.) The love story in *August King* amounts to a very tentative "brief encounter" that propels the story forward as this white man and this black woman climb higher toward home and freedom, respectively. It is also a tale of personal rejuvenation and even spiritual redemption for August King, though the terms of his psychological "journey" are not nearly as well developed in the film as they are in the book. (Ultimately, Jason Patric may be too bland an actor to dramatize such emotional complexities convincingly.)

As a historian, I am most impressed by the specificity of time and place in both the novel and the film. The movie's opening credits appear as the camera sweeps from east to west over an early nineteenth-century map of North Carolina, from the Atlantic coast to the mountains, lingering only as we see the names of the last settlements, "Wilkes" and "Morgantown." Just to the west, the words "Appalachian Mountains" arc in much larger letters across multiple mountain ranges, sketchily delineated. The date too is revealed early on. As August King makes a final mortgage payment on his small farm, his deed is marked paid and dated April 27, 1815.

Equally impressive is the careful—and I think remarkably accurate —re-creation of this remote frontier society. The Carolina highlanders depicted in the film are neither backwoods hillbillies nor "coonskin cap boys." They are hunters and farmers, most of them family men eking out modest livings on small landholdings. But they do not do so alone. Far from frontier loners enduring isolated existences amid an all-consuming wilderness, these early highlanders make up a thriving society driven by trade and commerce. There is a constant sense of movement throughout the film, as livestock and poultry crowd the roads as much as do people and wagons. The story is played out far more at trading posts, at drover stands, and along roads, fords, and campsites than it is on farms or in cabins.

One senses that it was through this market-driven mobility that mountain settlers most regularly encountered and kept in touch with one another. Another less obvious but ever-present subtheme of the film is the strong, if loose, sense of community among these Carolina highlanders. They interact as close neighbors, as casual acquaintances, as merchant and customer, as debtor and creditor, as counselor and client, as employer and hired hand. One of Ehle's most adept achievements, in fact, is to vividly illustrate these interpersonal bonds as forms of a greater connectedness inherent in this frontier society and at the same time to make equally compelling, through the character of August King in particular, the loneliness and isolation of highland life during those formative years. From Robert D. Mitchell to Durwood Dunn to David Hsiung and Wilma Dunaway, historians have wrestled with issues of connectedness and isolation and the dynamics of localism in early settlement patterns.[5] Again it is remarkable that all of these revelations by recent scholars merely confirm realities that John Ehle was already well aware of and conveyed with such insight in his novel more than thirty years ago.

Yet this sharply delineated sense of time, place, and socioeconomic development all serves as backdrop to a story that is at its heart a saga of slavery. Slavery in the mountains was well established by 1815, but few historians had acknowledged this basic fact at the time when Ehle wrote his book.[6] The presence of slaves played no part in the vast set of images, assumptions, and stereotypes on which popular—and even scholarly—understandings of Southern Appalachia were based. But indeed there were slaves: according to census analysis, roughly 15 percent of the Appalachian populace in 1820 was slave, though only 10 percent of highland households held slave property.[7] By coincidence, possibly the first slave in western North Carolina was a young girl named Liza, brought into the area of Old Fort where August and Annalees first cross paths. According to a long oral tradition among her descendants in the Asheville area, she accompanied Samuel Davidson, generally regarded as the "first white settler west of the Blue Ridge."[8] But although slaves were certainly present in the mountains from an early time, they were a limited presence, and the film reflects this fact. Besides Annalees and Sims—a fellow fugitive from whom she has become separated—the only other black characters are three or four servants who belong to the same owner, Olaf Singletary, and who attend him as a silent and begrudging entourage.

From beginning to end, this is a story of escape and pursuit, and in that respect it is very appropriate that it is set in Appalachia. The idea of the southern highlands as a refuge for fugitives of various sorts has long been an integral part of the higher moral ground that many have sought to bestow on the region. Abolitionist John Brown was by no means the first to acknowledge that the mountains of western Virginia, so integral to his Harpers Ferry scheme in 1859, "were intended by the Almighty for a refuge for the slave and a defense against the oppressor."[9] A recent scholar has echoed that theme, insisting that the region "was settled to a substantial degree by slaves and indentured white servants fleeing from exploitation and angry with established practices in Colonial America. The hills, in their exquisite isolation, became havens for the disenchanted black and white, who needed to escape burdensome drudgery and slavery."[10]

But Annalees is not a lowland fugitive who has lifted her eyes unto the hills. She is owned locally. Her master is well known to both August King and the others in the area, and she is simply moving deeper into the wilderness when she encounters King. Both novel and screenplay are vague about where she is heading or *thinks* she's heading. On their first encounter, King simply directs her to follow a stream headed north. At the film's end, he escorts her to a high ridge above his farm and points her to a "trail to the North." Whether or not the Underground Railroad ever moved through the southern highlands is open to debate. I have argued in the first chapter in this volume that there is no real evidence of its presence in the region.[11] Even if some regularized escape route developed later, it is highly improbable that it would have been established as early as 1815. But that is obviously what Ehle had in mind as King sends his fugitive charge off with no reference at all to a destination, either short- or long-term. "The trail has been used for years. It's marked," he tells her vaguely in the film. "People will show you kindness on the way."[12]

The pursuers are as vital as the pursued in demonstrating the complexities and variables that characterized mountain attitudes toward slavery. Olaf Singletary is the story's sole slaveholder, referred to early in the film as "the wealthiest man in the mountains." In rallying a search party to seek out his two runaways, Singletary at first finds few willing volunteers, which forces him to offer rewards and payment for their services and those of their dogs. In the wariness of other characters toward both the man and his mission, Ehle depicts the uneasiness with slaveholding and slaveholders that fueled Appalachian antislavery biases.

For some, the idea of the search itself is bothersome. One man states that it "hurts my conscience to set dogs on people," while another wonders about offering a horse as a reward for a human being. Such sentiments suggest a genuine sense of moral resentment at the dehumanization the "peculiar institution" imposed upon its victims. For many regional chroniclers, such qualms typified the views of freedom-loving southern highlanders. It fueled the image of "Holy Appalachia," where, according to one turn-of-the-century writer, those in the mountains "cherish liberty as a priceless heritage. They would never hold slaves and we may almost say they will never be enslaved. They are true democrats, holding all men to be equals in society, as they are taught that all of us are before God." Or as Harry Caudill put it, "These poorer mountaineers, fiercely independent as they were, found something abhorrent in the ownership of one person by another."[13]

Yet such idealized characterizations of antebellum Appalachian residents fail to acknowledge other, less noble factors that fueled their resentment toward slavery. Ehle lays them out as well. Alongside this indignation toward the debasement of slaves, he also reveals the class-based contempt toward the sole beneficiary of slavery in their midst. While his nonslaveholding neighbors fear Singletary and his power, they also see him as an object of derision and resentment. As such, they conform to what historian Carter Woodson once referred to as this "liberty-loving and tyrant-hating race" that exhibited "more prejudice against the slave holder than against the Negro."[14] For the first generations of southern highlanders, in particular, it was widely presumed that they moved into the hills when slavery and the plantation economy it supported pushed them out of the more desirable lowlands and fostered a resentment of the slaveholding class that had driven them away. According to one version of this premise, "The aristocratic slaveholder from his river-bottom plantation looked with scorn on the slaveless dweller among the hills; while the highlander repaid his scorn with high disdain and even hate."[15]

Though hardly "aristocratic," Olaf Singletary provides a ready target for such resentment by his nonslaveholding neighbors. And yet in characterizing the film's single slaveholder, Ehle has stacked the deck. Certainly the least subtle aspect of the film is that Singletary emerges as a rather one-dimensional villain. As portrayed by Larry

Drake, he is the least attractive character on-screen, fat and scowling, brutish and violent. His arrogant contempt for both his slaves and his poorer white neighbors is made abundantly clear.

From a dramatic standpoint, one can understand the need for a clear-cut villain, and who better but the man in pursuit of the film's heroine, the man who gives her the reason to flee in the first place? (It is very clear that it is sharing his bed that the seventeen-year-old Annalees found most unbearable; further complications not fully explored lie in her revelation that Singletary is her father as well.) He openly professes his love for her before the men he hires to retrieve her, but that does little to soften his portrayal or win him much sympathy from either the search party or from movie viewers. With this character as the sole embodiment of highland slaveholding, it is hard to distinguish between the personal hatred of so despicable a character by those who know him from a broader condemnation of the system and class he represents.

How much more interesting—and challenging—it would have been to present what I and others have suggested were more representative of the region's slaveholding class. More often than not, even in those formative years, mountain masters were merchants and professionals, doctors and lawyers. The commodities or services they provided the rest of the mountain populace made them integral and respected members of the community, which defused much of the resentment that their slaveowning might otherwise have generated.[16] None of those linkages are suggested here.

One must wonder, based on the film's depiction of such pervasive antislavery and antislaveholder sentiment in 1815, why these pioneers' descendants would so eagerly defend the institution two generations later and secede from the Union in order to do so. To have cast the upright, dignified, patrician Sam Waterston as Singletary, rather than the hulking Larry Drake, would have been both truer to history and more challenging for an audience who here finds much too comfortable a way out of the moral dilemma posed by the plot. We don't now want to think that our slaveowning ancestors could also have been attractive, high-minded, and morally fastidious. With Larry Drake as Olaf, it is too easy for us to dismiss both him and the institution of slavery. A more attractive man in the role of slave owner and captor would have provided even more subtle dimensions and moral shadings to this otherwise sophisticated treatment of the multiple components of a slaveholding society. (Sam Waterston all too predictably plays the dignified and impeccable Mooney Wright, who appears as the voice of antislavery in the film's closing scenes.)

Yet, to Ehle's credit, the despicable Singletary hardly carries the villainy of the film on his shoulders alone; his nonslaveholding neighbors can claim few moral exemptions of their own, as they reveal their own shades of race hatred. Once recruited for the pursuit of Annalees and her fellow fugitive Sims, Singletary's henchmen are fully contemptuous of their prey and, even though motivated by promises of material rewards, they are fully committed to seeing the system restored and those rebelling against it punished. The brutal lynching of Sims, once he is caught, evokes no apparent protest or even squeamishness among the many who witness it. They speculate openly as to the fate of Annalees upon her capture, debating casually whether she too will be executed or simply forced to return to her master's bed, without indicating any discomfort with whichever option he might take.

To me, the most blatant historical inaccuracy in the film lies in the shocking execution of Sims. In the midst of a bustling crossroads gathering, King detects from afar the fact that Annalees's male companion has been captured. Hearing cries of "String him up like a hog!" he watches in horror as just that takes place. Hung by his feet from a butcher's post, Sims refuses to reveal Annalees's location (which he doesn't know anyway); in anger, Singletary, with a single stroke of a butcher's cleaver, slices Sims down the middle, leaving witnesses to gawk at "the two halves of the brute turning just now in opposite directions so that the halves grossly formed the body of a man, then separated and became two men, one of them headless."[17]

Ehle surely included the scene in the film to convey the full sense of the brutality of the slave regime and perhaps the raw force of frontier violence. Yet it doesn't ring true. Slaves, particularly strong adult males like Sims, were valuable, representing a considerable financial investment for owners. This, of course, is why their capture was deemed so vital and why death as a punishment would have been so wasteful and irrational. Slaves were executed on occasion, but such incidents were relatively rare and usually resulted from court edicts following capital crimes of a far more serious nature than simply running away. Murder or attempts to murder a master or other whites or involvement in a rebellion conspiracy were virtually the only offenses for which courts would sentence a slave to death. Even then, the state compensated owners for such losses. The most severe punishments for runaways and other non-capital offenders—and even then usually applied only to repeat offenders—were brandings, shackles, stocks and pillories, isolation "sweat boxes," or deportation.[18]

Only in the story's final phase does Ehle present any sense of a communal abolitionist spirit within the region. King brings Annalees to his home in the remote cove settlement of Harristown, and after putting her up for a night in his cabin, he sends her off fortified with food and dressed in his dead wife's clothing. It is only after her departure that his neighbors gather, and August must finally account for his actions. King had stated earlier that "they don't allow slaves in the community I live in," and as its residents confront him, it becomes apparent that they are sympathetic toward his actions but wary of the consequences he soon must face from Singletary. Led by Mooney Wright, they urge King to lie in defending himself, and they offer their help in explaining away the circumstantial evidence linking him with Annalees. When in an informal trial "of a sort" inside his own cabin, King stands firm in declaring the truth before the man whose property he helped escape, his neighbors can only watch as Singletary and his men inflict a costly retribution by burning King's house to the ground and thus completing his economic ruin.

I question the extent of that retribution exacted by a slaveholder on one who has abetted his slave's escape and the passive compliance in such a punishment by all who witnessed it. I have never seen evidence of such extralegal measures in the mountains or elsewhere. Yet by depicting this punishment as an almost ritualistic act, and one that is fully expected and ultimately accepted even by those supportive of King's good deed, Ehle suggests that it was a common and generally accepted occurrence. (Another oddity in this scene is that it is one of only two in which white women appear, but they maintain their silence. Their marginalization in the film seems to undercut, or seriously distort, the gendered themes and tensions that derive from the relationship between August and Annalees.)

The antislavery sentiments that bound this community together, however, are somewhat more credible. There were indeed pockets of more remote highland settlement in which a black presence was unknown and unwelcome, though it was often antiblack prejudices more than antislavery sentiments that motivated such bans. As Frederick Law Olmsted noted in traveling through this very region several decades after the time of *The Journey of August King,* many highlanders found both the presence of blacks and the privileges that ownership of them bequeathed to other whites to be the worst features of a slaveholding society, and they fought to maintain their distance from both.[19]

Yet true antislavery activity spurred by humanitarian motives, such as those evident early in the film and embodied in Mooney Wright at the film's end, also found its place in Southern Appalachia. Sporadic efforts emerged then faded out throughout the antebellum era at Wheeling, Virginia; Berea, Kentucky; and Maryville, Tennessee. Yet it was in the area closest to the Harristown settlement— both geographically and chronologically—in which Appalachian abolitionism most flourished. In the 1810s and 1820s in northeastern Tennessee, just across the state line from Harristown's probable location, fledgling manumission societies and abolitionist publications emerged. They were usually based in towns and instigated by "New Light" Presbyterians and Quakers from Pennsylvania and Ohio.[20] Whereas such circumstances would hardly have penetrated into remote cove settlements like August King's, it would not have been improbable for a collective resentment to both the system and its beneficiaries to have developed in such communities. Mooney Wright makes it clear that he is acting from a sense of decency that opposes anyone's enslavement and that he silently applauds Annalees's triumph over the system. But it is never clear if the same higher ground lies behind the other neighbors' willingness to stand by August King. The basis for their opposition to Singletary and sympathy for Annalees is left—perhaps fittingly—ambivalent.

Part of the power of both the film and the novel lies in its early nineteenth-century setting, so early in the development of Appalachian society. These western Carolinians—and August King in particular—are forced to deal with a moral dilemma that has not been fully articulated as such up to that point. This is an escape story set well before the Underground Railroad was in place and in which characters wrestle with the wrongs of slavery well before a full-fledged abolition movement has articulated those evils. It is a relatively spontaneous situation with two opponents—one fighting for her freedom, the other fighting for the recovery of his legally owned property—that force this community of white highlanders to confront the legitimacy of the institution for the first time. They are well aware of the legalities of slavery. King's initial reaction to Annalees's request for help is "You know I can't do that. It's against the law." When King's complicity in her escape is revealed and he must face Singletary's retribution, Mooney Wright—in typical Sam Waterston deadpan—states simply the reason such punishment must be accepted: "Laws have been broken, property rights violated."

August King seems to have had little reason to question that truth until he makes this fateful journey. As played by Jason Patric, he is a simple farmer, an Everyman whose quiet strength and moral resolve audiences are meant to identify with. Neither he nor his neighbors own slaves, but neither have they taken any stand against a system that allowed "a horse in exchange for a man." Yet when the opportunity to fight that system presents itself in the form of this beautiful, vulnerable, and irresistible young woman, King rises to the moral challenge, and in his small way he helps to undermine the institution that had so victimized her. Both Ehle and the movie's casting director have perhaps stacked the deck here as well. Given the obvious charms of Thandie Newton as Annalees, one wonders if King's moral courage has received a true test. His explanation for his actions suggests his own ambivalence about his motives. "A spell came over me," he tells Mooney Wright and other neighbors. "I did a hundred things strange, nothing customary." Would he have driven as hard or risked as much if it were Sims he had first encountered or if Annalees were an old or even middle-aged woman? As it is, his libido never seems far from his conscience. (This point is more obvious in the film than in the book, with the casting of a much younger actor in the title role rather than the middle-aged protagonist Ehle originally created.)

Yet the power of the story derives in no small part from the sexual tensions that drive it, and it seems unfair to suggest that those dynamics in some way compromise the strong moral fiber that grounds not only the film's title character but its overall tone as well. It is a film that works on a variety of levels, of which history lessons are only one. But to see so compelling, if relatively unexplored, a part of the Appalachian experience portrayed with as much talent, sensitivity, sophistication, and integrity as is evident in *The Journey of August King* is reason for celebration, particularly in light of everything else the movies have done to the mountains.

In an interview just before the film's release, Borden Mace hoped that its universal theme and dramatic story would make it a commercial success. Alas, that was not meant to be. But Mace, John Ehle, and the many others who collaborated in transferring the novel to film should take great satisfaction in the fact that it did fulfill Mace's other great hope for it. "It would be great to have an honest depiction of one representative part of Southern Appalachia back on the silver screen," he said.[21] While it may be on a television screen or at the video store rather than at a movie theater that one discovers it, that goal was indeed achieved, and for that, all of us who cherish our region's rich past and the quest to make it real should be grateful.

Notes

1. J. W. Williamson, *Hillbillyland: What the Movies Did to the Mountains and What the Mountains Did to the Movies* (Chapel Hill: University of North Carolina Press, 1995); Thomas Cripps, *Slow Fade to Black: The Negro in American Film* (New York: Oxford University Press, 1977). Neither do other works on cinematic depictions of the South find anything to note on blacks as highlanders. See Edward D. C. Campbell Jr., *The Celluloid South: Hollywood and the Southern Myth* (Knoxville: University of Tennessee Press, 1981); and Jack Temple Kirby, *Media-Made Dixie: The South in the American Imagination,* rev. ed. (Athens: University of Georgia Press, 1986). John Sayles's *Matewan* (1987) is the only other film I know that explores racial tensions in an Appalachian setting, the coalfields of West Virginia in the 1920s; none of the books cited here deals with it.

2. John Ehle, *The Journey of August King* (New York: Harper & Row, 1971). This essay appeared as half of a "debate" with Jack Wright over the film's merits. For his more critical assessment of the film, see "Hollywood Does Antebellum Appalachia and Gets It (Half) Right: *The Journey of August King* on Film," *Appalachian Journal* 24 (Winter 1997): 192–204.

3. Steve Ward, Interview with Borden Mace, *Appalachian Journal* 23

(Fall 1995): 51. Much of this interview focuses on the production of *The Journey of August King.* See also Carol Boggess, interview with John Ehle, *Appalachian Journal* 31 (Fall 2006): 32–51.

4. Carter G. Woodson's seminal essay, "Freedom and Slavery in Appalachian America," *Journal of Negro History* 1 (April 1916): 132–50, stood alone on the subject for several decades. More recent treatments of these topics include Richard B. Drake, "Slavery and Antislavery in Appalachia," *Appalachian Heritage* 14 (Winter 1986): 25–33; John C. Inscoe, *Mountain Masters: Slavery and the Sectional Crisis in Western North Carolina* (Knoxville: University of Tennessee Press, 1989); Kenneth W. Noe, *Southwest Virginia's Railroad: Modernization and the Sectional Crisis* (Urbana: University of Illinois Press, 1994), esp. chap. 4; Wilma A. Dunaway, *Slavery in the American Mountain South* and *The African American Family in Slavery and Emancipation* (both, Cambridge, England: Cambridge University Press, 2003); and several essays in Edward J. Cabbell and William H. Turner, eds., *Blacks in Appalachia* (Lexington: University Press of Kentucky, 1985); and John C. Inscoe, ed., *Appalachians and Race: The Mountain South from Slavery to Segregation* (Lexington: University Press of Kentucky, 2001).

5. Robert D. Mitchell, *Commercialism and Frontier: Perspectives on the Early Shenandoah Valley* (Charlottesville: University Press of Virginia, 1977); Durwood Dunn, *Cade's Cove: The Life and Death of a Southern Appalachian Community, 1818–1937* (Knoxville: University of Tennessee Press, 1988); David Hsiung, *Two Worlds in the Tennessee Mountains: Exploring the Origins of Appalachian Stereotypes* (Lexington: University Press of Kentucky, 1997); Paul Salstrom, *Appalachia's Path to Dependency: Rethinking a Region's Economic History, 1730–1940* (Lexington: University Press of Kentucky, 1994); and Wilma A. Dunaway, *The First American Frontier: Transition to Capitalism in Southern Appalachia, 1700–1860* (Chapel Hill: University of North Carolina Press, 1996).

6. See titles listed in note 4, none of which, other than Woodson's essay, was published before Ehle published his novel.

7. William H. Turner, "The Demography of Black Appalachia: Past and Present," in Cabbell and Turner, eds., *Blacks in Appalachia,* 237–38.

8. Maggie Lauterer, interview with John Baxter, cited by Patricia D. Beaver in "African-American and Jewish Relations in Early Twentieth Century Asheville, North Carolina," paper delivered at Appalachian Studies Conference, Unicoi State Park, Georgia, March 1996.

9. Richard Hinton interview with John Brown and John Kagin in August 1858, reprinted in *John Brown,* ed. Richard Warch and Jonathan F. Fauton (Englewood Cliffs, N.J.: Prentice-Hall, 1973), 54.

10. Leon F. Williams, "The Vanishing Appalachian: How to 'Whiten' the Problem," in Cabbell and Turner, eds., *Blacks in Appalachia,* 201.

11. See "Race and Racism in Nineteenth-Century Appalachia," chap. 1 in this volume, n. 20.

12. For Ehle's explanation on this point, see Steve Ward's interview with Borden Mace, 66.

13. Julian Ralph, "Our Appalachian Americans," *Harper's Monthly Magazine* 107 (June 1903): 37. The term "Holy Appalachia" comes from Allen Batteau, *The Invention of Appalachia* (Tucson: University of Arizona Press, 1992); Harry M. Caudill, *Night Comes to the Cumberlands: A Biography of a Depressed Region* (Boston: Little, Brown, 1962), 38–39.

14. Woodson, "Freedom and Slavery in Appalachia," 147.

15. Samuel Tyndale Wilson, *The Southern Mountaineers* (New York: J. J. Little and Ives, 1914), 57.

16. Inscoe, *Mountain Masters,* chap. 3; Noe, *Southwest Virginia's Railroad,* chap. 4.

17. Ehle, *Journey of August King,* 139.

18. See, for example, Winthrop D. Jordan, *White over Black: American Attitudes toward the Negro, 1550–1812* (Chapel Hill: University of North Carolina Press, 1969); and Edward L. Ayers, *Vengeance and Justice: Crime and Punishment in the Nineteenth-Century South* (New York: Oxford University Press, 1984). For more succinct coverage of these issues, see Whittington B. Johnson, "Punishments," and Robert E. May, "Violence, Slave" in *Dictionary of Afro-American Slavery,* ed. Randall M. Miller and John David Smith (Westport, Conn.: Greenwood Press, 1988), 603–5, 776–79.

19. Frederick Law Olmsted, *A Journey through the Back Country in the Winter of 1853–54* (New York: Mission Brothers, 1860), 237–39. See also "Olmsted in Appalachia," chap. 3 in this volume.

20. On abolitionist activity in Southern Appalachia, see Woodson, "Freedom and Slavery in Appalachian America"; Drake, "Slavery and Antislavery in Appalachia"; Asa Earl Martin, "The Anti-Slavery Societies of Tennessee," *Tennessee Historical Magazine* 1 (1915): 261–81; Gordon E. Finnie, "The Antislavery Movement in the Upper South before 1840," *Journal of Southern History* 35 (1969): 319–42; and Durwood Dunn, *An Abolitionist in the Appalachian South: Ezekiel Birdseye on Slavery, Capitalism, and Separate Statehood in East Tennessee, 1841–1846* (Knoxville: University of Tennessee Press, 1997).

21. Steve Ward's interview with Borden Mace, 63.

12

"A Northern Wedge Thrust into the Heart of the Confederacy"

Explaining Civil War Loyalties in the Age of Appalachian Discovery, 1900–1921

The first comprehensive codification of Southern Appalachian life and culture came in the early twentieth century. Most regional commentaries throughout the nineteenth century had been travel narratives, firsthand descriptions of scenic vistas and flora and fauna along with observations of the often quaint customs and folk life of southern highlanders, or local-color writing, which conveyed much of the same in fictional form.[1] But by the turn of the century, these impressionistic, localized, and often anecdotal accounts began to give way to more serious and systematic ethnographic assessments of mountain people by missionaries, social workers, and academics. The work of Horace Kephart, William G. Frost, John C. Campbell, Emma Bell Miles, and others quickly became the foundational base for much of the way twentieth-century America came to know and understand the highland South.[2] Because of these writers' scholarly credentials and commitment to the region and its residents, their characterizations of its populace—even while perpetuating already established generalizations, distortions, and stereotypes—gave their work a credibility and endurance that came to be scrutinized and challenged only toward the end of the twentieth century.

Curiously, the Civil War played relatively little part in this particular body of work on Southern Appalachia. Only four or five decades removed from the conflict—and at a time when an obsession with "the late unpleasantness" manifested itself in the ideological and ceremonial trappings of the Lost Cause throughout much of the rest of the former Confederacy—the war's legacy became increasingly simplistic, vague, and detached from historical context in the master-works of this age of Appalachian discovery. And yet, even given the minimalist treatment that so many of these writers accorded the war, almost all of them draw upon the issue of southern highlanders' war-time loyalties as one means of gauging or explaining the character and ways of life of their subjects—sometimes in positive ways, some-times negative.

Henry Shapiro was the first modern scholar to seriously consider how the war's legacy was carefully shaped by Appalachians seeking to portray themselves and their region in a beneficial light. In his seminal *Appalachia on Our Mind* (1978), Shapiro suggested that there had been a concerted effort in the immediate postwar years to downplay or avoid any reference to the war in the outpouring of writ-ings on the southern highlands that appeared in the popular press. Only from about the mid-1880s on did regionalists come to acknowl-edge highlanders' role in the war, and then only as Unionists, whose loyalty became a valuable means of winning favor for southern moun-taineers as integral parts of the nation at large.[3]

More recent scholars have offered other perspectives on treatments of wartime Appalachia during the 1870s and 1880s. In perhaps the most pointed treatment of the "myth" of Unionist Appalachia, Ken-neth Noe has examined how and why "the southern mountains' slaves and Johnny Rebs [were] swept under the nation's intellectual rug." Looking at popular fiction produced in the first two postwar decades, Noe demonstrated that the war was not as ignored as Shapiro and oth-ers had claimed and that the assumption of a solidly Unionist Appala-chians was yet firmly in place, as indicated by portrayals of loyalist individuals and families as beleaguered minorities in Confederate-dominated parts of the region.[4] Shannon Wilson has explored more self-conscious efforts by educators within Appalachia to cast the re-gion as a bulwark of patriotism and loyalty to the Union cause, and even to embrace Abraham Lincoln himself as a product and reflection of highland character and virtues.[5] James Klotter and Nina Silber have explored the perceived "whiteness" of Southern Appala-chians after the war as explanations for its attraction to northern social workers and philanthropists, but only Silber made wartime loy-alties a significant part of her analysis.[6]

Yet none of these scholars pushed their examination of these issues past the turn of the century to examine how the far more influential writings of that era incorporated the Civil War into their portraits of the region and its people.[7] Whereas the trends detected in late nineteenth-century accounts of the war are very much in evidence in the outpouring of writing in the early twentieth century, significant variables emerged in that work as well that reflect newly evolved agendas and perspectives by this next generation of Appalachian chroniclers.

Several traits distinguish this new era of scholarship from the travel writing and local-color fiction of previous decades. By the end of the nineteenth century, Henry Shapiro has noted, "the 'old-fashioned' quality of mountain life seemed to demand explanation, both as an abstract problem and as an aspect of the American dialogue on the nature of American civilization." This in turn led to a redefinition of Appalachia as a discrete region of the nation and its residents as a distinct population, and also an assumption of a social and cultural coherence and homogeneity throughout this vast geographical entity that embraced parts of at least seven different states. From these new perceptions emerged a different stage of Appalachian portraiture that was far more systematic in its attempts to embrace the region as a whole.[8]

Just as they claimed to portray the region as a whole, these writers were also far more inclusive of the regional experience they chose to document. Adopting an emerging ethnographic approach taking shape among academics at the turn of the twentieth century, they devoted chapters or sections of their books to a vast range of topics such as religion, language, folkways, kinship, community, and work, as well as moonshine, humor, and other "quaint" attributes of Southern Appalachian life. Several worked from the assumption that southern highlanders had little sense of their own history—and they themselves vary in terms of their own use of the historical past as explanatory forces in assessing mountain life and culture.

Most of these new chroniclers were sympathetic toward their subjects; some displayed outright affection for mountaineers and admiration for their stalwart traditions, love of land, and the simplicity of their lifestyles. Whereas they often portrayed mountain life and attitudes in bemused or condescending tones, they saw themselves as advocates for, and often defenders of, this perceived constituency. Closely related to this attitude is the other biggest distinction in their writing over that of previous decades: all of these writers had specific agendas that drove their writings and shaped their characterizations for particular readerships. As ministers, educators, social workers, culture brokers, or merely as scholars, they sought to explain mountain people as worthy of attention and of help, and they worked to preserve and promote the distinctive music, folklore, and handicrafts of the region. In whatever form of "uplift" their agendas took, they looked to northern readers, benefactors, and organizations as their primary audiences. Although their characterization of highland life was basically presentist in outlook and emphasis, they also had to acknowledge the Civil War and to explain the role of southern highlander participants in it in ways conducive to what were, in effect, elaborate sales pitches for those very people.

The most seminal of these works was not a book but a mere eight-page article. Published in 1899 in the *Atlantic Monthly,* William Goodell Frost's "Our Contemporary Ancestors in the Southern Mountains" embodies almost all the traits just mentioned, and it has served as an influential model for much of the subsequent scholarship on the region.[9] The grandson of an abolitionist and son of a Congregational minister in upstate New York, Frost was educated and then taught at Oberlin College before moving to Berea College in Kentucky, which he served as president from 1892 to 1920. His leadership had much to do with reviving the college, which had faced serious financial and enrollment setbacks in the postwar decades. By shifting its mission and identity from a biracial student body to one that served the sons and daughters of Appalachia to its east, Frost made himself one of the era's most influential spokesmen for educating and uplifting the mountain people.[10]

In "Our Contemporary Ancestors," Frost articulated for a national readership a portrait of southern highland society that resonated for many years. Folklorist W. K. McNeil has called it "perhaps the most famous essay ever written about Appalachia," while Allen Batteau has credited Frost, in perhaps a bit of an exaggeration, with having "invented Appalachia as a social entity."[11] As the title of his essay suggests, Frost cast the region as a remnant of America's pioneer past, with highlanders living in log cabins and living off the land with none of the trappings of modern technology or ideas. While at first glance, an outsider might have found such backwardness "rude and repellent," Frost stressed the virtues they retained—among them, the purity of their Anglo-Saxon heritage, unpenetrated by foreign contamination, an abiding patriotism that emerged during the American Revolution, and an abhorrence of slavery. As a result of these traits, Frost maintained, "when civil war came, there was a great surprise for both the North and the South. Appalachian America clave to the old flag. It was this old-fashioned loyalty that held Kentucky in the Union, made West Virginia 'secede from secession,' and performed prodigies of valor in East Tennessee and even in the western Carolinas."[12] Somewhat more vaguely, he celebrated the "independent spirit" that inspired this loyalty and its rejection of slavery, though he did no better than any other writer of the era in clarifying the linkage between Unionism and this rugged individualism.

None of these ideas originated with Frost; the notion of the region's predominant Unionism, as we've seen, was well established by then. Yet by making them so integral a part of his sweeping characterization of mountain society and culture, Frost paved the way for much of the work on Appalachia that followed, and the traces of his claims, his assumptions, and even his phrases continued to appear in the work of his successors. It is clear that Frost was seeking substantial aid for the region; he even called his essay a "call for the intervention of intelligent, patriotic assistance." "Appalachian America is a ward of the nation," he claimed, and the means by which its residents "are to be put in step with the world is an educational one."[13] Essential to that effort was to create both sympathy and admiration for its people, and—as with an earlier generation making a similar plea— one means of doing so was to stress their devotion to the Union at a time when other southerners rebelled against it. Frost very consciously linked the word "Appalachian" with America, repeating the term at least seven times throughout the essay; thus he reminded readers of the most basic commonality they shared, even while delineating their "otherness."

Equally important to Frost, and to those who followed in his wake, was his emphasis on the Revolutionary War. That conflict proved a much safer historical context in which to place these high-landers, given that it evoked far more consensual sentiments among Americans, North and South. That most of Southern Appalachia was only sparsely settled in the 1770s, and that its few frontier inhabitants were likely as divided or detached as their descendants were during the Civil War were facts even easier to ignore than the messier realities of 1861–1865.[14] As evidence of that "Revolutionary patriotism," Frost posited a single event to stake his claim—the battle of King's Mountain, where, he claimed all too simply, "backwoodsmen of Appalachian America annihilated a British army." To further accentuate how closely tied later generations of Appalachians were to that era, he stated: "Cedar kegs used as canteens, and other accoutrements which saw service in that enterprise, may still be found in mountain cabins."[15]

Another, far more obscure essay produced at about the same time echoed Frost's themes. In an essay on "The Mountaineers of Madison County, N.C.," Mrs. D. L. Pierson, a Presbyterian mission worker based in the county at Hot Springs, just north of Asheville, dismissed the Civil War as irrelevant to their present backwardness. "We can not charge [the mountaineer's] poverty to the war," she wrote. "He never was a slaveowner and his uninviting little home was unmolested by the invading armies."[16] Such a claim took on particular irony, even absurdity, given that Madison County was notorious for the guerrilla warfare waged in its more remote sections, and was the site of one of the war's most notorious atrocities, the infamous Shelton Laurel massacre, in which a Confederate regiment, the 64th North Carolina—mostly home-grown and based in the county seat of Marshall—invaded the Shelton Laurel community, where it captured and then executed thirteen suspected Unionists.[17] To make no reference to that internecine violence a mere thirty-five years later seems to be a blatant oversight, intentional either on the part of the writer, or on that of the local populace who may have shielded her from that bitter but unspoken past.

Yet Pierson did not neglect that more common theme in such pleas for sympathy and support. "The mountain people have a peculiar claim upon us, because they are purely American born," she stated. "Probably ninety per cent of them would be eligible 'Sons and Daughters of the Revolution.'" In an even greater stretch than Frost's evoking of King's Mountain, she harkened back to pre-Revolutionary incidents, from the Battle of Alamance in 1771 and the Mecklenburg Declaration of Independence (1775), which she claimed were somehow the "work of their ancestors" and thus made them worthy of assistance now, though neither locale was even remotely Appalachian-based.[18]

Another Kentuckian, John Fox, was even more influential than William Frost in conveying southern highland life to a national readership in the early twentieth century. A native of the Bluegrass region, Fox spent most of his adult life in Big Stone Gap, in the heart of Virginia's Blue Ridge Mountains, though most of his writing focused on Kentucky.[19] Best known for his fiction (his novels *The Little Shepherd of Kingdom Come* [1903] and *The Trail of the Lonesome Pine* [1908] were significant best sellers), Fox wrote of encounters between uncouth and primitive mountaineers and urbane, sophisticated lowlanders, which manifested themselves through cross-regional romances, politics, and even the Civil War, the setting for *The Little Shepherd.* Fox characterized mountain life in nonfictional form as well. In 1901, he published a collection of twelve essays contrasting the two sections of the state, entitled *Bluegrass and Rhododendron: Outdoors in Old Kentucky.* In the first of those essays, a broad overview of "The Southern Mountaineer," Fox made a forceful case not only for Appalachia as a solid Unionist bastion, but also for its military significance in preventing the Confederacy from winning its independence, a claim made by few others referenced here.

Obviously influenced by Frost's 1899 essay, Fox took his argument to a new level, arguing that it was Confederate military leaders who first discovered the American mountaineer when they learned, through sad experience, that the Mason–Dixon Line was not necessarily a firm demarcation between northern and southern loyalties. He cited the plan of a Captain Garnett, who was charged with moving Confederate troops through the Virginia mountains and into Ohio in an effort to sever the Midwest from the Northeast, but got no farther than Harpers Ferry. "When he struck the mountains," Fox wrote, "he struck enemies who shot at his men from ambush, cut down bridges before him, carried the news of his march to the Feder-

262

als, and Garnett himself was felled with a bullet from a mountaineer's squirrel rifle at Harpers Ferry."[20]

Only then, Fox stated, "did the South begin to realize what a long, lean powerful arm of the Union it was that the southern mountaineer stretched through its very vitals." In a passage obviously derived from Frost's essay, he built his case state by state:

> For that arm helped hold Kentucky in the Union by giving preponderance to the Union sympathizers in the Blue-grass; it kept the East Tennesseans loyal to a man; it made West Virginia, as the phrase goes, "secede from secession"; it drew out a horde of one hundred thousand volunteers, when Lincoln called for troops, deleting Jackson County, Kentucky, for instance, of every male under sixty years of age and over fifteen; and it raised a hostile barrier between the armies of the coast and the armies of Mississippi.

In short, he concluded, "The North has never realized, perhaps, what it owes for its victory to this nonslaveholding southern mountaineer."[21]

Fox was highly selective in making his case for highlanders' attachment to the Union, having made no mention of those areas of Appalachia—in Virginia, the Carolinas, or Georgia—where Confederate sentiment was much more in evidence; nor did he acknowledge the guerrilla warfare waged not only in those areas, but in the very areas he suggests were solidly in support of the Union. Nevertheless, the very specificity with which he defined Unionist Appalachia lent credibility to that assumption, and he would reinforce it in the novels he had yet to write.

In 1906, another Presbyterian, also a college president, sought to explain *The Southern Mountaineers* to the rest of America. Samuel Tyndale Wilson, the president of Maryville College on the western edge of the Great Smokies in Tennessee and just east of Knoxville, published his small book through the Presbyterian Home Missions Board in New York City. Born to missionary parents in Syria and educated at Maryville, Wilson himself served a brief stint as a missionary in Mexico. He returned to teach at his alma mater in 1884 and spent the rest of his career there, assuming the presidency in 1901.[22] Wilson was forthright in stating of his title characters that his was a "story told by one who has been all of his lifetime identified with them, and loves them, and has been their ready champion whenever occasion offered." Wilson echoed the themes of both Frost and Fox. As a Presbyterian, he stressed the Scots-Irish roots of most highlanders; in an early section entitled "Service to the Nation," he declared them "possessed by a fierce love of freedom," and proceeded through the usual litany of the Mecklenburg Declaration of Independence and the Battle of King's Mountain, in which "mountaineers had, without order, without pay, without commission, without equipment, and without hope of monetary reward, struck a decisive blow for the entire country."[23]

For all of his rhapsodizing about highlanders' valor, patriotism, and sacrifice in America's wars—he gave nearly equal attention to their roles in the War of 1812, the Mexican War, and the Spanish American War—Wilson was more willing to acknowledge the very real divisions within the region during the Civil War, stating up front that "many on the Virginian side of the mountains and among the North Carolina, Georgia, and Alabama mountains espoused the cause of the Confederacy, and made as good soldiers as the valorous hosts of the South could boast." He also noted that Stonewall Jackson was a "mountaineer indubitably of the first class," and that his famous brigade was made up "largely of the men of the hills."[24]

Yet once he had given due lip service to the pro-Confederate Appalachians (in a mere two sentences), Wilson moved on to his real focus—nearly two pages extolling the Union loyalists of West Virginia, Kentucky, and East Tennessee. He made his case in quantitative terms: "The Federal forces actually recruited from the southern Appalachians were as considerable in number as were the armies of the American Revolution gathered from all the thirteen colonies," he asserted, "and considerably exceeded the total of both mighty armies that fought at Gettysburg." He boasted that his own congressional district "claims the distinction of having sent a larger percentage of its population into the Union army than did any other congressional district in the entire country." He noted that these Appalachian loyalists "cleft the Confederacy with a mighty hostile element that not merely subtracted great armies from the enrollment of the Confederacy, but even necessitated the presence of other armies for the control of so large a disaffected territory."[25]

Wilson stressed as well the risks taken by mountain Unionists and suggested that their contribution to Federal forces may have tipped the conflict's ultimate resolution. "Their soldiers," he maintained, "were not conscripted or attracted by bounty, but rather in most cases ran the gauntlet through hostile forces for one, two, or three hundred miles to reach a place where they could enlist under the flag of their country" (a half-truth at best, since it hardly applied to those very areas of Union strength that he had just documented so forcefully). Like both his predecessors and those who followed, he suggested that while it might have been an exaggeration to say that "the loyalty of the Appalachians decided the great contest, that loyalty certainly contributed substantially to the decision."[26]

The two most notable female chroniclers of the highland South during this era made little reference to the war and were less explicit or categorical in their characterizations of Appalachia's wartime loyalties. Both Emma Bell Miles in *The Spirit of the Mountains* (1905) and Margaret W. Morley in *The Carolina Mountains* (1913) wrote only fleetingly about the war, yet they made very different suggestions as to what it meant to their highland subjects.

Born in Indiana and raised, until the age of ten, in north central Kentucky, Miles spent her adolescence and most of her adult life in and around Chattanooga. Her parents taught school on Walden's Ridge (now known as Signal Mountain), which overlooked the city yet seemed quite remote from its influences, both economically and culturally. It was the residents of Walden's Ridge that Miles took as her archetype Appalachians, drawing on their customs, beliefs, and simple lifestyle to generalize about the southern highlanders as a whole. The result was a study that is as much that of a folklorist as an ethnographer. Whereas she exhibited a genuine affection for her subjects and frequently identified herself with them, Miles was often patronizing in extolling the virtues of their isolation, their harmony with the natural world, and their long-held traditions. She downplayed the more degenerate attributes of feuding and moonshine so prevalent at the time, dismissing them with only the slightest of lip service. "Feuds are part of the price we pay for the simplicity and beauty of mountain life—for its hospitality, for its true and far-reaching family ties," she wrote. She even suggested that they were a mere phase to be withstood: "I do not say the inevitable price, for the lawless fighter, along with illicit whiskey, is bound to disappear; but these ugly features are, under present conditions, the price of the tribal bond."[27]

Miles displayed remarkably little sense of history in her descriptions of southern mountain life. It seems especially odd that someone who spent so much of her life in and around Chattanooga would have no more sense of the Civil War's impact than Miles demonstrated in her book, given the tangible trappings so evident there—battlefields, monuments, and Confederate veterans' reunions, all of which made the most of the crucial engagements that played out in and around the city in 1863. And yet Miles devoted a mere two sentences to her highland subjects' role in the war.

She opened a chapter on "Neighbors" with the statement that there is no such thing as a community of mountaineers, one of the common misconceptions long perpetuated by outside observers of the region. "They are knit together, man to man, as friends," she suggests, "but not as a body of men." There was no core or axis between the family and the State in this remote rural setting that would fit the definition of a community. As a result, she concluded that "Our men are almost incapable of concerted action unless they are needed by the Government." It was, of course, war and war alone that defined that need in the nineteenth century, and Miles suggested that it was an innate impulse that drew southern highlanders into military service. "It was the living spirit of '76 that sent the mountaineer into the Civil War—they understood very little of what it was all about." But unlike most other regional chroniclers, she did not assume that they remained loyal to the Union. "I even venture to say that had the Southerners fought under the Stars and Stripes," she wrote, "most of our people would have been found on that side, following the flag they knew."[28] In short, she seemed to think that, like southern sheep, they blindly joined the Confederate cause, simply because their fellow southerners or the state of Tennessee did as much.

The fact that Miles assumed that her subjects were pro-southern

in their sympathies and service—even if rather indiscriminately so—
was most likely a function of her Chattanooga base. Compared with
other parts of heavily Unionist East Tennessee, there was certainly
more Confederate support in this crucial railroad center on the state's
southeastern border, but to assume that those in its highland outskirts were equally of one mind is, of course, a gross oversimplifica-
tion that is indicative of Miles's generalizations throughout her
book.[29]

Although *The Spirit of the Mountains* was the first book-length
treatment of Appalachia in this era of discovery, it seems to have enjoyed only limited sales and had relatively little influence compared to
the later successes of Kephart and Campbell; it was only with a 1975
reprint edition that scholars have embraced both Miles and her
work.[30] Similar in tone and sympathies, Margaret Morley's *The Carolina Mountains* proved much more popular than *The Spirit of the
Mountains* when it appeared eight years later. It was as much a travel
narrative as it was an analysis of mountain life, and more specifically
aimed at the many tourists who were finding their way to western
North Carolina at the turn of the century, which also contributed to
its wide circulation.[31] Perhaps for the same reasons, her book is much
less valued now and receives far less attention from current scholars.

Morley was far more of an outsider to the region than was Miles,
having discovered the area only in middle age, after a teaching and
writing career based in the Midwest and New England. In the early
1890s, she and a companion visited the summer home of prominent
actor, William Gillette, in Tryon, North Carolina. She became a regular visitor to this thriving artists' and writers' colony at the base of
the Blue Ridge Mountains, and she eventually moved there to practice
both pursuits. It proved to be a convenient base for exploring both the
Smokies and the Blue Ridge; as a result of her travels, she wrote *The
Carolina Mountains,* one of her last and most successful publications.
(Most of her earlier output had been children's books on botany, natural history, and even sex education.)[32]

Far more than Miles or any other regional chronicler of the era,
Morley was as fully attuned to the cities and the resorts of the highlands as she was to the primitive and picturesque "backcountry" to
which most others limited their attention. She seemed enamored of

the wealth in the region—perhaps because of her own social standing among New England intelligentsia—and devoted whole chapters to Asheville, Flat Rock, Highlands, and other tourist destinations, even the Biltmore House, with which she was particularly enthralled. Nevertheless, her primary focus remained on the same backward inhabitants. She describes their customs, beliefs, and way of life with the same fascination and interest as do her contemporaries, though occasionally she seemed more bemused than anything else. "We're powerful poor around here, but we don't mean no harm by it," she quoted one "ancient native of the forest who does not think himself poor at all."[33]

Morley demonstrated a far greater sense of the region's history than did Miles—and yet for her, too, the Civil War was never more than of marginal interest. Her several references to it throughout the book are brief and serve only to illustrate other points about her subjects. Like Miles, she granted the mountaineers very little agency or sense of purpose in terms of their military service in the war. She quoted another elderly highlander, who said that he had been drafted into Confederate service against his will, but claimed no understanding of the circumstances or the issues behind the war or his role in it. "When you asked him about it he knit his brows, 'studied' a minute, and then slowly said, 'Law, which side *was* I on?'" Although he may have been puzzled by "the meaning and the advantages [an odd term] of the War of the Rebellion," which he characterized simply as "a rich man's war and a poor man's fight," one should not attribute his disdain for participating as cowardice, Morley insisted. She was quick to remind her readers that when he did understand what the fight was about, as at King's Mountain, he was more than willing to join the Union cause.[34] Once again, the Revolution served as a far safer and less ambiguous touchstone than any reference to the Civil War.

Both Miles and Morley seemed to see the mountaineer's ignorance as a reflection of his innocence. He may have fought in the war—as either Confederate or Unionist—but he did so with either little sense of purpose or against his will, and thus he could be absolved of any allegiance that might offend current readers from either section of the country. Both women were quick to extrapolate from an individual to the populace as a whole; in so doing, they not only embraced the values of the current generation, but following Frost's lead, evoked the patriotic virtues of earlier generations as well.

Both women seemed to view their subjects as an endangered species in the wake of what Miles called "the oncoming tide of civilization, that drowns as many as it uplifts." For her, that meant an influx of summer people and the trappings of wealth that could prove so corruptible to the character and the simple lifestyle of the backwoodsmen she championed.[35] Morley, first and foremost a tourist at heart, acknowledged that the idea of progress may have scared the Carolina highlanders in its path, but she was optimistic as to its effects. "Let the new order be better than the old," she proclaimed, and prophesied, rather naively, that "the mountains [will] continue to develop in the direction of sanitation, safety, and ever-increasing beauty."[36] Yet neither scenario for the region's future relied much on its past, particularly that of the Civil War, which seemed to have been ultimately irrelevant to the circumstances in which the mountain people now found themselves.

Later in the same year in which Morley's book was first published, another far more influential and lasting work made its first appearance—Horace Kephart's *Our Southern Highlanders* (1913). Generally acknowledged as one of the two "classics" of its time and genre (John C. Campbell's *The Southern Highlander and His Homeland* being the other), Kephart undertook his masterwork with a less pronounced agenda than did most of his contemporaries. Also an outsider, with roots in the Northeast and much of his career spent in the Midwest, he was, in Allen Batteau's description, "an alcoholic-librarian-turned-journalist." His retreat to the Great Smokies in North Carolina in 1904 represented a retreat from academia and from his drinking problem into a natural world that satisfied what he called his "inborn taste for the wild and romantic" and his yearning "for a strange land and people that had the charm of originality."[37] At forty-two years of age, and nearing a nervous breakdown, he left family and career behind him and moved to North Carolina for therapeutic purposes as much as anything, ultimately settling in a remote settlement on Hazel's Creek in the heart of the Smokies. He later moved to nearby Bryson City, where he lived until his death in an automobile accident in 1931.[38]

Kephart's first books reflected his recreational interests in the area, *Camping and Woodcraft* (1906), *Camp Cookery* (1907), and *Sporting Firearms* (1907), but gradually he became more enamored of the people and culture in whose midst he found himself. Once an impassioned student of the American frontier, he discovered in the Smokies survivals of that early American history. "In Far Appalachia," he wrote, "it seemed that I might realize the past in the present, seeing with my own eyes what life must have been to my pioneer ancestors of a century or two ago."[39] Despite constant observation and notes made at Hazel Creek and Bryson City, Kephart hesitated to draw broad conclusions on the region based on those areas alone, but after travel throughout the highlands of Tennessee, Georgia, and Kentucky, he concluded that "southern mountaineers everywhere [were] one people." And whereas he fully acknowledged the socioeconomic variables within the towns, valleys, and highlands throughout the region, he devoted the vast majority of his attention to the same traditional "mountaineers" as did other authors, maintaining that the segment of the populace that most typified them were "the great multitude of little farmers living up the branches and on the steep hillsides, back from the main highways, and generally far from the railroads. These, the real mountaineers, were what interested me; and so I wrote them up."[40]

Some critics have found Kephart's book a significant step forward in terms of its approach to mountain life—one recent scholar called it "probably the most vigorous and honest book written on the Appalachian South"[41]—and yet his interest in his subjects lay largely in the more primal aspects of their existence. He devoted multiple chapters to moonshining, bear hunts, and other activities, along with the obligatory chapters on religion, dialect, and living off the land that differ from others of the genre only in the lively, engaging—sometimes sensationalistic—style and in the wide array of literary and historical allusions that he sprinkled throughout the narrative.

Yet Kephart's historical perspective is among the book's weakest and most pejorative components, and one built upon the worst of the stereotypes so rampant at the time. Despite an abiding interest in Daniel Boone and early settlement patterns, he was quick to portray Appalachia as a quagmire for the thousands of poor whites whose migration forced them into a land of no return. Their deterioration began as soon as "the best lands, the river valleys, were claimed by a class of citizens superior to the average mountaineers." Once pushed back along the creek branches and up along the steep, they quickly became the isolated and ignorant mountaineers with "nothing in [their] environment to arouse ambition. The hard, hopeless life of the mountain farm, sustained only by a meager and ill-cooked diet, begat laziness and shiftless unconcern." As for why they didn't take the option of so many other Americans who sought new opportunities farther west, Kephart's explanation adds insult to injury: "They were so immured in the mountains, so utterly cut off from communication with the outer world, that they did not know anything about the opportunities offered new settlers in far-way lands."[42]

And so they remained until the Civil War, which to Kephart served only as a "thunder-crash" that aroused those highlanders languishing in a "Rip Van Winkle sleep" (an image borrowed from Frost). Not that that was a good thing, given that "throughout that struggle, the mountain region was a nest of bushwhackers and bandits that preyed upon the aged and defenseless who were left at home," for which it paid a heavy price after the war—"an evil legacy of neighborhood wrongs and private grudges." And because most mountaineers incurred strong resentment from the rest of their states by remaining loyal to the Union, "after Appomattox, they were cast back into a worse isolation than they had ever known." That alienation from their states was compounded by new federal tyranny in the form of "a prohibitive excise tax imposed upon their chief merchantable commodity." So, Kephart concluded, "Inflamed by a multitude of personal wrongs [and] habituated to the shedding of human blood . . . it was inevitable that this fiery and vindictive race should speedily fall into warring among themselves. Old scores were not to be wiped out in a reign of terror. The open combat of bannered war was turned into the secret ferocity of family feuds."[43]

Kephart was thus the first of the twentieth-century writers to see the war as a significant turning point in the course of Appalachian development, and to acknowledge the internal warfare highlanders endured—even if, ironically, it returned them to the same primitive and unchecked impulses that had characterized them before the war.

Given the degenerate state to which the war had reduced (or merely returned?) these backwoodsmen, any progress—or civilization— imposed on the region, whether it be timber or mineral enterprises, could be nothing but uplifting for them. Kephart insisted that "this economic revolution," bringing with it "good schools, newspapers, a finer and more liberal social life," should be celebrated as a vast improvement in Appalachians' lives, whether or not they wanted it or recognized it as something better than their current way of life.[44]

Far different in both tone and purpose was John C. Campbell's posthumous treatise on the region that appeared in 1921, two years after Campbell's death—and perhaps not coincidentally, a year before a new and expanded edition of Kephart's *Our Southern Highlanders.* Campbell was a Midwesterner—Indiana born—who spent most of his early career as a teacher in the southernmost Appalachians, most notably at Piedmont College in the north Georgia mountains. A research grant from the newly established Russell Sage Foundation in New York led Campbell to mount an extensive and systematic study of Southern Appalachia's social and economic conditions. Based in Asheville from 1909 on, he was secretary of the foundation's Southern Highland Division. His book was the culmination of his research and increasing activism. He organized the Conference of Southern Mountain Workers, and worked closely with his wife, Olive Dame Campbell, who in her own right was a major force as both scholar and activist in pursuing and promoting the music, crafts, and folk life of the region for more than thirty years after John's death in 1919. The first major task she undertook as a widow, however, was the completion of his book, which was published by Russell Sage.[45]

Campbell's characterization of the region was both more sophisticated and more balanced than most of those that preceded it. An odd but often effective mix of social science data and literary descriptions (perhaps a function of Olive's input), the book recognized and readily acknowledged both the region's geographical variables and how they shaped a far more diverse socioeconomic structure among Southern Appalachians. Historian John Alexander Williams has even suggested that had Campbell lived longer, and been able to expand upon these ideas—indeed these realities—the scholarly stranglehold on the stereotypes and misconceptions of the region might have been broken a full half-century sooner than they were.[46]

Nevertheless, Campbell was not immune from many of the same generalizations and clichés already in circulation. He took on the war in a chapter of his book dealing with individualism. He opened the chapter by challenging both the notion that Appalachia "was thrust like a Northern wedge into the heart of the Confederacy," and the rationale behind that claim. He noted up front that "speakers who have sought to raise money in the North for mountain work have been wont to dwell upon the part played by the Highlander in the Civil War." The impression left by these claims is that "the Highlander is in reality a Northerner in a Southern environment. The impression is far from the real truth."[47] Yet Campbell was not willing to cast his stock highlander as fully southern either, hence his emphasis on his independence. "Heredity and environment have conspired to make him an extreme individualist," Campbell claimed. "His dominant trait is independence raised to the fourth power."[48]

In explaining the wartime loyalties and the reasons behind them, however, Campbell fell back on the same tenuous connections as his predecessors had propounded, which has little to do with any independence of thought or spirit. "They held, withal, a deep though distant attachment to the Federal Government, for which they had fought in the Revolution, the War of 1812, and that of Mexico." He did acknowledge the same general division as that laid out by Samuel Wilson: that West Virginia, eastern Kentucky, and East Tennessee "stood firm for the Union," whereas western North Carolina and Virginia "showed a larger Confederate element."[49]

Campbell admitted that the war provoked "the bitterest of feeling" among mountaineers, especially those from Tennessee and Kentucky, where "the roughness of the country led to a sort of border guerrilla warfare," and even provided anecdotal evidence of the harassment suffered by mountain women and children at the hands of bushwhackers and "rebel raiders." And yet he assured his readers that there were no lingering aftereffects from such atrocities, which he based on firsthand yet fairly impressionistic evidence. He noted that in the "little community at the southern end of the mountains" where he first taught—Joppa, Alabama—many veterans gathered, some Union and more Confederate. "At [a local] hearth sat often a man who had stood with the 'Rock of Chickamauga,' and another who had starved with Pemberton at Vicksburg or taken his tender farewell of Lee at Appomattox," and yet, Campbell claimed, "there was no bitterness or rancor between them." He told of another highland community where a Blue and Gray Camp was organized, due to the number of sympathizers from both sides. On Southern Memorial Day, veterans of both sides gathered at the school hall "to listen to declamations on patriotism by the school boys . . . while above them on one side hung the picture of Lee between the Stars and Stripes, and on the other, framed in Southern garlands, the picture of Grant."[50]

So what are we to make of these various treatments of the war's impact on Southern Appalachia or Southern Appalachians' impact on the war, given the agendas of their authors and the audiences they hoped to reach? Shannon Wilson has noted of certain higher-education administrators raising funds for their colleges in the region in the 1870s and 1880s: "The memory of the war experience was manipulated artfully to project a way of seeing and perhaps a means of thinking about Appalachia in a defined and particular manner."[51] Much the same could be said about those chronicling the region in the early twentieth century, although both how and why they "artfully manipulated" the war's legacy differed in several telling respects.

At one level, it is obvious that these authors still sought to woo northern philanthropists and organizations by depicting Appalachians as deserving and worthy recipients of their largesse. Certainly an easy means of winning that sympathy and support was to stress their wartime loyalty to the Union; thus it is no surprise that every writer but one made that loyalty integral to their coverage of the war. (Only Emma Bell Miles assumed a Confederate majority among her mountaineers, but even she held them blameless in that decision, asserting that they had little understanding of what they were doing or why.)

Of the rest, there was considerable variation in terms of the extent, the significance, and the rationale behind the Unionism they claimed was so predominant among southern highlanders. Only Wilson and Campbell took seriously the fact that some areas of Appalachia were more supportive of the Confederacy, but both minimized that reality, offering no explanation why some mountaineers would cast their lots with the South. Most followed the lead of Frost and Fox by linking Unionism to a deep-seated patriotism that mountain people had demonstrated from the American Revolution through even the Spanish American War, and falling back on the same few examples to demonstrate that point. On the other hand, some attributed that loyalty to less worthy motives: either to ignorance or apathy of the world beyond their own, and hence to a lack of ability to make a reasoned commitment to either cause. Even Frost quoted a "fine old Southern lady . . . in a border city," who, explaining mountain Unionism, told him: "If those mountain folks had been educated they would have gone with their states!" Frost's response: "Probably she was right."[52]

Curiously, the presence of slavery or the lack thereof played little part in the explanations offered. Only John Campbell even raised the issue directly, and said only: "The doctrine of States' Rights, separated from its slavery bias, was but an abstraction to them." In effect, he was suggesting, as others had, that the issues that drove the sectional crisis—whether slavery or something else—were irrelevant to mountain people.[53]

Others focused more on the effects than on the causes of Appalachian loyalties. Several suggested that the manpower the region provided to the Federal war effort and denied to the Confederacy was significant; indeed, it may even have tipped the scales in favor of the North and its ultimate victory. Both John Fox and Samuel Wilson pushed that claim, and insisted that such a commitment by highlanders entailed far more risk and sacrifice than joining Confederate forces would have been. Campbell's description of the region's role as "a northern wedge thrust into the heart of the Confederacy" vividly makes the same point.

On the other hand, it is equally striking that the coverage of the Civil War in all these works was so fleeting. One could hardly have written comprehensively about any other part of the South at the turn of the century and not made the war's impact a central part of a characterization of the region. And yet most of the book-length works examined here devoted no more than a page or two to the war, while the essays or journals included a paragraph or two at best. Such minimal attention, in part, reflects an ahistorical approach. In seeking to explain the origins of mountain people and what made them what they became, most of these writers fell back on the platitudes and misconceptions about patriotism, individualism, sacrifice, and other unspecific but value-laden terminology. Yet it may also have been that these writers felt that only by downplaying Appalachia's role in or impact on this most central event of the nation's history could they make a convincing case for the isolation or insulation of its inhabitants. If they were to remain the simple, backward "contemporary ancestors" that would make them so palatable to potential benefactors, the less said the better about the complexities of guerrilla warfare, divided loyalties, and home-front atrocities—not to mention the political wranglings of influential leaders such as Andrew Johnson, Zebulon Vance, and Joseph E. Brown, which would paint a far different and much messier portrait of southern highland agendas and agency.

Also curious is how little firsthand information about the war these chroniclers derived from the many local residents that they came to know and certainly relied on for much material on so many other topics. The fact that the only direct quote from Carolina highlanders that Morley could muster was the question "Law, which side *was* I on?" says a great deal about what she chose to overlook or not pursue in terms of local memories or sentiments, as was true for most of her fellow authors as well. John C. Campbell drew on firsthand observation only to stress the highlanders' reconciliatory spirit after the war's end, though one is sure that he must have heard just as many or more reminiscences about the waging of the war itself, none of which appears in his book.

By the same token, the fact that Campbell was based in Asheville, a center of Confederate enlistment, mobilization, and even manufacturing; that Emma Bell Miles was in Chattanooga, another center of Confederate activity and military action; and that Mrs. D. L. Pierson seemed so oblivious to the Shelton Laurel massacre in her portrait of Madison County, North Carolina—all suggest intentional silences in the face of a very different reality that would not have jibed with the sympathetic and simplistic portraits each sought to present.

In short, by the turn of the twentieth century, the particulars of how the war was actually fought in the mountain South, and why, entailed far more inconvenient truths—which did not lend themselves to the image of mountain people these writers worked so hard to create and convey. To sell the remoteness and "otherness" of highland life required that the Civil War—so central a trauma and turning point to the rest of the South—be granted only a marginal place in explaining Appalachia, where people were so set in their ways that even an upheaval of that nature had little lasting effect on their lives. And if their loyalties couldn't be linked to an innate—or even blind—patriotism or long-standing sense of duty to the federal government, then it could be explained as something far less flattering, but even more useful: the assumption that they simply didn't understand what the war was about, and were therefore innocent pawns drawn into the conflict—on whichever side—without even the option of making that decision themselves.

The easiest way to make that case was to minimize the war, its impact, and its relevance to Appalachia. Despite ample private and communal memories of the region's residents still very much alive during the 1900s and 1910s, these writers created a version of their war experiences all their own, and one that became firmly embedded in popular perceptions for far too much of the century to follow.

Notes

1. W. K. McNeil, ed., *Appalachian Images in Folk and Popular Culture*, 2nd ed. (Knoxville: University of Tennessee Press, 1995); Kevin E. O'Donnell and Helen Hollingsworth, eds., *Seekers of Scenery: Travel Writing from Southern Appalachia, 1840–1900* (Knoxville: University of Tennessee Press, 2004); and Katherine E. Ledford, "A Landscape and a People Set Apart: Narratives of Exploration and Travel in Early Appalachia," in *Confronting Appalachian Stereotypes: Back Talk from an American Region*, ed. Dwight B. Billings, Gurney Norman, and Katherine E. Ledford (Lexington: University Press of Kentucky, 1999), 47–66.

2. Henry Shapiro, *Appalachia on Our Mind: The Southern Mountains and Mountaineers in the American Consciousness, 1870–1920* (Chapel Hill: University of North Carolina Press, 1978); Cratis Williams, "The Southern Mountaineer in Fact and Fiction" (Ph.D. diss., New York University, 1961); and Allen W. Batteau, *The Invention of Appalachia* (Tucson: University of Arizona Press, 1990), chaps. 4 and 5.

3. Shapiro, *Appalachia on Our Mind*, 87–90, though most of Shapiro's

discussion of this issue focuses on East Tennesseans. Kenneth Noe has noted that of thirty-nine works considered by Shapiro published between 1865 and 1883, only nine made any reference to the Civil War. Kenneth W. Noe, "Toward the Myth of Unionist Appalachia, 1865–1883," *Journal of the Appalachian Studies Association* 6 (1994): 68.

4. Ibid., 67–74. The article appeared in an expanded version as "Deadened Color and Colder Horror: Rebecca Harding Davis and the Myth of Unionist Appalachia," in Billings et al., eds., *Confronting Appalachian Stereotypes*, 67–84.

5. Shannon H. Wilson, "Lincoln's Sons and Daughters: Berea College, Lincoln Memorial University, and the Myth of Unionist Appalachia, 1866–1910," in *The Civil War in Appalachia: Collected Essays,* ed. Kenneth W. Noe and Shannon H. Wilson (Knoxville: University of Tennessee Press, 1997), 242–64.

6. James C. Klotter, "The Black South and White Appalachia," *Journal of American History* 66 (March 1987): 42–62; and Nina Silber, "What Does America Need so Much as Americans? Race and Northern Reconciliation with Southern Appalachia, 1870–1900," in *Appalachians and Race: The Mountain South from Slavery to Segregation,* ed. John C. Inscoe (Lexington: University Press of Kentucky, 2001), 244–58.

7. Shapiro extends his treatment of Appalachia and its chroniclers to 1920, but he has nothing to say about the Civil War in his coverage of 1900–1920.

8. Shapiro, *Appalachia on Our Mind,* 116–17, 132–33. With the exceptions of John Fox and Margaret Morley, all the writers discussed in this chapter at least claimed that their observations and conclusions applied to all parts of Southern Appalachia.

9. William G. Frost, "Our Contemporary Ancestors in the Southern Mountains," *Atlantic Monthly* 83 (March 1899), reprinted in McNeil, ed., *Appalachian Images,* 91–106. (Subsequent references to the essay are to the version appearing in the McNeil volume.)

10. The best biographical data on Frost are found in his memoir, *For the Mountains: An Autobiography* (New York: Fleming H. Revell, 1937), and in two histories of Berea College: Elisabeth S. Peck, *Berea's First 125 Years, 1855–1980* (Lexington: University Press of Kentucky, 1982), 68–74; and Shannon H. Wilson, *Berea College: An Illustrated History* (Lexington: University Press of Kentucky, 2006), 78–81, 90–111.

11. McNeil, *Appalachian Imagery,* 91; Batteau, *Invention of Appalachia,* 74. Both Shapiro and Batteau offer insightful analyses of Frost's essay: Shapiro, *Appalachia on Our Mind,* chap. 8, and Batteau, *Invention of Appalachia,* 74–80.

12. Frost, "Our Contemporary Ancestors," 99.

13. Ibid., 105–6.

14. On the strength of British loyalists of the southern backcountry, see Robert S. Lambert, *South Carolina Loyalists in the American Revolution* (Columbia: University of South Carolina Press, 1987); Carole Watterson Troxler, *The Loyalist Experience in North Carolina* (Raleigh, N.C.: Division of Archives and History, 1976); and Robert M. Calhoon, *The Loyalists in Revolutionary America, 1760–1781* (New York: Harcourt Brace Jovanovich, 1973).

15. Frost, "Our Contemporary Ancestors," 99. John C. Campbell wryly noted, "Few discourses on mountain questions are complete without this reference [to King's Mountain]. The audiences for whom such addresses are given . . . would feel cheated without it. They look for it as expectantly as the Bostonian does for the closing phrase in the Governor's Thanksgiving Proclamation, 'God Save the Commonwealth of Massachusetts.'" John C. Campbell, *The Southern Highlander and His Homeland* (New York: Russell Sage Foundation, 1921), 8.

16. Mrs. D. L. Pierson, "The Mountaineers of Madison County, N.C.," *Missionary Review of the World* (November 1897): 823.

17. See "Unionists in the Attic," chap. 13 in this volume, for a more detailed account of the Shelton Laurel massacre and how it was remembered locally.

18. Pierson, "Mountaineers of Madison County," 828. The Battle of Alamance was the final showdown between the Regulators and North Carolina's royal governor, William Tryon. Both it and the Mecklenburg Declaration of Independence took place in North Carolina's backcountry, but far east of the mountains.

19. On Fox's life and Appalachian writing, see Darlene Wilson, "The Felicitous Convergence of Mythmaking and Capital Accumulation: John Fox Jr. and the Formation of An (other) Almost-White American Underclass," *Journal of Appalachian Studies* 1 (Fall 1995): 17–29; Wilson, "A Judicious Combination of Incident and Psychology: John Fox Jr. and the Southern Mountaineer Motif," in Billings, ed., *Confronting Appalachian Stereotypes*, 98–118; and Batteau, *Invention of Appalachia*, 64–74. On the significance of *The Little Shepherd of Kingdom Come* in particular, see Silber, "What Does America Need So Much as Americans?" 254–56.

20. John Fox Jr., *Bluegrass and Rhododendron: Outdoors in Old Kentucky* (New York: Charles Scribner and Sons, 1901), 6. Brigadier General Robert S. Garnett took Confederate command of northwestern Virginia in June 1861, having been informed beforehand that "there is great disaffection in this and adjoining counties and opposition to the lawful action of the State authorities is certainly contemplated." *Official Records of the War of the Rebellion* (Washington, D.C.: Government Printing Office, 1880), series I, vol. 2, 843. He was killed in a battle against General George McClellan's forces at Laurel Hill, in what would become West Virginia, on July 11, 1861.

21. Fox, *Bluegrass and Rhododendron*, 6–7.

22. Biographical data on Wilson are slim; this information comes from his own description of his early life in Samuel Tyndale Wilson, *A Century of Maryville College, 1819–1919: A Story of Altruism* (Maryville, Tenn.: Directors of Maryville College, 1919), 159.

23. Samuel Tyndale Wilson, *The Southern Mountaineers* (New York: Presbyterian Home Missions, 1906), preface, 27–31.

24. Ibid., 33.

25. Ibid., 34.

26. Ibid.

27. Emma Bell Miles, *The Spirit of the Mountains* (1905; rept., Knoxville: University of Tennessee Press, 1972), 82.

28. Ibid., 71–72.

29. On the stronger Confederate sentiment in the Chattanooga area than elsewhere in East Tennessee, see W. Todd Groce, *Mountain Rebels: East Tennessee Confederates and the Civil War, 1860–1870* (Knoxville: University of Tennessee Press, 1999), 39. Groce reports that 89 percent of the city's voters supported secession in the referendum of June 8, 1861, the highest concentration in the region. On Confederate enlistment in Chattanooga and elsewhere in East Tennessee, see John D. Fowler, *Mountaineers in Gray: The Nineteenth Tennessee Volunteer Infantry Regiment, C.S.A.* (Knoxville: University of Tennessee Press, 2004), 18–22.

30. David Whisnant, introduction to the University of Tennessee Press's reprint edition, xv. Other scholarly work on Miles includes Grace Toney Edwards, "Emma Bell Miles: Feminist Crusader in Appalachia," in *Appalachia Inside Out*, ed. Robert J. Higgs, Ambrose N. Manning, and Jim Wayne Miller, vol. 2 (Knoxville: University of Tennessee Press, 1995), 709–12; and Kay Baker Gaston, *Emma Bell Miles* (Signal Mountain, Tenn.: Walden Ridge Historical Society, 1985). For a particularly favorable assessment of *The Spirit of the Mountains* and of Miles's treatment of her subjects, see the introduction to McNeil, *Appalachian Images*, 3–4.

31. Foreword to Margaret W. Morley, *The Carolina Mountains* (1913; rept., Fairview, N.C: Historical Images, 2006), xix. In 1926, the Grove Park Inn in Asheville commissioned a special deluxe edition of *The Carolina Mountains* and placed it in each guest room.

32. "About Margaret W. Morley," in ibid., xi–xiv.

33. Ibid., 12–13.

34. Ibid., 13. Morley's other significant reference to the war is a chapter on the history of Asheville, in which she states, "Deserters from both sides took refuge in the mountains. Desperadoes of the worst sort lived in caves and raided the country" (102). While this is one of very few acknowledgments of guerrilla warfare in any of the works under discussion, Morley fails to mention that Asheville was a center of Confederate recruitment and ar-

mament production, a target of Stoneman's Raid at war's end, or the home base of Zebulon B. Vance, North Carolina's Civil War governor.

35. Miles, *Spirit of the Mountains,* chap. 10, quote on 190.

36. Morley, *Carolina Mountains,* 123; see also 292–95.

37. Batteau, *Invention of Appalachia,* 89; Horace Kephart, *Our Southern Highlanders: A Narrative of Adventure in the Southern Appalachians and a Study of Life among the Mountaineers* (New York: Macmillan, 1913, 1922), 29. The book was much expanded in 1922, when the subtitle was added. That edition is the one cited here.

38. The fullest biographical treatment of Kephart is George Ellison's introduction to a 1972 reprint of *Our Southern Highlanders,* ix–xlvi.

39. Kephart, *Our Southern Highlanders,* 29–30. More recent editions of Kephart's other books included *Camping and Woodcraft: A Handbook for Vacation Campers and for Travelers in the Wilderness* (Knoxville: University of Tennessee Press, 1988); and *Camp Cookery* (New York: Macmillan, 1924).

40. "Horce Kephart by Himself," *North Carolina Library Bulletin* 5 (June 1922): 52, quoted in Ellison, xxxvii.

41. Batteau, *Invention of Appalachia,* 90.

42. Kephart, *Our Southern Highlanders,* 429, 443–45. Nearly half of Kephart's coverage of the war consists of lengthy block quotes from John Fox and William Frost, discussed earlier in this chapter.

43. Ibid., 447, 449–50.

44. Ibid., 40–51.

45. Biographical information about Campbell remains surprisingly thin. Among the most thorough accounts of his life are found in the inventory to the John C. Campbell and Olive Dame Campbell Papers, Southern Historical Collection, UNC–Chapel Hill, and in David Whisnant, *All That Is Native and Fine: The Politics of Culture in an American Region* (Chapel Hill: University of North Carolina Press, 1983), 106–7, although Whisnant focuses more fully on Mrs. Campbell's work after her husband's death.

46. Williams, *Appalachia,* 207–8.

47. Campbell, *Southern Highlander,* 90.

48. Ibid., 90–91.

49. Ibid.

50. Ibid., 96–97.

51. Wilson, "Lincoln's Sons and Daughters," 244.

52. Frost, "Our Contemporary Ancestors," 99.

53. Campbell, *Southern Highlander,* 95. For more on how several of these authors dealt with race in their work, see "Race and Racism in Nineteenth-Century Appalachia," chap. 1 in this volume.

13

Unionists in the Attic

The Shelton Laurel Massacre Dramatized

Rarely, if ever, have southern Unionists been incorporated into the public memory or commemoration of the Civil War. For all of the many ways in which Tony Horwitz found interest in the war alive and thriving throughout the southern states, the quirkiest and most off-beat of which he described so colorfully in *Confederates in the Attic,* not once does the term "Unionist" appear in his text. Nor would one ever know of internal dissent or divided loyalties from watching Ken Burns's epic documentary treatment of the war.[1] While scholars over the past decade have made southern Unionism an increasingly significant part of Civil War studies,[2] that trend has not found its way into more popular perceptions of the war. The plight of those southerners who chose not to give their allegiance to the Confederacy or to in any way support its war of independence has been all too easily erased from the ways in which Americans collectively look back on the war and its legacy.

That is, until 2005, when an extraordinary play, commissioned and produced by the Southern Appalachian Repertory Theatre, debuted on the campus of Mars Hill College in the Blue Ridge Mountains of North Carolina. This dramatization of the infamous Shelton Laurel massacre, which occurred only twenty miles away, represented a significant new development in the war's public commemoration. Not only did it bring the Unionist experience fully into the spotlight, but it allowed—or forced?—descendants of both the victims and the perpetrators of that tragedy to confront that past in a very public forum. If Unionism and guerrilla warfare have been stored far more deeply in the attic where Tony Horwitz found so many Confederates, at least one particularly painful incident has been removed from storage and put on display in an unusual venue for wrestling with the complex issues it raises: the theater.

In mid-January 1863, two columns of the 64th North Carolina Regiment moved into the remote Shelton Laurel valley in the remote mountains of Madison County, North Carolina, seeking the men there who had been part of a raid on the county seat of Marshall two weeks earlier. Led by Colonel Lawrence Allen and Colonel James Keith, first cousins who were among Marshall's more prominent citizens, the troops sought retribution for the havoc wreaked by some fifty-odd men, many of them from Shelton Laurel and many of them deserters from the 64th. With somewhat ambiguous orders from General Henry Heth, the soldiers harassed—even tortured—local women and girls into giving up the hiding places of the men they sought. Over the course of two days, they arrested and held fifteen men and boys, with the stated intent of taking them to Knoxville, Tennessee, to be either imprisoned or conscripted into Confederate service. But on the morning of January 19, only a mile or two after their forced march began (and after two prisoners had escaped), either Keith or Allen—which one remains in doubt—ordered the thirteen prisoners into a nearby clearing, forced them into groups of five and three, and executed them all. Seven of the thirteen were named Shelton; both the oldest, sixty-five, and the youngest, twelve, were named David Shelton.[3]

The story is a familiar and oft-told one. It is as well documented as any single incident in the South's irregular war, and certainly as well known as any other event that occurred in wartime North Carolina. News of the massacre appeared in a Memphis newspaper in June 1863, which led to coverage soon thereafter in several northern papers, including the *New York Times*. Tennessee Union scout Daniel Ellis, in perhaps the most widely read memoir by a guerrilla warrior, devoted several pages to Shelton Laurel and its Unionist martyrs in his *Thrilling Adventures*, published in 1867. By century's end, Confederate participants in the massacre had had their say. In 1894, the commander of the 64th, then living in Arkansas, published a self-serving pamphlet titled *Partisan Campaigns of Col. Lawrence M. Allen*, followed in 1901 by a regimental history of the 64th by one of its officers, Captain B. T. Morris, who defended the actions of Allen and Keith and the men under their command.[4] The massacre received brief acknowledgment in regional histories by John Preston Arthur and Ora Blackmun, and rated a chapter in Manly Wade Wellman's lively and somewhat unorthodox county history, *The Kingdom of Madison.*[5]

In 1981, established Civil War scholar Phillip Paludan produced a masterful book-length study of the massacre, entitled simply *Victims*. It remains the fullest account of the incident and the circumstances surrounding it, but it was by no means the last word.[6] No fewer than three chapters of William R. Trotter's *Bushwhackers* (1988) focus on Shelton Laurel, and Sean O'Brien devotes both his prologue and first chapter to the incident in *Mountain Partisans* (1999), a broad-based study of guerrilla warfare in Southern Appalachia. Gordon McKinney and I added nothing new, but we provided a full account drawing on all of the above in our study *The Heart of Confederate North Carolina* (2000).[7] Even fiction writers have embraced the massacre in recent years. Two of region's most prominent novelists, Sharon McCrumb and Ron Rash, have incorporated the incident into their most recent works.[8]

Even without reference to any of the above, the story has held a firm place in the oral tradition over several generations of the Shelton family and other residents of the Shelton Laurel community. In 1989, Jim Taylor added significant details to the written record in a regimental newsletter, through interviews with Rena Shelton, a descendant of several of the massacre's victims and widely regarded as the family's matriarch and guardian of its historical legacy. She told Taylor that much of her information on the massacre was based on stories told her years earlier by a hundred-year-old woman who had witnessed much of what she related.[9]

Despite this oral legacy and the extensive scholarly record, probably few Shelton Laurel residents were ready to confront the most infamous event in their community's past in the far more public and pronounced rendition that faced them in 2005—the play produced at Mars Hill. Founded in 1975, the Southern Appalachian Repertory Theatre (SART) had long made a part of its mission "produce new plays, especially those that reflect the rich cultural heritage of the region."[10] Commissioned works focused on the story of Frankie Silvers, a notorious 1831 murder case that led to the first execution of a woman in North Carolina, and on geologist Elisha Mitchell's exploration of the nearby peak that bears his name. Both met with critical acclaim and local enthusiasm, but taking on the Shelton Laurel massacre raised the stakes considerably. The incident still carries considerable emotional baggage, with some residents—Rena Shelton among them—understandably leery of how outsiders might choose to interpret and dramatize a tragedy to which they lay such a personal claim. Complicating that issue was the fact that the perpetrators as well as the victims of the massacre were Madison County residents, and their descendants would likely scrutinize any dramatic treatment of the incident as fully as would those who counted Shelton Laurel residents among their ancestors.

SART's leadership—president Rick Morgan and artistic director Bill Gregg—took a significant first step in meeting these challenges by hiring playwright Sean O'Leary to write the play in the spring of 2004. O'Leary's credentials made him a natural choice for the task. Two of his previous plays had focused on historical subjects—one on Ezra Pound, the other on the Spanish Civil War—and had much impressed Morgan and Gregg.[11] O'Leary, who lives in Harpers Ferry, West Virginia, accepted the challenge of taking on Shelton Laurel; he researched deeply in the historical literature and made a close consultant of Dan Slagle, a Madison County native whose interest and expertise derived from genealogical research into his own background. (Slagle has traced at least three ancestors who served in the 64th.)

O'Leary came to Mars Hill in the spring of 2005 for a reading of an early draft of the play, then called *Beneath Shelton Laurel*. It was at that point that I became involved, having been invited to serve as a historical consultant, along with Slagle. I was very impressed with what O'Leary had done, and I offered only minor suggestions, as did several others in attendance. Much of the concern among the group revolved around the perspective to be taken—and how well the play represented the viewpoints of both Confederates and Unionists; all involved were conscious that the major players would have descendants, and thus partisans, in attendance at the performances. Most agreed that O'Leary had done a masterful job in keeping those very different perspectives in play; the primary sticking point was how to resolve the historical confusion as to which officer—Allen or Keith—actually gave the orders to execute their prisoners.[12]

The final version of *Shelton Laurel*, as produced by SART in August 2005, works on a number of levels—dramatically, emotionally, and historically. The basic situation around which the play is structured may seem contrived and stilted, and yet any such first impressions are quickly displaced by the dramatic repercussions of the setup unfolding on stage. O'Leary created a fictional scenario in which three key players in the massacre—Lawrence Allen, James Keith, and Patsy Shelton—come together in a Baptist church in Marshall in 1894 (the last year all three were still alive) to confront each other over the tragedy that still haunted them to one degree or another more than thirty years later. (Allen made a return visit to Madison County in 1892, to settle a land dispute, but there is no evidence that either Keith, who also lived in Arkansas, or Patsy Shelton, who had moved to East Tennessee, ever did so.)[13]

In O'Leary's play, Keith is particularly remorseful over his part in the massacre and has returned home to Marshall, sensing that he's close to the end of his life. He seeks penance, and perhaps some solace from the torment of "ghosts" from the past, by meeting with Mrs. Shelton, whose husband and two sons were among the thirteen victims. She arrives with no intention of offering either forgiveness or comfort to the man she holds responsible for the unjustified and meaningless murder of her family, and she insists that she is there merely to learn about their final hours and what, if anything, they had said before they were killed. Allen, like Keith, had moved to Arkansas shortly after the war's end, and he returns to this "haunted" place out of concern for his friend, explaining that Keith's wife had asked him to retrieve her husband from this place that could mean only trouble for him. (There's a hint that Keith may have been contemplating suicide.) Unlike Keith, Allen expresses no regrets and offers no condolences to Mrs. Shelton, and he fully defends his actions and the rationale behind the massacre.

O'Leary's decision to make Keith the conscience-torn penitent and Allen the hard-line defender of their actions works well dramatically, even if the historical record does not necessarily support that version of events. He knew that Keith became an active lay leader in the Baptist Church after moving to Arkansas, so it makes sense that he is wracked with guilt about his part in the massacre. Given the tone of Allen's 1894 memoir, O'Leary is on surer ground in making Allen unrepentant.

Much of the emotional and narrative power in O'Leary's play lies in the fact that it takes Keith's "haunting" literally. The voices of four of his three victims—Patsy Shelton's husband and two sons and a young girl whom he ordered to be flogged for refusing to reveal their location—disturb his conscience and his state of mind. They appear on stage as well, witnessing this meeting of their wife and mother with their murderers, seen and heard by the audience but not by the three principals (except being heard on occasion by Keith). As Patsy Shelton confronts Keith and Allen about not only what happened but why, these ghosts provide impassioned commentary on what they're hearing, and occasionally reenact that fateful day in effectively staged flashback scenes.

It is through the confrontation among the living characters in the 1890s that the circumstances surrounding the 1863 incident gradually emerge. Allen stubbornly insists that the thirteen executed prisoners were "traitors, criminals, deserters," men who had "murdered, raided our homes, stole from our children," whose actions invited—even demanded—Confederate retribution. When Mrs. Shelton insists that none of that justified the shooting of "mere boys—her boys," Allen is quick to dismiss their age. "And some of our men were boys. And some of the Yankees were boys. It was terrible. The war was terrible." She accuses him of being cold-blooded and having no feelings. Allen responds, "Despair—that's what I feel . . . despair because they made us stoop to their level."[14]

The earlier raid on Marshall was the immediate impetus for the 64th's retaliatory action. Mrs. Shelton is quick to explain the necessity behind that raid: not simply that those in the community were hungry, but that they were intentionally kept so by local authorities who, in carefully rationing salt, so vital to preserving hog meat, denied it to those families who failed to demonstrate adequate support of the Confederate war effort. The "crime" of which her family and others really stood accused, she insisted, was simply their neutrality

—their desire to be left alone. Their desperation for salt, along with their resentment of its denial by Marshall authorities, led to the raid: "If our men weren't willin' to die in your army on the battlefield," she asks Keith and Allen, "did y'all think they were gonna be willin' to die o' starvation in them hills along with their families?" When Keith suggests that "your men could have joined the effort," Mrs. Shelton responds: "All we knew was the Yankees weren't doin' nothin' to us, but them folks in Marshall were." (O'Leary adds a crucial fact that Phillip Paludan curiously overlooked in his book—that the raid was "organized" and led by an outsider, a Union lieutenant from Tennessee, John Kirk, whose brother George would later conduct several raids at Confederate targets elsewhere in western North Carolina.)[15]

It is left to Keith, in confessional mode, to acknowledge that he—like Allen, a resident of Marshall—sought authorization from General Henry Heth to put down this "insurrection." Heth had only recently taken command of the Department of East Tennessee, which one scholar has called "the most eagerly avoided command in the entire Confederacy,"[16] and issued orders that the Madison County insurrectionists be taken. The terms of how that order was executed were vague enough to add fuel to the later controversy over the executions. Keith explains to Mrs. Shelton: "He didn't think your men could ever be made into soldiers and he didn't want to be bothered with prisoners."[17] In a key flashback scene, Allen, Keith, and a Captain Nelson debate the fate of the prisoners they've taken and, in so doing, articulate the moral and practical dilemmas posed by this—or any other—guerrilla war. When Keith expresses qualms about executing the prisoners, feeling that they have not done enough to determine the guilt or innocence of those they so arbitrarily rounded up, Allen counters that Keith was "the one who went to Heth . . . who wanted two companies of men to finish off these damn savages." Nelson adds, "These people, if that's what you want to call them, threaten our towns, steal our supplies, harbor deserters and Union spies, and deplete our resources by diverting whole regiments to deal with them. My God! Half the generals in the Yankee army haven't accomplished as much."

Allen argues that their job is not to determine who was or was not part of the raid, and that this extreme punishment sends a signal to others who think they can act with impunity, that there will be consequences to pay, "if not by them, then by others, the ones who harbor them. If they put our families at risk, they put their own at risk as well." He also expresses his contempt for their effort to claim neutrality, and for hiding behind their civilian status while waging unconventional warfare: "There's no power on heaven or earth that will persuade me that we should treat some ragtag bunch of savages whose only concern is their own selfish interests better than we treat our own soldiers who fight and die to protect our families—our way of life." When Keith argues that war doesn't give them license to execute civilians for any crime, however awful, and asks "where do we draw the line?" Allen responds, "The line is drawn for us. We have orders," and reiterates: "I won't grieve as much as when it's our own men we have to execute or a Yankee for that matter. Even they're to be respected for having the courage to put on the uniform and accept the consequences."

The harshness of Allen's views are put into somewhat different focus when Keith reveals to Mrs. Shelton how the raid on Marshall inflicted a very personal loss on the Allen family. In looting stores and homes for far more than salt, the raiders ransacked Allen's home and took the blankets and sheets from the beds of his two children, who lay sick with scarlet fever. On the day before the Confederate assault on Shelton Laurel, Allen received word that both his son and daughter, ages six and four, had died, and he had returned to deal with the prisoners just after their funerals.[18] That revelation, held off until midway through the play, suddenly serves to humanize Allen, and to provide an even more understandable explanation for the bitterness he feels toward the prisoners and those they represent. Even Mrs. Shelton seems momentarily sympathetic, though she is quick to turn on Keith, saying, "But *you* knew what you were doing to my children was wrong." Keith answers simply, "I knew what duty demanded."

As Allen's language suggests, O'Leary is very much attuned to the class distinctions that played such an integral role in the war waged in North Carolina's mountain counties. The "county seat elite" represented by both Keith and Allen were indeed contemptuous of those more remotely situated residents of the county—for their insularity and backward ways as much as for their efforts to keep at arm's length the war and the ideological issues behind it. Those deep-rooted prejudices made it much easier for Allen, Keith, and their men to dehumanize the Sheltons and the other captives; it not only rationalized their right to put to them to death but also enabled them to do so.

Shelton Laurel residents were fully aware of that contempt. O'Leary constructs a particularly poignant scene in which, just after their capture, Jim Shelton and his sons speculate on their future. It becomes obvious that they underestimate the extent of the hatred directed toward them. Young Jim protests his innocence, insisting they tell their captors that they played no part in the raid, to which his father responds, "You done somethin' worse'n that." "What?" Young Jim inquires, and is told, "You was born, boy—born a barefoot, ridge-runnin', heathen savage. Ain't worthy o' the life the Lord give you."

But in response to the boys' worries over rumors that they were to be shot, Shelton assures them that being viewed in such terms does not make them worthy of slaughter, and that their common humanity will overcome any class differences. They won't kill us, he insists, "cuz they're flesh and blood and heart and soul just like you and me. Besides, they got orders to take us to Knoxville." Pushing the point even harder, he says that it isn't easy to kill a man in cold blood, and that soldiers only do so out of fear that "the other feller's trying to kill him." To fire point-blank at a man who poses no threat is beyond the capacity of most men, he insists. "Them soldiers ain't no different than us—even the ones like that Keith. He may think he can, but if that time ever came, he'd find out he's just like us."

Keith overhears this conversation and acknowledges both the basic truth of Jim Shelton's words and the irony in how naïve that statement proved to be. The climax of the play comes with a skillful staging of the execution itself, which shocks audiences even though they are fully aware of what's to come. The use of flashbacks and the constant presence of the Shelton "ghosts" adds to the ghastliness of seeing bodies crumple and fall even as they plead for their lives until bullets silence their pleas. (The last moments are based on details conveyed in the first newspaper accounts of the massacre.)

Much of the power of O'Leary's play comes from the complexities and moral ambiguities that he builds into his retelling of the slaughter.

While audiences never lose sympathy for Patsy Shelton and fully accept her tragedy as one compounded by the innocence of all three Shelton victims, the playwright's far more impressive achievement is that they are made to understand—if not condone—the frustration, anger, and even righteousness of the two Confederate leaders, at least one of whom feels justified in having taken such drastic action.

The play's critical success and sold-out performances in the summer of 2005 led SART to present the play again in September 2006, in a tightened version, in order to accommodate school groups and the post-play discussions in which Dan Slagle and I participated, along with Bill Gregg and Michael Mattison, the actor who so powerfully portrayed Colonel Allen. It was through those discussions that the current relevance of the issues debated in that Baptist church in 1894 came through loud and clear, issues that easily transcend the local context of O'Leary's play and would—or should—resonate as fully with any American audience as they do with those in and around Madison County.

This was not the first time that the Shelton Laurel story had been imbued with contemporary parallels. A number of commentators drew parallels between Shelton Laurel and the equally notorious My Lai massacre during the Vietnam War, in which Lieutenant William Calley led an American force to slaughter an entire village whose inhabitants were suspected of shielding and supplying the Viet Cong. When Paludan's book appeared in 1981, only six years after the Vietnam War era's end, he acknowledged that he was interested in Shelton Laurel "because I am concerned with My Lai and the Holocaust, in the tragic capacity that humans have shown throughout history—the capacity to commit atrocity."[19]

The war in Iraq now resonates in much the same way. In fact, it was during the play's run in early September 2006 that the debate over the use of torture in interrogating terrorist prisoners raged in Washington, and audiences easily recognized and eagerly discussed the parallels: how an occupying force controls insurgency; how one defines civilian combatants and to what extent they are subject to military justice when taken prisoner; where the chain of command stops and starts; at what point an individual soldier has the right to question orders that he sees as immoral or unauthorized; the accountability for such actions after the fact (although the play stops short of dealing with the charges made against Keith and Allen); and finally, what right one has to remain neutral, or merely disengaged, when one's country is at war.

Even in a civil war involving, for the most part, white men fighting each other, the basic contempt and/or prejudice an occupying army feels toward the civilian populace it seeks to control is as relevant in Madison County in 1863 as it was in Vietnam in the 1960s and in Iraq today. In O'Leary's script, Colonel Allen defends both their actions to Keith by noting that it was all a matter of survival, the survival of "our men, our boys." He adds, "Every day they're out there fighting, sacrificing for the Confederacy, for our cause. There's no power on heaven or earth that will persuade me that we should treat some ragtag bunch of savages whose only concern is their own selfish interests better than we treat our own soldiers who fight and die to protect our families—our way of life." How much different was the mind-set of William Calley toward the villagers at My Lai, or that of at least some American troops toward the Iraqis in whose midst they find themselves so vulnerably situated?

In post-performance forums, audiences recognized and jumped at the opportunity to discuss the timeliness of the questions raised by O'Leary's play. And yet its local context was never lost on them; just as many questions and comments focused on particularities of the war in Madison County, the massacre itself, and the fate of those participants who survived. In addition to the public performances at Mars Hill, and one in Asheville, some twenty miles to the south, generous support from the North Carolina Humanities Council and the National Endowment for the Arts allowed for two special performances for Madison County middle and high school students, nearly four hundred of whom attended with their teachers. For many, not only was it their first exposure to live theater, but it also served as their introduction to the incident that so defined the nature of the Civil War for their ancestors in their home county.

The highlight of the play's second-season run was a performance in Shelton Laurel itself. On Saturday night, September 16, 2006, the cast and crew moved the production to the gymnasium of the Laurel Elementary School. Some residents had seen the play the year before at Mars Hill, but the community remains relatively isolated, and many had not crossed the county to attend. With the encouragement of the school principal and support from the PTA, the volunteer fire department, and school staff, the dramatized version of this very local tragedy finally came home.

There was some uncertainty about how the play would be received there. Over the years, Shelton Laurel residents—so many of whom can trace their ancestry to one or more of the victims—had demonstrated considerable ambivalence regarding the massacre. Some seemed especially cautious, even suspicious, as to its commemoration, unsure that they wanted that painful past exposed in too visible or public a way. Some were most likely mistrustful of O'Leary, who had consciously resisted their offers of "help" in "getting it right" when they learned that he was taking on their story.[20]

While the oral tradition is remarkably strong, and a number of residents, including Rena Shelton, have been willing to share what they know with scholars and journalists, they have done very little to draw attention to the site of the massacre, and they intentionally downplay any physical reminders of it. The only tangible reminder in the area is a state historical marker at a highway juncture well before one enters the community itself. It states simply, "Shelton Laurel Massacre: Thirteen men and boys, suspected of Unionism, were killed by Confederate soldiers in early 1863. Graves 8 mi. E." There are no signs or directions to the obscure cemetery on a wooded knoll in which the victims are buried—most likely in a mass grave (though a large and well-maintained marble slab has marked the site since the 1970s). As the Civil War Trails project is rapidly being implemented in many counties throughout North Carolina, an inquiry about focusing one of Madison County's three such displays on the massacre and placing it in Shelton Laurel was quietly declined by one or more community leaders.[21] Jim Taylor's summation of the community's attitude in 1989 holds true even now. "To this day," he wrote, "the story is still told to the children in the area, and the older folks will tell it as if it happened yesterday. Some will refuse to speak of it because of the strong emotions it kindles, while others use a hushed tone out of a sense of grief that is still felt, even after all these years."[22]

But concerns about community response to having O'Leary's play

brought into their midst proved unfounded. About 120 people attended the performance at Laurel Elementary. The emotional impact
of the play's climax was particularly acute—for the actors as well as
the audience. Yet, at the end of the performance, something unexpected happened. After hearty applause and an announcement that
the panel discussion would begin momentarily, people rose from their
seats; some left the gymnasium with tears streaming down their
cheeks, but most moved forward to confront the actors, the crew, and
those of us who would have made up the panel, eager to engage in
one-on-one conversations about what they had just seen, and the
memories or associations it triggered.

Actress Marlene Earp was quickly surrounded by local residents
eager to thank her for her beautifully moving—and for them, quite
authentic—performance as Patsy Shelton, certainly the play's pivotal
character from their perspective. The rest of us heard family stories
full of details about the massacre and its impact on the community as
they had heard it over the years. One woman identified herself as a
descendant of Judy Shelton (Patsy's sister-in-law); she told me that
Judy had been one of the women who discovered the bodies of the
massacred men and boys, and then described the route by which they
were moved for a proper burial near Judy's house. An elderly man
told me that he counted among his ancestors Pete McCoy, one of the
two prisoners who managed to escape his captors the night before the
rest met their common fate. Others talked in more general terms
about their genealogical linkages to the victims, about various prop-
erties in the valley, and how they'd changed hands over the years,
which in turn led to other stories about earlier and later incidents in
the long life of the community.

The effect, in short, was cathartic, at both an individual and a
collective level. Much of the reaction must have been relief that nothing in their own understandings of the story had been challenged or
contradicted—rather it broadened, deepened, and added new levels of
meaning to what they already knew and felt about it. Rena Shelton,
ninety-two years old, had not been sure she had wanted to see the
play because, according to her daughters, it might not tell the story
the same way she had told it for so long. Thus all associated with the
production were much relieved with her pronouncement at its end:

"It's as good as it could be to have been written by someone not from here." Yet another elderly resident reiterated that judgment when he commented, "Well, it's not exactly the way I've always heard the story, but it's not wrong."

For all of the scholarship on the Shelton Laurel massacre, much of which Mrs. Shelton and her family and neighbors are familiar with, there must have been some sense of satisfaction in seeing a dramatization that spoke even more eloquently and movingly about the tragic plight of their ancestors. Certainly little in the public memory of the war beyond their own community had ever acknowledged or validated that reality. Within the shared belief system that emerged in the South in the years after the Civil War, there was no place for divided loyalties, for internal dissent, or for guerrilla warfare. Such ambivalence or complexity in southern wartime behavior would have seriously undermined the basic, clear-cut interpretation of regional solidarity to the cause in which white southerners so wanted, indeed needed, to believe. For most of them, the Civil War era became, to paraphrase a quote by Harold Pinter, "a past that they remembered, imagined they remembered, convinced themselves that they remembered, or pretended to remember."[23]

Shelton Laurel was not the only Appalachian community that sought to sidestep the traumas of the guerrilla warfare that had so divided them for that brief period. Recent studies of the war in north Georgia indicate that within a decade or so after the war's end, communal memory began to find no place for the divisiveness in that region, and created instead a public myth of Confederate southern solidarity throughout the conflict, fully embracing the "Lost Cause" ideology.[24] A similar study of Haywood County's postwar legacy suggests similarly sanitized versions of its part in the war perpetuated by local veterans groups, historical societies, and county histories, in which, according to historian Richard Starnes, "unpleasant topics such as desertion, internal dissent, and outright disloyalty were replaced by images of Confederate solidarity, bravery in battle, and devotion to duty."[25]

Such claims of Confederate solidarity and the neglect of less pleasant realities continue into our own time, and they are often based on similar sentiments. In a recent study of tourism and historical memory in Southern Appalachia, Brenden Martin notes that during and after the civil rights movement, "symbols of Dixie"—most notably the Confederate flag—at tourist attractions such as Gatlinburg and Pigeon Forge became as prominent as the hillbilly/redneck image in terms of memorabilia sold and the image projected to a vastly white clientele. Martin notes the presentism in these marketing ploys, as well as the irony: Tennessee's Sevier County was among the most solidly Unionist of any in the state during the sectional crisis and the war itself, but visitors would find no sign of that reality conveyed in anything offered for their consumption.[26]

Yet perhaps the closest parallel to the Shelton Laurel incident and how it was remembered lay at the far end of the Confederacy. In a wave of hysteria in and around Cooke County, Texas, in the fall of 1862, more than two hundred Unionists were arrested and tried by local and state Confederate authorities; forty-four were executed in the county seat of Gainesville over several days, after conviction by a "citizen's court." Quite understandably, that event, which came to be known as "the Great Hanging," inspired protests and repercussions even greater than those that followed the Shelton Laurel massacre. After the war, it led to increasing reticence on the part of local citizens, who preferred to remember it more privately than publicly. Thomas Barrett, a former minister who had actually participated in the trials and the hangings, published a full account of it all in pamphlet form in 1885. In attempting to generate interest and sales in the area, he found little interest. According to Richard McCaslin's definitive history of the Great Hanging, Barrett "encountered opposition based on the enduring animosities between Unionists and ex-Confederates and the desire of many people to let the past lie undisturbed." The reaction led him to become "close-mouthed" about the incident, and even in the 1890s, when asked about it, he said that it was still unsafe to reveal all that he knew.[27]

If the messiness of guerrilla warfare and its tragic consequences were both an embarrassment and counterproductive to the New South aims of postwar elites in the mountains, and thus was erased from the cleaner and less ambivalent public memories shaped by that elite, it was left to individual families and households to preserve the painful legacy of the internal strife they experienced through much more private and obscure venues. It is obvious that the Shelton Laurel community, particularly the Shelton family, have perpetuated but also carefully guarded its own version of the particular tragedy that has so "haunted" their Civil War history.

This then is why O'Leary's play has proved to be such a landmark event. Not only is it one of the only visible and public commemorations of the Unionist experience anywhere within the bounds of the former Confederacy; it also represents a serious and factually accurate re-creation and explanation of a profound tragedy in the very county where it for so long was so divisive, and where it has been remembered in personal terms and hushed tones.

This public commemoration of so controversial and unsavory a piece of local history suggests parallels with other such events in the southern past. What C. Vann Woodward termed the "burden of southern history" continues to haunt other communities. Not surprisingly, those dealing with race are among the most subject to communal negligence, either intentional or unintentional. The "collective amnesia" of white residents of Wilmington, North Carolina, and Atlanta in writing out of their history the brutal race riots those cities experienced in 1898 and 1906, respectively, are prime examples of the deniability of the historical record. City leaders quickly wiped them from collective or institutional memory, and local historians for much of the twentieth century complied in ignoring these "unpleasantries" in their celebratory chronicles of those cities, especially in Atlanta, that most self-conscious and boosterish of southern cities.[28] By the same token, whites in many other communities, North and South, have long suppressed any collective memories of racial violence, particularly lynchings, leaving it to the private and more informal oral traditions of black communities to keep those traumatic memories alive among themselves.

The Shelton Laurel legacy differs from that of lynchings and race riots in that it has been the victimized community itself that has sought to keep the memory of the massacre alive, but only on its own terms and within its own bounds. For much of the nearly century and a half since the Civil War, it did not have to work particularly hard at doing so. While scholars over the past couple of decades have certainly acknowledged and treated the incident seriously, those within the region seemed content to let its memorialization remain the responsibility of the victims' descendants. It does not seem to have been a major component of the historical consciousness of people elsewhere in Madison County, much less the rest of the region. I've sensed this myself: in giving lectures or doing book signings in adjacent Asheville and even elsewhere in western North Carolina, audiences frequently ask about the Battle of Asheville, a rather insignificant skirmish with no casualties and no discernible effects. Yet the same audiences seem surprised to learn that only a few miles and one county away, one of the war's most notorious atrocities took place—one that reflects far more accurately the nature of the conflict in this region and many other parts of Southern Appalachia than does the botched raid that was so easily beaten back in Asheville.[29]

Yet if the tensions that so characterized southern race relations for much of the past century render at least more understandable the reasons behind the suppression of riots and lynchings from local white histories, similar agendas, on a rather grander scale, led to the initial suppression of Civil War realities such as Shelton Laurel by southern whites: for political and racial reasons, they depicted the Confederate cause as far more united and honorable than it actually was. To have celebrated or even acknowledged what happened at Shelton Laurel would have seriously contradicted that consciously devised and perpetuated image.

Sometimes it takes unorthodox methods and more creative genres to overcome long-standing popular perceptions and to bring the reality of the stories back into public consciousness. In reviewing Charles Frazier's second novel *Thirteen Moons* in 2005, novelist Adam Goodheart began by stating: "There's a certain kind of history that's made in out-of-the-way places: the swamps, the borderlands, the barren mountain ranges that no one claims. No grand political gestures, or even any memorable battles, unfold here. It's the terrain, rather, of squalid little deals, nasty skirmishes and forgotten massacres—where the reverberations of great events wreak distant havoc on singular, unchronicled lives." Goodheart goes on to suggest that "this is territory where historical novelists, not historians sometimes make the truest guides." This, he claims, is perhaps the one thing historical fiction is good for: "the reconstruction of . . . what went unrecorded, the countless vanished moments and ordinary gestures that constitute the past."[30]

If that indeed is what Charles Frazier has done in both *Thirteen Moons* and *Cold Mountain,* it also describes Sean O'Leary's accomplishment in documenting another aspect of western North Carolina's Civil War. He is meticulously faithful to almost all the facts of the massacre as we know them. It is in the imagined framework of an 1894 reunion of three key players that he becomes at least as true a guide as we historians have been in making meaningful and all too human the "reverberations of great events wreaking distant havoc" on a decidedly out-of-the-way place. In so doing, he brings into a very public forum not only the dilemma and tragedy suffered by southern Unionists there and elsewhere, but also the inhumanity of civil war imposed on all of those caught up in its throes.

Notes

1. Tony Horwitz, *Confederates in the Attic: Dispatches from the Unfinished Civil War* (New York: Pantheon Books, 1998); Geoffrey C. Ward with Ric and Ken Burns, *The Civil War: An Illustrated History* (New York: Alfred A. Knopf, 1990).

2. A selective list of the growing literature on Unionism includes Richard N. Current, *Lincoln's Loyalists: Union Soldiers from the Confederacy* (Boston: Northeastern University Press, 1992); Jon L. Wakelyn, ed., *Southern Unionist Pamphlets and the Civil War* (Columbia: University of Missouri Press, 1999); Daniel E. Sutherland, ed., *Guerrillas, Unionists, and Violence on the Confederate Home Front* (Fayetteville: University of Arkansas Press, 1999); John C. Inscoe and Robert C. Kenzer, eds., *Enemies of the Country: New Perspectives on Unionists in the Civil War South* (Athens: University of Georgia Press, 2001); and William W. Freehling, *The South vs. the South: How Anti-Confederate Southerners Shaped the Course of the Civil War* (New York: Oxford University Press, 2002).

Local and regional studies include Thomas G. Dyer, *Secret Yankees: The Unionist Circle in Confederate Atlanta* (Baltimore: Johns Hopkins University Press, 1999); Margaret M. Storey, *Loyalty and Loss: Alabama's Unionists in the Civil War and Reconstruction* (Baton Rouge: LSU Press, 2004); and Robert Tracy McKenzie, *Lincolnites and Rebels: A Divided Town in the American Civil War* (New York: Oxford University Press, 2006).

3. Jim Taylor, "The Killings on the Shelton Laurel," *Company Front* (August/September 1989): 5–12.

4. Lawrence M. Allen, *Partisan Campaigns of Col. Lawrence M. Allen*

(Raleigh, N.C.: Edwards and Broughton, 1894); and B. T. Morris, "Sixty-fourth Regiment," in *Histories of the Several Regiments and Battalions from North Carolina in the Great War, 1861–1865,* ed. Walter Clark (Greensboro, N.C.: Nash Bros., 1901), 3:659–71.

5. John Preston Arthur, *Western North Carolina: A History* (Raleigh, N.C.: Edwards and Broughton, 1914), 603; Ora Blackmun, *Western North Carolina: Its Mountains and Its People in 1880* (Boone, N.C.: Appalachian Consortium Press, 1977), 345–46; Manly Wade Wellman, *The Kingdom of Madison: A Southern Mountain Fastness and Its People* (Chapel Hill: University of North Carolina Press, 1973), 81–83.

6. Phillip Shaw Paludan, *Victims: A True Story of the Civil War* (Knoxville: University of Tennessee Press, 1984).

7. William R. Trotter, *Bushwhackers! The Civil War in North Carolina,* vol. 2: *The Mountains* (Greensboro, N.C.: Signal Research, 1988), 209–32; Sean Michael O'Brien, *Mountain Partisans: Guerrilla Warfare in the Southern Appalachians, 1861–1865* (Westport, Conn.: Praeger, 1999), ix–x, 3–14; John C. Inscoe and Gordon B. McKinney, *The Heart of Confederate Appalachia: Western North Carolina in the Civil War* (Chapel Hill: University of North Carolina Press, 2000), 117–20.

8. Sharon McCrumb, *Ghost Riders* (New York: Dutton, 2003), and Ron Rash, *The World Made Straight* (New York: Henry Holt, 2006).

9. Taylor, "Killings on the Shelton Laurel," 5–12.

10. Statement by SART artistic director William Gregg. See its Web site, www.sartheatre.com.

11. See O'Leary's Web site, www.olearyonstage.com.

12. Paludan maintains that Keith was the only one of the two on-site and thus in command on the day of the massacre, citing the earliest newspaper reports at the time, and official military reports. Jim Taylor, whose account differs from Paludan's on several significant points, agrees that Keith was in command. O'Leary chooses to put Allen on the spot, with Keith momentarily absent, but attributes the actual order to fire on the prisoners to a Captain Nelson, who had led his company on an earlier expedition to put down the resistance in the Laurel valley. Paludan, *Victims,* 89, 96–97; Taylor, "Killings on the Shelton Laurel," 9–10.

13. Paludan, *Victims,* 121.

14. All quotes come from the working script of *Beneath Shelton Laurel* as produced in 2005. It differs slightly from a tightened 2006 version of the play, also produced by SART, and from an expanded version by O'Leary to be performed in workshop in New York City.

15. Kirk's role is laid out in Inscoe and McKinney, *Heart of Confederate Appalachia,* 118, where we cite Lawrence Allen's *Partisan Campaign* as our source.

16. Taylor, "Killings on the Shelton Laurel," 8. See also Paludan, *Victims*, 55.

17. Keith and Heth gave slightly differing versions of the exact language Heth used to order Keith to move his troops into Shelton Laurel. O'Leary provides an accurate version of what Keith claimed he'd been told. Both sources admitted that Heth had said that there was no need to take prisoners because "these men had forfeited their right to be treated according to the rules of war." Paludan, *Victims*, 87–88.

18. The timing of that revelation in relation to the massacre is one point of discrepancy among the various historical accounts.

19. Paludan, *Victims*, x.

20. O'Leary explained his decision in an e-mail message to me, December 5, 2006: "I felt justified in declining their assistance because even 'historical plays' are at their core works of fiction and in a case such as this in which no living person personally knew any of the characters, their 'memories' would have been at best unreliable and from a dramatic standpoint probably not useful. The other problem was that some folks clearly had axes to grind, so I thought it better to insulate myself and SART from charges of favoritism."

21. The three markers installed in Madison County in December 2006 for the North Carolina Civil War Trails project are located at Mars Hill, Marshall, and Warm Springs. Each refers to events that took place at those locations, but each also makes reference to the Shelton Laurel incident. For the text of those markers, written by Dan Slagle, see www.civilwartrails.com.

22. Taylor, "Killings on the Shelton Laurel," 11.

23. Harold Pinter's actual statement was "The past is what you remember, imagine you remember, convince yourself you remember, or pretend to remember," quoted in W. Fitzhugh Brundage, *The Southern Past: A Clash of Race and Memory* (Cambridge: Harvard University Press, 2005), 4. The recent scholarship on memory and the Civil War has also neglected any mention of Unionism or guerrilla warfare: David W. Blight, *Race and Reunion: The Civil War in American Memory* (Cambridge, Mass.: Harvard University Press, 2001); Horwitz, *Confederates in the Attic*; David Goldfield, *Still Fighting the Civil War: The American South and Southern History* (Baton Rouge: Louisiana State University Press, 2002); Alice Fahs and Joan Waugh, eds., *The Memory of the Civil War in American Culture* (Chapel Hill: University of North Carolina Press, 2004).

24. Jonathan D. Sarris, "The Lost Cause in Appalachia: (Re)constructing Memories of the Civil War in the Southern Mountains, 1865–1900," paper delivered at Southern Historical Association annual meeting, November 2004; Rod Andrew, "Martial Spirit, Christian Virtue, and the Lost Cause: Military Education at North Georgia College, 1871–1915," *Georgia His-*

torical Quarterly 80 (Fall 1996): 486–505; and Sarris, *A Separate Civil War: Communities in Conflict in the Mountain South* (Charlottesville: University of Virginia Press, 2006), chap. 5.

25. Richard D. Starnes, "'The Stirring Strains of Dixie': The Civil War and Southern Identity in Haywood County, North Carolina," *North Carolina Historical Review* 74 (July 1997): 237–59; quotes on 257 and 259.

26. C. Brenden Martin, "To Keep the Spirit of Mountain Culture Alive: Tourism and Historical Memory in the Southern Highlands," in *Where These Memories Grow: History, Memory, and Southern Identity,* ed. W. Fitzhugh Brundage (Chapel Hill: University of North Carolina Press, 2000), 259–60.

27. Richard B. McCaslin, *Tainted Breeze: The Great Hanging at Gainesville, Texas, 1862* (Baton Rouge: LSU Press, 1994), 190–93; quote on 190.

28. Joel Williamson, *The Crucible of Race: Black-White Relations in the American South since Emancipation* (New York: Oxford University Press, 1984), 86–88; and Brundage, *Southern Past,* 47. Both cities used the centennials of the riots, in 1998 and 2006 respectively, to compensate for those long years of neglect through scholarly conferences and public forums.

29. The definitive account of the Battle of Asheville, which took place April 5, 1865, is a pamphlet by George W. McCoy, "The Battle of Asheville" (Asheville, N.C.: Buncombe County Confederate Centennial Commission, 1965), and Trotter, *Bushwhackers!* chap. 25. Trotter stated that it was "as close to bloodless as a five-hour firefight can get," with both sides "just going through the motions" (294).

30. Adam Goodheart, "Trail of Tears," a review of Charles Frazier's *Thirteen Moons,* in the *New York Times Book Review,* October 29, 2006, p. 14.

14

Appalachian Odysseus

Love, War, and Best-sellerdom in the Blue Ridge

Late in the summer of 1997, Charles Frazier's *Cold Mountain* hit the top of the *New York Times* best seller list in fiction, a remarkable achievement for any first-time novelist, but particularly so for a book set in Civil War Appalachia. Not since John Jakes's *North and South* has a Civil War novel ever made its way into that top spot; the only other novel set in the southern highlands to have appeared on the list was *Deliverance,* more than a quarter of a century earlier.[1] *Cold Mountain* enjoyed widespread praise and much media attention upon its publication.[2]

What is it about Frazier's book that accounts for its remarkable success? Why did Frazier, a western North Carolina native, suddenly attract more readers than Patricia Cornwall, Danielle Steele, or John Grisham? Independent booksellers, with an extraordinary boost from local stores in Raleigh, where Frazier then lived, claimed much of the credit, as they did with *The Bridges of Madison County* and *Snow Falling on Cedars.* The book fully warrants its success. It is a sensitive, delicately wrought romance between two complex and memorable characters and an intimate wartime epic that conveys, in unconventional ways, the impact of the Civil War both on its hero and on its heroine. If it drags in places (and I for one think it does), it also builds toward so powerful and surprising a climax in its last forty or so pages that readers were left both satisfied and dazzled. Word-of-mouth was perhaps the most potent sales pitch of all.

Can the tale's Appalachian setting take any claim for the book's appeal? Alas, probably not. This is no reason to think that the same story, as beautifully told but set in some other part of the war-torn South, would not have been equally popular. And yet the Blue Ridge Mountains are an integral part of the novel, and Frazier's treatment of the region and his characters' relationship to it are among the narrative's most intriguing and enriching aspects.

Frazier based his story on the experience of his own great-great uncle, Confederate enlistee W. P. Inman, who in late 1864 escaped from an Illinois prison camp and made the trek home—on foot!—to his North Carolina home near Cold Mountain, a high but fairly nondescript peak some twenty miles southwest of Asheville, where the Blue Ridge mountains merge with the Great Smokies. He was within three miles of home when he met his death in a skirmish at the hands of a particularly notorious Home Guard unit that had plagued local residents for much of the war.[3]

In fictional form, Inman (the only name given to him) does much the same, though Frazier places him in a Confederate hospital in Raleigh in the summer of 1864, having been wounded in the neck during the siege of Petersburg. Fearful that he will be sent back into the hellish fray that the Virginia theater had become, Inman deserts and begins a long cross-state trek, moving toward home and a mountain that "soared in his mind as a place where all his scattered forces might gather" (17). Also drawing him home is his fiancée, Ada Monroe, though he is wracked with doubts as to whether she will want the demoralized shell of a man the war has made of him. He is a loner, a stolid, introspective man whose sensitivity and virtue would render him a rather one-dimensional character were it not for the self-doubt and urgent sense of despair and survival that humanize him and assure our continued interest in his fate.

Ada emerges as an even more carefully delineated character. Her romance with Inman develops fitfully (and remarkably briefly, in relative page count) in the few months before he leaves for Confederate service. With missionary zeal, her father had taken her from a comfortable Charleston existence and brought her into the wilds of the Carolina highlands to enlighten what their Low Country friends saw as "a heathenish part of creation," to a people so uncivilized that "only men of gentry affected underdrawers, and women of every station suckled their young, leaving the civilized trade of wet nurse unknown" (42). (Has anyone so cleverly and succinctly satirized the elitism of Appalachia's lowland detractors?) Ada's father dies soon after the war begins, and she chooses to remain rather than return to Charleston, primarily to await Inman's return.

It is refreshing to see a home-front heroine as unabashedly helpless as Ada is, at least in the beginning of the novel. Given our celebration of southern women's fortitude and resourcefulness (and several of us maintain that highland women held their own with the best of their Confederate sisters, as I do in several chapters in this volume), it is Ada's very frailties and her obliviousness to even the rudiments of mountain life that make her so compelling a character. Her pampered upbringing in Charleston and her father's own apathy toward farm management leave her bewildered, musing to herself about "how a human being could be raised more impractically for the demands of an exposed life." She is not alone long, as she teams up with a local woman, Ruby, who is in all respects her opposite—unschooled but with a vast reservoir of physical strength and native know-how that ultimately assures both women's survival. In effect, Frazier ends up celebrating, as we historians have, the achievement of these home-front heroines, even if it takes this oddly matched sisterhood to pull it off.

Just as Homer's *Odyssey* alternated between Odysseus's attempt to make his way home from war and Penelope's struggles at home as she awaits his return, so Frazier devotes alternating chapters to the very different plights of his lovers as the narrative propels them toward the reunion that ultimately makes the novel so powerful. The parallels between Greek and North Carolina epics are not especially subtle, given that Ada reads Homer to Ruby, who in pondering the trials and tribulations of the Ithacan couple, concludes that "all in all, not much has altered in the way of things despite the passage of a great volume of time" (108).

Inman's journey across North Carolina sometimes seems rather formulaic as he moves chapter by chapter from one encounter to another, some war-related, some not. In this sense, the book is not unlike the postwar accounts of Civil War veterans, particularly of the subgenre of "escape" narratives by fugitive prisoners (most from Confederate prisons), several of which Frazier obviously has used as a model.[4] Yet as episodic as these chapters can be, the incidents and characters grow increasingly intense as Inman approaches the foot-hills and then the mountains themselves. If Frazier strains credibility with his protagonist's luck and skill in overcoming so constant a bar-rage of adversaries—con men, jealous husbands, beguiling widows, Home Guardsmen, bandits, and even a bear—more often than not he creates something compelling, sometimes horrific, and often quite un-expected from these vignettes.

This is not the Civil War or the Confederate South that we usu-ally see in historical fiction. There are few if any plantations, slave-holders, or slaves on this home front. The many characters who people Frazier's saga are far removed from those in Margaret Mitch-ell's or John Jakes's fictionalized Confederacy. With very few excep-tions, these people are poor, leading lives of quiet—and often not so quiet—desperation. For all participants, the war has become one of disillusionment, resentment, desolation, and brutality as they engage in a primal quest for sheer survival.

Both hero and heroine recognize this much grimmer face of war and articulate it. Inman, who fought under Robert E. Lee, is troubled by the general who "seemed to think battle—among all the acts man might commit—stood outranked in sacredness only by prayer and Bi-ble reading." He thinks to himself with much resentment that "he did not enlist to take on a Marse, even one as solemn and noble-looking as Lee" (8). Ada takes issue with a neighbor who "found the fighting glorious and tragic and heroic," asserting instead that "she found it, even at a great distance, brutal and benighted on both sides about equally. Degrading to all" (140–41). And so, in Frazier's narrative, it proves to be.[5]

Frazier's historical grasp of this late-war reality in the southern highlands is impressive and effectively conveyed. In addition to the "family stories" about his great-great uncle, Frazier acknowledges a dozen or so rather mixed sources for his research, including Horace Kephart and James Mooney, Richard Chase's "Jack Tales," Walter Clark's North Carolina regimental histories, and firsthand narratives of regional renegades such as Daniel Ellis and J. V. Hadley. Real fig-ures and incidents—from William Holland Thomas and his famous Cherokee legion to the infamous bushwhacker Robert Teague, who terrorized deserters in that very area of Haywood County—make brief but indelible appearances.

Frazier does not depict the war in the mountains with much complexity; very little is made of the ideological splits and confusions, though clashes between bushwhackers, deserters, Home Guards, and even Heroes of America regularly occur throughout Inman's cross-state odyssey. Frazier draws heavily from Phillip Paludan's *Victims,* but he sets his version of the infamous Shelton Laurel massacre in the piedmont rather than in remote, mountainous Madison County, and he makes Inman the sole, if unintended, survivor of an extralegal mass execution by local Confederates. He is left for dead and even buried with his less fortunate fellow captives, owing his ultimate resurrection to feral hogs rooting in the shallow grave—yet another bit of luck that strains credibility.[6]

Union marauders, lonely women coping on their own, poverty and war weariness, and Home Guard units that harass "outliers" are as prevalent as Inman moves through the piedmont as they are in the mountains, a reality those of us chronicling the war in the highlands perhaps need to be reminded of. Nevertheless, as Inman moves beyond Salisbury into Wilkes County and on toward Grandfather Mountain (a rather circuitous route for one headed toward Haywood County), the intensity of civilian and paramilitary terrorism and the danger they pose become ever more ominous.

Though he never dwells on it, Frazier acknowledges, with his usual economy of form, the class resentment that the war spawned in the mountain South and that would eventually pervade much of the rest of the Confederacy. As Inman moves through Happy Valley, certainly among the most affluent enclaves of western North Carolina slave-holders, he notes the "big houses with white columns . . . ringed around with scattered hovels so that the valley land seems cut up into fiefdoms." He looks at the lights in these houses as he sneaks by them at night: he "knew he had been fighting for such men as lived in them, and it made him sick" (205). Frazier never uses the words "slaves" or "slavery" here, and the white columns are a rare bow to stereotypical convention. Yet the resentment stirred over who was fighting and who was not and why was certainly central to the tensions that plagued the mountains as well as much of the rest of the South by late 1864, even if Inman's sense of justice is far more enlightened than that which motivated most highland yeomen.

Personal grudges lead to blatant forms of revenge and brutality. In a later incident, as related to Ada by Ruby's father, "one of the county's few gentry, a leading slaveholder . . . fell afoul of the cave society," meaning Teague and his bushwhacking terrorists in Haywood County. Walker, the target of this retribution, "had long been a high-handed bastard with all he considered his lessers, which in his estimation included most everybody. Punishment, the cavers had decided, was in order" (264). And delivered it is, in a vividly described raid on Walker's home.

Frazier even explores the origins of the war fever that would later degenerate into such disillusionment and internalized conflict. A female hermit, or "goat woman," eking out a living in the crevasses on Grandfather Mountain forces Inman to articulate why he went to war in the first place. In one of the book's most intriguing chapters, this oracle, "a pinched-off little scrag of a person" with whom our hero takes shelter for several days, asks him why men go to war and why he himself felt compelled to join this war in particular. Inman is quick to deny that "fighting for the big man's nigger" motivated him; he feebly responds instead, "I reckon many of us fought to drive off invaders." But in later pondering what really drove him and his fellow highlanders to respond so readily to the call to arms in 1861, Inman is forced to admit to his hostess that even that rationale holds little weight and that the real reason was in fact "change" or "the promise of it that made up the war frenzy in the early days. The powerful draw of new faces, new places, new lives. And new laws whereunder you might kill all you wanted and not be jailed, but be decorated." He goes on to reflect:

> Men talked of war as if they committed it to preserve what they had and what they believed. But Inman guessed that it was boredom with the repetition of the daily rounds that had made them take up weapons. The endless arc of the sun, wheel of seasons. War took men out of that circle of regular life and made a season of its own, not much dependent on anything else. He had not been immune to its pull. (218)

Here, as at other points throughout the novel, Frazier encapsulates through his deceptively spare and simple prose the essence of issues with which historians have grappled for years.

Much of the beauty and emotional depth of this saga lie in the intense love Inman and others feel for their highland home, which stands in stark contrast to the sheer revulsion they feel for any area outside their mountain region. After many months of fighting far from the Blue Ridge, Inman has come to hate "these planed-off, tangled pinebrakes. All this flat land. Red dirt. Mean towns. He had fought over ground like this from the piedmont to the sea, and it seemed like nothing but the place where all that was foul and sorry had flowed downhill and pooled in the low spots" (53). Those who never left the mountains have similar disgust for those "low spots." The very name of Georgia conjures up dismal imagery to these western Carolinians. One of a roving band of "outliers" is a young deserter from Georgia seeking his way home with little success through the Blue Ridge. One of his companions—perhaps the novel's lowest and most contemptible character—says of him, "I feel sorry for that boy. . . . He's wishing he'd never left home, but he's not even got sense to know what kind of vile state he's from. If I had a brother in jail and one in Georgia, I'd try to bust the one out of Georgia first" (286). Ruby, offering direction to the same boy, states simply, "They say you know Georgia when you come to it, for it's nothing but red dirt and rough roads" (296).

At the same time, the more articulate and sensitive of these highland-based characters, whether native or transplanted, find something mystical, even spiritual and life-affirming, about the grandeur and beauty of the mountains. This is especially true both of Inman, so desperately trying to return to them, and of Ada, so desperately trying to survive within them. From his hospital bed in Raleigh, Inman is sustained by his yearnings for Cold Mountain and the antidote it provided for the horrors he's experienced on Virginia battlefields. "He could not abide by a universe composed only of what he could see, especially when it was so frequently foul. So he held to the idea of another world, a better place, and he figured he might as well consider Cold Mountain to be the location of it as anywhere" (17).

Once in the mountains and nearing home, Inman stands atop a peak from which he "achieved a vista of what for him was homeland." He takes great joy in seeing "the leap of hearth smoke from the houses of people he had known all his life. People he would not be called upon to hate or fear." As comforting a thought as that is, it is the sheer physical world he is reentering that seems most to exhilarate him. Frazier's writing is at its most eloquent when describing Inman's feelings:

> As he studied on it, he recognized the line of every far ridge and valley to be remembered. They seemed long ago scribed indelibly on his corneas with a sharp instrument. He looked out at this highland and knew the names of places and things. He said them aloud: Little Beartail Ridge, Wagon Road Gap, Ripshin, Hunger Creek, Clawhammer Knob, Rocky Face. Not a mountain or watercourse lacked denomination. Not a bird or bush anonymous. His Place. (281)

Ada too, though a relative newcomer, is caught up in the power of place. To her and her father, "this mountain country was so dark and inclined to the vertical compared with Charleston." But within a few days after their arrival on Cold Mountain, Ada's father notes that "like all elements of nature, the features of this magnificent topography were simply tokens of some other world, some deeper life with a whole other existence toward which we ought to aim all our yearning" (112). After his death, "outsider though she was, this place, the blue mountains, seemed to be holding [Ada] where she was. From any direction she came at it, the only conclusion that left her any hope of self-content was this; what she could see around her was all that she could count on" (50).

Despite her helplessness to survive alone in this harsh setting, made all the more bleak by the ravages of war, Ada is as fully attuned to the beauty and the wonder of the natural world around her as Inman is. Just as William Bartram's vivid descriptions of the area a century earlier sustain and inspire Inman as he moves toward the highlands, so she comes to find very little outside of her mountain world to be of much comfort or meaning. She becomes increasingly bored reading *Adam Bede* and wishes that its characters could be "more expansive, not so cramped by circumstance. What they needed was more scope, greater range. Go to the Indies, she directed them. Or to the Andes" (259). Her own life is expanding, with more scope and greater range, so that by the time she and her lover are reunited, she has undergone a transformation fully as profound as that inflicted on Inman by the traumas of war.

Thus in a number of ways and at a number of levels, *Cold Mountain* is a profound and deeply moving novel. There is something quite edifying in seeing a work of this depth and power, and grounded so richly in the historical and geographical realities of the mountain South, claim so vast a national readership. Never before in American literature has the Civil War been depicted in quite this way, though it is a side of that experience that is readily recognizable to those of us (and our numbers are legion) researching the war in the southern highlands. Nor have nineteenth-century Appalachia or Appalachians been rendered in fictional form in quite this way. An outsider stuck in the mountains by circumstances beyond her control, and a native highlander, stuck outside the mountains for reasons not of his own making, yearn for each other and somehow find their strength and their drive within and through the mountains themselves. If it is not necessarily these attributes that account for the extraordinary popularity of Frazier's work, they will undoubtedly have much to do with its lasting significance as historical fiction and as Appalachian literature.

As a film, *Cold Mountain* is part of a genre of intimate historical epics —*Dr. Zhivago, Reds, The English Patient, Pearl Harbor*—in which war serves as the catalyst for doomed romance. It is often war that brings lovers together and then pulls them apart—sometimes temporarily, sometimes for good. As Humphrey Bogart's Rick Blaine states in *Casablanca*, a somewhat less-than-epic variation of this Hollywood type, "The problems of three little people don't amount to a hill of beans in this crazy world." But of course, it is just that—the problems of these "little people"—that draws us in as viewers and allows us to relate to a particular "crazy world," the chaos and trauma of war, on such a personal and tangible level.

Curiously, the Civil War has only rarely provided the setting for these film spectacles, although *Gone with the Wind* is, of course, the granddaddy of them all. But other than that and *Shenandoah,* a 1965 drama starring Jimmy Stewart as a Virginia farmer determined to keep his family out of the conflict, no major Hollywood film has dealt as fully with southerners and their home-front plight as does *Cold Mountain*.[7] And even more than other such epics, Anthony Minghella's elaborate production does so through its dramatization of lovers' separation and their desperation to reunite in a narrative so emotionally compelling that it assured its success both on best seller lists in the late 1990s and at the box office in 2003 and 2004.

Minghella's film is unusually faithful to the book in recreating Inman's encounters with beleaguered widows, bushwhackers, Union renegades, fellow deserters, and the seemingly omnipresent Home Guardsmen, who collectively suggest the disorder, desperation, and corruption that characterized southerners' struggle to survive in an increasingly lawless and dysfunctional society. One of the film's great strengths is that these struggles are presented in such graphic, unflinching form, more often than not with violent resolutions that genuinely shock. Rarely has the collective plight of a people at war been conveyed to movie audiences as effectively as in this series of disturbing and emotionally charged episodes.

The screen adaptation does almost as well with the home-front situation, embodied most notably in the unlikely partnership between the overeducated but hapless Ada Monroe, and Ruby, the brash native woman, portrayed by Nicole Kidman and Renée Zellweger (who won an Oscar for her efforts). Their teaming makes for the film's most appealing and satisfying development, with the cultural disconnect between them providing much needed comic relief.

Yet as vividly as the impact of the war on southern civilians is rendered, this is a war devoid of much meaning. The film does not address the issues behind the struggle or why those from Cold Mountain choose to fight for the Confederacy. When a church service is interrupted with the news that the war has begun, local men and boys are excited and express their eagerness to fight. It is very much like the scene at Twelve Oaks in *Gone with the Wind* where the same news is met with equal enthusiasm; but in that film, an earlier scene of Rhett Butler debating with hot-headed young Georgians at least provides some context and meaning for their exuberant response. In *Cold Mountain,* there is no such rationale for these highlanders' almost mindless revelry, the most distinguishable dialogue in the scene being, "We got our war, man! We got our war." (It's not even clear what spurs this particular moment: Is it the attack on Fort Sumter? Lincoln's call for troops to put down the rebellion? North Carolina's secession vote a month later?)

Neither slaves nor slavery plays much part in the film; only fleeting references are made to both. Inman crosses paths with a band of African American refugees as he treks through eastern North Carolina; it could have been a very revealing scene if they hadn't merely fled from each other. A particularly odd moment has Ada taking refreshments out to her slaves—never seen—during a party at her home. Even the otherwise meticulously re-created Battle of the Crater at Petersburg, which opens the film, fails to portray the many black Union troops who played such a key role there.

If the film captures the sheer messiness of this internalized Appalachian war, it vastly oversimplifies the forces of good and evil that do battle in the region. Perhaps because the protagonist, Inman, is first and foremost a deserter, all other deserters become sympathetic characters and innocent victims who pose little threat to anyone else. It is those who seek them out—the Home Guard—who become the film's unequivocal villains. From the war's beginning, Captain Robert Teague (a historical figure) and his self-appointed band of local vigilantes are portrayed as menacing, power-hungry thugs who become increasingly ruthless, cruel, and destructive in their harassment of the very civilian population they are charged with protecting. In actuality, it was often the deserters, along with those avoiding conscription, escaped prisoners of war, and other renegades who made up the bushwhacking bands who hid out in the more remote Carolina highlands and wreaked such havoc on nearby towns and farms. While Home Guard units did engage in unauthorized violence and harassment, they often served, if not always very effectively, as the only protectors and restorers of order for many communities so plagued by these lawless bands.

Perhaps Minghella's most serious deviation from Frazier's book is the elimination of Inman's internalized thoughts and feelings as he heads home. The novel is infused with a palpable sense of place; it especially comes through in Inman's yearning for his Blue Ridge mountain home that—along with his beloved Ada—he counts on to restore his sanity, indeed his humanity. The beauty of North Carolina's mountains (which this native western Carolinian must grudgingly admit is fairly convincingly portrayed by the Romanian Alps) is apparent throughout the film; it poses a striking visual contrast to the wretched Virginia battlefields with which it is juxtaposed in alternating opening scenes. One of Minghella's strengths as a filmmaker is his ability to create a compelling sense of place, as he did so beautifully for both Italy and North Africa in his Oscar-winning adaptation of *The English Patient* (1996). This film's landscapes are just as stunning, yet little of that love of the mountains is seen or felt through Inman's eyes or memories. As a man of so few words, he only briefly acknowledges his revulsion of war or his longing for the comfort and refuge of his highland home, which make up some of the most moving and meaningful passages in Frazier's novel. We see nothing of his love of the highland flora and fauna, or the inspiration he derives from the descriptions of William Bartram, which in the novel provide him with an intellectual dimension and sensitivity that account for much of his appeal. (Bartram's *Travels* makes it into the film, but only in an offhanded way: Ada hands the book to Inman as he's departing for war, saying, "They tell me it's good; I think he writes about these parts." Thereafter the book's function seems to be little more than a place for him to store Ada's picture.) With this side of the character so diminished, Jude Law's Inman thus is far more an Everyman—reacting to a range of far livelier and more colorful characters, than is his prose counterpart. In the book, Inman's intellect, sensitivity, and emotional depth make him a far more compelling and complex character than the "average" Confederate soldier or deserter.

One of the more striking and fully developed themes in the film is the plight of women caught up in guerrilla warfare. Historians of the Civil War in Appalachia and other fringes of the Confederacy have described the wartime breakdown of conventional gender roles. Left without male protection, women either had to participate in the war or were forced to serve as the first and last line of defense of their households and often of their husbands, sons, or other male relatives, many of whom were forced into hiding close to home.[8] Michael Fellman's characterization of women caught up in Missouri's guerrilla conflict during the war years—"disintegration, demoralization, and perverse adaptation" in which women became forced participants, with "varying degrees of enthusiasm, rage, and fear"[9]—is fully applicable to the women of western North Carolina and specifically to the female characters of *Cold Mountain*. Two of the film's three central characters are women, of course, but so are several of the more vivid supporting characters, and their roles tell us much about the war and its often devastating impact on their real-life counterparts.

Historically accurate women at war are new to film depictions of Appalachia, but strong women who are forced into traditionally masculine roles are not. As with all facets of Hollywood's depiction of southern mountain life, Jerry Williamson in his book *Hillbillyland* gives full attention to portrayals of women. "Hillbillyland grants extraordinary equality to women. At times," Williamson notes. "Strong backwoods women with weapons have regularly appeared in movies . . . , fighting back against whatever threatened them—with guns especially."[10] In his chapter on "Hillbilly Gals," he devotes sections to "Uppity Women," "Cross-Dressers," and "Mannish Misfits." One can certainly see in Zellweger's brash rendering of Ruby elements of all three, and several of the other female characters exhibit "mannish" behavior or character traits. In fact, in both her feminine appearance and gentle demeanor, Kidman's Ada Monroe is perhaps most distinguished from anyone else in the film. Even when she ultimately resorts to wearing men's clothes—a sign that she's about to enter the fray in a serious way—little else about her appearance or demeanor seems to change.

If such women are not unusual in the Appalachian-based movies Williamson analyzed so brilliantly in *Hillbillyland,* much rarer are Hollywood productions that have dramatized the struggle of southern women during the Civil War. Again, the obvious exception is *Gone with the Wind,* but few others since have even focused on the Civil War home front, much less on how its women coped. In *Shenandoah,* Yankee renegades murder Jimmy Stewart's new daughter-in-law, and his daughter wears men's clothes to join her brothers in taking revenge, but the women's roles are never more than marginal.

In *Cold Mountain,* however, female characters respond in a variety of ways to the violence and hardship forced upon them as the war disrupts their households and communities. By the war's final months, when most of the film takes place, several characters fall victim to the desperation and lawlessness that has overtaken the highland home front. In one encounter during his arduous trek home through North Carolina, Inman is taken in by Sara, a teenage war widow and mother (played by Natalie Portman), who is struggling on her own in an isolated mountain cabin to keep herself and her sickly newborn alive. Soon after his arrival, three Union renegades approach her cabin, demanding whatever food she has. They bind her to a post outside and expose her baby to the elements in an effort to force her to reveal where she's hidden her hog and chickens. Inman, on hearing them approach, escapes out the back, where he watches and schemes how to rescue his young hostess.

Here Minghella provides an intriguing twist on Frazier's narrative. In one of the novel's most riveting passages, Inman stalks the men as they depart with Sara's hog and several chickens, her only means of support. Inman follows them to their camp, where he picks them off one by one, and returns to Sara with her hog, as yet unkilled, and the chickens, one living, two dead. On-screen, Minghella compresses this sequence considerably by having Inman ambush and kill two of the three Federals inside Sara's house, one as he attempts to rape her. Inman is willing to let the youngest and least malicious of the three men, by then cowered and fully repentant, leave unharmed, but as this young renegade scurries away from the scene, he is suddenly shot in the back . . . by Sara. This is a war that has made killers of women and girls; in this case the woman kills out of vengeance and hatred, showing more of those emotions than Inman, that most sensitive and compassionate of Confederate soldiers. As Williamson found to be the case in early silent movies, a "hillbilly gal" is allowed a symbolic moment "of equal power through violence."[11]

Equally as harrowing is an incident in which a woman is more brutally victimized and left without recourse to fighting back. Sally Swanger, a very minor character in Frazier's novel, emerges in the film as the most prominent female in the Cold Mountain community, the wife of one of its more prosperous farmers and a neighbor fully sympathetic to the plight of the hapless Ada. Like many mountain women, she is forced to hide her two sons, who have deserted the

Confederate army and returned home. The suspicious Home Guard, in an effort to either force her to reveal their hiding place or force them out to rescue their mother, bind Sally to a rail fence with a noose around her neck and place her fingers between the top rails. The youngest and least scrupulous of this gang of thugs dances sadistically along the top of the rail, in the process breaking her hands.

The historical record includes numerous accounts of just this sort of torture—both with nooses and rail fences and, for that matter, babies exposed to the elements and pets shot—applied to women in western North Carolina. The incidents involving Sara and Sally Swanger were likely based on the brutalities inflicted upon Unionist wives and mothers as prologue to the infamous Shelton Laurel massacre in early 1863, as well as the experience of another Madison County woman, whose story is related in Muriel Shepherd's *Cabins in the Laurel*.[12] Torture on a rail fence occurs in the opening pages of Wilma Dykeman's novel *The Tall Woman,* in which the heroine's mother falls victim to a sadistic group of "outliers" seeking the meat supply that she has carefully hidden.[13] Frazier made only fleeting reference to such abuses in his novel, but Minghella included an extended scene in the film, which is all the more powerful because he turned Sally into a more fully developed character (well played by Kathy Baker), who in addition to her physical torture must watch as her husband and both sons are gunned down in front of her.[14]

Like Sally defending her deserting sons, other women serve as protectors and caretakers for men at war, whether stranger or friend. In one of the novel's most revealing chapters, Inman encounters the "goat woman" setting traps in the woods around Grandfather Mountain. When he asks for food, this elderly woman leads him to her remote encampment on the side of the mountain, where she allows him to stay with her and her small herd for a day or so. The power of this episode is not only that this hermit/oracle is such an intriguing character in her independence and eccentricity; it is also that she forces Inman to confront and articulate the meaningless of the war and of his participation in it.

Yet in the film, this character, vividly brought to life by the great British actress Eileen Atkins, offers much more, though in a considerably condensed scene. For Minghella, she becomes Inman's savior:

she finds him unconscious but still chained to an otherwise dead band of prisoners, all victims of cross-fire in a skirmish between their Confederate captors and a small Union force who stumble upon them. With great effort, the goat woman manages to get Inman to her shelter, where she treats his wounds and nurses him back to health over several days. She thus becomes an even more integral determinant of Inman's ever-questionable fate; more important, however, her role stands as yet another indication of the degree to which men at war depended on women—known or unknown—for their very survival.

So it is that the film's central characters, Ada and Ruby, are also drawn more inextricably into the guerrilla warfare waged around them. Like Sally Swanger, they find themselves forced to protect and provide for Ruby's brutish father and his renegade companions, who have deserted the Confederate army and become outliers (though rather more benign and thus far more sympathetic than their real-life counterparts). Ada and Ruby are forced to move from the comforts of home and farm—where providing sustenance and protection to these men was relatively easy, even though it rendered them far more vulnerable to harassment by the Home Guard—into the thick of the mountain wilderness, where they learn that their male charges have been attacked and are in need of their attention. In taking off on this rescue mission, the two women arm themselves, dress as men, and—in the words of a Cherokee County woman in 1863—"assumed all the duties of the sterner sex." They thus further blur gender roles as they engage in a shoot-out that serves as the film's climax.[15]

Mary Bell of neighboring Macon County, whose story is told earlier in this volume, confided to her husband in the spring of 1862 that "I wish I could be both man and woman until the war ends."[16] She was referring primarily to the sometimes overwhelming burdens she faced in managing her farm without her husband's help. Many women throughout the Confederacy faced this challenge and probably felt about it as Mary Bell did. *Cold Mountain*'s Ada Monroe experiences these burdens with her father's death, and her first attempts at taking charge reflected how totally helpless she is to assume any such manly roles. It takes another woman, one of Williamson's "mannish misfits," the irrepressible Ruby, to save Ada by saving her farm. It is only later in the war, and primarily in this highland environment, that many women were forced to take on even more of a man's role by engaging in the horrific guerrilla warfare that engulfed them.

It is here that Anthony Minghella altered Frazier's novel for the screen by amplifying the roles of women as participants and partners in that "inner war" that so plagued western North Carolina. Far more than is the case in the book, women become in Minghella's screenplay far more active agents in their own defense and in the care and protection they provide for males. Certainly in no other film set in Appalachia and in no other Civil War film since Scarlett O'Hara vowed that she would never go hungry again has this point been dramatized as vividly or as centrally as it is in *Cold Mountain*. For all of the other problems from which the film suffers in terms of how historic reality is compromised—and there are several—Minghella deserves much credit for how effectively he portrays the gendered nature of this very messy war as it played out on the many home fronts of Southern Appalachia.

When the book was published, a colleague of mine, a distinguished Civil War historian and biographer of Robert E. Lee, read it and wryly pronounced it to be a cross between Larry McMurtry and Cormac McCarthy, with most of its characters "trailer park trash before there were trailer parks." *Cold Mountain* indeed depicts a war and a people that Lee would probably not have recognized; neither gods nor generals play much of a role here. It is thus all the more remarkable that, despite the limitations and concessions imposed by a major Hollywood production, the final product should demonstrate so much respect for the novel on which it is based and provide so unflinching a portrayal of the bleak and unsettling realities of the Civil War as it was waged throughout Appalachia and other parts of the war-torn South. It is a far less familiar version of the war, but it is one that would have been all too recognizable to thousands of hardscrabble southern men and women who lived through it.

Notes

1. Charles Frazier, *Cold Mountain* (New York: Atlantic Monthly Press, 1997); John Jakes, *North and South* (New York: Harcourt Brace Jovanovich, 1982); James Dickey, *Deliverance* (Boston: Houghton Mifflin, 1970). A television miniseries of *North and South* first aired in 1985; a film version of *Deliverance* debuted in 1972.

2. *Cold Mountain* won the National Book Award for Fiction in 1997.

3. Frazier has given different versions of this story in interviews over the years since *Cold Mountain*'s publication. For two particularly revealing interviews conducted soon after the book's publication, see Charles Frazier on *Cold Mountain* at www.bookbrowse.com, and "Cold Mountain Diary: How the Author Found the Inspiration for His Novel among the Secrets Buried in the Backwoods of the Smoky Mountains," Salon.com (July 9, 1997). For another treatment of the original William P. Inman, see Rob Neufeld, *A Popular History of Western North Carolina: Mountains, Heroes, and Hootnoggers* (Charleston, S.C.: History Press, 2007), 68–71.

4. See chap. 8 in this volume, "'Moving through Deserter Country': Fugitive Accounts of Southern Appalachia's Inner Civil War."

5. For a different, very perceptive assessment of the historical accuracy of the novel, see Martin Crawford, "*Cold Mountain* Fictions, Appalachian Half-Truths," *Appalachian Journal* 30 (Winter/Spring 2003): 182–95.

6. Phillip Shaw Paludan, *Victims: A True Story of the Civil War* (Knoxville: University of Tennessee Press, 1981). The detail of rooting hogs comes from a gruesome reality at Shelton Laurel, where wild hogs who dug up the Madison County mass grave chewed the head off one of the victims rather than saving him.

7. On Hollywood depictions of the Civil War, see Brian S. Wills, *Gone with the Glory: The History of the Civil War in Cinema* (New York: Rowan & Littlefield, 2006); David B. Sachsman, S. Kittrell Rushing, and Roy Morris Jr., eds., *Memory and Myth: The Civil War in Fiction and Film from Uncle Tom's Cabin to Cold Mountain* (West Lafayette, Ind.: Purdue University Press, 2007); and Gary W. Gallagher, *Causes Won, Lost, and Forgotten: How Hollywood and Popular Art Shape What We Know about the Civil War* (Chapel Hill: University of North Carolina Press, 2008).

8. See particularly Gordon B. McKinney, "Women's Roles in Civil War Western North Carolina," *North Carolina Historical Review* 69 (January 1992): 37–56; Ralph Mann, "Guerrilla Warfare and Gender Roles: Sandy Basin, Virginia, as Test Case," *Journal of the Appalachian Studies Association* 5 (1993): 59–66; and John C. Inscoe and Gordon B. McKinney, *The Heart of Confederate Appalachia: Western North Carolina in the Civil War* (Chapel Hill: University of North Carolina Press, 2000), chap. 8.

9. Michael Fellman, *Inside War: The Guerrilla Conflict in Missouri during the American Civil War* (New York: Oxford University Press, 1989), 193.

10. J. W. Williamson, *Hillbillyland: What the Movies Did to the Mountains & What the Mountains Did to the Movies* (Chapel Hill: University of North Carolina Press, 1995), 225.

11. Ibid., 233.

12. On the women of Shelton Laurel, see Paludan, *Victims,* 96–97; James O. Hall, "The Shelton Laurel Massacre: Murder in the North Carolina

Mountains," *Blue & Gray* (February 1991): 20–26; and chap. 13 in this volume, "Unionists in the Attic," which discusses a dramatized treatment of that massacre and its repercussions. On other such incidents, see Muriel Sheppard, *Cabins in the Laurel* (Chapel Hill: University of North Carolina Press, 1935), 64; Margaret Walker Freel, *Unto the Hills* (Andrew, N.C.: privately printed, 1976), 139–40; and Inscoe and McKinney, *Heart of Confederate Appalachia,* 194–96.

13. Wilma Dykeman, *The Tall Woman* (New York: Holt, Rinehart, and Winston, 1962), 30–31.

14. For a very different interpretation of the abuse of women in the film, see Anna Creadick's comments in "A Roundtable Discussion of *Cold Mountain,* the Film," *Appalachian Journal* 31 (Spring/Summer 2004): 330–31, 347–48.

15. Quote from anonymous "Voice from Cherokee County," *North Carolina Standard* (Raleigh), August 19, 1863, quoted in Inscoe and McKinney, *Heart of Confederate Appalachia,* 187.

16. Mary Bell to Alfred Bell, May 22, 1862, Alfred Bell Papers, Duke University Library. For a full account of the wartime travails of Mary Bell, see "Coping in Confederate Appalachia," chap. 7 in this volume.

15

Guerrilla War and Remembrance

Reconstructing a Father's Murder and a Community's Civil War

On June 17, 1864, Isaac Wilson, a forty-two-year-old farmer and Confederate lieutenant from the North Fork community of Ashe County, North Carolina, decided to spend the last morning of his furlough plowing his cornfield. Soon after leaving his wife and eight children to undertake that task, he was shot from a distance and killed by a group of Unionists who also happened to be his neighbors. While by no means the first such incident to take place in this tension-filled area only a few miles from the Tennessee border, Wilson's murder reverberated in especially potent ways, and it intensified the level of local violence that would continue through much of the war's remaining ten months. The story is well known locally and has been retold in numerous accounts of the war in Ashe County and western North Carolina. Yet the most thorough and moving account of the incident is in a memoir produced in the 1940s by Isaac's third son.[1]

William Albert Wilson's memoir is extraordinary for a variety of reasons, not the least of which is the fact that he was only two and a half years old when his father was killed. Although he is rarely explicit about how much of his narrative comes from his own memory and how much comes from the memories of others, it is obvious that most of this remarkably vivid and detailed account of Isaac's death and the final months of the war and its aftermath in Ashe County's North Fork community is built from stories told to him—perhaps repeatedly and over many years—by family and local acquaintances.

The value of this document then lies not only in its meticulous re-creation of the guerrilla warfare that proved so destructive to this

322

Appalachian community, and by implication, to so many other highland communities like it. Equally intriguing is the way in which Will (as he seems to have been called)[2] Wilson constructed his memoir. The nature and number of sources on which he drew to tell this story in itself tells us as much about the legacy of the war as it does about the nature both of memory, individual and collective, and of oral history in shaping that legacy.

Within the vast and growing scholarship on memory and its relationship to history, the Civil War looms large. "The Civil War is, for the American imagination, the great single event of our history," Robert Penn Warren wrote at the beginning of the war's centennial in 1961. It is "our only *felt* history . . . an overwhelming and vital image of human, and national, experience."[3] For many white southerners who lived through the war, that "felt history" was determined not only by individual recollections of their own experiences over the course of the conflict and its aftermath, but also (and perhaps even more) by the collective memories that emerged at various levels—from households, neighborhoods, and communities, to states and throughout the region as a whole. What Warren refers to as "national imagination" was, for southern whites, an impressive feat of carefully constructed public memory meant for mass consumption and consensus.

In the decades after the war's end, largely elite groups of men and women throughout the former Confederacy shaped a very selective, subjective and politically useful version of the war for public memory. Codified and labeled early on as the "Lost Cause," this version of the war in the national—or regional—imagination was a series of rationales for why the South seceded from the Union and why it lost the war, with neither immoral aims nor internal failings of either Confederate leadership or citizenry playing any part. The Lost Cause served instead to honor and even ennoble the military effort made by the Confederacy and the men who fought on its behalf. The fervor with which these beliefs were embraced and promoted made it almost a religion, and the commitment to these beliefs was manifested in a vast array of monuments and memorials, ceremonies and parades, veterans' organizations and reunions, battlefield preservation and museums, political rhetoric, regimental histories and hagiographic biographies, children's literature, and even the censorship of textbooks.[4]

Within this shared belief system, there was no room for any mention of divided loyalties, for internal dissent, or for guerrilla warfare. Such ambivalence or complexity in southern wartime behavior would have seriously undermined the basic, clear-cut interpretation of regional solidarity to the Cause in which white southerners so wanted, indeed needed, to believe. For most of them, the Civil War era became, to paraphrase British playwright Harold Pinter, a past that they remembered, imagined they remembered, convinced themselves that they remembered, or pretended to remember.[5] And because of its absence in the legacy shaped by the post–Civil War generation itself, recent scholarship on memory and the Civil War has also neglected the much messier reality that characterized the war in many parts of the more marginalized South.[6]

Even within those areas of Southern Appalachia so consumed by the traumas of guerrilla warfare, that less sanctioned warfare was largely "written out" of the public memory that shaped how communities chose to recall and derive meaning from it. Historian Jonathan Sarris has written about the blatant attempts by pro-Confederates in the north Georgia mountains to expunge from communal memory any sense of divisiveness in that region and to create instead a public myth of southern solidarity throughout the conflict and fully embrace the Lost Cause ideology. In so doing, they not only excised the activities of Unionists and other dissenters who created internalized strife in Dahlonega and other mountain communities from official and unofficial accounts of their war, but they also chose to forget their own brutal and lawless repression of those who defied them.[7]

Richard Starnes found much the same historical amnesia among North Carolina's highlanders. In a study of the war's historical legacy in Haywood County, he found that from Confederate veterans' groups to county historians, from the 1870s until well into the twentieth century, the consensus of opinion was, as W. W. Stringfield declared, "no people were more zealous for the South than Western North Carolinians." In all four published histories of the county and of Waynesville, its seat, Starnes noted, "unpleasant topics such as desertion, internal dissent, and outright disloyalty were replaced by images of Confederate solidarity, bravery in battle, and devotion to duty."[8]

The messiness of guerrilla warfare was embarrassing and counterproductive to the New South aims of postwar elites in the mountains; thus the local establishment "erased" it from public memory, preferring a cleaner and less ambivalent version of what had happened. Part of the ease in doing so lay in the fact that Unionist activity— and harassment—was often hidden from view within and beyond the communities of which those Unionists were a part. As historian Martin Crawford has noted in his study of the war in Ashe County itself, "By its very nature, Southern Unionism failed to generate the large-scale public commitment and ritual participation associated with community involvement in the Civil War. . . . Here there were no formalized enlistment procedures, no exhortatory speeches, no ceremonial presentations of company flags, and as a consequence, one might infer, precious little sustaining identification with the local or wider state community."[9]

Because this was so often the case, memories of that other reality were left to individuals and families, who preserved in far more private ways the painful legacy of the internal strife they experienced. A number of men and women recounted on paper those experiences as either participants or victims in this inner civil war. Their personal narratives—in the form of correspondence, diaries, letters, memoirs, or family histories—have provided historians with testimony that informs our understanding of this inner war as it played out especially in more remote areas.

Individual partisans occasionally earned enough notoriety during the war to have their stories published at war's end, either by themselves or others. Confederate renegades such as Champ Ferguson and John Hunt Morgan earned considerable attention for their ruthless harassment of Unionists in the Tennessee, Kentucky, and Virginia mountains, though neither survived to provide firsthand narratives of their experiences.[10] Daniel Ellis, a Unionist guerrilla from East Tennessee, did survive and sought to establish his own celebrity with the publication—by Harper Bros. of New York, no less—of his *Thrilling Adventures* in 1867. A native of Carter County, Tennessee (almost adjacent to Ashe County, North Carolina), Ellis was a wagon maker who found himself caught up in the bridge burnings by East Tennessee loyalists early in the war, and soon he became a civilian river pilot, guiding hundreds of endangered Unionists from Confederate-occupied Tennessee to safety in Kentucky. He also engaged in bushwhacking attacks on Confederate residents and soldiers in and around Carter County and provided full—perhaps much exaggerated—accounts of his exploits in his book.[11]

But the guerrilla warfare that took place in Ashe County and most other parts of western North Carolina was not like the sustained irregular campaigns targeting both troops and civilians mounted by partisans such as Morgan, Ferguson, and Ellis. It consisted instead of localized acts of violence sporadically waged by neighbors against neighbors, and families against families, attacks that grew especially intense during the latter part of the war.[12] Accounts of those home-front experiences, many of them written by victims rather than by the perpetrators of those attacks, have been discovered only recently, after having been long stashed away in archives or among privately held family papers.

Among the most unusual of such memoirs are those of Horatio and Margaret Hennion. As an outspoken Unionist in the north Georgia mountains, Hennion was a constant target of Confederate persecution, and as is so often the case in a guerrilla war, the terrorist tactics were often equally aimed at his wife and children. Both husband and wife recalled those experiences separately in dictated statements to a daughter—Horatio in 1892 and Margaret in 1900. Together they confirm harrowing conditions that both suffered, and yet their separate voices reveal distinct, gender-linked perspectives on the same events. Horatio seemed to rally to the challenges he faced in outwitting and harassing his Confederate antagonists, and he tells of his exploits with considerable self-satisfaction. Margaret, on the other hand, while always supportive of her husband, never took any joy or pride in enduring these burdens, which apparently left her more emotionally and physically drained than Horatio.[13]

Just as southern women were on the forefront of efforts to commemorate the Confederacy and impose the values of the Lost Cause on a new generation of southern youth, so too were many Appalachian women intent on chronicling the hardships they had faced when caught up in the guerrilla warfare in their region.[14] Margaret Hennion was by no means alone in leaving vivid testimony of harrowing experiences endured in remote pockets of the Blue Ridge or Smoky

Mountains. North Carolinians Margaret Walker of Cherokee County and Mary Orr of Transylvania County also penned lengthy narratives of their ordeals. Walker was forced to watch as Unionist bushwhackers abducted and then murdered her husband, the reputed head of the Home Guard, though she was never able to find or bury his corpse. Orr and her mother were harassed by local Confederates because their husbands had defected to Union companies in East Tennessee, and they were forced to become roaming refugees themselves for the last few months of the war.[15] Though probably not meant for public consumption, these women's stories found their way into the hands of descendants or local historians who preserved them—and, in Walker's case, published them—thus allowing historians to incorporate them into the vast mosaic they are constructing of the turbulent Appalachian home front.[16]

Fugitive prisoners of war, along with other transients who moved through Southern Appalachia, often left vivid accounts of their observations of the inner Civil War into which they were inadvertently drawn either as targets or as collaborators. Junius Browne of Connecticut, for instance, was shocked at the brutality of the irregular warfare he encountered in the Carolina highlands as he fled from a Salisbury prison toward the safety of Union-occupied East Tennessee. "It is not difficult to conceive," he wrote, "how a few months of such an experience would transform a man from an enduring saint to an aggressive demon." Others were more partisan in their sympathies, acknowledging only the abuse suffered by the compatriots they encountered in the mountains. A Wisconsin officer, John Azor Kellogg, also a prison escapee, commented that those he saw "were compelled to defend themselves against the North American savages in a war persecuted without regard to the laws governing civilized nations."[17]

In many cases, local histories of guerrilla warfare remained part of nothing more than a strong oral tradition, with stories passed by family members from one generation to another. Only when someone committed those distant memories, often blurred or distorted through generations of retelling, to the written page did they become available to others elsewhere. One of the most unusual of such efforts was undertaken by a local historian, Elihu J. Sutherland in the Sandy Basin of southwestern Virginia, a community very much like Ashe County's

North Fork. In the 1920s and beyond, he conducted oral interviews with more than a hundred fellow residents in an attempt to construct family histories and, through them, a "folk history" of the community, with the Civil War a central focus of the interviewees' own memories or those of their parents and grandparents. More recently, historian Ralph Mann has used that exceptional collection of remembrances to reveal a great deal about the nature of Appalachia's guerrilla warfare and the ways in which it shaped and was shaped by kinship networks, gender roles, and community dynamics.[18]

Some of the more familiar wartime incidents in western North Carolina, from the Shelton Laurel massacre in Madison County to exploits of the infamous Keith and Malinda Blalock in and around Grandfather Mountain, have come to us as much through local lore as through official records.[19] Certainly the best-known product of that family-shared oral legacy is Charles Frazier's *Cold Mountain*. In stumbling over an obscure grave in the Smoky Mountains, Frazier found that it held two bodies—those of a local fiddler and a retarded adolescent. Both were civilians murdered by Captain Robert Teague's notorious Home Guardsmen, who terrorized deserters and others of questionable loyalties in Haywood and surrounding counties. That discovery led Frazier's father to tell him of an ancestor of their own, Inman, who was also a victim of Teague's gang. A Confederate soldier wounded in battle, Inman escaped from an Illinois prison and trekked home on foot, only to be confronted and killed by local Home Guardsmen within a few miles of his destination. From these basic facts, transmitted purely from memory by family members and area residents, Frazier constructed his best-selling saga of the war in these mountains.[20]

All of these accounts lead us back to William Albert Wilson and his version of this mountain war. If Charles Frazier chose to tell the tragic consequences of the brutal, internalized conflict on his ancestors in fictional form, Wilson chose a somewhat more conventional means of doing so. Yet his narrative of the war as experienced on the farms, households, and crossroads that made up the North Fork community of Ashe County is distinctive because it is far more than simply a memoir: it is the reconstruction not of an individual's experience, and not of a family's, as is true of most other such firsthand chronicles. It is rather a comprehensive record of a full community's wartime ordeal, one in which his family played an integral part. His testimonial ranks among the most meticulous and comprehensive we have of the many households, neighborhoods, and kinship networks for an Appalachian, even a southern, populace. What emerges from his narrative is a full-blown portrait of this most divided area of Ashe County, a community wracked by violence and destruction inflicted both from within and without, and of the multiple forces that drove an otherwise peaceful people to such extremes of hatred, cruelty, and vindictiveness.

Again, perhaps the most striking aspect of Wilson's account is that it was written by a man who was born only after the war was well under way. (He must have been conceived at about the time of Lincoln's inauguration in early March 1861.) Wilson states up front that "I, who as a child witnessed many cruel and tragic deeds, have undertaken to narrate what I saw as well as what I learned from others." It soon becomes obvious that it is the latter—what he learned from others—that makes up most of his narrative of the war years.[21]

A close analysis of the most central and traumatic of those deeds—the murder of his father, Isaac Wilson, on June 17, 1864—demonstrates how Will, many decades later, relied on the memories of other participants and witnesses to reconstruct so complete an account of that tragedy. Curiously, he begins that particular story—understandably, the first told in his memoir—by stating that he was four years old at the time.[22] Having been born December 20, 1861, Will was in actuality a mere two and a half. Although nothing else in his narrative ever suggests that he relied on his own recollection of his father's death (only the funeral a day later seems to have made a lasting impression on his young mind), it seems obvious, at least by implication, that he wanted to present himself, probably more than was actually the case, as a conscious participant in that central event of his young life and those surrounding it.[23]

Wilson provides only vague information about his family background or the events leading up to his father's death. Well into his narrative he states that his father "had engaged in wagoning to Salisbury" for several years prior to the war's outbreak, an explanation of the considerable material goods the family owned and feared losing to bushwhacking thievery.[24] In a letter to his older brother, Robert, in 1941 (a letter that in many respects seems to be the initial basis for this memoir, which he composed later that decade), he adds only fleeting bits of background. Oddly, he does not repeat or elaborate on these facts in the otherwise much fuller memoir. He informs his brother that their great-grandparents have moved from Lexington, North Carolina, to a farm on Forge Creek in Johnson County, Tennessee, just over the state line from Ashe County, though he does not say when they moved, or at what point his own father moved back across the line into North Carolina. He also refers to tensions between the Potter family and the Wilsons, dating from the marriage of his father's first cousin to Andy Potter, a union much opposed by her parents and grandparents.[25]

Will has nothing specific to say about Isaac's Confederate enlistment in 1861, giving no specific date for that momentous event; even more striking, he makes no reference to the company or regiment his father joined. (We know from other sources that he served in Company E of the 37th North Carolina Regiment.) In fact, he has nothing to say about his father's wartime service or even where he fought, prior to the summer of 1864, when he returned home for that fateful furlough. Nor does he have anything to say about the war itself, in the North Fork or elsewhere, prior to 1864, a rather glaring omission given the exceptional level of detail with which he describes the sequence of events once Isaac returned home.

Will gives a full account of Isaac's activity during his furlough. One can attribute many of the specific details to a strong sense of hindsight in others; incidents in the days and hours before Isaac's murder took on added significance and heightened remembrance for those who shared his final moments. Caroline Wilson, Isaac's wife and Will's mother, is obviously the primary source of information here. Not only does she become a prominent figure in Will's telling of those events, but the narrative takes her point of view at crucial points. What she told her husband about not visiting acquaintances whom she suspected of malevolent motives and her growing concern over his safety at home situate us as readers within her point of view and keep us there through the murder itself. We know that she spent a restless night beforehand and that she was increasingly uneasy about Isaac's decision to plow a cornfield before he departed. We know exactly what Isaac did that morning before he left the house—the chores he performed, the timing of his departure, and which ones of their eight children accompanied him and why. We know of the suspicious activity of other men moving along the road in front of the house, of Caroline's sending the younger children to see who else might be in the vicinity, and—based on their report—of her decision to go find Isaac and warn him yet again to leave immediately. Finally, we know exactly where she was as she heard the three shots that downed her husband, and we know that because she was walking past an almost empty barn at that moment, "the shots seemed to her to have a distinct echo."[26]

Once those shots were fired and Isaac fell dead in his field, Will draws on other voices and perspectives to reconstruct the sequence of events—from Polly Jones, Caroline's sister, and from Caroline's grandfather, Jesse Greer, both of whom were on the scene at the time or just afterward. Most astonishing of all is that Will quickly shifts the narrative to the point of view of his father's killers, as he recounts their plans for the assassination and how they carried it out. Their version of events came from boasts the Potter family made throughout the community—obviously to sympathetic neighbors—only days after their crime. That "full account of the plot and the dastardly deed," as Will calls it, must have been circulated widely and perhaps often, for he is able to re-create the movements of the Potters and Tom Stout, whom he calls "rabid Union men," on that fateful morning in as much detail as he is the movements of his own father. Women re-emerge as important catalysts and chroniclers as well, both in spreading word of the murder within the community at the time, and in adding details that would have been otherwise unavailable to Will later. Through their accounts, particularly that of Polly Jones, who repeated what she had learned from Liz Stout and Peggy Potter (the wife and sister-in-law, respectively, of two of Isaac's killers), these women's complicity in the plot becomes apparent.

The Potters spread the word of their involvement in Wilson's death with bravado, and they also explained their reasons for targeting him. The fact that it resulted from a case of mistaken identity only adds to the tragedy. As part of a conscription roundup for Confederate service, another Isaac Wilson (distinguished from his second cousin as "Big Ike") had had a confrontation with Jack Potter that resulted in the latter's death.[27] With little or no remorse for having shot the wrong Isaac Wilson, the Potters proceeded to seek out "Big Ike," attacking him in his own home, where they left him for dead, though he survived. While the culprits themselves obviously told this story in a form that eventually reached Will Wilson's ears, this is the first element of his narrative for which he credits other, more direct sources from his own adulthood: he uses personal interviews in 1939 with two of Big Ike's relatives, who sheltered him in their home after he was shot, and letters from the 1880s from other relatives involved in the incident.

There follows an extended and equally detailed description of the retribution sought for Isaac's murder by the Wilson and Greer families. Will's source of information for these events is not as obvious as the sources of his earlier material. Wilburn Greer, Caroline's brother, played the most prominent part in the pursuit of the Potters and other conspirators and may well have provided his nephew Will with such details as the route the pursuers took, the names of those questioned along that route, those who provided information, their ultimate apprehension, and finally the execution of one of Wilson's killers, a man named Silvers Arnold. Significantly, the one name Will chooses not to divulge in his narrative is that of the individual who "fired the fatal shot," although he is quick to note that Arnold's executioner "wore the uniform of a Confederate soldier."[28] Thus justice, in Will's mind, had been appropriately served.

One of Will's most unusual passages is his extended description of his father's funeral. It is the first event that Will actually claims to remember himself even though he was just a toddler. "As a child," he writes, "I was actually deeply impressed by what seemed to be a vast crowd of people but other incidents were indelibly impressed on my mind." The building of his father's coffin, the decisions made regarding the burial site and the funeral itself, and who performed what parts of the service are all details that most likely came from either Will's mother or his grandfather. Will knows—and records—who provided the cherry planks for the coffin, and who shaved his father before he was placed in it. In his letter to his brother, Will claims that he himself remembered "many of the things that took place while the corpse was being laid out."[29]

But Will credits yet another source much more explicitly. In 1889, in Franklin, North Carolina, he encountered a Methodist minister, Mr. Cooper, who told him he had officiated at his father's funeral and "related many incidents my child mind had failed to register." Cooper's contribution to the story seems to be rather trivial. He confirmed an odd incident that Will himself recalled, in which an unruly dog attacked an overwrought woman, who was rescued by a slave woman. Incidentally, this is the only reference to a slave or slavery in Wilson's narrative, yet as brief as it is, his explanation of who she was and why she was present suggests the sort of disruption and displacement that characterized the rapidly deteriorating "peculiar institution" during the war's latter months in western North Carolina and in many other parts of the South. (Also typical of Wilson's all-inclusive narrative style, he provides nearly as much background on the dog, Turk—who else he bit and how he met his end—as he does on the slave, Letty.) Such details, recalled a quarter of a century later, attest to the quirkiness of memory of both young and old, with the odd blend of significant and insignificant in terms of what the human mind chooses to retain and recall.

Perhaps the most significant fact that Will relates about his father's funeral is that one of his murderers, Tom Stout, was present. Stout was under arrest at the time and seems to have been forced to attend his victim's burial simply because his captors attended. Just afterward, they escorted him far from that scene to carry out what seems to have been a well-laid plan—his hanging. This execution is yet another event that Will is able to recount in remarkably precise terms: he tells us who participated, the site of the execution and the route taken to get there, how Stout's body was disposed of, and how his family was told where they could find it.

The events surrounding his father's death and its immediate repercussions make up merely the first few pages of what becomes an extended chronicle of other such atrocities that North Fork residents continued to inflict upon each other over the remaining ten months of the war. Will Wilson notes that his father's murder was a turning point of sorts and served to escalate the violent recrimination that characterized the area's internalized conflict. It brought new attention to the North Fork community from both Confederate conscription officers and Home Guard units who more actively sought out dissenters and forced confrontations that often resulted in killings by both sides. "From this time," Wilson notes, "animosities sprang up and the words 'Yankee' and 'Rebels' signified the opposing camps and untold suffering and violence were ushered in."[30]

The rest of his narrative of the war years—a total of about forty pages of the eighty-six-page transcript of Will's memoir—are very much like that of the early section on the circumstances surrounding Isaac's death. Will defines bushwhackers as "men who profess to be neutral and refuse to join either side, openly, but as individuals or small bands, using ambush tactics, attack, kill or plunder the homes of those unable to defend themselves."[31] That description is fitting for much of the ruthless activity of bushwhackers in many parts of the mountains, yet curiously it is at odds with the actual circumstances in the North Fork community. Far from any claims of neutrality, Will clearly identifies the men who engaged in this guerrilla war, either individually or in small bands, as either Confederate or Unionist. It is their loyalties to—or assumed affiliation with—one side or the other that ignites the antagonisms that in turn spur the many ambushes, murders, and executions that occupy so much of the narrative. Martin Crawford has noted of the North Fork that no part of the county was less supportive of secession or contributed fewer enlistees to Confederate service.[32] The intensity of that anti-Confederate sentiment, combined with much resented efforts at conscription and, by 1864, a general war weariness, created the volatile situation in the area that Wilson describes so vividly. Only in the conflict's final days does Wilson note any blurring of ideological lines. He states that by this point the people of the North Fork township were "so split up among themselves sometimes as not to be able to know who inclined to the 'Union' or who was a 'Rebel.'"[33]

Just as a confrontation over conscription resulted in Unionist Jack Potter's death, which in turn set off the chain of events that resulted in six other deaths, including that of Confederate Lieutenant Isaac Wilson, similar situations led to remarkably similar outcomes. Will tells the story of yet another Unionist, Tom Osborn, who ambushed and murdered a distant relative, Alex Osburn, just as the latter was preparing to join a Confederate company. Friends of Alex's then sought out and hanged Tom to avenge Alex's death. Will Wilson acknowledges the parallels to his father's death and its aftermath, saying, "The Osborn family and our own even then were intimate but the similarity of the tragedies that had visited our homes bound us more closely."[34]

That cycle played out repeatedly, and Will provides the same painstaking treatment of numerous atrocities, supplying names, places, and anecdotal details that often serve as the only distinguishing features of this continuous wave of North Fork violence. In re-creating the course of this localized war, he in effect embraces a cast of characters that comprised much of the local populace. A total of 284 different names appear in the wartime section of his narrative alone (not including Turk, the dog). He not only tells us who was killed (a total of nineteen people) but also identifies the family members of these men, how they were related to other families in the community, and—most significant—who was involved in their killings. We know by name most of those who made up the various groups that served as law enforcement, Home Guardsmen, search parties, executioners, and looting mobs. Nothing brings home the localized nature of guerrilla warfare as experienced in Southern Appalachia more than the fact that both sides knew each other so well.[35] Few if any of the men who were casualties of this North Fork conflict could not have recognized and named their attackers and killers. Only with Stoneman's Raid of April 1865, the largest incursion of Union forces to move through western North Carolina, does Will describe a wartime event involving nameless enemies. (He states that only later did local residents come to know that these troops were from Stoneman's Brigade.)

But for all the attention to the community dynamics at play in this turbulent warfare that erupted on the North Fork, Will never loses for long his focus on his own family—particularly the plight of his mother and his grandparents who, on several occasions, are victimized by bushwhackers and who, at other times, aid and abet friends and neighbors also under attack. Thus, even when his own family forms the centerpiece of his narrative, their experiences are integrally linked to those of the community at large.

The hardships of home-front life also emerge as a significant theme of Wilson's narrative, and he gives equal attention, also in great detail, to the material aspects of the war's latter months. He carefully chronicles shortages of clothing and food, as well as transactions in property, farm equipment, and livestock that were bought, sold, and negotiated among multiple families, much of which was a function of wartime deaths or the displacement of families forced out of this increasingly destabilized society. As both the theft and destruction of property became more prevalent, the defense of one's home and the protection of one's goods became a more constant concern. Will recounts quite specifically, both for his own family and for others, what items were hidden and where, what was stolen and by whom. In one of many striking instances, he records the way that a neighbor, Tom Stewart, managed to prevent a robbery of the Wilsons' home by first pretending to be part of the mob who broke into the house and then holding the other robbers at gunpoint and forcing them to leave, an act that made Stewart, as Will recalls it, both "an idol and a hero" to Caroline Wilson.[36]

Of course, very little of this memoir could be re-created from the memory of an under-three-year-old. As with Isaac Wilson's death, Will must have drawn on the individual and collective memories of adult witnesses and participants to reconstruct the many events that occurred in its wake. His mother remained a major source of the information; so too did his maternal grandparents, Jesse and Frankie Greer, who spent much of the war's remaining months living with their widowed daughter and her eight children. Yet many others contributed to the rich oral tradition on which Wilson built his narrative. Both in relating other incidents not involving his family and—more often—reinforcing or elaborating on events in which they were involved, Wilson takes full advantage of the memories of neighbors and acquaintances that he encountered in adulthood.

To cite one example of the multiple sources at his disposal: After a lengthy account of a shoot-out waged in protection of an elderly man named Landrine Eggers and the circumstances surrounding it, Wilson states, "I passed the place many times before Eggers died, sometimes with my mother and listened to the story firsthand." In the next paragraph, he notes that in 1909, as he and several men were surveying land, one said, "Tell Will Wilson about going over to Landrine Eggers' place after the body," a reference to the unclaimed body of a young man accidentally shot by Eggers's daughter. His companion, who had obviously been a participant in that gruesome series of events, complied. Wilson concludes that "as told by him, it harmonized with what I heard from others."[37]

These two offhand remarks with which Will concludes this story are no doubt indicative of how he absorbed many of his stories—through repeated recitations by his mother and grandparents and through enhanced or corroborated retellings over the years by other local residents, whose powers of recalling what they had seen or done seem as sharp and as vivid as those of his family. Although Wilson rarely acknowledges the sources of his information, he does so just enough to make it apparent that his narrative is an amalgamation of many minds, memories, and perspectives accumulated and filtered over nearly the full range of his long life. Perhaps most impressive is that for the vast majority of that life, the forty-two years he spent as a missionary in Japan, and then nearly twenty years in retirement in Durham, North Carolina, Wilson spent very little time in the North Fork community. Thus he accumulated his vast store of anecdotes mostly from oral sources within the community either before he left home in the 1880s or on sporadic visits back—in 1901–1902, 1909, and 1939—when on furlough from Japan. He apparently committed the stories to paper only during those retirement years. [38]

Integral to this internalized and civilian-driven conflict were the women caught up in it as both participants and chroniclers. Caroline Wilson was certainly a key player in many of the incidents her son relates and the most important source of much of that information. She lived until 1911, and there is no evidence that she ever wrote down her version of these events; rather, it is obvious that she told them to her children many times over the years, and that Will absorbed them, and in such vivid detail that he could reproduce them on paper nearly eighty years later. He introduces a number of incidents in his narrative with the phrases "The story was often related to me" or "As I often heard it told"; most of the time he is referring to his mother. Occasionally he is more specific about the circumstances under which he absorbed her stories. For example, Will states that after

Tom Stewart protected the family from looters or worse late in the war, whenever Stewart passed their house, his mother would insist that he and his brothers and sisters stop so that they could thank him again for his good deed. Of another incident involving Landrine Eggers, he notes that "I passed the place many times before Eggers died, sometimes with my mother and listened to the story firsthand."[39]

So too were other wives and mothers vital parts of this localized, home-grown conflict. But they were not merely the targets of harassment by bushwhackers and renegades or victims of their threats and intimidation. As Wilson's account makes abundantly clear, they were far more proactive than that. Throughout his narrative, women act as messengers, informants, protectors, collaborators, accomplices, and co-conspirators, and even on occasion as combatants. Hardly a page in the narrative does not include the name of at least one woman—and often several women are mentioned. Given their high level of involvement, it should come as no surprise that the women of this community, like those in so many other guerrilla-torn areas, also shouldered much of the burden of remembering and retelling the stories of what they suffered and what they endured in the postwar era and beyond.

Caroline Wilson's constant recitation of wartime events to her children brings to mind an observation of other western Carolina women displaced by the brutality of this mountain war. A Federal soldier who served at a refugee camp for Unionist civilians in Alabama at the war's end recalled the Appalachian women who had sought safe haven there. "I heard them repeat over and over to their children the names of men which they were never to forget, and whom they were to kill when they had sufficient strength to hold a rifle," he wrote. "These women, who have been driven from their homes by the most savage warfare our country has been cursed with . . . impressed me as living wholly to revenge their wrongs."[40]

In Caroline Wilson's case, at least, such vendettas were not the primary motives behind the constant telling and retelling of these stories to her children. Despite the strength of her Confederate loyalties throughout the war (her son writes that she "never forgave anyone who turned his back on the Confederacy"),[41] she actively sought and fully embraced reconciliatory efforts with most neighbors and acquaintances at war's end. And yet, for her and many mountain women like her, the war was their "felt history," to quote Robert Penn Warren again; who they were and who they became, as individuals, as families, and as parts of a community were all inexorably altered by what happened in the North Fork between 1861 and 1865. Even if they failed to hold grudges or continued wartime vendettas into the postwar era, these women nevertheless felt compelled to keep alive, through their children, stories of what they had endured. In part, they were testifying as to their own strength and courage in confronting this enemy and taking pride in their resolve to stand firm in the wake of the many dangers and threats they faced. (This seems especially true of Frankie Greer, Caroline's mother.)[42] But these stories no doubt also served to shape the values and identities of their children through recounting those actions and behaviors of their own—courage, fortitude, loyalty, endurance—those same qualities in which they took such self-satisfaction.

Equally as prominent as the centrality of women are the dense and overlapping kinship networks that pervade Will Wilson's narrative. He calls nearly three hundred individuals by name; like many of his sources, he was no doubt constantly attuned to the identity of his characters by the families they belong to and their relationship to others in the narrative. More often than not, he introduces an individual to the reader by laying out his or her genealogy. Very early in the memoir, for example, Will explains the plot to entrap his father and murder him. He states that the wife of Andy Potter had sent a message to Isaac asking him to come see her before he returned to his command. Will then proceeds to tell us that Mrs. Potter's mother was Elisabeth Heath, who was the sister of Hiram Wilson, Isaac's father, which made her Isaac's first cousin.[43] That relationship makes it evident that blood ties were not necessarily to be trusted, since she was an integral part of the plan by Andy and other Potters to lure her cousin into a situation in which he would be ambushed and killed.

Many historians have written about the key role played by family and kinship in determining loyalties and identity in Appalachia's inner civil war, but the sheer complexity and overlapping layers of family connections in the North Fork make such patterns less detectable there. It's very clear, though, that husband and wife, Isaac and Caroline (like her parents, Jesse and Frankie Greer), were of one mind in their commitment to the southern cause. This was not always the case in a region with divided households, with even husband and wife giv-ing allegiance to different sides.[44]

Finally, it is worth noting that Wilson's is not the only account we have of his father's murder. Not surprisingly, the incident long re-mained a major part of the oral history of the war in both Ashe and Watauga counties. In 1915, John Preston Arthur referred to it briefly, along with many other local atrocities, in his history of Watauga County. In it, he names most of the names that Will does in his ac-count, and he devotes as many words to the retribution exacted from Tom Stout as he does to the shooting of Isaac. Given that macabre elements are often those most remembered and transmitted through oral tradition, it is perhaps not surprising that Arthur quotes a local man who claimed that on April 10, 1865, while near the "little cavi-ty" of Rich Mountain, he heard someone sobbing, and following the sound, encountered Mrs. Tom Stout, sitting at the base of a tree with the bones of her husband in her apron, "crying as if her heart would break."[45]

Will Wilson's own account of his father's death and the circum-stances surrounding it were widely circulated within the county at some point in the 1940s, when as part of a senior journalism class project at Northwestern Ashe High School in Warrenton, the full text of his letter to his brother Robert, "R.B.," was published in its student newspaper, *Mountaineer Heritage,* under the title "The Wilson–Potter Feud." The only statement made by way of introduction was "The Wilson–Potter feud is more widely known in and around Ashe County than the Hat-fields and McCoys," which suggests that, for many of those reading this version of events and even those students involved in reproducing it for circulation, the story was still a vital part of the local oral tradition in that part of the county. The students provide no context or editorial-izing about the narrative, but state simply at its conclusion, "May the Wilson–Potter feud forever rest in peace."[46]

Despite the presumably widespread dissemination of the student paper, it somehow seems to have escaped the notice of the county historian, Arthur Fletcher, who would publish the first full history of Ashe in 1963. Oddly, he makes no mention of the Wilson murder, and his coverage of any guerrilla warfare in the county is fleeting. Fletcher begins his brief section on the war years in the county by blithely stating, "Practically every household in Ashe County today has its cherished memories of father, grandfather, great-grandfather or other ancestor, who answered the call for arms and fought bravely for the Confederacy." As with many such nuts-and-bolts accounts of local historians, Fletcher focuses his attention primarily on how many Ashe residents enlisted and in what companies and regiments they served, much more so than he does on anything that happened within the county itself.[47] His version of the war parallels that of that first generation of postwar historians in Haywood County and north Georgia, cited earlier, whose selectivity "wrote out" most of the internalized war that so consumed the North Fork corner of Ashe County.

Even more surprising is Stephen William Foster's anthropological analysis of Ashe County residents, published in 1988, in which he focuses specifically on their kinship and genealogical awareness, their collective self-image, and their historical consciousness. And yet, other than a single reference, the Civil War plays no part in his largely theory-driven study. He quotes from one family's oral history, in which one ancestor was identified as "a captain in the Home Guard during the Civil War and helped hang a bunch of bushwhackers. After which he went West in a hurry." Foster himself makes no comment on this passage, and he apparently found no one else who ever referred to the war or found no reason to cite such references if they were made.[48]

On the other hand, probably no county in what was once the Confederate South has as sophisticated, as comprehensive, and as insightful a history of its Civil War era as does Ashe County, thanks to the work of British historian Martin Crawford, whose book, *Ashe County's Civil War,* appeared in 2001. For Crawford, an inherent interest in the social history of the war itself, and not an interest in the county per se, drove his study. This particular locale merely served as the conduit through which he, like Foster, asked very large questions of a very small place; in Crawford's case, he began a study "preoccupied with internal relationships and dynamics" that evolved into one that "equally insists on the centrality of the external experience to an American community's life and identity." He ultimately argues that "the experiences of Ashe County men and women were shaped as much by their membership in the wider American society, by its values, its institutions, and its shared crises, as by local factors," which he by no means short-changes. A dogged detective, Crawford made full use of both Will Wilson's 1941 letter and his later memoir to recount in full the events they chronicle.[49]

Will Wilson's memoir apparently serves much the same purpose. It is, at one level, a remarkably rich factual description of the "shared crises" of North Fork residents during the Civil War's final and most destructive year; and yet it also serves as an intriguing exercise in the multiple ways in which memory—public and private, individual and collective, firsthand and secondhand—all function as part of an effort to create a communal sense of history and historical consciousness.

In a recent essay on "Writing the Individual Back into Collective Memory," historian Susan A. Crane grapples with theoretical questions such as "who has history and/or memory, who represents it, who experiences it, and how is it perpetuated?" She distinguishes between "collective memory" and "historical memory" as that between lived experiences common to a group and the preservation of that lived experience by descendants of those in that group. "Collective memory," states Crane, "exists and is perpetuated in specific groups . . . who maintain a living relation to [it]; and it is only within such groups that any individual can remember and express personal memories."[50]

Such seems to be the case for Will Wilson and his written record of the Civil War. Only through the collective memories of his elders in the North Fork, those who maintained a living relation to the war, was he able to place himself within that experience and express any personal memories of it. At the same time, the sheer distance between those experiences—his own and others—and his committing them to paper renders them "historical memory," to use Crane's term.

Yet another characterization of Will Wilson's role in the perpetuation of memory can be drawn from theorization of an early twentieth-century French sociologist, Maurice Halbwachs, who noted in 1922: "The totality of past events can be put together in a single record only by separating them from the memory of the groups who preserved them and by severing the bonds that held them close to the psychological life of the social milieus where they occurred, while retaining the group's chronological and spatial outline of them."[51] Is that, indeed, the function served by the "single record" Wilson produced? Just how much was he separated from the group memories or the "psychological life of the social milieu" about which he wrote? On the one hand, his chronicle is extremely personal and emotionally linked to the events he describes; yet on the other, given that he was no more than a toddler when these events took place, that his historical record of them was produced much later, in the 1930s and 1940s, and that he had not lived among those he wrote about for more than half a century at the time, he does seem to have achieved the distance that Halbwachs claimed was essential for historical memory, as opposed to collective memory.

In essence, Wilson's age allowed him to maintain a foothold in each camp, to bridge the gap, in effect, between lived experience and its preservation, between collective memory and historical memory. But Wilson's is by no means the only individual memory at play here, for, as Crane reminds us, "Individuals provide interpretations for other individuals, and these are dealt with as information to be assimilated, remembered, and archived," and "individual experience is never remembered without reference to a shared context."[52]

Perhaps this dynamic serves as the most apt characterization of Will Wilson's memoir: it is a carefully constructed product of an accumulation of individual memories, including his own. But in the latter stages of his life, when he seems to have made a conscious decision to write a narrative of the Civil War in the North Fork community, Wilson became a historian: he conducted oral interviews with members of the community, made notes of what they told him, and consulted written records, from household inventories to land deeds, thus supplementing, much enhancing, and perhaps further authenticating the primary basis of his narrative—those early memories of his own and those so deeply instilled in him by others.

Finally, the multiple versions of those stories to which Wilson had access over a nearly eighty-year period testify to the communal nature of guerrilla warfare itself. The residents of the North Fork community inflicted it upon each other, endured it together, and long remembered afterward what was done to them and by whom and what they themselves did and who they did it to. The very fact that almost every aspect of Wilson's story involved not just himself or his family but other families, neighbors, and acquaintances is, in effect, what makes guerrilla warfare a unique manifestation of this or any war. As a result, it is likely that from the beginning, distinctions between personal and collective memories were both reinforced but blurred in ways that would not have been true for those who experienced this war in more conventional ways. In repeating those stories over the years, Wilson's family, friends, and neighbors were integral to his own understanding and remembrance of the North Fork's Civil War, and thanks to that one small boy in that wartime community—so much a part of that lived experience but ultimately removed from it—his community's story became his own, as he "assimilated, remembered, and archived" it in a way that few others have.

Notes

1. Wilson's memoir is reproduced, along with background information on the circumstances under which it was written, in *Neighbor to Neighbor: A Memoir of Family, Community, and Civil War in an Appalachian Community,* ed. Sandra L. Ballard and Leila E. Weinstein (Boone, N.C.: Center for Appalachian Studies, 2007); it appeared previously in *Appalachian Journal* 34 (Fall 2006): 42–72. All quoted material in this chapter will reference this version of the memoir. Equally valuable is Patricia D. Beaver's introductory essay in the same issue, "The Civil War on the North Fork of the New River: The Cultural Politics of Elevation and Sustaining Community," 98–116.

2. There is evidence that suggests that at various stages of his life, he was also called Billy and Will, and later, during and after his career as a missionary, as "Jay-pan Billy."

3. Robert Penn Warren, *The Legacy of the Civil War: Meditations on the Centennial* (New York: Random House, 1961), 3–4; quote on 1.

4. On the "Lost Cause," see Charles Reagan Wilson, *Baptized in Blood: The Religion of the Lost Cause* (Athens: University of Georgia Press, 1980); Gaines Foster, *Ghosts of the Confederacy: Defeat, the Lost Cause, and the Emergence of the New South* (New York: Oxford University Press, 1987); Gary W. Gallagher and Alan T. Nolan, *The Myth of the Lost Cause and Civil War History* (Bloomington: Indiana University Press, 2000); and David Goldfield, "Whose Southern History Is It Anyway?" chap. 1 in *Southern Histories: Public, Personal, and Sacred* (Athens: University of Georgia Press, 2003), 4–22.

5. Harold Pinter's actual statement was "The past is what you remember, imagine you remember, convince yourself you remember, or pretend to re-

member," quoted in W. Fitzhugh Brundage, *The Southern Past: A Clash of Race and Memory* (Cambridge, Mass.: Harvard University Press, 2005), 4.

6. None of the following recent studies of the war and its legacy makes any mention of guerrilla warfare: David W. Blight, *Race and Reunion: The Civil War in American Memory* (Cambridge, Mass.: Harvard University Press, 2001); Tony Horowitz, *Confederates in the Attic: Dispatches from an Unfinished Civil War* (New York: Pantheon, 1998); David Goldfield, *Still Fighting the Civil War: The American South and Southern History* (Baton Rouge: Louisiana State University Press, 2002); Alice Fahs and Joan Waugh, eds., *The Memory of the Civil War in American Culture* (Chapel Hill: University of North Carolina Press, 2004).

7. Jonathan D. Sarris, "The Lost Cause in Appalachia: (Re)constructing Memories of the Civil War in the Southern Mountains, 1865–1900," paper delivered at Southern Historical Association annual meeting, November 2004. See also Rod Andrew, "Martial Spirit, Christian Virtue, and the Lost Cause: Military Education at North Georgia College, 1871–1915," *Georgia Historical Quarterly* 80 (Fall 1996): 486–505; and Sarris, *A Separate Civil War: Communities in Conflict in the Mountain South* (Charlottesville: University of Virginia Press, 2006), chap. 5.

8. Richard D. Starnes, "'The Stirring Strains of Dixie': The Civil War and Southern Identity in Haywood County, North Carolina," *North Carolina Historical Review* 74 (July 1997): 237–59; quotes on 257 and 259.

9. Martin Crawford, *Ashe County's Civil War: Community and Society in the Appalachian South* (Charlottesville: University Press of Virginia, 2001), 126.

10. Morgan, a Kentucky native, was ambushed and killed in September 1864 in Greeneville, Tennessee; Fergeson, who had murdered or mutilated more than a hundred Unionists over the course of the war, was captured at war's end, tried, and hanged in October 1865. See Noel C. Fisher, *War at Every Door: Partisan Politics and Guerrilla Violence in East Tennessee, 1860–1869* (Chapel Hill: University of North Carolina Press, 1997); Sean Michael O'Brien, *Mountain Partisans: Guerrilla Warfare in the Southern Appalachians, 1861–1865* (Westport, Conn.: Praeger, 1999); Robert R. Mackey, *The Uncivil War: Irregular Warfare in the Upper South, 1861–1865* (Norman: University of Oklahoma Press, 2004); and Daniel E. Sutherland, ed., *Guerrillas, Unionists, and Violence on the Confederate Homefront* (Fayetteville: University of Arkansas Press, 1999).

11. Daniel Ellis, *The Thrilling Adventures of Daniel Ellis* (New York: Harper & Bros., 1867). For a study of how much of Ellis's book is authentic and how much of it he actually wrote, see Allen Ellis, "The Lost Adventures of Daniel Ellis," *Journal of East Tennessee History* 74 (2002): 58–68. For recent work that puts Ellis in the broader context of guerrilla warfare in Appalachia, see the titles listed in the previous note, plus William R. Trotter,

Bushwhackers: The Civil War in North Carolina, vol. 2: *The Mountains* (Greensboro, N.C.: Piedmont Impressions, 1988); and several essays in Kenneth W. Noe and Shannon H. Wilson, eds., *The Civil War in Appalachia* (Knoxville: University of Tennessee Press, 1997).

12. For two useful overviews of recent scholarship on guerrilla warfare and on the distinction between these two very different models of irregular conflict in the Civil War South, see Daniel E. Sutherland, "Sideshow No Longer: A Historiographical Review of the Guerrilla War," *Civil War History* 46 (March 2000): 5–23; and James A. Ramage, "Recent Historiography of Guerrilla Warfare in the Civil War—A Review Essay," *The Register of the Kentucky Historical Society* 103 (Summer 2005): 517–41. See also Sutherland, "Guerrilla Warfare, Democracy, and the Fate of the Confederacy," *Journal of Southern History* 68 (May 2002): 259–92.

13. Keith S. Bohannon discovered both memoirs in the Horatio Hennion Papers at the U.S. Army Military History Institute, Carlisle Barracks, Pennsylvania, and wrote an essay based on their contents: "'They Were Determined to Root Us Out': Dual Memoirs by a Unionist Couple in Blue Ridge Georgia," in *Enemies of the Country: New Perspectives on Unionists in the Civil War South,* ed. John C. Inscoe and Robert C. Kenzer (Athens: University of Georgia Press, 2001), 97–120.

14. On southern women's roles in shaping the war's legacy, see Catherine Clinton, *Tara Revisited: Women, War, and the Plantation Legend* (New York: Abbeville Press, 2001); Karen L. Cox, *Dixie's Daughters: The United Daughters of the Confederacy and the Preservation of Confederate Culture* (Gainesville: University Press of Florida, 2003); and Tara McPherson, *Reconstructing Dixie: Race, Gender, and Nostalgia in the Imagined South* (Durham, N.C.: Duke University Press, 2003).

15. Margaret Walker, "Story of the Life of Margaret Walker during the Civil War," typescript, William Walker Papers, Special Collections, Hunter Library, Western Carolina University, Cullowhee, N.C., reprinted in expanded form in Margaret Walker Freel, *Unto the Hills* (Andrews, N.C.: privately published, 1976), 154–61; and Mary Middleton Orr, "The Experience of a Soldier's Wife in the Civil War," privately held typescript. See Gordon B. McKinney, "Women's Role in Civil War Western North Carolina," *North Carolina Historical Review* 69 (January 1992): 37–56; and William A. Strasser, "'A Terrible Calamity Has Befallen Us': Unionist Women in Civil War East Tennessee," *Journal of East Tennessee History* 71 (1999): 66–88.

16. For vivid accounts by other Appalachian women—Confederates hounded by both Union guerrillas and regular troops—see John N. Fain, ed., *Sanctified Trial: The Diary of Eliza Rhea Anderson Fain, A Confederate Woman in East Tennessee* (Knoxville: University of Tennessee Press, 2004); see also Daniel W. Stowell, "'A Family of Women and Children': The Fains of East Tennessee during Wartime," in *Southern Families at War:*

Loyalty and Conflict in the Civil War South, ed. Catherine Clinton (New York: Oxford University Press, 2000), 155–73; and Cornelia Peake McDonald, *A Woman's Civil War: A Diary, with Reminiscences of the War, from March 1862,* ed. Minrose C. Gwin (New York: Gramercy Books, 2003). McDonald lived in Winchester, Virginia, at the northernmost end of the Shenandoah Valley.

17. Junius Henri Browne, *Four Years in Secessia: Adventures Within and Beyond the Union Lines* (Hartford, Conn.: O. D. Case, 1865), 351–52; John Azor Kellogg, *Capture and Escape: A Narrative of Army and Prison Life* (Madison: Wisconsin Historical Commission, 1908), 165. For a thorough treatment of this genre of wartime accounts, see "'Moving through Deserter Country': Fugitive Accounts of Southern Appalachia's Inner Civil War," chap. 8 in this volume.

18. Ralph Mann, "Family Group, Family Migration, and the Civil War in the Sandy Basin of Virginia," *Appalachian Journal* 19 (Summer 1992): 374–93; and "Guerrilla Warfare and Gender Roles: Sandy Basin, Virginia as a Test Case," *Journal of the Appalachian Studies Association* 5 (1993): 59–66.

19. There are now multiple scholarly sources for both of these incidents. On Shelton Laurel, see Phillip S. Paludan, *Victims: A True Story of the Civil War* (Knoxville: University of Tennessee Press, 1981); on the Blalocks, see Trotter, *Bushwhackers,* chap. 14. For accounts of both, see John C. Inscoe and Gordon B. McKinney, *The Heart of Confederate Appalachia: The Civil War in Western North Carolina* (Chapel Hill: University of North Carolina Press, 2000), 117–20, 189–90. Both stories have, in very recent years, inspired fictional accounts as well. Sean O'Leary wrote an original play, *Shelton Laurel,* first produced at Mars Hill College in August 2005 (see chap. 13 in this volume); the massacre also plays an integral part in Ron Rash's novel *The World Made Straight* (2006). Sharon McCrumb's novel *Ghost Riders* (2004) is, in part, a fictional rendering of the Keith and Malinda Blalock story.

20. Charles Frazier, "*Cold Mountain* Diary: How the Author Found the Inspiration for His Novel among the Secrets Buried in the Backwoods of the Smoky Mountains," Salon.com (July 9, 1997); see also chap. 14 in this volume, which discusses *Cold Mountain.*

21. Wilson seems to have laid out much of this narrative first in the form of letters to his brothers in 1940 and 1941, just after he had retired from his mission work in Japan and moved to Durham, North Carolina. Patricia Beaver has obtained copies of four such letters, still owned by Wilson descendants, dated December 15, 1940, and January 7, February 25, and February 27, 1941.

22. "Early Life of William Albert Wilson," 45.

23. For an essay on how young people remember historical or traumatic events, see the work of two Danish psychologists, Dorthe Berntsen and Dorthe K. Thomsen, "Personal Memories for Remote Historical Events: Ac-

curacy and Clarity of Flashbulb Memories Related to World War II," *Journal of Experimental Psychology* 134 (May 2005): 242–57. I thank Judkin Browning for alerting me to this work.

24. "Early Life of William Albert Wilson," 64.

25. W. A. Wilson to R. B. Wilson, January 7, 1941, in private hands, though it was reproduced in the student newspaper of Northwest Ashe High School, *Mountaineer Heritage,* vol. 2, undated, 32–34, under the title "The Wilson-Potter Feud."

26. "Early Life of William Albert Wilson," 45–46.

27. In his letter to his brother, cited in note 25, Wilson suggests deeper underlying tensions with the Potters, and makes clearer that other Wilson family members—three sons of Lemuel Wilson, Isaac's brother—served as part of the Home Guard that so harassed the Potters for their resistance to Confederate service, and were responsible for Jack Potter's death.

28. "Early Life of William Albert Wilson," 50.

29. W. A. Wilson to R .B. Wilson, January 7, 1941. Curiously, one of the most significant discrepancies in Wilson's letter to his brother and his memoir is that in the former, he states that his father did not die in the field but was carried home and placed on a cot, where he lingered for less than an hour. Here, too, Wilson claims personal recollection of that moment: "I was the youngest of seven children but as I remember, even I could see that he was dying," he informed R. B.

30. "Early Life of William Albert Wilson," 54.

31. Ibid., 44–45.

32. Crawford, *Ashe County's Civil War,* 92–94; see also Crawford, "The Dynamics of Mountain Unionism: Federal Volunteers of Ashe County, North Carolina," in Noe and Wilson, eds., *Civil War in Appalachia,* 55–77. For another perspective on wavering commitments to the Confederacy in this region, see Gordon B. McKinney, "Layers of Loyalty: Confederate Nationalism and Amnesty Letters from Western North Carolina," *Civil War History* 51 (January 2005): 5–22.

33. Quote from the typescript of the Wilson memoir, p. 33, not included in the published version.

34. "Early Life of William Albert Wilson," 54.

35. I am grateful to Steve Nash, a University of Georgia graduate student working on Reconstruction in western North Carolina, for making a precise count of the names in Wilson's narrative of the war years, 1–54, and of the body count accrued in those same pages; also to Patricia Beaver, for sharing with me the meticulous family trees she has constructed, which provide a vast and growing genealogical re-creation of the North Fork community.

36. "Early Life of William Albert Wilson," 66–67.

37. Ibid., 69–70.

38. For background on Will Wilson's later life and how he came to write

his memoir, see the introduction to the published memoir by his grand-daughter, Frances Bivens Smith Rector, *Appalachian Journal* 34 (Fall 2006): 42–44.

39. Ibid.

40. Frank Wilkeson, *Recollections of a Private Soldier* (New York: Putnam, 1887), 232–33, quoted in Phillip Shaw Paludan, *Victims: A True Story of the Civil War* (Knoxville: University of Tennessee Press, 1981), 21.

41. "Early Life of William Albert Wilson," 56.

42. For other examples of such self-celebration among mountain women after the war, see "Talking Heroines," chap. 9 in this volume. See also McKinney, "Women's Role in Civil War Western North Carolina," 37–56; and Mann, "Guerrilla Warfare and Gender Roles."

43. "Early Life of William Albert Wilson," 47.

44. On the nature of family loyalties, see Mann, "Family Group, Family Migration, and the Civil War"; Jonathan D. Sarris, *A Separate Civil War: Communities in Conflict in the Mountain South* (Charlottesville: University of Virginia Press, 2006). On divisions within families in Appalachia and in the border South, see Inscoe and McKinney, "Highland Households Divided: Familial Deceptions, Diversions, and Divisions in Southern Appalachia's Inner Civil War," chap. 6 in this volume; and Amy Murrell Taylor, *The Divided Family in Civil War America* (Chapel Hill: University of North Carolina Press, 2005).

45. John Preston Arthur, *A History of Watauga County, North Carolina, with Sketches of Prominent Families* (Richmond, Va.: Everett Waddey, 1915), 170–71. E. B. Miller of Meat Camp is the man to whom Arthur attributes the story of Mrs. Stout. In *Ashe County's Civil War*, 205–6, nn. 40, 41, Martin Crawford relates another version of this story that found its way into a much more recent compilation of Ashe County family histories: Clarice B. Weaver, ed., *The Heritage of Ashe County*, vol. 2 (West Jefferson, N.C.: privately printed, 1994).

46. "Wilson-Potter Feud," *Mountaineer Heritage*, 2:32–34.

47. Arthur L. Fletcher, *Ashe County: A History* (Jefferson, N.C.: Ashe County Research Associates, 1963), 137–40; quote on 138.

48. Stephen William Foster, *The Past Is Another Country: Representation, Historical Consciousness, and Resistance in the Blue Ridge* (Berkeley: University of California Press, 1988), 69.

49. Crawford, *Ashe County's Civil War*, xi. His coverage of Isaac Wilson's death and its repercussions is on 142–44.

50. Susan A. Crane, "Writing the Individual Back into Collective Memory," *American Historical Review* (December 1997): 1372–85; quote on 1376.

51. Maurice Halbwachs, "Historical Memory and Collective Memory," in *The Collective Memory* (New York: Harper & Row, 1980), 84, quoted in ibid., 1376.

52. Crane, "Writing the Individual," 1378, 1381.

16

Race and Remembrance in West Virginia

John Henry for a Postmodernist Age

Surprisingly, one of the acclaimed novels of 2001 seems to have received very little, if any, attention from Appalachian literary critics or historians. A finalist for the Pulitzer Prize, *John Henry Days* was the much-anticipated second novel by Colin Whitehead, who made a considerable literary splash with his debut effort, *The Intuitionist,* in 1998.[1] As its title suggests, *John Henry Days* is firmly set in West Virginia, which alone should make those of us in Appalachian Studies sit up and take notice. But even more important for those of us seeking to understand the region, its image, and its hold on the rest of the country, it grapples with themes often quite familiar but cast in new and occasionally profound terms.

In 1996, the U.S. Post Office issued a commemorative series of four stamps focused on American folk heroes—Paul Bunyan, Pecos Bill, Casey at the Bat, and John Henry. Whitehead, Brooklyn born and bred and African American, had long nurtured an interest in John Henry, but it was the stamp that served as the impetus for his novel. "I knew vaguely that I wanted to do a modern update of the John Henry story," he explains in an online essay. The postal commemoration provided him with "a nice modern hook—a real live contemporary event that I could pin the story to. What kind of monument is a postage stamp? It was so banal that it addressed something about our debased age."

To top it off, Whitehead found that the town of Talcott, West Virginia, had been the site of the stamp's official "unveiling," an event that became the first in what is now an annual John Henry Days festival. "I hit the motherlode," he writes. "Now I really had my ingre-dients together. Except for characters, plot, and sentences, but who cares about that?"[2]

Talcott, in the southernmost part of the state, is a mile east of the Big Bend Tunnel of the Chesapeake & Ohio Railroad, which was constructed between 1870 and 1872. It is estimated that nearly a thousand workers, most of them black, worked on the mile-and-a-quarter tunnel over the two-year period of its construction and hun-dreds may have died under the grueling and dangerous circumstances of the work there.[3] It was there, according to most versions of the legend, that one of those workers, former slave and steel-driver John Henry, took on a contest against a new steam-operated drill that threatened to make him and his fellow workers obsolete. He beat the machine, but then he dropped dead. The novel is for the most part set in Talcott and nearby Hinton ("Talcott's pretty small," one character explains, "which is why most of the stuff this weekend is being orga-nized in Hinton") over the course of that three-day festival in 1996.

The protagonist, J. Sutter, is a cynical young African American freelance journalist who views the occasion as but one more in a long series of press junkets, in which he joins with other "hacks" like him-self for whom bragging rights consist of how many such publicity occasions they've attended and how much free food and booze they've consumed as a result. Sutter and his fellow "junketeers" spend their days in Talcott reminiscing about other boondoggles they've shared, and commiserating over the limited entertainment value Talcott of-fers, even though its residents have gone all out to make the most of the newfound national attention the U.S. Postal Service has bestowed by commemorating the town's sole claim to fame: the legendary John Henry.

The most obvious theme arising from this scenario—the discom-fort of an urban black New Yorker who finds himself deep in the West Virginia mountains—plays out only in the novel's very early stages. In flying toward this latest assignment, Sutter sees it as merely the South, for which he "possesses the standard amount of black Yankee scorn . . . a studied disdain that attempts to make a callus of history. It *manifests itself in various guises*: sophisticated contempt, a healthy stock of white trash jokes, things of that nature, an instinctual stiffening to the words County Sheriff." He has, Whitehead writes, "arrived at a different America he does not live in." Other than a few trips to Atlanta (which after all, is "a chocolate city") and once covering Mardi Gras, Sutter has conscientiously stayed away from the South, "the forge of his race's history" (14–15).

Once on the ground, and being chauffeured from Charleston to Talcott, Sutter finds that it's the terrain that first gives him pause: It's "a concatenation of cliffs and banks, as if some hobgoblin roosting on the side of the hills had shoved up the earth. Like a giant kicking a bunch of green carpet. Hearty folk, the mountain people." Though he makes a concerted effort to enjoy the scenery, "It is hard; all the trees look alike to him. The route slips between the places the government blasted through, the hills, and the scarred rock faces stare at each other from the sides of the road, grim, still grudgeful after all these years at their sunderance" (18–19).

In striking up a conversation with Arnie, his driver, Sutter betrays his misgivings about his surroundings. In response to the chauffeur's comment that Sutter sounds like a southern name, he quips, "Maybe my ancestors were owned down here at some point," which Arnie finds amusing. Sutter experiences a "burp of paranoia" as they move farther and farther off the interstate along ever more desolate back roads. With images of *Deliverance* or perhaps the West Virginia–based *Silence of the Lambs* in mind, he muses: "What if Caleb here is driving him up into the mountains, down to the creek, out to the lonesome spot where his family performs rituals. Boil him up in a pot, ritual sacrifice that helps the crops grow." Sutter worries whether the FBI will be able to follow his trail, thinking it unlikely, given that Arnie's cousin is probably the local constable. As they leave him boiling in a pot, "they watch wrestling on TV. He figures that even the most remote shack has a TV these days. The cable carrier in this region serves a special clientele, entire public access shows devoted to dark meat recipes" (22–23).

Whitehead is at his most clever and entertaining in these satiric takes on outsiders' fears and stereotypes of Appalachian people, but he quickly abandons the comic and dramatic possibilities of this rather conventional scenario to explore other, more original issues. The menacing mountaineers fade away as the scene shifts to Talcott and

Hinton and more traditional small-town folks become the social reality of this "new America" Sutter faces. Once there, other characters and subplots are introduced and then interspersed throughout—a postmodernist collage that never fully untangles itself. Postal officials, stamp collectors, folksingers, journalists, publicity agents, local officials, and entrepreneurs—all interact in a swirl of culture clashes, cynicism, and self-interest. Yet the heart of the novel lies in the fact that, for certain key figures, it is John Henry himself who holds special meaning, though in very different ways that are revealed only sporadically over the course of the fragmented narrative.

Parker Smith is a Postal Service public relations man from Washington charged with staging the stamp's unveiling. For him, John Henry provides a chance to plug into small-town Americana that national media all too often bypass. "If no one gets excited about presidential candidates anymore," he reasons, "they certainly come out in droves to support their beloved heroes and artifacts. On stamps" (295). He talks in the typical banalities of "official" endorsements: "Part of what we at the Post Office hope to achieve by our issue of the Folk Hero commemoratives is to create awareness of the trials of men like John Henry, to invite Americans to walk in his shoes. That each time they use one of our Folk Heroes stamps they think about the men who died to get us where we are today." In response, one cynical observer asks, "Is this man talking about a stamp or taking the beach on Normandy?" (66).

Yet in observing the town's own overzealous take on the occasion, Smith finds himself baffled why John Henry means so much to them. Given the illusory nature of his fatal feat—whether it ever took place, and if so, whether it had indeed happened here—Parker muses on the town's commitment to that legacy. "There are canned preserves and old men walking around in old conductor uniforms," he observes. "Is this really homey or is it constructed in some way? Is their sincerity actually the hapless grasping for something they believed their fathers possessed? There's a safe deposit box containing their heritage, but they don't possess the right documentation" (295).

Pamela Street, a young black woman also from New York—to whom Sutter is immediately attracted—is drawn to Talcott because of her father's interest in John Henry. A hardware store owner in Harlem, he had become intrigued by the legend after picking up a ceramic figure of "the hunched black man with a hammer poised to slam a railroad spike" in an antique shop. Pamela, then six years old, asked her father who the figure was. "He told her it was John Henry, and John Henry sat in the back seat with her all the way back to Harlem, swaddled in her favorite red blanket, her blanket." So, she muses in reflecting on that first encounter with the legend, she felt was sibling rivalry: "John Henry took her blanket" (114).

Beginning with that initial acquisition, Pamela's father found a hobby in collecting John Henry memorabilia—from sheet music to records and cassettes, from playbills to hammers to the pants that Paul Robeson had worn when he played John Henry on Broadway. It became a fixation: "Some sixties guy catching that nationalist fever, getting radicalized by Frantz Fanon, save up for a dashiki, revolutionary consciousness. Latches on the steel-driver as an ideal of black masculinity in a castrating country" (189). He created a museum—or shrine—to John Henry in his Harlem apartment, but few people ever saw it. Now Pamela has come to Talcott to deliver all of the boxes of papers and artifacts—the largest such collection in the world—to the town, which has purchased it as the basis for a new museum it plans to build. She brings her father's ashes as well, which she plans to scatter on the supposed site of John Henry's own grave.

Whitehead creates other, seemingly random vignettes that flash back to earlier days and other ways in which John Henry's legacy affected earlier generations in equally diverse ways. There is the great actor Paul Robeson playing John Henry on Broadway in 1940 between engagements as the Emperor Jones and Othello, just after a controversial European tour that took him from Russia to civil war–torn Spain. Robeson returns to America a more radicalized man, and he announces that "I have found that where forces have been the same, whether people weave, build, pick cotton, or dig in the mines, they understand the common language of work, suffering and protest." Now playing John Henry on stage, he realizes "the dialogue is terrible, the characters racist, the situation appalling." In John Henry, "a man of the land," Whitehead says, "Paul Robeson sees the folks. The masses. He wants to represent the experiences of the common man." But it was not to be. The production was a flop, with one critic stating that even Robeson "could not carry on his back 800 pounds of bad play" (229).[4]

Whitehead also dramatizes the efforts of University of North Carolina sociologist Guy B. Johnson to trace the roots of the ballad that by the 1920s had become so pervasive and had so many variations among American blacks, from the Deep South to the Midwest. Johnson quickly became overwhelmed with all that he found: "'The Ballad of John Henry' had picked up freight from every work camp, wharf and saloon in the land; its route is wherever men work and live, and now its cars brim with what the men have hoisted aboard, their passions and dreams" (154–55).

Johnson eventually zeroes in on Talcott, West Virginia, as the source of the legend and the song, yet even after three days of researching there, he finds that he is "one man against the mountain of contradictory evidence! Three days, and Guy thinks he can see a little into John Henry's dilemma: the farther he drives, the deeper the darkness he creates around himself" (155). In what becomes one of his richest chapters (at least for a historian), Whitehead explores the fluid and subjective nature of memory and oral history and the challenges it poses to any quest for truth. Johnson finds that people who claim to remember John Henry change their stories, contradict themselves, or admit that what they'd first claimed as firsthand knowledge was merely hearsay or some vague combination of recall and invention.

As a black man in Whitehead's narrative, Johnson's challenges as a visitor are complicated by the fact that he is still in the segregated South, even as far northward as he has traveled from Chapel Hill. Finding the room that he had reserved through correspondence denied him when he appears in person, Johnson realizes that "his earnestness to get to Hinton, coupled with the numerous dispatches he had posted under the whiteface of scholarly research, had caused him to forget the grip of Jim Crow, ever clenched around his people. Unlikely yes, but there he was with sweat on his neck and dumb embarrassment on his face." The point of this section, which Whitehead conveys in subtle and not so subtle ways, is, as Johnson states it, "A Negro in the world of academics must be twice the scholar, and twice the tactician, of his white colleagues" (157).

As powerful as these passages are, it is here that Whitehead unfortunately makes an egregious mistake, in historical terms at least: Guy B. Johnson was white, not black! The author picks up on an error made by anthropologist Brett Williams, who mistakenly identified Johnson as African American in her 1983 bibliographical study of the John Henry story.[5] (Did it not occur to either writer that a black man could not get a Ph.D. at Chapel Hill in the 1920s, much less serve on its faculty, as Johnson did?) Johnson's study, *John Henry: Tracking Down a Negro Legend,* published in 1929, was one of several books that established him as not only one of the foremost scholars of black culture, folklore, and dialect, but also as one of several influential white liberals from the University of North Carolina who sought to improve southern race relations during the height of the Jim Crow era.

The "real" Guy B. Johnson could have made an equally interesting character for Whitehead to imagine in Talcott in 1927. Instead, by turning him into a black man, the author unintentionally creates a strange mix of fact and fiction. Whitehead makes the most of the dilemma—and even the opportunities—of a black scholar's quest for the truth of John Henry and why African Americans had more of a stake in that truth than did whites. Whitehead has Pamela Street speculate on the differences between what white and black researchers concluded about John Henry's actually existence. In lecturing Sutter on the two foremost authorities on the subject (her father's collection included first editions of each of their books), she points out that Johnson and Louis Chappell "each came down in the twenties or thirties to interview people around here and find out if he really lived or not. They found some people who said he did and some who said he didn't." The bottom line, according to Street, was that the white man, Chappell, believed that the contest actually took place, whereas the black man remained more skeptical. "They interviewed the same people, a year or two apart, and got different stories from them" (187).

There does indeed seem to be some truth to the discrepancies between the two men's findings, even if different racial identities can't explain them. Louis Chappell, like Johnson a white man, was an English professor and musicologist at West Virginia University. The two scholars did indeed become rivals, in that they covered much the same turf at about the same time. Chappell's book, *John Henry: A Folk-Lore Study,* was published in 1933, four years after Johnson's. Both men used similar research methods—on-site interviews along with massive collections of testimony solicited through ads in both black and white newspapers. Despite a similar array of evidence drawn from these sources, Chappell concluded with far more certainty that John Henry was indeed a historical figure, and he seemed to take great offense at the UNC sociologist's reluctance to reach the same conclusion.[6]

As a prologue to his novel, Whitehead has compiled excerpts from the testimonials and memories drawn from both Johnson's and Chappell's books. This device effectively alerts readers up front about how pervasive the John Henry legend had become in American oral tradition and folk culture by the 1920s, and indicates the remarkable contradictions and variations it had by then taken on. These quotes establish as well just how ubiquitous the ballad of John Henry was, and how little either the character or his story was tied to West Virginia, much less Appalachia. Of the fifteen or so responses that Whitehead quotes verbatim, some claim that Henry was from Alabama, some that he was from Mississippi, and some that he was from Jamaica—and that his mighty feat had been performed in as wide a range of locales. One testimonial even claimed that he was hanged for murder in Welch, Virginia (3–6).[7]

Yet most of these claims seem to agree that Henry lived and died in the Big Bend Tunnel, on the C&O Railroad, and in West Virginia, even though other details are murky or nonexistent.[8] Thus, from the novel's opening, the reader is hit by the uncertainty of truth, the vagaries of memory, and even the personal agendas that account for the particular versions of the story told, themes that will remain in play throughout the book.

Whitehead reconstructs the final days of the great "steel-driving man" himself in a series of vividly rendered three-page vignettes interspersed, seemingly at random, throughout his novel. Though far too fragmented to carry the impact they would have if presented as a more sustained and coherent narrative, these passages serve to humanize the legend. In his sharply delineated re-creation of the hostile and high-risk environment in which Henry lived and died, Whitehead provides a poignant and complex portrait of a man who seemed to know that he was doomed and of the multiple pressures he faced—

from his bosses, from racist Irish workers, and from his fellow black workers.

When a salesman hauls the new steam drill to the worksite and shows it to the gawking workers, only Henry sees his fate as sealed: "He looked at the thing in the cart and saw tomorrows. Tomorrows and all the tomorrows after that because he understood as he had always understood that that was what this machine was going to take away from him. He saw the future, the very thing the machine would steal from him. Just as he stole from the mountain every day with his steel that which made the mountain what it was" (358). In bringing John Henry so vividly to life in passages such as these, though in the guise of a tragic hero—even a noble tragic hero—Whitehead gives credence to the reality of both the man and the final act that made him a legend, even if his modern-day characters never reach any conclusion—or "truth"—in that regard.

The most central of these characters remains Sutter; it is his own relationship with the steel-driving man that emerges as the novel's most meaningful. He sees himself as little more than a "hack-for-hire" who has been commissioned to write up Talcott and the festival as a feature for a new travel Web site. The trip for him means nothing more than a weekend of free food, drink, and promotional materials thrown at him, and ultimately a paycheck for the story he will produce from it all. Sutter arrives as both cynic and skeptic, and only gradually does he come to recognize some linkage between the dilemma of the doomed steel-driver and his own fate.

It's not that Sutter hadn't known about John Henry prior to this. He recalls his first exposure to the folk hero was when his fifth-grade teacher showed the class a cartoon. As the only black student in his class, he was intrigued to see black characters—particularly slaves, as John Henry had been born—animated in film. (This incident seems particularly autobiographical, as Whitehead has stated that this was his own first exposure to the subject, most likely a 1974 cartoon, *The Legend of John Henry*, narrated and sung by Roberta Flack.)[9] The mythic nature of his feats, including the claim he made to his parents just after his own birth that he would die at the Big Bend Tunnel on the C&O Railroad, didn't particularly phase Sutter. After all, "They were taught about Greek gods, and prophesying witches popped up everywhere you looked. . . . Curses, omens, the odd swan rapist: they were as common as eviction notices, overdue bills, utilities shut off for lack of payment," so why not, he asked, in the "glowing shack of this cartoon . . . where a young black boy was born with a hammer in his hand?" (138).

An impressionable Sutter recalls in vivid detail the cartoon's narrative, remembering that it had mesmerized his white classmates as much as it had him. "John Henry mashed the spikes into the ground, driving a mythology into the ground, as if carving it letter by letter into the earth would make the dreams of men live" (141). In some of his most beautifully rendered prose, Whitehead describes John Henry's opponent, the new-fangled steam drill against which he competed in the famous contest that would kill him, as portrayed in animated form for schoolchildren: "Clouds of steam exited pipes, the metal creature shook furiously, all to a ridiculous chorus of toots and whistles. It was the foolish dream of a mad scientist, and yet the railroad workers were in awe. In fear. Except for our man John Henry, who saw in this comic and elaborate concoction the seamless assembly of his fate." (It is revealing that the same fatalistic tragic hero portrayed by Whitehead was inspired perhaps by a cartoon.) When the film ended, Sutter was sure the teacher had led a discussion about the lessons to be learned from the story, and about its "ambiguous ending," though he can't recall anything now but the questions raised: "Mrs. Goodwin, why did he die at the end? Mrs. Goodwin, if he beat the steam engine, why did he have to die? Did he win or lose?" (142).

As an adult though, it is only over the course of the weekend, and particularly through his association with Pamela, that Sutter comes to view John Henry and his story with any personal relevance. Initially a skeptic, Sutter comes to identify and to appreciate both the man and the myth in a cathartic moment when he and Pamela visit the Big Bend Tunnel. "He thought it would be bigger. This is the John Henry tunnel, not the one over there that has replaced it. The functional tunnel draws in the modern freight, the John Henry tunnel old wives' tales. Rain and dirt have sullied the dignity of the entrance but the cut and arranged stones announce a tamed mountain. The message out of the black mouth is not that of conquest but shrugged failure" (319–20).

Stepping just inside the tunnel, Sutter asks himself, "What if this were your work? To best the mountain. Come to work every day, two, three years of work, into this death and murk, each day your progress measured by the extent to which you extend the darkness. How deep you dig your grave." He recognizes that the mountain retains its power over modernization even into the present. "This place," he concludes, "confounds devices, the steam drill and all that follows. This place defeats the frequencies that are the currency of his life. Email and pagers, cell phones, step in here and fall away from the information age, into the mountain" (321–22).

If the legend represents a parable of man versus machine, of tradition over modernization, then Sutter sees himself caught in a parallel dilemma in a postmodernist era. If John Henry was consumed by—indeed a martyr to—the Industrial Revolution, then Sutter can be seen as a casualty of the Digital Age, where he is a mere pawn whose vapid writings only add to the vast stockpile of information doled out to cyberspace consumers who have been swindled into believing it has some worth. As Sutter wonders what the modern equivalent for John Henry's martyrdom might be, he remains unaware that his own destruction—in the book's all-too-melodramatic conclusion—will provide the answer.

So what does all this tell us about the racial legacy of either John Henry or the efforts by a seemingly all-white community to celebrate that legacy more than a century later? And what does it add to our understanding of that cultural legacy within the context of Appalachia? Ultimately, place seems to matter very little to Whitehead once he has grounded his protagonist in Talcott after moving him along the winding and ever more ominous back roads of West Virginia in his opening pages. Appalachian residents appear only as marginal characters, and locals appear to be of far less interest than the variety of outsiders who find themselves thrown together in this remote mountain town with little regard for or sense of relevance to the region.[10]

But if place and people in Appalachia seem peripheral to what ultimately interests Whitehead, his commentary on image, legend, oral tradition, and the powerful hold all three continue to exert does speak to central concerns for those of us in Appalachian studies. One is reminded of Allen Batteau's thesis in *The Invention of Appalachia*, that the region has meant very different things and served very different agendas generated by individuals and groups far removed from the southern highlands.[11] Just as these outside forces shaped the region's image and played on its stereotypes for a variety of purposes, so it is that an array of people, past and present, black and white, insiders and outsiders, have seen meanings that serve their own needs in the story of John Henry, who just happened to be the product of a particular place and time in Appalachia's history.

Pamela Street quotes her father, the obsessive collector from Harlem, as she and Sutter are burying his ashes on the site of John Henry's own grave. Commenting on the many versions of the ballad, she recalls his observation: "Passed between work gangs and families and friends in the old days of folk music, on record, on the radio. You could split the song into so-called official versions, her father used to say, the ones made by established singers and put on vinyl, cassette, and CD, and the songs of the people, entirely different, the mis-sung versions, belted out by people who misremembered the lyrics and supplied their own haphazard verses." For those parts one couldn't recall, "her father used to say that what you put in those gaps was you—what you inserted said a lot about you. . . . Then you've assembled your own John Henry" (373).

This is a novel of many such John Henrys created by many perceived gaps, both racial and regional, past and present. If the full work never quite rises to the level of several of its multiple parts, *John Henry Days* offers challenging and often profound commentary on memory, on history, on heritage, and on identity in a postmodernist age. All of these loaded terms take on new significance and mixed meanings as New Yorkers and Washingtonians, government officials and journalists, performers and collectors, all converge in search of themselves for three days in West Virginia.

Notes

1. Colson Whitehead, *The Intuitionist* (New York: Anchor Books, 1998); Whitehead, *John Henry Days* (New York: Doubleday, 2001).

2. Colson Whitehead, "I Worked at an Ill-Conceived Internet Start-up and All I Got Was This Lousy Idea for a Novel," http://www.randomhouse .com/whitehead/essay.html.

3. Guy B. Johnson, *John Henry: Tracking Down a Negro Legend* (Cha-

pel Hill: University of North Carolina Press, 1929), 27; Louis Chappell, *John Henry: A Folk-Lore Study* (1933; rpt., Port Washington, N.Y.: Kennikat Press, 1968), 61–69. For a useful bibliography on the literature on John Henry and Appalachian race relations, see the "Resource Guide" in *Blacks in Appalachia,* ed. William H. Turner and Edward J. Cabbell (Lexington: University Press of Kentucky, 1985), 267–74.

4. Here Whitehead draws from Brett Williams's coverage of Roark Bradford's adaptation of his novel *John Henry* (New York: Harper and Bros., 1931) as a musical and why it failed, even with Robeson in the title role. See Brett Williams, *John Henry: A Bio-Bibliography* (Westport, Conn.: Greenwood Press, 1983), 81–84.

5. Ibid., 59.

6. For a thorough discussion of the rivalry between Johnson and Chappell, and the source from which Whitehead obviously drew, see Williams, *John Henry,* 59–62. Williams concludes, "The two books complement each other very nicely, with Johnson's perhaps more useful to the artist, and Chappell's most helpful to those seeking substantive information on the Big Bend Tunnel community" (61). Both Johnson's and Chappell's work has been superseded by a far more sophisticated and definitive account of John Henry's life and legacy. Scott Reynolds Nelson, *Steel Drivin' Man: John Henry, The Untold Story of an American Legend* (New York: Oxford University Press, 2006). I have resisted the urge to overhaul this essay to incorporate Nelson's book into it, and will limit to the notes acknowledgment of its contributions, one of the most significant of which is the detective work by which he has established, once and for all, the reality of John Henry's existence.

7. Whitehead acknowledges that five of the quotes in his prologue came from Johnson's book, six from Chappell's, and one from yet another folklorist of the era, John Harrington Cox, "John Hardy," *Journal of American Folk-Lore* (October–December 1919), 505–20.

8. A University of Georgia chemistry professor has recently claimed to have evidence that the John Henry contest took place in Leeds, Alabama, in 1887. "Challenging the Legend: Professor Driving Home New Evidence on Life of John Henry," *Athens Banner-Herald,* February 4, 2002. Scott Nelson concludes the Lewis Tunnel, several miles east of the Big Bend Tunnel, was the site of John Henry's death. Nelson, *Steel Drivin' Man,* 81–86.

9. Colson Whitehead interview, *Houston Chronicle,* September 14, 2001; and Daniel Zalewski, "Tunnel Vision: An Interview with Colson Whitehead," *New York Times Book Review* (May 13, 2001), 8, 15. For a listing of some films and filmstrips (mostly brief and produced for classroom use), see Williams, *John Henry,* 138–39.

10. Allen Batteau, *The Invention of Appalachia* (Tucson: University of Arizona Press, 1991). It is revealing that neither this book nor a more recent

book on Appalachian identity and imagery makes any mention of John Henry, which suggests that his story has never been integral to perceptions of the region. Dwight B. Billings, Gurney Norman, and Katherine Ledford, eds., *Confronting Appalachian Stereotypes: Back Talk from an American Region* (Lexington: University Press of Kentucky, 1999).

11. Nor does Scott Nelson in *Steel Drivin' Man* provide much of an Appalachian context for his account of John Henry's life and death, although he provides a meticulous geographical description of its West Virginia setting (pp. 10–18) and describes Edward J. Cabbell's efforts to use the John Henry legend to draw new attention to the African American experience in the region (p. 167).

17

In Defense of Appalachia on Film

Hollywood, History, and the
Highland South

One of the courses that I most enjoy teaching is a freshman seminar called "Appalachia on Film." As an academic exile from the region (though I occasionally take comfort that Athens, Georgia, is only one county away from official Appalachia, according to the Appalachian Regional Commission's skewed reasoning), I rarely get the chance to teach Appalachian history at the undergraduate level. I thus jumped at the chance to develop this course when freshman seminars were added as a curricular option at the University of Georgia a few years ago. Many faculty members take this opportunity to bring to the classroom interests that are sometimes far afield from their home disciplines; it has been fun to see a microbiologist offer a course on Wagnerian opera, a physicist take on Tolstoy and his philosophy of war, and a mathematician teach baseball statistics (sabermetrics). Many of us in the History Department seem to be film buffs. Although we don't seem to stray very far from our areas of historical expertise, my colleagues have designed seminars focused on screen depictions of scientists, the French Revolution, the civil rights movement, and the Middle East.

Perhaps too predictably, I focus on the region I know best, Southern Appalachia. I have built my course around nine films:

- *The Journey of August King* (1995): a well-received production of a yeoman farmer in frontier North Carolina who aids a fugitive slave girl at great sacrifice to himself, based on a John Ehle novel

- *Cold Mountain* (2003): the big-budget version of Charles Frazier's best-selling saga of the Civil War among Carolina highlanders and its protagonist's odyssey home to the woman he loves
- *Songcatcher* (2000): an independent film based loosely on Olive Dame Campbell's discovery and documentation of English ballads and folk music in the Blue Ridge Mountains at the turn of the century
- *Sergeant York* (1941): Gary Cooper's Oscar-winning portrayal of Alvin York, the homespun Tennessee pacifist who became the most celebrated hero of World War I
- *Matewan* (1987): John Sayles's meticulous re-creation of a West Virginia coal-mining community and the strike that led to an infamous "massacre" in 1920
- *Wild River* (1960): director Elia Kazan's story of a TVA agent's struggle to remove a determined old woman from her island home on the Tennessee River just before it's to be flooded
- *The Dollmaker* (1984): Jane Fonda playing Gertie Nevels in a faithful, if much compressed, adaptation of Harriett Arnow's classic novel of Appalachian displacement during World War II
- *Deliverance* (1972): a wilderness horror story of Atlanta canoers who find themselves in "hillbilly hell," based on James Dickey's best-selling 1970 novel
- *Foxfire* (1987): a television adaptation of a Broadway play based on the clash between real estate dealers and an elderly widow clinging to her right to live out her life on her north Georgia farm

These films cover a broad spectrum of types: three are major studio productions and box-office hits (*Sergeant York, Deliverance,* and *Cold Mountain;* the first two were Hollywood's biggest moneymakers of 1941 and 1972); two were more modest studio productions (*Wild River* and *The Journal of August King*); two were independent films (*Matewan* and *Songcatcher*), and two were television productions, both part of CBS's "Hallmark Hall of Fame" (*The Dollmaker* and *Foxfire*).[1] Four were adapted from novels (*August King, Dollmaker, Cold Mountain,* and *Deliverance*), two were original screenplays that adhered reasonably close to historical events (*Sergeant York* and *Matewan*), and the other two (*Songcatcher* and *Foxfire*) are heavily fictionalized stories based loosely on real characters or situations.

I cannot claim any overarching rationale for these selections— other than that they are all films I very much like and thus enjoy teaching; in different ways, each engages students at some, often multiple levels, and as such, they easily evoke discussion or debate; and perhaps most important, each offers some element of "truth" regarding the historical realities of Appalachia.

We spend the first week discussing major themes in Appalachian history and the reasons behind the many misconceptions and stereotypes to which the region has long been subjected.[2] I have found particularly useful as a working theme for the course a statement by David Whisnant explaining Olive Campbell's mission in the 1920s in his book *All That Is Native and Fine*: "Popular understanding of the Appalachian South at the time [early 20th century] reflected every shade of opinion. While for some, mountain people were 'backward,' unhealthy, unchurched, ignorant, violent, and morally degenerate social misfits who were a national liability, for others they were pure, uncorrupted 100 per cent American, picturesque, and photogenic pre-moderns who were a great untapped national treasure."[3] This vast range of perceptions applies to far more than the early twentieth century; it encapsulates to varying degrees nearly all the depictions the students will see on-screen.

Hollywood has never been known for its historical accuracy, and yet it has been too easy for historians to throw out the baby with the bathwater, dismissing any value in cinematic treatments of historical subjects. In a recent study, *Reel History: In Defense of Hollywood*, Robert Brent Toplin urges his fellow historians to take a more open-minded view of cinema; he argues that movies can communicate important ideas about the past to students of history. The very nature of the medium prevents it from presenting factual realities in the same way one would expect of a written work of history, or even a documentary film. Nevertheless, Toplin insists, "in many important respects, the two-hour movie can arouse emotions, stir curiosity, and prompt viewers to consider significant questions."[4]

I admit that I originally conceived this course as one that would examine these films in terms of how they perpetuate misconceptions, stereotypes, or clichés. Yet early on I came around to Toplin's perspective. Most of the films have plenty of stereotypes and distortions to discuss; more important, though, each of these stories depicts the human struggles that arose in real historical situations, which skilled writing and often great acting bring to life. As such, I see these films as appealing and accessible means of drawing students into discussions of the historic realities conveyed—or at least suggested—on-screen. Students are certainly astute enough not to accept what they see on-screen as literal truth or documentary filmmaking, and thus we don't spend much class time separating fact from fiction, which is what I had anticipated when designing the course.

I show and discuss the films in chronological order by content, rather than by their date of production. For all but the last two, *Deliverance* and *Foxfire*, we have specific dates in which each is set: 1815, 1864–1865, 1907, 1917–1918, 1920, 1935, and 1944–1945. The last two are contemporary depictions of the times in which they were made—the 1970s and 1980s. There are merits to both chronological approaches. In a freshman seminar I teach on southern race relations on film, the order in which the films were produced is far more integral, as we use those films to explore the changing racial attitudes of Hollywood itself and how it reflected—or failed to reflect—such attitudes in the rest of the country and in the South. For my "Appalachia on Film" course, the films' production dates are less integral to my purposes than their historical subject matter. Six of these nine films were made since 1984 (only *Sergeant York, Wild River*, and *Deliverance* were not), so they do not lend themselves to an assessment of changing views of Appalachia over the course of the twentieth century.

The class meets twice a week. On Tuesdays, we view a film after I offer fairly brief and basic introductory remarks. Based on notes made during the screening, students write a three- to four-page analysis, which they turn in on Thursday. I ask them to respond in some way to a set of questions centered on the tone each film takes toward Appalachian life (contemptuous? respectful? romanticized? satiric? etc.); the virtues and vices of the characters, major and minor; the narrative techniques that shape viewers' attitudes toward the region; what aspects of the film—music, speech patterns, location shooting—contribute to or detract from its regional authenticity; and what impact the movie likely had on how American filmgoers view Appalachia.

On Thursdays, when we convene again, I provide far more historical context on the film, and then we spend most of the class period discussing the issues the students have written about. Discussions grow richer and more rewarding over the course of the semester, as each film builds on those seen earlier, and students are able to assess the films in increasingly comparative terms. It was only as I taught the course for the first time that I came to fully appreciate this cumulative effect: that the juxtaposition of these particular films offered far more insight into both realities and perceptions of Appalachia than one would have any right to expect from southern California's "dream factory" or than any one or two of these films alone could offer. And I took great satisfaction that, more often than not, the students themselves picked up on these parallels and comparisons, and in so doing, often drew their own conclusions about the region and its depiction in film.

The most obvious commonality shared by all but one of these films is the interaction of southern highlanders with outsiders—either through the incursion of outsiders into the region, or through Appalachian natives' movement elsewhere. (Only *August King* is regionally self-contained, with all the characters and conflict limited to Appalachian residents, though its plot is centered on the efforts of one native —a slave—to move beyond the region.) The intentions of the strangers coming into the region vary greatly in these films, as has indeed been the case historically, particularly over the course of the twentieth century. Academic field-workers, union organizers and company agents, government officials, tourists, and the developers who cater to those tourists—all serve as catalysts who drive the story lines of *Matewan, Songcatcher, Wild River, Deliverance,* and *Foxfire.* In each, it is the reactions of local highlanders to these individuals or groups and their various agendas that provide the dramatic tension, conflict, and emotional weight that propels the plot.

For those highlanders who move beyond the bounds of home and region, it is usually larger historical forces that push them away; none leave willingly. It is war that takes Inman, Alvin York, and Gertie Nevels far from home and into alien environments. They carry with them skills honed in the mountains—whether shooting prowess or woodcarving—that have much to do with their survival in hostile circumstances far from home. Yet all are profoundly troubled by their displacement and seek desperately to return to the comfort and security of their highland households and communities—or merely the natural world. (Inman, in particular, seems drawn back home by the aesthetics of the mountains themselves—oh, and by Ada Monroe.)

A related theme that students readily detect is Appalachians' strong attachment to land. August King, Alvin York, and Gertie Nevels seek to own it. ("I know a piece of bottomland to be had and I'm a gonna' git it," says York; Nevels declares to her youngest son, "You ain't goin' work your life away plowing another man's land"). The plots of both *Wild River* and *Foxfire* are driven by desperate struggles to hold on to land already owned. In both cases, elderly widows are forced to defend their property against forces far more powerful than they are: TVA officials and real estate developers, respectively. A somewhat vaguer, but equally pervasive, sense of loss is evident in *Deliverance*. As in Elia Kazan's *Wild River,* the damming of a river is the impetus for the threats felt by its central characters, though the losses they fear couldn't be more different. While Ella Garth has far more at stake in defying the TVA, which is about to flood her island home and destroy her way of life, the suburban adventurers on the Cahulawassee are merely interested in "doing the river" one last time before it is turned into a lake. Yet *Deliverance* director John Boorman suggests that more than a wild river is about to be destroyed. Perhaps borrowing from Kazan's film, the final scene of *Deliverance* depicts graves being dug up prior to the cemetery's flooding, a ritual no doubt reenacted many times during TVA's incursion throughout the region, and a major point of concern to Ella Garth.

The moral dilemmas that stem from these conflicts are often obvious in these films, with right and wrong, and good and evil, characterized in fairly simplistic form. Yet closer examinations often reveal more subtle and complex factors that defy such easy judgments. August King (portrayed by Jason Patric) is obviously on the side of angels as he facilitates a slave's escape and makes increasingly bigger sacrifices to protect the seventeen-year-old girl, Annalees, as she eludes her brutish master. No question of good guys or bad guys here, but students enjoy discussing the sexual attraction that might well have been behind King's willingness to give up so much to protect this alluring young woman (played by Thandie Newton). Would he have risked as much for a male fugitive, or for an elderly or unattractive woman?[5] And while students recognize the strong antiwar message of *Cold Mountain,* the movie strips any moral ambivalence from the internal strife that plagued Carolina highlanders: Home Guardsmen are consigned the roles of villains in far too simplistic a take on the realities of guerrilla warfare that so wracked much of that society from 1861 to 1865.

Much of the effectiveness of Kazan's *Wild River* lies in the moral ambivalence of the protagonist, TVA agent Chuck Glover (Montgomery Clift)—who fully recognizes that the TVA and the New Deal will improve the lives of East Tennesseans but also develops increasing sensitivity to and admiration for Ella Garth (Jo Van Fleet), the elderly woman who refuses to abandon her island farm. In an interview, Kazan said of these characters, "I think Miss Ella's right to want to stay on her land. I think Glover is right, too. There's a need to do things for the good of the majority, which in this case is to establish inexpensive electric power and to control the erratic, devastating flooding of the Tennessee River. . . . But when you do that, some individuals are just ruled out, and I think that's a real loss and should not be ignored."[6]

In *Foxfire,* students recognize the similar dilemma facing Annie Nations (portrayed by British actress Jessica Tandy, who spent much of her latter career playing Georgia women).[7] This elderly widow faces pressures from land-hungry developers to give up her north Georgia farmstead so that they can make big profits from the scenic vistas of that mountain-top property. The more ambiguous, and perhaps universal, issue in her story is simply her age, and the concern of her son (John Denver) as to how much longer she can live independently in that remote environment and the physical demands required to sustain a life on it.

Some of my students at UGA are familiar with the scenario behind Annie Nations's story—the incursion of tourism and second-home development in the north Georgia mountains. The families of some have vacation homes there, and others have visited friends or relatives who do. But they admit that their contacts with natives of the area have been minimal, and they've never thought in terms of the human and cultural costs of that development. Given how many of our students come from suburban Atlanta, they react even more strongly to *Deliverance*. (Some female students are repulsed by the film and find it very difficult to sit through the rape scene at its core, a reaction I don't recall when the film first appeared in 1972 and became the biggest box-office hit of that year.) But as Jerry Williamson has so astutely observed, "*Deliverance* is not about mountain people; it is rather a critique of city people."[8] By shifting discussion from the harassment by grotesque hillbillies and viewing the four Atlantans as something other than simply the victims of mountain violence, we open a new frame of reference that informs several of the other films as well.

These films also provide very effective means through which to explore gender issues. Strong women play key roles in so many of these films that students could easily conclude, based on Hollywood's version of southern mountain life, that Appalachia was a matriarchal society. In a chapter of *Hillbillyland* devoted to "Hillbilly Gals," Jerry Williamson notes, "If a hillbilly is a democrat, then hillbillyland grants extraordinary equality to women. . . . At times." It certainly does so in the films under consideration here; one cannot help but be struck by the nearly reverential treatment afforded mountain women in nearly all these movies—only *Deliverance* lacks a memorable female character.

Jane Fonda, Jessica Tandy, Nicole Kidman, and Renée Zellweger made the most of formidable yet vulnerable heroines in *The Doll-maker*, *Foxfire*, and *Cold Mountain*. All these characters face seemingly overwhelming odds that force them to fight for their families, their homes, or their own survivals, usually with little or no support from men. Fonda's performance, in particular, is an extraordinary blend of fortitude and vulnerability that embodies much of both the stereotypes and the reality of Appalachian women. (She has said that Gertie Nevels is the role of which she is most proud; she won an Emmy for it.)[9] Jessica Tandy plays an equally poignant character in *Foxfire*, whose fragility—due only to age—and stubborn attachment to her way of life, her land, and her memories suggest what Gertie Nevels might have become in thirty years.

Equally memorable and worthy of analysis are the rich array of secondary female characters in almost all these films. They are even stronger mountain women, played by able character actresses: Jo Van Fleet as the island matriarch of *Wild River;* Pat Carroll as Viney Butler, the curmudgeonly midwife who becomes the champion of *Songcatcher's* title character Lily Penlaric (Janet McTeer) and the most authentic source of the music Penlaric is collecting; Mary McDonnell as Elma, the boardinghouse operator and widow in *Matewan,* who stands her ground in supporting the strike and factors prominently— and triumphantly—in the film's climactic shoot-out; Eileen Atkins as the "goat woman" who rescues Inman and nurses him back to health in *Cold Mountain;* and the British stage actress Margaret Wycherly as Ma York, perhaps the ultimate of mountain matriarchs, whose stalwart dignity commands the respect and submission of her wayward son Alvin (Gary Cooper) and makes their relationship as much the emotional center of *Sergeant York* as his courtship of his young sweetheart Gracie (Joan Leslie).[10]

Not all such women are admirable: Geraldine Page plays Gertie Nevels's overbearing and needy mother, who insists that Gertie join her husband in Detroit, which in effect forces her daughter to give up the farm she had scraped and saved so hard to acquire. In *Matewan,* Bridey Mae, a rather empty-headed and man-hungry young widow (played by Nancy Mette) is easily manipulated into betraying the coal miners and their community, of which she herself had been a part.

None of these women bows to the authority or power of men (though Gertie's mother forces her daughter to do so); on the other hand, only Ma York is defined by her influence on a male. Her quiet authority and moral suasion over not only Alvin but her entire household of children render her a pivotal character despite what is a surprisingly small speaking part. Although her role is based heavily on the real Mary York and her relationship with her son, one cannot help but wonder if another influence on screenwriters was the character of Ma Joad in *The Grapes of Wrath,* produced a year earlier. (The role won an Academy Award for actress Jane Darwell.) In her influence over her grown son (Tom, played by Henry Fonda) and her management of a large family, Ma Joad is much like Ma York; both films served as tribute to American motherhood as the backbone of the nation's pioneering spirit in an era of strong patriotic and historic sentiment. (There are perhaps even stronger parallels between *The Grapes of Wrath* and *The Dollmaker,* and of the stalwart women, Ma Joad and Gertie Nevels, who attempt to hold their families together during the traumatic displacement forced upon each by the Great Depression.)

These films provide plenty of opportunity for students to scrutinize masculinity as well. It is the very essence of *Deliverance*—and by this point in the course students recognize that this film is the only one we view that depicts a mountain society devoid of women, and they are struck by how that makes the society appear far bleaker and more threatening. (Is it mere coincidence that Drew [Ronny Cox], the most sensitive of the four Atlantans, and the only one to connect with a local resident—through their banjo duet—is the only one killed by those locals?) There is no shortage of violence in these films, but only occasionally is it portrayed as endemic to mountain society—the decadent brutality in *Deliverance;* the good-ole-boy rowdiness and barroom brawls in several films, from *Sergeant York* to *Songcatcher;* a gut-wrenching execution of a slave in *The Journey of August King;* and vigilante retribution rendered by local hoodlums upon Montgomery Clift's TVA agent in *Wild River.* Just as often, if not more frequently, the violence is instigated by outsiders, as in *Matewan,* or results from larger outside forces, such as the guerrilla warfare in *Cold Mountain.*

If one were to keep score, it quickly becomes apparent that mountain men are not nearly as appreciated by filmmakers as are mountain women. Of male protagonists, only August King, Inman, and Sergeant York qualify as heroes in terms of standing up for principles (and in each case, a woman is behind much of their motivation in doing so); in *Matewan* and *Wild River,* it is outsiders—pacifist union organizer Joe Kenehan (Chris Cooper) and TVA agent Chuck Glover—who serve as the moral compasses when confronted with wrongs that need to be righted. More often than not, the native men in these movies are seen as weak, irresponsible, rowdy, even emasculated, malevolent, or intolerant. Women emerge as the guardians, even the repositories, of values, of culture, and of tradition. This is particularly evident in *Songcatcher,* which features no fewer than six major female characters; it is probably no coincidence that it is also the only film in the course that was both written and directed by a woman, Maggie Greenwald. For the most part, these films affirm the final speech delivered by that archetypal screen matriarch, Ma Joad, in *The Grapes of Wrath*. Just before her upbeat declaration "We're the people," she notes how her family has responded to the challenges and crises they've faced in seeking work as California migrants: "A woman can change better than a man. Man, he lives in fits and jerks. Woman, it's all one flow, like a stream." And so it seems with Hollywood's Appalachian men and women as well.

These films can trigger fruitful discussion of other key topics in Appalachian history, such as race, religion, and community. Slavery is central to *August King,* of course, although Annalees is the only black character with a speaking part in the film, and despite her tough, determined exterior, she remains a rather passive character whose fate remains fully in the hands of men. Racial divisions among labor forces are evident in the strikebreakers (led by James Earl Jones, no less) who so alter the dynamics of organizing efforts in *Matewan,* and in local white resentments over the New Deal policy of equal wages to black workers in *Wild River.* The sheer absence of racial issues can generate good class discussion as well, the most conspicuous example being the lack of African American characters in *Cold Mountain,* even though Ada Monroe is depicted as a slaveholder.[11]

Preachers appear as influential members of Appalachian communities in *Sergeant York, Matewan, Cold Mountain,* and *Songcatcher,* sometimes as social activists, sometimes as their moral consciences. Each of these films features at least one church scene that serves to reveal vital truths about local values and/or prejudices. It's a fourteen-year-old preacher, Danny (Will Oldham) whose perspective provides the crucial narrative thread through which the Matewan massacre is told in hindsight. And, as the local community is forced to deal with its persecution of the mission workers in its midst, a church meeting makes up the climax of *Songcatcher* (which ends, rather improbably, with a woman shooting her abusive husband in front of the congregation).

Sergeant York opens with a church service, the primary point of which is the rowdy Alvin's absence from it. His conversion experience, along with his quest for bottomland (and a marriage that's contingent on that land), form the dramatic crux of the movie's first half.

"Folks say you're no good 'cept for fightin' and hell-raisin'," says his sweetheart (Joan Leslie), "and I'm thinkin' they're plumb right." Prodded by Pastor Pile (Walter Brennan) and the two women in his life, York quickly matures into a responsible adult, and his newfound faith spurs the pacifist convictions and the resultant moral struggle he confronts in becoming a soldier.

The sense of community is more sharply defined in some of these films than in others. John Sayles's *Matewan* is certainly the epitome of community studies; in fact, I would argue that no other film has ever portrayed as complete and complex a portrait of a single community. Others, such as *The Journey of August King, Sergeant York,* and *Cold Mountain,* make the collective values and agendas of particular communities central to their protagonists' own dilemmas and actions, though *Cold Mountain* does so far more superficially than the others; students notice that particularly when they compare the three films. All three, like *Matewan,* thus provide useful reference points for discussions of class differences, of shifts in power and powerlessness, of mob (or mere group) mentalities, and of how outside forces serve either to unite or to divide local residents.

Revealing too are characters such as August King, Inman, Gertie Nevels, and Annie Nations who for various reasons, either forced upon them or self-imposed, are alienated or removed from the communities of which they once were or could have been a part. The resulting tensions between these characters and those in whose midst they live can tell us much about the shifting dynamics within Appalachian society at various eras in its history.

Students become sensitized to the use of music and settings as barometers of how authentic an Appalachian experience filmmakers seek to capture on celluloid. With only two exceptions (*Sergeant York,* filmed entirely in Hollywood, and more famously, *Cold Mountain,* filmed in Romania), these films were produced on location in or near the regions in which they are set, and they are generally effective in making not only the mountain scenery, but mountain life—buildings; agriculture; flora, fauna, and other natural resources; and physical isolation or remoteness—integral elements of the highland experience.[12]

Nearly all these filmmakers use authentic music to add credibility to their productions and to enhance the sense of mountain life and culture—English ballads and folk tunes, gospel music and labor songs, and of course "Dueling Banjos." Most hired established musicians from the region as either consultants or performers or both. It is interesting to explore correlations between the authenticity of depictions of Appalachia and the choices of music and the locales at which a movie is shot. It is obvious that Georgia's Chattooga River is integral to *Deliverance*'s impact, but what effect does the banjo score have on the film's tone and mood? How much do the blending of multiple musical traditions in *Matewan* reflect the multicultural components—Baptist, Italian, African American, and so on—that so characterized the workers' struggle there?[13] Are the relatively minor though egregious stereotypes and inaccuracies in *Songcatcher* ultimately redeemed by the filmmakers' close attention to what most matters in the film—its music, so meticulously re-created under the supervision of Sheila Kay Adams? And what of the irony that *Sergeant York*, the most romanticized and stereotyped depiction of the region among these films and the only one in which no attempt was made to shoot on location or to incorporate mountain-based music, may have been the most authentic film of all? After all, it was made in consultation with Alvin York himself, who had not only full script approval but specified that Gary Cooper should portray him on-screen.[14]

Unlike the hillbilly images stressed by Jerry Williamson (through mostly different films than those discussed here), there is a pervasive sense in these films of Appalachians fighting back. They are constantly under siege and regularly exploited, and yet they never become merely victims. These characters don't take their oppression lying down. Whether they're fighting for property, for family, for community, for tradition, for culture or a way of life, or for their very lives, they all take on heroic qualities that make us admire their willpower, their courage, and their determination, sometimes against unbeatable odds. That this spirit is captured so effectively and through so many different stories and such a range of multifaceted characters brought to life in powerful performances is a point not often appreciated by those who have focused on the misrepresentations of Appalachia by outsiders—journalists, fiction writers, and playwrights as well as filmmakers. (Given the dominance of this view, it is no wonder that *Deliverance* has received far more attention from Appalachian scholars—and almost always in defensive mode—than nearly all the rest of these films combined.)

These are of course partial truths, often oversimplified, romanticized, or much embellished. Again, no one expects historical authenticity from Hollywood. And yet each of these films gives students entrée into very real issues and aspects of the Appalachian experience, which allows them to recognize and examine them in very concrete and tangible terms.[15] In his book *The Invention of Appalachia*, Allen Batteau stresses the extent to which the region has often served far more national than regional agendas; he points out that in the American imagination Appalachia has long represented far more than deprived and depraved hillbillies. As pervasive as those images are, Batteau argues that they have been offset by more positive images, which "have become less symbols of Appalachian particularity than of shared American values—the dignity of labor, self-sufficiency, pioneering spirit, patriotism, and independence."[16] In essence, much of what he labels "Holy Appalachia" was also Hollywood's Appalachia. That's certainly the case in most of the films considered here.

Alvin York and the filmmakers reproducing his story on-screen certainly bought into this notion that "Appalachia is somehow a special repository of 'fundamental Americanism,'" the one region in the country that has "preserved traditional American values in their purest form."[17] York, his family, and his neighbors represented for filmgoers as well the spirit of what made this nation great; that these patriotic sentiments were expressed on the eve of the United States' entry into another world war no doubt contributed to the film's success.

But Hollywood's sense of "Holy Appalachia" was neither unique to 1941 nor limited to periods of national crisis. In some sense, almost all these films share to one degree or another ennobling depictions of the values of home, of family, of land, of tradition, and it is as important to recognize and discuss these themes as "inventions" as it is to debunk more denigrating stereotypes and distortions. Yet even if those positive images of the region are not necessarily any more historically accurate than the negatives are, the mere fact that these films take on real issues and events should allow us to approach them as glasses half full rather than dismiss them as glasses half empty.

This is certainly the approach Robert Toplin has taken in his defense of Hollywood history. To grant him the last word, he claims that such screen depictions of the past are successful when "audiences receive a modicum of information about broad historical events but are, nevertheless, emotionally and conceptually rewarded. Memorable films address important questions about the past and attach viewers' emotions to them. Hollywood gives life and personality to individuals and groups that often appear rather sterilely in the pages of history books. Cinema helps transform stale, one-dimensional stories into lively, two-dimensional experiences to which audiences can relate."[18]

So it is, I would argue, for all of the films discussed here. Their redeeming value lies not in any literal truths that they convey, but in the mere fact that they embrace real issues and present them in dramatic contexts that provide students—as they have American moviegoers for much of the past century—accessible, appealing, and multifaceted introductions to the region, its people, and the struggles they have undergone.

Notes

1. For brief descriptions of each of these films except *Foxfire,* see individual entries in Rudy Abramson and Jean Haskell, eds., *Encyclopedia of Appalachia* (Knoxville: University of Tennessee Press, 2006). The fullest scholarly assessment of Appalachia on film is J. W. Williamson, *Hillbillyland: What the Movies Did to the Mountains and What the Mountains Did to the Movies* (Chapel Hill: University of North Carolina Press, 1995). Three of the films I teach were released after the publication of *Hillbillyland;* of the others I use, Williamson offers extensive commentary on only two: *Sergeant York* (207–24) and *Deliverance* (155–67).

2. The literature on Appalachian stereotypes and imagery is increasingly vast. The best of these works include Cratis D. Williams, "The Southern Mountaineer in Fact and Fiction" (Ph.D. diss., Columbia University, 1961); Henry D. Shapiro, *Appalachia on Our Mind: The Southern Mountains and Mountaineers in the American Consciousness, 1870–1920* (Chapel Hill: University of North Carolina Press, 1978); Rodger Cunningham, *Apples on the Flood: The Southern Mountain Experience* (Knoxville: University of Tennessee Press, 1987); Allen W. Batteau, *The Invention of Appalachia* (Tucson: University of Arizona Press, 1990); and Dwight B. Billings, Gurney Norman, and Katherine Ledford, eds., *Confronting Appalachian Stereotypes: Back Talk from an American Region* (Lexington: University Press of Kentucky, 1999).

3. David Whisnant, *All That Is Native and Fine: The Politics of Culture in an American Region* (Chapel Hill: University of North Carolina Press, 1983), 110.

4. Robert Brent Toplin, *Reel History: In Defense of Hollywood* (Lawrence: University Press of Kansas, 2002), 1.

5. For a debate on the merits of *The Journey of August King,* see Jack Wright and John C. Inscoe, "Hollywood Does Antebellum Appalachia and Gets It (Half) Right," *Appalachian Journal* 24 (Winter 1997): 192–215. My half of that debate appears as chap. 11 in this volume.

6. Jeff Young, *Kazan: The Master Director Discusses His Films—Interviews with Elia Kazan* (New York: Newmarket Press, 1999), 258–59. See also William Baer, ed., *Elia Kazan: Interviews* (Jackson: University Press of Mississippi, 2000).

7. Tandy followed *Foxfire,* for which she won an Emmy, with starring roles in *Driving Miss Daisy* (1989), *Fried Green Tomatoes* (1991), and the television film *To Dance with a White Dog* (1993).

8. Williamson, *Hillbillyland,* 157–58.

9. Fonda made the statement on "Private Screenings: Jane Fonda," an interview with Robert Osborne on Turner Classic Movies, March 28, 2007.

10. For a full discussion of Ma York's pivotal role in *Sergeant York,* see Williamson's chapter on "The Mama's Boys," in *Hillbillyland*, esp. 215–22.

11. For a discussion of the role of race in *Cold Mountain,* both book and film, see "Appalachian Odysseus," chap. 14 in this volume; Martin Crawford, "*Cold Mountain* Fictions, Appalachian Half-Truths," *Appalachian Journal* 30 (Winter–Spring 2003): 182–95; "Roundtable Discussion on *Cold Mountain,* the Film," especially comments by Tyler Blethen, John Crutchfield, and Gordon McKinney, *Appalachian Journal* 31 (Spring–Summer 2004): 316–53; and a film review by Inscoe in *Journal of American History* 91 (December 2004): 1127–29.

12. *Matewan* was filmed in Thurmond, West Virginia; *Deliverance* and *Foxfire* in Rabun County, Georgia; *Wild River* in and around Cleveland and the Hiawassee River in Tennessee; *Songcatcher* primarily in Madison County, North Carolina; and *The Journey of August King* in several other western North Carolina counties. The Kentucky-based scenes in the first third of *The Dollmaker* were filmed in Sevier County, Tennessee, and Chicago doubled for Detroit. Excellent book-length accounts of the filming of two of these films are John Sayles's *Thinking in Pictures: The Making of the Movie Matewan* (Boston: Houghton Mifflin, 1987), and Christopher Dickey's *Summer of Deliverance* (New York: Simon and Schuster, 1998). Christopher Dickey is the son of James Dickey, who was with his father during the making of the film.

13. See a chapter on the scoring of *Matewan* in Sayles, *Thinking in Pictures,* 107–13. For another good discussion of the film, see Eric Foner,

"Matewan," in *Past Imperfect: History According to the Movies,* ed. Mark C. Carnes (New York: Henry Holt, 1995), 204–7.

14. The details of *Sergeant York's* production are recounted in Williamson, *Hillbillyland,* 207–24; Robert Brent Toplin, *History by Hollywood: The Use and Abuse of the American Past* (Urbana: University of Illinois Press, 1996), chap. 3; and David D. Lee, *Sergeant York: An American Hero* (Lexington: University Press of Kentucky, 1985), chap. 6. For a discussion of the film within the context of other frontier films of the era, see J. E. Smyth, *Reconstructing American Historical Cinema: From* Cimarron *to* Citizen Kane (Lexington: University Press of Kentucky, 2006), chap. 8.

15. Other films might reveal different patterns and different "truths" about the southern highlands. *Thunder Road* (1958), *The Trail of the Lonesome Pine* (1936), *I'd Climb the Highest Mountain* (1951), *Coal Miner's Daughter* (1980), *The Molly Maguires* (1970), and *October Sky* (1999) are all mainstream films that I would consider adding to an expanded version of my course, either because they address other significant aspects of the Appalachian experience, or because they offer contrasting views and treatments of issues covered in the nine films I currently teach.

16. Allen Batteau, *The Invention of Appalachia* (Tucson: University of Arizona Press, 1990), 17–18.

17. Lee, *Sergeant York,* 104. Jerry Williamson has noted the irony in the fact that in *Tobacco Road,* another major film released in 1941, filmmakers applied some of the same hillbilly stereotypes to portray its characters as degenerates that were used in *Sergeant York* to "stoke the fires of patriotism in painting the young ne'er-do-well Alvin York as an ideal foot soldier in the nation's defense." J. W. Williamson, "Feature Films," in Abramson and Haskell, eds., *Encyclopedia of Appalachia,* 1710.

18. Toplin, *Reel History,* 204.

Credits

"Appalachian Odysseus: Love, War, and Best-sellerdom in the Blue Ridge" is a composite of a review essay of the novel that first appeared in *Appalachian Journal* 25 (Spring 1998), the author's section of a roundtable discussion of the film version of *Cold Mountain* entitled "Mountain Women, Mountain War" in *Appalachian Journal* 31 (Spring/Summer 2004), and a review of the film in the *Journal of American History* 91 (December 2004). Reprinted with the permission of *Appalachian Journal* and *Journal of American History*.

"Between Bondage and Freedom: Confronting the Variables of Appalachian Slavery and Slaveholding" is an expanded version of a lecture delivered at Berea College in October 2005 as part of a symposium on the black experience in Appalachia and America, in commemoration of the college's sesquicentennial.

"Coping in Confederate Appalachia: Portrait of a Mountain Woman and Her Community at War" originally appeared in *North Carolina Historical Review* 59 (October 1992), and is reprinted with the permission of the *North Carolina Historical Review*.

"A Fugitive Slave in Frontier Appalachia: *The Journey of August King* on Film" appeared as half of a "debate" with Jack Wright in "Slavery, Freedom, Frontier . . . and Hollywood? 'The Journey of August King' in Historical Perspective" in *Appalachian Journal* 24 (Winter 1997). Reprinted with the permission of *Appalachian Journal*.

"Guerrilla War and Remembrance: Reconstructing a Father's Murder and a Community's Civil War" is an expanded version of an essay that appeared in *Appalachian Journal* 34 (Fall 2006). Wilson's memoir is reproduced, along with background information on the circumstances under which it was written, in *Neighbor to Neighbor: A Memoir of Family, Community, and Civil War in an Appalachian Community,* ed. Sandra L. Ballard and Leila E. Weinstein. Boone, N.C.: Center for Appalachian Studies, 2007. Reprinted with the permission of the Center for Appalachian Studies, Boone, N.C.

"Highland Households Divided: Familial Deceptions, Diversions, and Divisions in Southern Appalachia's Inner Civil War." From *Enemies of the Country: New Perspectives on Unionists in the Civil War South,* ed. John C. Inscoe and Robert C. Kenzer. Athens: University of Georgia Press, 2001. Reprinted with the permission of the University of Georgia Press.

"In Defense of Appalachia on Film: Hollywood, History, and the Highland South" was commissioned for an essay collection, Patricia Gantt, ed., *Appalachia in the Classroom* (Athens: Ohio University Press), forthcoming in 2009.

"Mountain Masters as Confederate Opportunists: The Slave Trade in Western North Carolina, 1861–1865" originally appeared in *Slavery & Abolition* 16 (April 1995).

"'Moving through Deserter Country': Fugitive Accounts of Southern Appalachia's Inner Civil War." From *The Civil War in Appalachia: Collected Essays,* ed. Kenneth W. Noe and Shannon H. Wilson. Knoxville: University of Tennessee Press, 1997. Reprinted with the permission of the University of Tennessee Press.

"'A Northern Wedge Thrust into the Heart of the Confederacy': Explaining Civil War Loyalties in the Age of Appalachian Discovery, 1900–1921" was commissioned for Andrew L. Slap, ed., *The Civil War's Aftermath in Appalachia* (forthcoming from the University Press of Kentucky).

Index

Abbott, Shirley, 145
Abingdon, Va., 30, 67, 74
Abolitionism, 50, 58, 72
  in Appalachia, 22, 24, 27, 115–16,
    197, 237, 246, 250–52, 260
Absalom, Absalom! (Faulkner) 227,
    230–32, 237–38
Adams, Sheila Kay, 376
Agriculture, Appalachian, 81, 157–
    61, 166
Alabama, 67, 68, 191, 338, 357
Alamance, Battle of, 262, 279n18
Alcoholism, 151–52, 159
Alleghania, 1–2
Allen, Lawrence, 283, 286–90
American Revolution, 260–61, 264,
    268, 273, 275
Andrews, Raymond, 19
Annalees (slave), 243–52, 370, 374
Appalachia
  black population of, 15–17, 25–26,
    32, 59, 67, 75, 98n8, 105–6,
    229–30
  class divisions in, 206, 211–15,
    219–20, 230–33, 375
  and Confederacy, 1, 4–5, 89, 111–
    12, 219–20
  contrasted with South, 2–5, 13,
    111–12, 231–33, 277, 304–6
  discovery of, 196–97
  as frontier, 244–45
  geographical definition of, 3–4, 6–7

influx of blacks into, 31, 83–85,
    245–46
  mission workers to, 256, 258, 273
  patriotism in, 260–62, 264, 269,
    275–78
  stereotypes of, 2, 75, 175, 197–98,
    245, 256, 258, 272–73, 352–53,
    366–67
  whiteness of, 3, 4, 15–17, 21, 197,
    227–32, 235, 257
Appalachian Regional Commission,
    364
Appalachia on Our Mind (Shapiro),
    257
Arkansas, 283, 286–87
Army of Northern Virginia, 182
Arthur, John Preston, 284, 340
Ashe County, N.C., 80, 129–31, 134,
    322–44, 340
  guerrilla warfare in, 325–44
  histories of, 340–41
Asheville, N.C., 17, 50, 67, 74, 84,
    105, 112, 147, 150, 272
  battle of, 298, 302n29
  Civil War in, 206–7, 276, 280n34
  Confederate armory in, 85–86, 87
  race riot in, 31, 34
  and Stoneman's Raid, 205–11, 216–
    20
  as tourist resort, 268
Atkins, Eileen, 317–18
Atlanta, Ga., 34, 154, 158, 184

Augusta County, Va., 46
Avery, W. W., 82, 96n3, 106
Ayers, Edward J., 31–32

Baker, Abner, 49
Bakersville, N.C., 67
Banner, Napoleon, 138–39
Bartram, William, 310, 314
Bates, Daniel, 48–49, 55, 63n6
Bates, John, 49
Bates, Stephen, 49
Batteau, Allen, 4, 7–8, 196–97, 259,
    360–61, 377
Bell, Alfred, 90–94, 144–68
Bell, John, 106
Bell, Mary, 90–94, 144–68, 208, 318
Berea, Ky., 251
Berea College, 22, 23, 259
Berwanger, Eugene, 27
Big Bend Tunnel, W.Va., 351, 357–59
Biggers, Jeff, 4
Billings, Dwight, 48
Biltmore House, 268
Birdseye, Ezekiel, 47–48, 58
Blackmun, Ora, 284
Blalock, Keith, 328
Blalock, Malinda, 328
Blee, Kathleen, 48
Blue Ridge Mountains, 104, 207, 245,
    262, 267, 304, 313–14
Boone, Daniel, 242, 270
Boone, N.C., 209–10
Boorman, John, 369
Bower, George, 80–81
Bread riot, in Jonesville, N.C., 208
Breckinridge, John, 106
Bristol, Tenn., 17, 30, 105
Brown, John, 20–21, 245–46
Brown, Joseph E., 30, 276
Brown, Mary Taylor, 216–17
Brown, W. Vance, 216–17
Brown, William Vance, 82
Browne, Junius, 176, 186, 192–93, 327
Brownlow, William G., 28, 107, 109–
    11, 115
Brundage, W. Fitzhugh, 32

Bryson City, N.C., 270
Buffalo Forge, Va., 51–52
Bull Run, battle of, 183
Buncombe County, N.C., 86, 220
Burke County, N.C., 49–50, 56, 105,
    215
Burkes Garden, Va., 134
Burns, Ken, 282
Burnsville, N.C., 67, 71
Burson, William, 186–87
Bushwhackers, 127, 131, 166–67,
    180–81, 214, 271, 273, 308, 312,
    326–27, 334–38, 341

Cabbell, Edward J., 17, 363n11
Cabins in the Laurel (Shepherd), 317
Cades Cove, Tenn., 134, 190
Cain, Sarah Bailey, 218, 219
Caldwell County, N.C., 87, 88–90,
    94, 124–25, 180
Calley, William, 291–92
Campbell, John C., 18, 70, 236, 256,
    269–76
Campbell, Olive Dame, 272, 365–66
Camp Sorghum, S.C., 127, 177, 193
Carnesville, Ga., 184
Carolina Mountains, The (Morley),
    265–68
Carroll, Edith, 129–31, 134
Carson, Logan, 210–11
Carter County, Tenn., 325
Cash, W. J., 17–18, 71, 238
Cashiers, N.C., 190
Caudill, Harry, 21, 247
Chapman, Verena, 213, 219
Chappell, Louis, 356–57, 362n6
Charleston, S.C., 83, 86–87, 92, 112,
    163, 304–5, 310
Charlotte, N.C., 209–10
Chattanooga, Tenn., 17, 30–31, 67,
    74, 105, 184, 265–67, 276
Chattooga River, 376
Cherokee County, N.C., 144, 167,
    318
Chesapeake & Ohio Railroad, 351,
    357–58

Chesnut, Mary Boykin, 84
Chickamauga, battle of, 274
Civil War Trails project, 293, 301n21
Clark, Walter, 306
Clay County, Ky., 48–49
Clingman, Thomas L., 106, 112, 118–19
Cobb, Irwin S., 233
Cold Mountain, 135, 298–99, 303–
    19, 328, 365, 370–75
Cold Mountain, N.C., 304, 309
Coleman, David, 151–54, 171n23
Colonization, African, 73
Columbia, S.C., 177, 179, 209
Confederacy, 206
  support of in Appalachia, 89, 111–
    12, 219–20, 264, 274–75, 312–
    13
Confederate currency, 89–91, 95
Confederates in the Attic (Horwitz),
    282
Conference of Southern Mountain
    Workers, 272
Confessions of Nat Turner, The (Sty-
    ron), 19
Conscription, 150, 170n19, 331–32,
    334
Cooper, Alonzo, 176, 187–88
Cooper, Gary, 376
Corpening, Joseph, 87
Cotton, 89, 104
Cowles, Calvin J., 80, 85–86, 87–88
Cowles, Mary, 94–95
Cranberry, N.C., 138–39
Crane, Susan A., 342–43
Crawford, Martin, 134, 334,
    341–42
Cripps, Thomas, 242
Crockett, Davy, 242
Cumberland Mountains, 14, 21, 23,
    104
Cunningham, Rodger, 27

Dahlonega, Ga., 324
Danville, Va., 177, 185
Davidson, Allen, 86
Davidson, Samuel, 245

Davis, Jefferson, 83, 148–49, 165
Davis-DeEulis, Marilyn, 54
de Tocqueville, Alexis, 27
Deaderick, David, 20
Degler, Carl, 26
Deliverance, 303, 352, 365–73
Democratic Party, 105–6, 116
Denver, John, 370
Desertion, 136, 148, 154, 178, 181–
    82, 186, 214, 280n34, 288, 309,
    312–13, 316–17
D'lea (slave), 47, 54
Dollmaker, The, 365, 371, 373
Douglass, Frederick, 20, 60–61
Drake, Madison, 124–25, 136, 176,
    180, 191–92
"Dueling Banjos," 376
Dugger, G. W., 138–39
Dugger, Shepherd, 139
Dunaway, Wilma, 245
Dunn, Durwood, 134, 245
Dykeman, Wilma, 317

Earp, Marlene, 294
East Tennessee, 14–15, 16, 22–23,
    25, 27–28, 58, 72, 260
  economy of, 104–5, 114, 116–17
  escaped prisoners in, 179–96
  racial violence in, 228–30
  secession from Tennessee, 117, 263
  stories set in, 228–30, 233–34
  Union troops from, 103, 209
East Tennessee and Virginia Rail-
    road, 105
Eaton, John, 18, 34
Egan, Michael, 129, 136, 187
Eggers, Landrine, 336–37
Ehle, John, 242–50, 364
Elizabethton, Tenn., 67, 72
Ellis, Daniel, 192, 283, 306, 325–26
Ellis, John, 147, 150
Emancipation, 34. *See also* Slavery,
    end of
Emancipation Proclamation, 28
Enlistment, Confederate, 147–48,
    267, 268, 308, 330

Equiano, Olaudah, 60–61
Erwin, Marcus, 82, 106

Families, divided loyalties of, 125–39, 267, 337–40
Faulkner, William, 14–15, 18, 227–38
Faust, Drew Gilpin, 165, 193
Fayetteville, N.C., 218
Featherstonaugh, George, 30, 146
Federal Writers Project, 50–51
Fee, John, 23
Fellman, Michael, 125, 136, 190, 314
Ferguson, Champ, 325–26
Feuding, 265–66, 271
Fields, Barbara, 20, 34–35
Film
    Appalachian women on, 250, 312–16
    Appalachia on, 242–50, 253, 303, 312–16, 364–78
    blacks in, 242, 313, 374
Flat Rock, N.C., 83, 97n3, 112–13, 127–28, 193, 268
Fletcher, Arthur, 340–41
Fonda, Jane, 365, 371
Fort Defiance, N.C., 88
Fort Sumter, attack on, 107, 126, 313
Foster, Stephen William, 341
Fox, John, 14–15, 22, 262–63, 275
Foxfire, 365, 369–71
Franklin, John Hope, 60–61
Franklin, N.C., 91, 146–47, 150, 166–67, 208, 333
Franklin, State of, 117
Frazier, Charles, 135, 298–99, 303–6, 313, 328
Fredericksburg, Va., 183
Free blacks, 17, 46–47, 52, 56, 59–60, 72–73, 189, 197
Freedman's Bureau, 18, 236
Free Masonry, 212
Free Soil movement, 20
French Broad River, 112, 185, 206
Frost, William G., 202n55, 256, 259, 275

Fugitive prisoner narratives, 176–98, 305
Fugitive prisoners of war, 140n7, 327

Gale, Katherine Polk, 206–7, 217–18, 220
Garnett, Robert S., 262–63, 279n20
Garth, Ella, 370–71
Gastonia, N.C., 234–35
Gatlinburg, Tenn., 296
Genovese, Eugene, 65
Georgia, 16, 19, 24, 86, 112, 126, 309
    racial violence in, 31–32
    See also North Georgia
Gettysburg, battle of, 264
Ghormley, Nancy, 132–33, 138
Gillem, Alvan C., 210–17
Gilmore, James R., 1–2, 6–7, 188
Glatthaar, Joseph, 195
Gold rush
    California, 49–50, 56
    western North Carolina, 49
Gone With the Wind, 311, 312, 315
Goodheart, Adam, 298–99
Goodrich, William, 21
Graham, William A., 205
Grandfather Mountain, N.C., 307–8, 317, 328
Grant, Ulysses S., 209, 274
Grapes of Wrath, The, 372, 374
Great Hanging (Cooke Co., Tex.), 296
Great Smoky Mountains, 104, 127–28, 132–33, 146, 179, 207, 267, 270
Great Wagon Road, Va., 46
Greeneville, Tenn., 52–53, 55, 110, 132
Greenville, S.C., 184
Greenwald, Maggie, 374
Greer, Jesse, 331, 336, 340
Greer family, 332
Gregg, Bill, 285, 291
Griffin, Larry, 4–5
Gudger, Sarah, 31, 50–51, 55

Guerrilla warfare, 5, 125–37, 180–
    81, 265, 271, 273, 276, 280n34,
    288
  on film, 312–16, 370
  memories of, 282–98, 322–44
  women and, 125–37, 207, 213, 273,
    314–19
Gurney, Joseph John, 31, 33
Gwyn, James, 89–90, 135

Hadley, J. V., 193, 306
Halbwachs, Maurice, 342–43
Hall, Van Beck, 33
Hannibal (slave), 48, 57–58
Happy Valley, N.C., 307
Harper, Ella, 207, 215
Harpers Ferry, Va., 20–21, 245–46
Harris, George Washington, 233–34
Harris, Isham, 110
Hatfield-McCoy feud, 29, 134
Hayes, Rutherford B., 194–95
Haywood County, N.C., 86, 88–90,
    233, 295, 306–8, 328, 341
Hemp, 47
Hemphill, William, 50–51, 55
Henderson, N.C., 190
Henderson County, N.C., 28, 113,
    193
Hendersonville, N.C., 83, 95, 112–
    13, 214, 216
Hennion, Horatio, 326
Hennion, Margaret, 326
Henry, John, 350–63
Heroes of America, 307
Hesseltine, William, 176, 196
Heth, Henry, 283, 288
Highlander Folk School, 23–24
Highlands, N.C., 268, 352–53
Hillbillyland (Williamson), 242, 315,
    371
Hills Beyond, The (Wolfe), 16
Hinton, W.Va., 351
Holden, William W., 80
Hollinger family, 127–28, 134, 137
Holmes, William F., 32
"Holy Appalachia," 21, 197, 247, 377

Home Guard, 162–63, 181, 186–87,
    304, 306–7, 312–18, 327, 334,
    341
Horwitz, Tony, 282–83
Hot Springs, N.C., 261
Howe, Irving, 228
Hsiung, David, 245
Humes, Thomas, 25, 27–28

Inman, W. P., 135–36, 304–10, 368–
    69, 375
Internal improvements, 104–5, 118
Invention of Appalachia, The (Bat-
    teau), 360–61, 377
Iraq, war in, 291–92
Ironworks, 57, 138–39

Jackson, Stonewall, 264
Jacobs, Harriet, 60–61
Joad, Ma, 372–74
John Henry Days (Whitehead), 350–
    63
Johnson, Andrew, 28, 55, 107, 110,
    114, 132, 276
  as slaveholder, 29, 52–53, 114
Johnson, Charles, 53
Johnson, Guy B., 355–57, 362n6
Johnson County, Tenn., 330
Johnston, Joseph E., 209
Johnstone, Andrew, 97n3
Jones, Alexander H., 28, 95
Jones, James Earl, 374
Jones, Loyal, 19, 70
Jonesboro, Tenn., 30, 117
Jonesville, N.C., 208
Joppa, Ala., 274
Journal of Negro History, 23
Journey of August King, The, 242–
    53, 364, 368–70, 373

Kazan, Elia, 365
Keith, James, 283, 286–90, 300n12,
    301n17
Kellogg, John Azor, 182, 184, 188,
    327
Kentucky, 14–15, 23, 47, 263, 264

Kentucky *(continued)*
  divided loyalties of, 260
  racial violence in, 32
Kephart, Horace, 236, 256, 269–72, 306
Kidman, Nicole, 312, 315, 371
King, August, 243–52, 369–70, 373, 375
King's Mountain, battle of, 261–62, 264, 268, 279n15
Kinston, N.C., 88
Kinston, Tenn., 111
Kirk, George, 288
Kirk, John, 288
Kirke, Edmund, 189
Kirk's Raid, 96–97n3
Klotter, James, 3, 16, 197, 257
Knox County, Tenn., 105
Knoxville, Tenn., 17, 22, 30–31, 105, 109–10, 116, 128, 132, 283
  destination for fugitive prisoners, 179, 184
Kousser, J. Morgan, 34
Ku Klux Klan, 32

Lancaster, Pa., 46
Lanman, Charles, 33, 147
Last Ninety Days of the War in North Carolina, The (Spencer), 204
Law, Jude, 314
Lee, Robert E., 94, 209, 274, 306, 319
Lenoir, Lizzie, 208
Lenoir, N.C., 86, 207–8, 213–14
Lenoir, Rufus, 88–90, 94
Lenoir, Thomas, 88
Lenoir, Walter, 88–90, 94
Lenoir family, 88–91, 94
Lexington, Va., 51
Libby Prison, 189
Liberia, 22, 72
Lincoln, Abraham, 111, 150, 257
  call for troops, 107, 263, 313
  election of, 28, 29, 103, 106
  inauguration of, 329
Little Shepherd of Kingdom Come, The (Fox), 14–15, 22, 262

Little Tennessee River, 146–47
Livestock, 68, 104
London, Ky., 30
"Lost Cause," 29
Lost Cause, 256–57, 295–96, 323–24, 326
Love, Dillard, 91, 93, 147
Loyalties, divided, 324–25
  in Appalachia, 124–39, 256–77
Lumpkin, Grace, 233
Lundy, Benjamin, 22, 30
Lynchburg, Va., 67
Lynchings, 32, 249, 297

Mabry, Jeannette, 128–29, 137
Mace, Borden, 243, 253
Macon County, N.C., 90–91, 144, 147, 208, 307, 318
Madison County, N.C., 133, 261, 276, 283–95
Manley, Charles, 107–8
Mann, Ralph, 134, 328
Manumission, slave, 33, 49, 55–56, 115
Marshall, N.C., 283
  raid on, 287–289
Mars Hill College, 282, 284–85, 292–93
Martin, Brenden, 296
Martin, James G., 210, 217
Maryville, Tenn., 251
Maryville College, 16, 263
Mason-Dixon line, 36, 262
Massey, Mary Elizabeth, 164
Masur, Louis, 175
Matewan, 365, 372–75
Mattocks, Charles, 179, 185
McCaslin, Richard, 296
McCrumb, Sharon, 284
McDowell, Tom, 148–49
McDowell County, N.C., 207, 210–11
McElrath, Robert, 49–50, 56
McKenzie, Tracy, 134
McKinney, Gordon B., 33–34, 166, 284
McNeil, W. K., 259
Mecklenburg Declaration of Independence, 262, 264, 279n18

Memminger, Christopher, 84, 113, 128
Memory, 7–8, 355, 361
  and guerrilla warfare, 294–98, 325–44
  historical, 294–98, 342–44
Mexican War, 76
Miles, Emma Bell, 256, 265–69, 274
Mind of the South, The (Cash), 17–18, 71, 238
Minghella, Anthony, 312, 313, 319
Mississippi, 227, 228–30, 233, 263, 357
Missouri, 190, 314
Mitchell, Elisha, 112, 285
Mitchell, Robert D., 245
Mitchell County, N.C., 19, 71
Monroe, Ada, 304–11, 369, 374
Mooney, James, 306
Moonshiners, 32, 265–66, 270
Moravians, 46
Morgan, John Hunt, 137, 325–26
  murder of, 132
Morgan, Rick, 285
Morganton, N.C., 104, 210, 214–15, 244
Morley, Margaret, 265–69, 276
Morris, B. T., 284
Mountain Born (Gowen), 233–34
"Mountain Victory" (Faulkner), 227–30, 237–38
Murphy, N.C., 67
Music, Appalachian, 259, 374–75
My Lai massacre, 291–92

Nashville, Tenn., 110, 116–17
Natchez, Miss., 30, 69
Nations, Annie, 370, 375
Nelson, Scott R., 362n6, 363n11
Nelson, Thomas A. R., 107, 109–10, 116
Nevels, Gertie, 368–369, 371–73, 375
New Orleans, La., 84
Newport, Tenn., 47–48
New River Valley, 30
Newton, Thandie, 243–44, 252, 370
New York City, 50, 75–76
Nicholas, Wilson Cary, 47

Noe, Kenneth, 194, 257
Nolichucky River, 192
Nonslaveholders, 184, 271
  in Appalachia, 67–77, 112–13, 227–32, 247–49, 271
North Carolina, 204
  secession of, 313
  Sherman's troops in, 209
  See also Western North Carolina
North Carolina regiments. *See* Regiments, North Carolina
North Fork, N.C., 131, 322–44
North Georgia, 15, 23–24, 29, 30, 67, 235, 341
  Lost Cause in, 324
  racial violence in, 31–32
  tourism in, 370–71
  Unionism in, 180–82
Northwest Territory, 27
Norwood, Joseph, 214
Norwood, Laura, 212

Oberlin College, 259
O'Brien, Sean, 284
O'Connor, Flannery, 16
Odyssey, The (Homer), 305
O'Hara, Scarlett, 319
Ohio Valley, 54
Old Fort, N.C., 31, 243
O'Leary, Sean, 285–89, 297, 299, 301n20
Olmsted, Frederick Law, 7, 25–26, 33, 65–77, 81–82, 251
Olson, Eric, 31, 34
Osburn, Tom, 334–35
Our Southern Highlanders (Kephart), 236, 269–72

Page, Geraldine, 372
Palmer, William, 210, 212
Paludan, Philip, 284, 288, 307
Parish, Peter, 59
Parkins, W. H., 176, 192
Patric, Jason, 243–44, 252
Patriotic Gore (Wilson), 175
Patsy (slave), 92–93
Patterson, Rufus, 95

Pearson, Robert C., 215
Petersburg, siege of, 304
Philanthropists, northern, 274
Phillips, U. B., 13, 65
Piedmont College, 272
Pierson, Mrs. D. L., 261–62, 276
Pigeon Forge, Tenn., 296
Pikeville, Ky., 30
Pinter, Harold, 295, 324
Polk, Leonidas, 84
Polk County, Tenn., 67
Poor whites. *See* Nonslaveholders
Potter, Andy, 330–32, 339
Potter, Jack, 332, 334
Potter family, 330–34, 339, 348n27
Presbyterian Home Mission Board, 263
Presbyterians, "New Light," 22, 251
Prisoners of war, 206, 211, 288
Prisoners of war, fugitive, 7, 28, 124–25, 140n7, 176–98, 218, 305, 313
Prisons, Confederate, 124, 127, 176–77
Prosser, Gabriel, 33
Prostitution, 151, 170n20

Quakers, 22, 46, 107, 115–16, 251

Rabun County, Ga., 59
Race riots
in Asheville, N.C., 31, 34
in Atlanta, 34, 297
in Wilmington, N.C., 297
Racial demographics of Appalachia, 1–2, 5, 14–17, 59, 67, 237
Racial violence
in Georgia, 31–32
in Kentucky, 32
Racism, in Appalachia, 25–27, 34–36, 70–74, 115, 235–36, 251–52
Railroads, 209, 267
in Appalachia, 84, 102, 104–5, 113
Raleigh, N.C., 118, 309
Ramsey, J. G. M., 116
Rankin, Emma L., 207, 210–11, 216
Rash, Ron, 284

Reconstruction, 31–32, 33–34, 197, 235–38
Reed, John Shelton, 4
Refugees, war time, 83, 178, 189, 327, 338
Regiments, North Carolina
37th, 330
39th, 148
64th, 261, 283
Reid, John, 154–55
Reid, Salena, 154
Religion, in Appalachian films, 374–75
Republican Party, in Appalachia, 33–34
Rice, John Andrew, 167
Richardson, Albert, 181–82, 185–86, 188
Richmond, Va., 33, 88, 111
Roanoke, Va., 17
Robeson, Paul, 354
Rockbridge County, Va., 22, 51–52
Rome, Ga., 146
Rosa (slave), 92–93
Ruby (*Cold Mountain*), 305–9, 315, 318, 371
Ruffin, Thomas, 205
Ruffner, Henry, 22
Russell Sage Foundation, 272
Rutherford County, N.C., 87, 214

Salem, N.C., 210
Salisbury, N.C., 177, 179, 209, 307, 329
Confederate prison in, 124, 209, 327
Salt, 287–88
Salt mining, 48–49, 57
Sam (slave), 52–53
Sandy Basin, Va., 134, 327–28
Sarris, Jonathan, 134, 324
Savannah, Ga., 86–87
Sayles, John, 365, 375
Schweninger, Loren, 60
Scotch-Irish, 23, 264
Scott, Anne Firor, 164
Secession, 32, 275
in East Tennessee, 103–4, 109–10, 112, 117–19

in Georgia, 30
in North Carolina, 81–82, 103–4,
    107–9, 118–19
in Virginia, 29, 30, 107
Semmes, Thomas J., 84
Semple, Ellen, 15, 23
Sergeant York, 365, 372–75
Sevier County, Tenn., 296
Shaler, Nathaniel S., 16
Shanks, Henry, 29
Shapiro, Henry, 257, 258
Shelton, David, 283
Shelton, Jim, 290
Shelton, Patsy, 286–91
Shelton, Rena, 284–85, 292–95
Shelton Laurel (play), 282, 285–97
Shelton Laurel, N.C., 292–95
    massacre, 133, 261, 276, 282–98,
    307, 317, 328
Shenandoah (film), 311–12, 315
Shenandoah Valley, Va., 22
Shepherd, Muriel, 19, 317
Sherman's troops, 184, 195, 209, 218
Silber, Nina, 17, 257
Silence of the Lambs, 352
Silvers, Frankie, 285
Slagle, Dan, 285, 291
Slaveholders, 47–62, 68–77
    Appalachian views of, 2, 71, 73–74,
    114–15
    in East Tennessee, 105
    murder of, 48–49, 58
    in western North Carolina, 81–84,
    105, 183–84, 205–6, 248, 307
Slave labor, 47, 49–52, 56–57, 83–85
    competition with poor whites, 72–
    73, 75
Slave narratives, 60–61
Slavery
    in Appalachia, 1–2, 5, 14–16, 25–
    26, 47–61, 67, 74–76, 333
    in Appalachian films, 374
    end of, in Appalachia, 93–96, 220
    profitability of, 81, 89–90
    as secession issue, 29–30, 105, 275
Slaves, 55–56
    aiding fugitive prisoners, 183–89

execution of, 47, 48, 58, 249–50
hired out, 53, 83, 84–87, 91, 146,
    158–59, 164, 183
insurrectionary activity of, 82, 95,
    160
literacy of, 47
manumission of, 33, 49, 55–56, 115
runaways, 87–88, 186–87, 245–46,
    249, 313
sales of, 51, 52–53, 55, 57, 83, 91–
    95
treatment of, in Appalachia, 33, 47,
    47–62, 211
Slave trade, 30–31, 163–64
    in western North Carolina, 81–96
Smith, Lillian, 26, 58–59
Smoky Mountains. *See* Great Smoky
    Mountains
Songcatcher, 365, 372–74
South Carolina, 83–84, 86, 112, 185,
    233
    secession of, 106
Southern Appalachian Repertory
    Theatre, 282, 284–85, 291
*Southern Highlander and His Home-
    land, The* (Campbell), 236, 269
South Mountains, N.C., 49, 215,
    234–35
Spanish-American War, 275
Spencer, Cornelia Phillips, 204–5,
    212–15
Spirit of the Mountains, The (Miles),
    265–67
Stampp, Kenneth, 65
Starnes, Richard, 295, 324
Staunton, Va., 47
Stoneman, George, 205, 209
Stoneman's Raid, 205–6, 209–20,
    336
Stout, Tom, 333–34, 340
Stringfield, W. W., 324
Stuckert, Robert, 32
Styron, William, 19
Surry County, N.C., 233
Sutherland, Elihu J., 327–28
Sut Lovingood (Harris), 233–34
Sutpen, Thomas, 230–32, 238

Swain, David L., 85, 204
Swanger, Sally, 316–17, 318
Swannanoa Valley, N.C., 50–51

Talcott, W.Va., 350–56, 360
Tall Woman, The (Dykeman), 317
Tandy, Jessica, 370–71
Tarr, Edward, 46–47, 56
Taylor, James W., 1, 6–7
Taylor, Jim, 284, 293, 300n12
Teague, Robert, 306, 308, 313, 328
Temple, Oliver, 27, 109–10, 115–16,
    128–29, 135
Tennessee, 18, 20. *See also* East
    Tennessee
Tennessee River, 105
Tennessee Valley Authority, 370–71
Tennessee Wesleyan College, 41n32
Thirteen Moons (Frazier), 298–99
Thomas, William Holland, 106, 113,
    306
Tobacco Road, 380n17
To Make My Bread (Lumpkin),
    233–35
Toplin, Robert Brent, 366, 378
Tourism in Appalachia, 74, 267–69
Trail of the Lonesome Pine, The
    (Fox), 262
Travel accounts
    antebellum, 175–76
    late nineteenth century, 236, 256
Trim (slave), 92–93
Trotter, William R., 284
Trowbridge, J. T., 236
Tryon, N.C., 267
Tug River Valley, 29, 47

Uncle Tom's Cabin (Stowe), 72
Underground Railroad, 19–20,
    39n20, 128, 246, 252
Unionism, 27–28, 125–26, 150, 184,
    237
    in Appalachia, 1–3, 21–22, 111,
        137–39, 177–82, 257–77
    in Ashe County, N.C., 325
    conditional, 107, 121n9

    in East Tennessee, 27–28, 109–10,
        126, 128–29, 236, 325–27
    in Georgia, 29, 326
    in Kentucky, 29, 325–36
    memories of, 324–25
    in North Carolina, 129–35, 150,
        166
Union troops
    African American, 216, 218
    from Appalachia, 265
University of North Carolina, 204,
    355–56

Vance, Zebulon B., 28, 81, 83, 84,
    107, 165, 205, 207, 276
    as slaveholder, 29
Van Fleet, Jo, 371, 373
Veterans, Confederate, 274, 305, 324
    reunions, 267
Vietnam War, 291–92
Virginia, 26, 47, 67, 194
    free blacks in, 33
    secession vote in, 29
    Tidewater, 56, 228, 238

Waller, Altina, 29, 134
Warm Springs, N.C., 112
Warren, Robert Penn, 323, 339
Washington, D.C., 109, 118
Washington College, 22
Watauga County, N.C., 131, 340
Waterston, Sam, 248, 252
Waynesville, N.C., 67, 324
Weaver, William, 51–52, 57
Wellman, Manly Wade, 284
West, Don, 23–24
Western North Carolina, 28, 31, 50–
    51
    class divisions in, 289–90
    economy of, 104, 112–13, 118,
        244–45
    escaped prisoners in, 179–96
    gold rush in, 49
    raids on, 96–97n3, 205–18, 288
    secession vote in, 29
    slavery in, 33, 80–96, 206, 245

Western North Carolina Railroad, 84, 104
West Virginia, 4, 17, 179, 260, 263, 264, 350–63
West Virginia University, 356–57
Wheeling, W.Va., 22, 30, 251
Whig Party, 105, 106, 111, 114, 116
Whisnant, David, 13, 366
"Whitecapping," 32
Whitehead, Colson, 350–59
Whiteness. *See* Appalachia: whiteness of
White Sulphur Springs, Va., 31
Whitfield County, Ga., 31–32
Wild River, 365, 369–70, 372–73
Wilkesboro, N.C., 188
Wilkes County, N.C., 85, 90, 135, 187, 208, 212, 307
Wilkeson, Frank, 191
Williams, Brett, 356
Williams, Catherine, 132
Williams, John Alexander, 2, 272
Williams, Leon, 20
Williams, Lucy, 132, 137–38
Williams, Nancy, 51–52, 57
Williams, Sam, 51–52, 57
Williamson, Jerry, 4, 242, 315, 318, 371, 376, 380n17
Williamson, Joel, 227, 238
Wilson, Caroline, 330–32, 335–37
Wilson, Edmund, 175
Wilson, Isaac, 330–31
  murder of, 131, 134–35, 322, 328–33

Wilson, Robert (R. B.), 330, 340
Wilson, Samuel Tyndale, 16, 263–65, 275
Wilson, Shannon, 257, 274
Wilson, William Albert, 322–44
Winchester, Va., 30, 137, 205
Winston, N.C., 210
Wolfe, Thomas, 16
Women
  in Appalachia, 69, 189–94, 204–19
  and bread riots, 208
  Confederate, 144–45, 155, 164–65, 305, 318
  film treatments of Appalachian, 250, 314–19, 371–74
  in Franklin, N.C., 153–55
  and guerrilla warfare, 125–37, 207, 213, 273, 314–19, 326–27, 331–32, 337–39
  postwar narratives of, 206, 218–20, 221n6
  Unionist, 190–96, 317, 326
Woodfin, Elizabeth, 154
Woodfin, John W., 96n3
Woodfin, Nicholas W., 84, 87–88
Woodson, Carter G., 23–24, 70, 247
Woodward, C. Vann, 297

Yeomen. *See* Nonslaveholders
York, Alvin, 365, 368, 372, 374–75, 377, 380n17
Younce, W. H., 129–31, 134

Zellweger, Renée, 312, 315, 371

LaVergne, TN USA
07 May 2010
181947LV00003B/5/P